Stages of Life

Stages of Life
Indian Theatre Autobiographies

Kathryn Hansen

ANTHEM PRESS
LONDON · NEW YORK · DELHI

Anthem Press
An imprint of Wimbledon Publishing Company
www.anthempress.com

This edition first published in UK and USA 2013
by ANTHEM PRESS
75–76 Blackfriars Road, London SE1 8HA, UK
or PO Box 9779, London SW19 7ZG, UK
and
244 Madison Ave. #116, New York, NY 10016, USA

Published in India by Permanent Black 2011;
first published in hardback in UK and USA by Anthem Press in 2011

Copyright © Kathryn Hansen 2013

The author asserts the moral right to be identified as the author of this work.

This publication is supported by a University Co-operative Society
Subvention Grant awarded by the University of Texas at Austin.

All rights reserved. Without limiting the rights under copyright reserved above,
no part of this publication may be reproduced, stored or introduced into
a retrieval system, or transmitted, in any form or by any means
(electronic, mechanical, photocopying, recording or otherwise),
without the prior written permission of both the copyright
owner and the above publisher of this book.

British Library Cataloguing-in-Publication Data
A catalogue record for this book is available from the British Library.

Library of Congress Cataloging-in-Publication Data
The Library of Congress has cataloged the hardcover edition as follows:
Hansen, Kathryn.
Stages of life : Indian theatre autobiographies / Kathryn Hansen.
p. cm.
Includes bibliographical references and index.
ISBN 978-0-85728-660-4 (hardcover : alk. paper)
1. Actors–India–Biography. 2. Dramatists, Indic–Biography.
3. Autobiography–Indic authors–History and criticism.
4. Theater–India–History–20th century. I. Title.
PN2887.H28 2011
791.43'028092354–dc23
[B]
2011035910

ISBN-13: 978 1 78308 068 7 (Pbk)
ISBN-10: 1 78308 068 X (Pbk)

This title is also available as an ebook.

Contents

Illustrations		vii
Preface		ix
Acknowledgments		xv

Part 1

1	Pioneers to Professionals: A Retrospective of the Parsi Theatre	3
2	Theatrical Memoirs and the Archives of Autobiography	26

Part 2

3	Narayan Prasad Betab, *The Deeds of Betab*	51
4	Radheshyam Kathavachak, *My Theatre Days*	102
5	Jayshankar Sundari, *Some Blossoms, Some Tears*	170
6	Fida Husain, *Fifty Years in the Parsi Theatre*	246

Part 3

7	Self and Subjectivity in Autobiographical Criticism	299
8	Voices and Silences: Reading the Texts	315
	Appendix 1: Historical Personages and Institutions	336
	Appendix 2: List of Plays and Films	347
	Glossary: Hindi and Urdu Terms	351
	Bibliography	355
	Index	361

Illustrations

1	Victoria Theatre, 1870	12
2	*Indar Sabha* Handbill	13
3	Agha Hashr Kashmiri	22
4	Helen Theatrical Company, 1908	23
5	Jamshedji Framji Madan	24
6	Narayan Prasad Betab	52
7	Scene from *Zahri Sanp*	54
8	Vidyavati Namra	56
9	Amrit Keshav Nayak	81
10	Postcard of Gauhar Jan	83
11	Gold Medal Given to Betab	93
12	Miss Gohar in the Film *Barrister's Wife*	99
13	*Radheshyam Ramayan*	103
14	*Krishna Avatar* Handbill	141
15	Radheshyam Kathavachak	164
16	Bapulal Nayak and Jayshankar Sundari in *Sneh Sarita*	174
17	Jayshankar Sundari Receives Padma Bhushan	175
18	Gaiety Theatre, now Capitol Cinema	201

19	Dayashankar Girnara	202
20	Jayshankar Sundari	244
21	*Mastar Fida Husain* Book Cover	250
22	Fida Husain	264
23	Fida Husain in *Krishna Sudama*	279

Preface

This book tells the stories of four men whose lives were profoundly touched by the Parsi theatre. Their tales begin near the end of the nineteenth century. In 1898, a boy named Jayshankar began his career as a 9-year-old child actor. Recruited from Visnagar, a small town in Gujarat north of Ahmedabad, he traveled the long distance to Calcutta to join a Parsi theatrical company. In the same year, hit tunes from the Parsi theatre were echoing through the lanes of Bareli (Bareilly), in what is now northern Uttar Pradesh. There a boy named Radheshyam, almost the same age as Jayshankar, took to singing in the Ram Lila. A third young man, a poet named Betab, was then working at the Kaiser-i Hind Printing Press in Delhi. A restless theatre enthusiast of 24, he had just started writing plays for the Parsi stage. In the following year, 1899, the youngest in our quartet, Fida Husain, was born in Muradabad (Moradabad), a center for artisans not far from Bareli. Although singing was forbidden in his household, he too became infatuated with the Parsi theatre. When he reached adolescence, he ran away from home to join a traveling company.

The lives of these boys were to be irrevocably altered by the Parsi theatre of the early twentieth century. Raised in humble circumstances, they grew up poor and unlettered. They went on to earn fame and fortune in their theatrical careers. The stage became their schoolhouse, bestowing on them its store of knowledge. When the tours of the companies separated them from their homes, they found surrogate families in the troupes they joined. Here they received sustenance and affection, imbibed discipline and respect for authority. The theatre took advantage of them, used them, and broke their health and spirit from time to time. But it also enabled them to develop their gifts, and they blossomed as singers, dancers, and poets. Through the professional stage these boys entered a larger world, an arena of possibility. The Parsi theatre turned these boys into men.

Jayshankar and Fida Husain became well-known actors; Betab and Radheshyam achieved fame mainly as playwrights and publishers. Each made valuable contributions to India's theatrical history. Jayshankar crafted a new feminine persona through his seductive impersonations of respectable young women. Fida Husain too excelled as a female impersonator, but he became most famous for his enactment of religious devotion in the role of the saint-poet Narsi Mehta. Both Betab and Radheshyam popularized the Hindu mythological genre in a period of national awakening. These achievements reoriented the half-century-old Parsi theatre, shifting it toward new agendas and audiences. It is because of these four men, and one or two others such as the playwright Agha Hashr Kashmiri, that the Parsi theatre continued to thrive well into the twentieth century. Through their life-work, the popular stage was able to retain its audience even after cinema made inroads in South Asia.

The end of the nineteenth century, when these impressionable boys took to the stage, was an age of infectious song and story. Every region of India possessed its own mix of popular oral genres. Frequently, these forms were central to the repertoires of hereditary performing groups or subcastes. Radheshyam, like his father, was a *kathavachak*, a storyteller who expounded upon religious verse for a living. Jayshankar was from the Nayak or Bhojak community who recited genealogies and narrative song-cycles for Jain patrons. Coming from artisan backgrounds, Betab and Fida Husain were not born into performing communities. They inherited the secular songs and theatre forms of North India: *lavani,* Svang, and Nautanki.

Then, from the port city of Bombay came a cosmopolitan entertainment culture carried by traveling theatre companies run by Parsi businessmen. These drama troupes brought a new level of sophistication to popular performance. Capitalizing on technologies introduced by European thespians, they paraded showy styles of acting, singing, and emplotting drama. The proscenium stage was newly adopted and outfitted for theatrical representation. Roving companies stayed for months in small towns like Bareli, where they rented family mansions for rehearsals and erected tin-roofed playhouses for their shows.

For provincial audiences, a night at the theatre meant dazzling lights, glittering costumes, and heart-stopping trick effects. Most memorable was the catchy music. Tunes from the Parsi companies soon infiltrated the soundscape. Singers of all stripes reworked familiar genres—sacred or profane—around the melodies, rhythms, and phrasing of the glamorous theatre companies. The allure of the new mode was so great that by the turn of the century the Parsi theatre had become a ubiquitous part of public culture across the subcontinent, its audience comprising people of every class. It knew no religious, linguistic, or ethnic bounds either. All the way from Quetta to Calcutta, an evening's fun could be had for the price of a ticket.

This colorful world of urban entertainment, transported to the tracts of northern India, comes alive in the life-stories contained in this book. Presented here are the autobiographies of Betab, Radheshyam, Jayshankar Sundari, and Fida Husain. As witnesses of epochal change, these men lived lives of inestimable value to historians. Their autobiographical writings capture a moment in India's cultural development that is largely forgotten. The four texts in this volume also introduce a new genre: the theatrical memoir, a variety of autobiographical narrative that emerged in India in the early twentieth century. The evidence of life-writing by theatre performers and poets raises important questions for the study of autobiography. Firmly planted in vernacular, largely oral, systems of communication and knowledge, these artists possess voices that speak in stylized performative registers. Through their work, the reader encounters not only a record of theatrical history but a living transcript, an oral performance in itself.

This book combines different objectives and is divided into several parts. Principally, it makes available a set of autobiographical texts by celebrated figures associated with the Parsi theatre. Written originally in either Hindi or Gujarati, the four accounts are here translated into English for the first time. The translations attempt to carry over the formal features and stylistic idiosyncrasies of the originals, while aiming for fluidity and easy access.

To explain specialized information, an apparatus of footnotes, appendices, and glossary has been provided. These aids synthesize a decade and more of research, and draw on an extensive archive including nineteenth-century newspapers and rare books in Gujarati,

Urdu, and Hindi. Their purpose is not only to render the texts more intelligible, but to trace the lineaments of the dense theatrical culture in which the autobiographers' activities were embedded. The footnotes interpret literary allusions and puns, and insert information omitted in the originals. Historical personages mentioned in the autobiographies, and institutions such as theatrical companies, are annotated in Appendix 1. Titles of plays and films in the texts are referenced with their authors or directors and dates in Appendix 2. The glossary defines Hindi and Urdu words that remain untranslated because of their specialized usage.

Each autobiography is preceded by an introduction specific to that work. Although arranged in chronological order, the autobiographies are self-contained narratives and may be read in any sequence. The introductions outline the life and achievements of the autobiographer and list his most important performances or works. Such topics as the style of the original, translation issues, the publication history of the text, and how it came to be written are also discussed.

The translations with their attached introductions in Part 2 are preceded in Part 1 by two chapters that supply contexts for the autobiographies, drawing on the approaches of cultural history and literary criticism. The aim of the first of these two chapters is to insert the autobiographies within an account of a historically specific form of theatrical practice. The Parsi theatre had been in existence for forty-five years by 1898, when Jayshankar entered the scene. Herein I present a synoptic view of its development, beginning with the first Parsi-sponsored drama performances in Bombay in 1853. This chapter explains how from its roots in amateur dramatics the Parsi theatre became a middle-brow commercial enterprise, in the process fanning out from Bombay to all parts of India, especially Delhi and the North.

The objective of the second chapter is to problematize autobiographical writing in India and focus on the theatrical memoir as a distinct genre. To this end, I enter the debates about the origins of autobiography and propose a definition of autobiography that is transcultural and transregional. Turning to the emergence of theatrical reminiscences within print culture in India, I then trace the context of literary production for the autobiographies within this volume. In the second part of this chapter, I discuss the ways in which theatrical memoirs constitute archives for examining histories of cultural formation, theatrical practice, and oral performance. This analysis entails a thematic reading of the texts for their documentary value.

The chapters in Part 1 do not presuppose any acquaintance with the autobiographies. Their purpose is to introduce the reader to the broad contours of the Parsi theatre and to establish the significance of theatrical autobiographies as cultural documents, thereby allowing for an informed encounter with the texts that follow. In Part 3, by contrast, the endeavor is to engage with the autobiographies fully from a position of foreknowledge and reflection. Here, I first look closely at the act of self-presentation at the heart of autobiographical writing. I begin with the axiom that life narratives are crafted by design and cannot simply be read as factual accounts. The reading of autobiography is connected to the way in which the self is understood, and the chapter therefore takes up the culturally and critically divergent forms of selfhood that have attained most notice in the literature.

In the final chapter I explore the voices articulated specifically in these life stories. My readings capture the differences among and within these memoirs in regard to narratorial manner and style, from Radheshyam's tone of supercilious superiority to Betab's mix of feistiness and self-deprecation. I highlight autobiographical templates such as the *bildungsroman* and consider the persistence of the didactic voice. The analysis responds to each autobiography in its own right, while marking the common ways in which childhood, education, maturation, success, and destiny are represented. Listening for what is omitted or elided as well as what is articulated, I direct attention to silences in the texts and point to instances in which silence, surprisingly, is broken.

These readings provide no closure; they are meant rather to spark questions and encourage a range of responses. Ultimately, they return us to the texts. In their performative ebullience, the narratives transcend analysis, suggesting the multifarious modes of being and vitality of their subjects—which, in the end, make their survival seem so worthwhile.

Acknowledgments

Scholarly projects, like autobiographies, are almost always collaborative acts. Many people have assisted me directly or indirectly, and many have been part of my life while this project evolved, sustaining me through their love and friendship. Those closest to home deserve credit first, especially my life-partner Carla Petievich, my parents Yvonne and Charles Hansen, and my in-laws Zaida and George Petievich. Their strength and support carried me through many a passage.

Among those who helped shape this book, I am most grateful to my friend Cynthia Talbot for perusing the entire manuscript with a historian's keen eye, and to my editor Rukun Advani for his unflagging enthusiasm and ear for the musicality of language. The dear colleagues who stimulated me over the past decade with their thoughtful remarks include Rimli Bhattacharya, Stuart Blackburn, Uma Chakravarti, Shohini Ghosh, Svati Joshi, Saleem Kidwai, Amrit Srinivasan, Rosie Thomas, Patricia Uberoi, Ravi Vasudevan, and Sylvia Vatuk. Santwana Nigam, Rajinder Nath, Govind and Roshan Shahani, Tara and Sidharth Sinha, Veena and Phil Oldenburg, Kirti Singh and Y.P. Narula, and Salima and Shoaib Hashmi turned each visit to South Asia into a homecoming with their hospitality.

I am indebted to Samira Sheikh, Sushma Merh-Ashraf, and Sucharita Apte for their help in reading and translating material from Gujarati. For questions related to Hindi and Urdu literature, I thank my esteemed colleagues Ulrike Stark and Allison Busch. A more general vote of thanks for supporting this project in myriad ways is due to Richard Allen, Shahid Amin, Ira Bhaskar, Vasudha Dalmia, Rachel Dwyer, Sabeena Gadihoke, Christine Gledhill, Jack Hawley, Kajri Jain, Nemichandra Jain, Anuradha Kapur, Jim Masselos, Christina

Oesterheld, Francesca Orsini, Chris Pinney, Sunil Sharma, and Sanjay Srivastava.

The translations in this book were undertaken between 2004 and 2006, while I was supported by the National Endowment for the Humanities, the Fulbright-Hays Faculty Research Abroad Program, and a Faculty Research Assignment from the University of Texas at Austin. I am deeply grateful for this research funding. The Department of Asian Studies and the Center for Asian Studies at UT, led by Patrick Olivelle and Joel Brereton, facilitated travel and leaves of absence.

The conception of the book developed during an earlier period of research. Between 1997 and 2001, I visited South Asia three times with funding from the American Council of Learned Societies, the USIA Fulbright Senior Scholar Program, the National Endowment for the Humanities, and the American Institute of Indian Studies. My thanks go to each organization for underwriting my research on the Parsi theatre. I am grateful to the Institute for Research on Women at Rutgers University, especially its director Bonnie Smith and the associate director Beth Hutchison for welcoming me as a visiting scholar, and to the Southern Asian Institute at Columbia University for the courtesy of a research affiliation.

In South Asia, I thank the following for the kindness of hosting me during research visits: Manju Jain, Department of English, Delhi University; Devraj Ankur, National School of Drama, Delhi; Vijaya Mehta, National Centre for the Performing Arts, Mumbai; Kishwar Naheed, Pakistan National Council of the Arts, Islamabad; Rajni Nair, Delhi Office, and Uma Das Gupta, Calcutta Office, United States Educational Foundation in India; Peter Dodd, Fulbright Country Director, Islamabad; Pradeep Mehendiratta, American Institute of Indian Studies, Delhi.

For archival assistance and access to records, special thanks go to Shrimati Madiman and Sucharita Apte, NCPA Library, Mumbai; Pratibha Agraval, Natya Shodh Sansthan, Kolkata; P. Sankaralingam and S. Ramakrishnan, Roja Muthiah Research Library, Chennai; Himani Pandey, Indira Gandhi National Centre for the Arts, Delhi. I am grateful as well to the libraries of the National School of Drama, Sahitya Akademi, Sangeet Natak Akademi, India International Centre, Natrang Pratishthan, and Jawaharlal Nehru Memorial Library in

Delhi; University of Bombay (Fort and Kalina campuses), K.R. Cama Oriental Research Institute, and Centre for Education and Documentation in Mumbai; National Film Archive of India in Pune; and Bholabhai Jesingbhai Institute in Ahmedabad.

I also benefited from the services extended to me by James Nye, William Alspaugh, and Marlys Rudeen, Regenstein Library, University of Chicago; David Magier, Butler Library, Columbia University; and Merry Burlingham, Perry-Castañeda Library, University of Texas at Austin. I owe a special word of thanks to Allen Thrasher at the U.S. Library of Congress, and to the Center for Research Libraries in Chicago. The former India Office Library and present British Library in London have also been invaluable resources.

Certain of the illustrations are reproduced with permission from the following archives: Natya Shodh Sansthan (nos. 2, 3, 14, 22), Indira Gandhi National Centre for the Arts (no. 4, 19), British Library (no. 9), Phillips Antiques, Mumbai (no. 10). Gool Madan Ardeshir generously allowed me to include a rare image of her great-grandfather, J.F. Madan (no. 5). I am grateful to Pratibha Agraval for permission to publish the translated text of, and reprint two illustrations (nos. 21 and 23) from, *Mastar Fida Husain: Parsi Thiyetar men Pachas Varsh* (1986). I thank B.D. Garga for his permission to reproduce an illustration (no. 12) from *So Many Cinemas: The Motion Picture in India* (1996). Credits for other illustrations are as follows: no. 1: Charles Sisson, *Shakespeare in India: Popular Adaptations on the Bombay Stage* (1926); nos. 6, 7, 8, 11: Vidyavati Namra, *Hindi Rangmanch aur Pandit Narayanprasad Betab* (1972); no. 15: Lakshmi Narain Lal, *Parsi-Hindi Rangmanch* (1973); no. 16: Suresh Nayak, *Bapulal Nayak* (1980); nos. 17, 20: Jayshankar Sundari, *Thodan Ansu: Thodan Phul: Jayshankar "Sundari" ni Atmakatha* (1976); nos. 13, 18: photographs by the author. Every attempt has been made to trace the names and addresses of copyrightholders and secure permission for the illustrations reproduced herein. Any omissions brought to the notice of the author or publisher will be remedied in subsequent printings.

Part 1

1

Pioneers to Professionals
A Retrospective of the Parsi Theatre

In South Asia, new forms of theatre stemming from the European encounter developed around 1850. The Parsis of Bombay, Zoroastrians who had come from Iran a millennium earlier, were one of the first groups to adopt Western modes of stagecraft and organize dramatic companies. They were not alone: the Gujarati, Marathi, Bengali, and other Indian-language theatres offered spectators comparable diversions by the early twentieth century. Regardless of ethnic or regional affiliation, all participated in a commercial entertainment economy and played to a bourgeois class of spectators in cities with rapid economic growth. Everywhere, forms of music, dance, and drama once restricted to aristocratic groups became ready commodities. The theatre experience became a defining feature of colonial modernity across South Asia.

Within this overall transformation, the Parsi theatre occupied a distinct space. It was identified by its entrepreneurial backbone, not by its performers, audience, language, or content. The Parsi theatre companies contained a mix of Parsis and non-Parsis, as did their audiences, and the dramatic fare they offered rarely referred to Parsi religion or culture. In fact, Parsi theatre, both by the composition of its personnel and the sorts of plays it staged, synthesized elements of Asian and European origin, lending it a hybrid, middle-brow character. Most unusually, its large companies circulated throughout the subcontinent. Touring by rail and ship, they reached a vast territory and achieved a remarkable degree of popularity. The rubric "Parsi theatre" came to signify glamor and sophistication wherever the mobile units went.

For this reason, possibly, the designation stuck, despite its somewhat misleading reference to a specific community.

The Parsi theatre held sway as a major component of South Asian popular culture for almost a hundred years. During this span, it mushroomed from a few groups of aficionados in Bombay to a pan-Indian phenomenon. How did the Parsi theatre come to figure so significantly on the map of popular entertainment? This chapter provides a history of the dynamic process of its growth. It outlines the important shifts in theatrical organization, language, and repertoire that enabled the theatre to remain vital to several generations of spectators.

The period begins with the seeds of a new theatrical culture in 1853 and ends with the arrival of another entertainment medium, the talkies, in 1931. The autobiographers whose life stories form the substance of this book were key players in this history, even if their arrival on the scene did not take place until the late 1890s. This allows for a retrospective which creates a larger context for the autobiographies, and for sketching the conditions that led to their appearance. It positions these stories against a larger painted curtain, as it were, illuminating the lives of our four protagonists.

Pioneers of the Parsi Theatre, 1853–1868

At the dawn of the Parsi theatre era, the idea of performing dramas in Indian languages on a proscenium stage was a novelty in Bombay. The first theatre house built on the Western model had opened in 1776 on the Bombay Green, in the heart of the British settlement. By the 1820s, amateur theatricals had acquired a modest following in colonial society. The dramas enacted were recent imports from the British stage, and the ambience derived from the London theatres. Nonetheless, members of the local elite began to take an interest in these English-language productions. In the face of mounting debt, the Bombay Amateur Theatre was sold in 1835, and for a decade Bombay lacked a public playhouse. When a large group of citizens petitioned the Governor in 1840 for funds to construct a new theatre, prominent Parsis topped the list of signators and provided financial aid.

The Grant Road Theatre opened in 1846 under English management, and the first plays were performed in English. Yet soon the new playhouse proved an ideal setting for Indian theatrical ventures. A group of players led by Vishnudas Bhave staged dramas based on the Hindu epics there in 1853. Parsi drama clubs also chose this venue for their earliest efforts. Their performances offered Indian spectators the opportunity to behold their costumed brethren acting, and they produced on the proscenium stage the cadences and witticisms of their own languages. From the performers' perspective, the pleasures of mounting productions in such a milieu must have been enormous. After witnessing English dramas for several decades, they now took up the reins themselves.

The social environment in which these activities occurred was rather circumscribed. In the main, two groups were pivotal to sustaining the Parsi theatre's early growth. The patron class was comprised of the mercantile elite, or *shetias,* leaders in the city's economic, cultural, and political life. *Shetias* had been active during the campaign to construct the Grant Road Theatre in 1840.[1] These wealthy backers were tapped when the first Parsi troupes appeared in 1853. Their largesse was crucial because, for the first fifteen years of its existence, the Parsi theatre was an operation of amateurs. Only after 1868 did *shetias* begin holding shares and the companies become commercial enterprises.

The second group of pivotal importance was the professional middle class, which yielded the majority of the players. The earliest Parsi Dramatic Corps members were educated youths from respectable families, gentlemen who made their living in journalism, law, and medicine. Their exposure to English education and Western literature had developed in them a passion for amateur theatricals. With their penchant for performing and desire to educate and reform society, these middle-class actors supplemented the *shetias'* cultural philanthropy.

Both groups conceived of theatre as an agent of moral betterment. The stage was understood as created by men of refinement for the edification of their class of society. The new theatrical experiments required careful nurturing, and the English newspapers were only too happy to commend them:

---

[1] Hansen (2002): 40.

> A Parsi Theatre will be opened before the rich, the gay, and the pleasure-loving of this island [Bombay], by a Company of respectable young men who intend to make their first appearance, on the boards of the Grant Road Theatre, about the middle of this month.... Nothing can be farther from their minds than any hope of pecuniary advantage—the highest wish of their hearts is to see the springing up of a taste among the Parsis for the Noble and the Beautiful, and for the enjoyment of those etherial pleasures which the Drama is sure to provide for them, if only kept in subordination to Morality and Virtue.[2]

Thus was heralded the first Parsi production of *Rustam and Sohrab*, a tale from Firdausi's Persian epic, the *Shahnama*. In the following months, five similar performances were publicized in the newspapers.

Although not intended exclusively for Parsis, these early shows were oriented primarily towards this community. As the playwright Edalji Jamshedji Khori, author of the first dramatic script, put it: "This play has the most intimate relation with Parsis. Its matters relate to Parsis. Its writer is a Parsi, its producer is Parsi, and the main audience is Parsi."[3] The *Shahnama* corpus set the Parsi theatre apart from folk-theatre forms based on the Hindu epics. It strengthened the early theatre's identity by reproducing tales from Iran, the Parsi mythic homeland, which were already in circulation within the community. And such early plays were enacted in Gujarati, the language of the region where the Parsis first settled in India.

Firdausi was not the only source, however. Parsi theatre buffs demonstrated an early penchant for Shakespeare. Gujarati-language productions of *The Taming of the Shrew*, *The Merchant of Venice*, *Two Gentlemen of Verona*, and *Timon of Athens* were presented in the late 1850s.[4] Elphinstone College youths also experimented with performing Shakespeare in English. Kunvarji Nazir established the Elphinstone Dramatic Society, a student group that earned kudos for its public performances in the Grant Road Theatre. The Shakespeare Society, another student club, mounted productions in the more private confines of the college.[5]

---

[2] *Bombay Telegraph and Courier*, Oct. 4, 1853.
[3] Khori (1870): Preface, 3, trans. Samira Sheikh.
[4] *Bombay Times*, May 13, 1857; Nov. 18, 1858; April 9, 1859; Aug. 4, 1859.
[5] Mehta (1960): 178–88.

The third kind of play was the farce, typically performed as a "tailpiece." At its debut in 1853, the Parsi Dramatic Corps presented *Dhanji Garak* after the main drama. In this playlet, a Goan watchmaker is brought to trial and the magistrate satirized.[6] Many farces focused on gender norms and family life. When performed for women-only audiences, they inculcated "scientific" attitudes toward religion, hygiene, and family welfare. Women were warned against blindly imitating their European sisters in *Freedom to Native Females*. Other farces, performed for mixed audiences, were intended to correct the behavior of men. *The Mahlarees* urged youths not to frequent lewd song-and-dance shows; men were instructed to avoid the excesses of the traditional marriage system. Although played for laughs, these farces defended modernity, reform, and colonial rule. The butt of humor was often the "unenlightened native." Some perpetuated the myth of the Oriental despot, indirectly promoting British rule. *The Folly of Indian Princes* portrayed the Oriental nabob and his sycophants. Anglo-Indian courts of law were also lampooned. One skit showed the judge, barristers, and functionaries in their flowing robes and "superfluous ribbons," and the plaintiff was ridiculed as a rogue, rascal, and perjurer.[7]

In both the serious play and the farce, dramatic narratives were harnessed to agendas of improvement and instruction. This civilizing discourse was used to gain elite support for initial theatrical efforts in modern Indian languages. By the early nineteenth century, most popular theatre forms in the Indian vernaculars had fallen into disrepute. When the Parsi theatre was gaining a footing, it was often contrasted with the Bhavai, a folk theatre of Gujarat, and the dances of Mahlaris and nautch girls. Against their supposed decadence, the new theatrical mode claimed to impart reason, virtue, and civility.[8]

The new spatial set-up of the playhouse also distinguished the Parsi theatre. The European-style theatre served to contain the transgressive energies of popular performance. Its gates and guards restricted access,

[6] Willmer (1999): 174–6.
[7] *Bombay Times*, May 31, 1858.
[8] Hansen (2003): 392–3. Similarly in Calcutta, the English-educated gentry held Jatra in contempt and tried to shed its influence, albeit unsuccessfully. Lal (2004): 40. On Bengali theatre in this period, see also Bhattacharya (1998), Chatterjee (2008), Das Gupta (1934).

while audiences were segregated by seating in separate classes: the pit, galleries, stalls, boxes. The proscenium arch positioned the players within an expansive picture frame, placing them at a distance from the audience. Announced times for starting and stopping asserted a new temporal discipline.

Despite these advantages, theatrical productions were limited by the poor quality of scripts, acting, costumes, and scenery. According to one journalist, "The Grant Road theatre in those days [*circa* 1863] was a picture of Gujarati translations of other plays, gaudy and loud costumes with gold and silver drapery, metal and silver-paper coated bamboo strips for swords, and only one type of curtain used as a backdrop."[9] Shows were sporadic and poorly funded, and the musical aspect not well developed. The stage scenery, routinely considered inadequate by reviewers, was improved by the addition of gas lighting after the visit of an Italian opera company and the repainting of the proscenium in 1872.[10]

By the end of the 1860s, as many as twenty Parsi theatre companies existed; almost all were amateur troupes. Few playscripts had been published, and very little is known about the playwrights.[11] Nor did the actors achieve much fame, the notable exception to this being female impersonators. Unlike their forebears in folk theatre, these were young men of social standing. D.N. Parekh, who played Portia in *The Merchant of Venice*, became a medical doctor and lieutenant colonel in the Indian Medical Service. Framji Joshi, the female lead in *The Lady of Lyons*, became superintendent of the Government Central Press.[12]

During this preliminary phase, Parsi amateurs regularly performed at the Grant Road Theatre and occasionally at Elphinstone College and elsewhere. Educated youths formed clubs and attracted sponsorship from wealthy citizens. Audiences were attracted through publicity in the newspapers, and a rudimentary theatrical public came into being, closely identified with the middle and upper classes of the Parsi community. Most of the serious dramas were presented in Gujarati.

---

[9] *Kaiser-i Hind*, Mar. 25, 1888, p. 342, trans. Sucharita Apte.
[10] Mehta (1960): 204–6.
[11] The earliest published plays from the Parsi theatre are in Ranina (1865).
[12] Hansen (1998): 2292.

Farces used a variety of speech registers, including Hindustani, to caricature different ethnic groups. Through theatrical activity, Parsis were able to buttress their economic position with an image of cultural cosmopolitanism. They also established a public sphere in which issues of group identity, history, reform, and morality could be debated. The early Parsi theatre helped to consolidate and legitimize Parsi influence in the metropolis, even as it planted the seeds of an entertainment culture that was to extend far beyond Bombay and its founder community.

Expansion and Professionalization, 1868–1891

In the next few decades, the theatrical enterprise underwent major economic, social, and aesthetic reorganization. Drama companies were restructured as profit-making concerns. Actors, playwrights, musicians, and stage crew were recruited, hired on contracts, and paid regular salaries. Theatre companies and private publishers issued dramatic texts and songbooks, selling them to add to ticket sales. The largest companies started touring at home and abroad. As new technologies of stagecraft were adopted, theatrical effects became more and more spectacular. To meet the demands of more diverse audiences, dramatic construction, plot types, and language usage shifted over this period.

This efflorescence was made possible by urban growth, prosperity, and social change. It also owed much to the favorable reception accorded theatregoing as a respectable activity. Playwrights expounded upon the moralizing effects of drama and encouraged audiences to appreciate its pedagogical utility. In the preface to his Gujarati *Romeo and Juliet*, Delta praised "the blameless amusement of theatre [that] enlarges the mind, gladdens the heart, cools the eyes, and speeds morality."[13] K.N. Kabra exhorted his spectators to consider the playhouse (*natakshala*) as a schoolhouse (*vidyashala*), only superior to it. Title pages of printed plays displayed the dictum, "Rational entertainment, in which popular amusement was combined with moral instruction and intellectual culture," attributed to Prince Albert.[14]

---

[13] Delta (1876): Preface, trans. Samira Sheikh.
[14] See Kabra (1869): title page.

During this time, audiences became more inclusive in class and ethnic composition and less specifically Parsi. Both trends were promoted by company owners: these remained exclusively Parsis. The actors who emerged now as celebrities, pre-dating the cinematic star system, were also Parsis. Even the first actress of note, Mary Fenton, although of Irish ancestry, married a Parsi and adopted a Parsi name. The Parsiness of the companies was heralded on tours outside of Bombay. Local companies often adopted the rubric "Parsi" or added "of Bombay" to their names, even when based elsewhere.

And yet the special relationship between the Parsi theatre and the Parsis of Bombay gradually weakened. The use of Urdu, a primarily North Indian language, was introduced in 1871 and quickly caught on. As Urdu romances and musicals proliferated, Gujarati was no longer the sole medium of Parsi-produced drama. *Shahnama* historicals were joined by other genres, not only Indo-Muslim adventure stories and fantasies but also topical contemporary plays or "socials." The repertoire grew in a number of directions, and plays came to be written and even performed by non-Parsis, diluting the Parsiness of the Parsi theatre.

The most influential and long-lived companies date to the beginning of this period. Foremost was the Victoria Theatrical Company, established by K.N. Kabra in 1868. Among its original four owners was Dadi Thunthi, who thirty years later would become Jayshankar Sundari's mentor in Calcutta. The second great company was the Alfred Theatrical Company, founded in 1871 by Framji Joshi. The third was the Elphinstone, the only company from the 1860s that survived and turned professional.

The actor-director came into his own in this phase of development. The most successful companies—the Victoria, the Alfred, the Elphinstone—were identified by their charismatic managing directors: K.M. Balivala, K.P. Khatau, and C.S. Nazir. Balivala starred in *Sone ke Mol ki Khurshed* in 1871 and became the Victoria's director in 1878.[15] As the theatre professionalized, a larger proportion of its actors was drawn from the lower classes. Khatau, Nazir, and others lived in Dhobi Talao, a poor neighborhood located in the city center. Khatau,

---

[15] Gupt (2005): 157–9.

a singing tragedian, was born to an indigent Parsi family. He joined the stage in 1875 and took over as manager of the Alfred Company in 1886, running it successfully for thirty years. Khatau was playwright Betab's boss and a major influence on his writing career.

The top companies vied with each other to obtain the best scripts, engage the most popular actors, and produce the grandest spectacles. Companies would send spies to view and learn by heart their rivals' new plays. Sometimes they planted disruptive elements in the audience to create mischief. The newspapers often served as a forum for mutual antagonisms. Writing under pseudonyms, company directors would attack each other in print. Even painters of curtains and scenery were enlisted in disputes. When the mercurial Dadi Patel wished to insult his rival Nazir, he had a drop scene especially prepared. It pictured himself as a beautiful youth and Nazir as a huge snake, recalling Lord Krishna subduing the serpent-demon Kaliya.[16]

Jealousies developed within companies too. Many a time an actor in pique would break away and start his own company, enticing his colleagues to come with him. The new actor-manager claimed that his was the original branch of the company, or he would devise a new company name that was easily confused with the old one. Thus, the Victoria sprouted two offshoots in the 1870s: the Original Victoria led by Dadi Patel, and the Empress Victoria of Jahangir Khambata, as opposed to the pre-existing Victoria, which continued as the Parsi Victoria or the Balivala (Balliwala) Victoria.

From 1868 onward, fierce demands were made to book the Grant Road Theatre, the most desirable playhouse in Bombay. Rival companies rented it out on different nights of the week. As an alternative method of earning revenue, companies began touring outside the city. The Victoria Company started the trend with its tour to Hyderabad in 1872. With the coming of transcontinental railways, theatrical companies hired special bogeys and sometimes took over entire trains for their luggage, trappings, performers, and laborers. The Victoria visited Delhi, Lucknow, Calcutta, Banaras, Jaipur, Lahore, and Poona in the 1870s. In the 1880s, Balivala led an excursion to Mandalay in Burma; the Elphinstone Company ventured across the seas to

[16] Ibid.: 179.

Colombo, and the Victoria followed; visits to Penang and Singapore began; and the Victoria Company sailed to London, England.[17]

The supply of playhouses in Bombay eventually improved. The Victoria Theatre was constructed on Grant Road at the recommendation of Dadi Patel, although it was reserved for his company. Dadi Thunthi also established a theatre there, and several other playhouses came up nearby.[18] Grant Road was located at what was then the extreme northern boundary of Bombay. Its position in the Native Town attracted a mixed crowd of Indian spectators. The long journey for a night's amusement, however, was difficult for European theatregoers and elite Indians residing to the south.

The addition of theatre houses in the affluent Fort district was thus welcomed. Opposite the massive Victoria railway terminus, two European-style playhouses opened. The first was the Gaiety Theatre, built by Nazir. The second, the Novelty Theatre, was constructed by Balivala and his partner Moghul. Both had impressive painted curtains and large stages; the Novelty seated 1400. The upmarket location of the Gaiety and Novelty stimulated elite taste for theatrical entertainment. Gujarati and Marathi dramas as well as European shows were featured alongside Parsi theatre fare at these venues.

1. Victoria Theatre, 1870

[17] Ibid.: 116–21.
[18] Ibid.: 36–40.

In these years, a fierce competition erupted between two Parsi theatrical companies, the Elphinstone and the Victoria. Each wished to exceed the other in its revival of a specific musical pageant, the *Indar Sabha*. This was an Urdu romance from 1853 that had originated in the court at Lucknow. The rage for the *Indar Sabha* increased the popularity of Urdu among spectators. The piece continued to be produced for decades all over India, being translated into various languages and often reprinted.[19]

2. *Indar Sabha* Handbill

---

[19] See Hansen (2001).

Having served as a lingua franca in British India, Urdu was used for education and governance in the nineteenth century. More importantly from the point of view of stage history, the language connected the Parsi theatre to well-endowed narrative and lyric traditions. The first Urdu plays were fanciful romances or adventure tales full of desirable women, supernatural beings, and heroic struggles. Such material, derived mainly from Persian and Urdu *dastan*s, proved appealing on stage. Urdu and the Islamicate court culture in which it was embedded also conveyed rich strains of poetry and music. Plays in Urdu were full of ghazals, lyric poems exuding love and desire. Even dialogues and soliloquys took the form of rhymed prose, with lines ending in multisyllabic refrains following poetic convention.

The shift to Urdu was linked with a greater use of music, and many plays in Urdu were advertised as "opera." These plays made use of Hindustani ragas and *tala*s for their ghazals and other song genres. The musical settings were imported from the salon or *kotha* of North India, heir to refined amusement in the post-Mughal period.[20] Parsi-Urdu dramas featured a number of visual innovations as well. Stories abounding in giants, spirits, and magic weapons were the forerunners of the "action" film. The fantasy was another common genre, focusing on erotic attraction between denizens of different realms: fairies, mortals, demons. Both types of narrative made sophisticated use of stage apparatus such as trapdoors, flying machines, lighting effects, and multiple curtains. Transformation sets executed by mechanical devices also came into vogue, and painted curtains were sometimes replaced by three-dimensional constructed sets. The addition of technology to stage production was understood as an advancement in knowledge and linked to scientific progress. Special value was placed on "realistic" displays such as live horses and running water. A reviewer found fault with a production of *Ali Baba* for not meeting the expectation of numerical realism: he wanted all forty thieves on stage. Still, his disappointment seems to have been compensated somewhat: he praises the company for importing a living tree from England.[21]

These strides in visual realism coincided with the rise of another kind of spectacle—that of "woman." The quest for verisimilitude was

---

[20] Hansen (2003): 401.
[21] *Kaiser-i Hind*, Feb. 16, 1890, p. 11, trans. Sucharita Apte.

even more complex in this case. Female characters were customarily represented by male actors, and by the 1870s female impersonators had become valued company assets. Those who earned kudos were known by the role they had performed to acclaim: Pestanji Madan became Pesu Avan, after his character Avan in *Pericles*. Young men of pleasing figure and superlative voice became especially important as music gained a greater role on the Parsi stage. J.F. Madan, who later in life founded a Calcutta-based entertainment conglomerate, got his start playing women's roles. He was considered a fine singer and danced the *jhumar* gracefully with a pot on his head.[22] Naslu Sarkari, famed for his sweet "cuckoo" voice, regularly took the female parts opposite Khatau as leading man. Another famous impersonator, Kavasji Contractor, was affectionately called Bahuji, meaning "young wife, daughter-in-law."

Simultaneously, female performers began to appear on the Parsi stage. In 1872, one Latifa Begam was abducted from backstage following her performance for the Parsi Theatrical Company. In another anecdote, Dadi Patel brought four female performers along when he returned from a tour to Hyderabad. He introduced these "Hyderabadi begams" as the four fairies in his production of the *Indar Sabha*. Balivala also inducted female performers into the Victoria Company.[23]

There was initially an outcry from journalists and reformers against women performers. Professional actresses were understood to be immoral and unruly, a stigma on the theatre. On the other hand, in the discourse of colonial modernity respectable family women were considered a civilizing force, and the Parsi theatre had from the outset encouraged attendance by such women. It had devised various strategies, holding women-only or family shows, and even providing childcare. In time, therefore, the appearance of Indian women in public became more acceptable, and perhaps this led to greater opportunities for female performers. By the late 1880s, progressive opinion had softened to the point of favoring women in female roles.

The question remained, which women? The burden of representing Indian womanhood could not be borne by all. One journalist argued in favor of a particular actress by citing her marital status and class

---

[22] Patel (1931): 257, trans. Sushma Merh-Ashraf.
[23] Ibid.: 181–2, 358.

background: "We are happy to know that the female artiste whom the owners have employed is a respectable woman. She is a good singer from North India. She does not belong to the lowly groups who constitute the singing profession. She is a married lady with children . . . This is enough proof of her respectability."[24] Ideally, actresses should be respectable women, but the Parsi community's own women had to be kept strictly apart from the acting profession, else they would be branded as disreputable and damage the reputation of the entire group.

So, "other" women, non-Parsis, were the preferred category from which actresses were recruited. One possibility was the class of courtesan-entertainers, who were primarily Muslim or chose to represent themselves as such. Another was the foreigner or "madam" actress. Earlier, in Calcutta, English actresses had emerged from the ranks of officers' wives and daughters and participated in amateur theatricals. European actresses also traveled to India specifically to work in colonial society. Mrs Deacle, who was recruited for the Sans Souci Theatre in Calcutta, subsequently moved to Bombay to manage the Grant Road Theatre. Under the stage name of Grace Darling, she played a Parsi woman opposite actor-manager Nazir.[25]

There was a precedent, then, for the first white woman to achieve celebrity in the Parsi theatre. The offspring of Jannette and Matthew (an Irish soldier), she was born in Landour and baptized as Mary Jane Fenton. Nothing is known of her upbringing and education. She was on tour as a magic lantern entertainer when Khatau discovered her in the 1870s and began tutoring her for roles on stage. Fenton's appearance in public created an immediate sensation, buttressed by rumors of her intimacy with Khatau. Her touching singing, accurate pronunciation of Hindi and Urdu, and ability to mimic Parsi modes of femininity were an instant hit. She later changed her name to Mehrbai, married Khatau, and bore a son named Jahangir.[26] Nevertheless, her presence in the Alfred Company was a source of discord. Several of its owners objected and eventually left the company to form their own. Even a madam-turned-Parsi could not quell the anxieties associated with performing women.

---

[24] *Kaiser-i Hind*, Mar. 23, 1890, p. 10, trans. Sucharita Apte.
[25] Das Gupta (1934): 207–14, 268–70; Patel (1931): 17–18.
[26] Gupt (2005): 164.

Such scandals notwithstanding, the Parsi theatre became a renowned and seemingly permanent fixture in the city's cultural life during this period. Although it competed with Gujarati and Marathi drama troupes for space in the urban playhouses, the Parsi theatre offered its audiences an unprecedented degree of spectacle and an ever-changing repertoire. Its audiences were no longer dominated by Parsis. As touring companies roamed the countryside, Parsi theatre shows appealed across linguistic and ethnic lines, communicating through the universal languages of song, dance, and mime. Traveling actors absorbed influences from their contact with others, inspiring countless local imitators. Regardless, the cosmopolitan core of the popular art remained intact, and its economic foundation was fundamentally secure.

Challenge and Opportunity, 1891–1931

During the third phase of Parsi theatrical history, many of the trends of the previous decades continued. This is the period during which our autobiographers make their entrance. As before, new companies arose to challenge the dominion of the established troupes. Most significant was the New Alfred Theatrical Company, founded in 1891. It became the flagship company of the twentieth century, employing both Radheshyam Kathavachak and Fida Husain in its heyday. Betab too was affected by its extraordinary influence. The Parsi theatre extended its outward reach, with many companies traveling widely, shifting their operations away from Bombay. Numerous companies sprang up in the provinces, and the Parsi theatre's organizational practices and presentational style exerted a major influence on vernacular drama all over India.

Innovations and artistic growth marked this period. The companies reached more heterogeneous audiences and employed a more variegated cast of artistic personnel. New languages and genres found favor with spectators who were often less cosmopolitan than the Bombay public. As religious reformers and nationalists sought to enforce puritanical restrictions on popular entertainment, the Parsi theatre lost some of the moral high ground it had claimed. A new social conservatism emerged in companies such as the New Alfred, marked by stern adherence to traditional gender norms. Yet these pressures led to creative advances too. Female impersonation reached a pinnacle of artistic perfection, embodied in the graceful enactments of Jayshankar Sundari. The mythological genre was invigorated to address spectators who now understood themselves as Hindus. Hindi as a language of the Parsi theatre thrived among North Indians, reaching far-flung audiences such as the Marwaris of Calcutta. Simultaneously, Urdu drama flourished as never before. It left a popular legacy that found a receptive haven in the early sound cinema.

The New Alfred Company encapsulated the tensions of this period. It prospered under the directorial hand of Sohrabji Ogra, a Parsi who also played comic roles. One of its managers, Manikji Jivanji Master, was a Parsi, but its actors and musicians were mainly Hindus and Muslims from outside Bombay, especially Gujarat and North India. The New Alfred pursued a policy of gender segregation and forbade actresses from appearing on stage. It imposed strict rules with regard to training and disciplined behavior within the company. This principled approach buttressed its reputation as a source of wholesome family entertainment. The New Alfred's staid image impressed the Hindi literatteur Premchand, and nationalist leaders such as Madan Mohan Malviya and Motilal Nehru attended its performances and praised them.

Like its parent company the Alfred, the New Alfred traveled across North India and far west into what is now Pakistan. The companies' successes in this territory were aided by the fact that Urdu had become the prevailing language of the Parsi stage. Many Urdu playwrights were employed as *munshis* and contributed to the sizeable corpus of dramas that were performed and published. The North Indian orientation was reinforced by the recruitment of actors, musicians, dancers, and artisans from UP and the Punjab.

Simultaneous with this development, the Gujarati-language theatre was becoming increasingly popular in western India. Aided to no small extent by stars like Jayshankar Sundari, the Mumbai Gujarati Natak Mandali and other companies began to threaten the Parsi theatre on its old turf. Although Gujarati productions were stylistically similar to those in the Parsi theatre, the two were now differentiated by language and community. The Gujarati theatre was identified with its Hindu patrons and performers, whereas the Parsi-Urdu theatre had become infused with Indo-Muslim culture and was linked now to Muslims as well as Parsis. In the face of a looming divide between the two, the mythological, a genre laden with Hindu religious and nationalist meanings, entered the Parsi theatre.

Through the efforts of Betab and Radheshyam, epic and devotional themes from Hindu tradition were revived and adapted for the Parsi stage. The mythological provided the companies with a vehicle to recapture a pan-Indian audience and unify it under the banner of national identity. It also entailed a shift of language. With the appearance of Betab's *Mahabharat* in 1913, Hindi was, for the first time on stage, seriously proposed as an alternative to Urdu. Announcing itself triumphally, the language of the new dramas was rich in Sanskritisms and printed in the Devanagari script.[27]

Cross-currents also developed over the representation of gender and were manifest in the rivalry between the two top companies—the Alfred and the New Alfred. The New Alfred was established, it is said, in protest at Khatau's showcasing of Mary Fenton. After the split, Khatau regained control of the Alfred and sponsored a series of star appearances featuring Fenton.[28] The shows were a hit, Fenton's cachet as a foreigner adding to her allure. The "madam" phenomenon continued to gain ground in the twentieth century. Women understood as European or Anglo-Indian were commonly employed by theatre companies. Their racial identities were often blurred, perhaps on purpose. An actress like Patience Cooper, who starred in Radheshyam's and Agha Hashr's plays in Calcutta, was usually thought to be an Anglo-Indian of mixed parentage. She was actually from the Baghdadi Jewish community, a group that had settled in India in the early nineteenth century. So was Sulochana, the stage-name of the actress Ruby Myers.[29]

The New Alfred responded to the vogue for actresses by taking the phenomenon of female impersonation to a higher level. The company found a new source of artistic energy in the Nayak or Bhojak community of Gujarat. This was a hereditary group that specialized in music

---

[27] Hansen (2006).
[28] Hansen (1998): 2293.
[29] Ibid.: 2297.

and dance. In the late nineteenth century, urban theatre companies began to send agents to villages in Gujarat for the purpose of recruiting Nayak boys. When these boys arrived in Bombay or Calcutta, they were trained to become professional dancers and sing in chorus lines dressed as females. The most outstanding from their ranks matured into the leading female impersonators of the day.

Amritlal Keshav Nayak was one such who joined the theatre at the age of 11.[30] He became Ogra's assistant director in the New Alfred four years later. With his literary proclivities in several languages, Amritlal proved himself a successful song-writer and director. He was also instrumental in bringing a number of other Nayak boys into the New Alfred. Under his guidance, Bhogilal, Purushottam, and Narmada Shankar became its new generation of heroines. They went on to contribute to the development of choreography, stage direction, music, and acting.

The actor Jayshankar Sundari was the most famous Nayak of them all. Although primarily associated with the Gujarati stage, he received his training in the Parsi theatre. His stage roles created prototypes for the ideal Indian woman of the early twentieth century. By embodying feminine sensibility and decorum, his persona exemplified the companionate heroine. Sundari's art was such that spectators insisted he could surpass any woman in his representation of the beauty of womanly suffering. His appeal to spectators of both sexes makes it evident that female impersonators were not simply substitutes for actresses. They coexisted and competed with actresses and could exceed them in popularity and artistry.

Both Sundari and Fenton found social drama the ideal medium for modeling feminine behavior. This genre focused upon domestic matters relating to family and marriage. "Socials" in this period were often written in Gujarati. The most memorable were those of B.N. Kabra, who wrote for the Parsi theatre, and Mulshankar Mulani of the Gujarati theatre. Notwithstanding these efforts, the majority of plays were written in Urdu. Murad worked as the leading dramatist of the Alfred Company under Khatau; he later joined the New Alfred.[31] Betab's encounter

---

[30] Lal (2004): 313.
[31] Gupt (2005): 130–2.

with him had a tremendous effect on the budding poet. Another popular playwright was Ahsan, who hailed from a lineage of Urdu poets in Lucknow.[32] Although best known for his Urdu adaptations of Shakespeare, Ahsan also wrote the play *Chalta Purza* which was set in contemporary times. Its performance in the New Alfred featured Amritlal Nayak and Narmada Shankar in female roles. Another important Urdu writer was Talib, a Hindu Kayasth from Banaras. He was associated with the Victoria Theatrical Company.[33]

The career of the prolific playwright Agha Hashr Kashmiri illustrates the scope of Urdu playwriting in this period.[34] Born in Banaras to a family of shawl merchants, Hashr wrote for a series of companies, including the Alfred, the New Alfred, and the Corinthian in Calcutta. He established and ran several companies himself, such as the Indian Shakespeare Theatrical Company, but these did not endure for long. He authored more than thirty dramas in all the leading genres: romantic, historical, social, and mythological. Hashr also wrote many screenplays, mostly adapted from his dramas. During the silent film era, his socials and mythologicals contributed to the development of Indian cinema. Later, with the arrival of sound, his work for the cinema industry more effectively incorporated Parsi theatre style. Hashr's dialogues and lyrics for *Shirin Farhad* were famously enacted by the singing duo Kajjan and Nisar. Several of his Shakespearean plays came to life on screen with the famous Parsi actor Sohrab Modi in title roles. His most influential play, *Yahudi ki Larki*, was remade several times as a film.

During these years, Parsi-organized troupes traveled to Lahore, Karachi, Quetta, and Peshawar. Radheshyam reports visiting the Khyber Pass and setting foot in Afghanistan. When Betab was working for the Alfred Company, the troupe toured the hills of Baluchistan. Betab's play *Gorakhdhandha* opened in Quetta. Even Jayshankar Sundari spent eight months in Karachi performing his signature play, *Saubhagya Sundari*. A number of spin-off Parsi theatre companies developed in the western Punjab and beyond. Meanwhile, in the

---

[32] Ibid.: 86–92; Lal (2004): 6.
[33] Gupt (2005): 68–80; Lal (2004): 465.
[34] Gupt (2005): 84–6; Lal (2004): 149–50.

3. Agha Hashr Kashmiri

Deccan the Nizam of Hyderabad patronized Parsi-led troupes such as the Helen Theatrical Company, which was photographed by Raja Deen Dayal.

It is noteworthy that the Parsi theatre also established itself firmly in Calcutta. In the 1890s, J.F. Madan purchased the Corinthian Hall and acquired ownership of the Elphinstone Theatrical Company, transferring its operations to Calcutta. This was the beginning of the entertainment empire that developed into the Madan Theatres.[35]

[35] Lal (2004): 241; Rajadhyaksha (1999): 139.

4. Helen Theatrical Company, 1908

Madan encouraged the Alfred Theatrical Company to perform in Calcutta, and it was to this eastern city that Betab traveled when he answered the company's call in 1909. The illustrious Victoria Company was absorbed by the Madan empire in 1913. Many smaller companies were taken over as the Madans built cinema halls and expanded into film exhibition and distribution. Eventually, even the original Alfred Company merged with Madan Theatres. However, as Radheshyam recounts, the New Alfred Company resisted all invitations to perform in Calcutta, and thus it retained its autonomy and avoided being bought out.

The restructuring of the industry around the Madan-family monopoly naturally led to resentment among old-line companies like the New Alfred. In the 1920s, the success of Betab's and Radheshyam's mythologicals persuaded Hindi nationalists like Premchand to moot the possibility of the Parsi theatre achieving a sufficiently high artistic and moral standard to serve the nation. These expectations ultimately came to naught. The Madans are often blamed in hindsight for debasing the quality of the Parsi theatre and hastening its demise through their rampant capitalistic ventures. The historical evidence, however, suggests a more complex set of factors. The struggle for financial survival grew more acute in this period. With the professional Gujarati

5. Jamshedji Framji Madan

theatre taking off in Bombay, Parsi-run companies were compelled to seek other markets, incurring new entrepreneurial expenses. The salaries demanded by star performers, scriptwriters, musicians, and designers of sets and costumes soared. In this capital-hungry climate, the rulers of native states, India's rajas and maharajas, moved in on the business of running theatre companies. They often took extraordinary risks, enticed by the prestige of possessing their own troupe of actors (and actresses), but their ventures usually ended in financial disaster.[36] To add to these pressures, slowly the cinema was gaining ground, pushing the theatre literally out the door as old playhouses were converted into motion picture palaces.

The third period ends, then, not with the arrival of silent films, which did little to threaten the appeal of the Parsi theatre, but with the advent of talking and singing motion pictures. Three of our autobiographers—Betab, Radheshyam, and Fida Husain—went to work for film production studios, as did many actors, musicians, scenarists, and playwrights from the remaining Parsi theatrical companies. Yet the Parsi theatre did not come to a complete halt. As Fida Husain's narrative makes clear, vestiges of the Parsi theatre in Calcutta survived through World War II and continued into the postcolonial era. The Parsi theatre had developed for more than a century, remaking itself for every generation of spectators through the process of adaptation and change. But its glory days were over. Luckily, the four autobiographies within this volume eloquently recapture those days.

---

[36] In 1927, the Maharaja of Charkhari, a princely state in central India, purchased the Corinthian Company of Calcutta along with the services of famed playwright Agha Hashr and the actress Sharifa, with whom the maharaja was smitten. The stage properties, costumes, and assets were valued at forty lakhs; they were later sold to Fida Husain for Rs 7000.

2
Theatrical Memoirs and the Archives of Autobiography

Autobiographical accounts by people in the theatrical profession began to appear in India in the early twentieth century. Binodini Dasi, the well-known actress from Calcutta, published *Abhinetrir Atmakatha* (Autobiography of an Actress) in a magazine in 1910, and hers is likely the first of such writings. In the decades that followed, men and women of the Indian theatre—actors, actresses, playwrights, managers, and directors—recounted their lives in print for public consumption. Writing in Bengali, Hindi, Gujarati, Marathi, Tamil, and other languages of the professional stage, they created a unique type of autobiography and a distinct category of literature.

This chapter situates the four narratives in this volume within this newly created class of theatrical memoirs. To understand its evolution, I backtrack in the first section to consider the development of autobiography in India and debates about the definition of the genre. In the second section, I describe the emergence of theatrical reminiscences within print journalism and introduce several leading memoirs. Lastly, I characterize this class of texts as important to three historical archives: the archive of India's cultural formation in the nationalist era, the archive of dramatic practice and theatre as an institution, and the archive of oral performance and performers.

Autobiography in India

Autobiography as a separate literary genre came into being and acquired a following in a number of Indian languages in the second half of the nineteenth century. These autobiographies identified themselves as *atmakatha* (self-story), *atmacharit* (self-chronicle), and *apbiti* (one's own experiences). Other terms used were *jivani* and *zindaginama*. Rashsundari Debi's autobiography, quite possibly the first published in an Indian language, was entitled *Amar Jiban* (My Life; first published in 1868). These labels were the Indic equivalents of "autobiography," the English term also known and used in India at this time.

Before the nineteenth century, self-referential texts produced in the subcontinent can be traced back to passages in the works of Bana, Bilhana, and Dandin in Sanskrit. The Mughal emperors introduced autobiographical writing when the *Baburnama* was translated into Persian during Akbar's reign. The first known Indic-language autobiography was Banarasi Das's *Ardhakathanaka* (Half a Tale), composed in 1641 in a mixture of Brajbhasha and Khariboli Hindi. Banarasi Das wrote it when he was 55, and since the Jains considered the lifespan to be 110, he gave the work this title. As in many premodern life-stories, the author focused on his experiences of travel and the evolution of his religious beliefs.[1] In the modern era, the autobiographical account of the secluded housewife Rashsundari Debi recounts how she taught herself to read with the goal of studying the Vaishnava religious canon. Rashsundari imbued her work with devotional yearnings and described events in her upper-caste household.[2]

These early autobiographical writings from India correspond with others like them elsewhere. In Japanese literature, autobiographical works were first written by women dating to the tenth century. Arabic writing of an autobiographical nature was clearly established by the twelfth century. Around 1700, the golden age of Chinese autobiography was already ending, just as the genre arose in the West. These non-European bodies of literature do not disprove the familiar assertion that autobiography is a distinctively modern literary form. They do, however, compel recognition that autobiography is not *exclusively* modern. They also challenge the notion that the genre originated in Europe and diffused outward from there.[3]

---

[1] See Babayan (2008) and Malhotra (2009) for examples.
[2] Sarkar (1999): 2.
[3] See Bowring (1987), Reynolds (2001), Wu (1990), and Kaviraj (2004).

These qualifications are important, given the prevalence of arguments that connect autobiography in India to the encounter with the West and the formation of colonial modernity. A widely held view stresses the necessity of written models of the autobiographical genre, tracing a narrative of influence through English education and exposure to English literature. Contact with the West, it is thought, introduced the textualized form of the exemplary life, which became a useable template for imitation. Yet narratives such as Banarasi Das's clearly pre-date English-language autobiographies. As far as later autobiographies are concerned, English literary antecedents played a role from the nineteenth century onward. However, indigenous genres such as *charit*, *tazkira*, hagiographies, and oral modes of performance also shaped life narrative in India.[4]

Another popular opinion regarding the rise of autobiography emphasizes a particular kind of individualism related to the modern concept of the self. For scholars such as Kaviraj, the crucial precondition for autobiography is "the invention of private life," which enables a reorientation toward the self and interrogation of normative structures, especially the family.[5] Focusing similarly on the private self, the Rudolphs assert that Amar Singh's act of writing a diary established a private space and thus was "culturally deviant" and "smacked of rebellious consciousness."[6] A concept of the individual as separate from the community or collective body is considered necessary not only to writing about the self, but to creating introspection and interiority, the hallmarks of autobiography. According to an often-cited formulation by Weintraub, "Autobiography presupposes a writer intent upon reflection on this inward realm of experience, someone for whom this inner world of experience is important."[7]

Yet Indian autobiographies rarely meet the test of introspection. Lath, the editor and translator of *Ardhakathanaka*, judged Banarasi Das's narrative deficient in "introspective complexity."[8] Fisher, in his analysis of an eighteenth-century traveler, commented upon the same

---

[4] Arnold and Blackburn (2004): 6–9.
[5] Kaviraj (2004): 95–8.
[6] Rudolph and Rudolph (2002): 31.
[7] Weintraub (1975): 823.
[8] Lath, in Banarasi Das (1981): lxxi.

lack: "Dean Mahomet did not explicitly examine his inner self."[9] Such findings also pepper the analysis of other contemporary autobiographies from India. However, the expectation of interiority is largely derivative of Western norms and seems misplaced in the Indian context. One may imagine alternative modes of self-narration that rely less on introspection, and these ought not be judged as deficient or inferior. As Waghorne demonstrates in the case of C. Rajagopalachari, the personal is often narrated through story-telling and myth in India. Variations in the form of the autobiography may well occur where "the subjective is experienced as objective,"[10] as she neatly puts it.

More could be added to illustrate how autobiography is constrained, how the capacity of the genre is narrowed when understood as the byproduct of European modernity. In Chapter 7, I will problematize at some length concepts of the self and the writing of autobiography. At this juncture, let me situate Indian autobiography with respect to more expansive constructs. I refer to the set of terms, "life narrative," "life history," and "life writing," as used by Smith and Watson in *Reading Autobiography*, as well as Arnold and Blackburn in *Telling Lives in India*. In their usage, such terms of reference have become maximally inclusive.

"Life writing," according to Smith and Watson, encompasses biographical, novelistic, historical, and other kinds of writing that take a life as their subject. "Life narrative" by contrast is restricted to the writing of one's own life. Nonetheless it is still a broad term, extending to genres such as the chronicle, diary, memoir, and autobiography. By studying life narratives in their diverse forms, the authors highlight the commonalities across autobiographical genres and invoke a shared history of critical appreciation. This strategy seems beneficial because it softens boundaries and allows more space for postmodern forms of self-writing. On the other hand, the authors unnecessarily fortify the boundaries around "autobiography," dismissing it as an outmoded project tainted by its alleged origins in the European Enlightenment. As the "master narrative of the sovereign self," autobiography has in their eyes become an oppressive, exclusionary genre. It is therefore

---

[9] Fisher (1998): 896.
[10] Waghorne (1981): 599–600.

rejected in favor of "life narrative," an open category more appropriate to a postcolonial and globalized history of the field.[11]

Arnold and Blackburn adopt the even more elastic term "life history" as their category of choice. They include within it both biographical and autobiographical texts, but they rule out novels and fiction. In order not to privilege print over orality, they extend the category to written and spoken forms of narration. Thus oral histories and folktales, of which India has an almost infinite number, are admissible. By virtually equating "life history" with "life story" as understood by anthropologists, they further broaden the canvas to the lives of gods, saints, and ordinary men and women.[12] This strategy, like Smith and Watson's, resists "artificial boundaries." It attempts to make connections between first-person and third-person narration, and between stories told and heard as well as stories written and read. The storytelling category that emerges, however, lacks analytic power. Life history may designate a broad field useful for certain types of study, but it is far removed from the specific genre of autobiography.

My method, by contrast, is to reclaim autobiography from its detractors and reinstate it as a useful descriptor for the purposes of this book. I intend to use the term for life narratives written by the subject herself or himself. Autobiography, unlike oral history, is a literary genre grounded in the materiality of writing. It is also clearly legible as an enunciation of the self. However, "self," "writing," and even "life" are invariably inflected by culture, convention, place, and time. Beyond this basic definition, the autobiographical text may be in prose or verse, singly authored or written in collaboration, fragmentary or comprehensive, descriptive of outer worlds or focused inward. The definition I pose encompasses cultural diversity and is flexible enough to include variant forms.

Returning to the autobiographies of nineteenth-century India, these works were predicated upon print culture, as against the oral modes of life narration that had long prevailed. The genre could not thrive before the consolidation of reading publics in the Indian languages. New readerships coalesced around commercial book publishing in

---

[11] Smith and Watson (2001): 3–4, 197.
[12] Arnold and Blackburn (2004): 9–14.

the mid- to late-nineteenth century, making genres like vernacular novels accessible to diverse audiences. The growth of reading communities accelerated with the spread of newspapers, magazines, and journals. Many life histories were produced, usually in the form of brief biographies, for the print media.[13] First-person accounts enlivened the reportage that filled the pages of the popular press. During the same period, sustained autobiographical writing in book format began to be produced by reformists and cultural innovators.

Among the men who wrote the pioneering Indian-language autobiographies, many were public figures affiliated with literary, educational, social, and political circles. A few examples should suffice. Ishwar Chandra Vidyasagar was a major Bengali writer, Sanskrit educator, and humanist who campaigned against polygamy and in support of widow remarriage. Upon his death in 1891, he left a fragmentary account of himself that was published by his son.[14] A more substantial Bengali work was the autobiography of Debendranath Thakur (1898), founder of the reformist Brahmo Samaj movement. His illustrious son Rabindranath Tagore published his own autobiography in 1912. In Hindi, the Arya Samaj founder Swami Dayanand Sarasvati published his autobiography in the journal *Theosophist* between 1879 and 1880. In the South, the nationalist poet Subramaniya Bharati wrote an autobiography using traditional Tamil poetic meters. A notable early autobiography in Telugu was that of Kandukuri Veersalingam, a pioneering figure in Telugu literature and keen social activist on behalf of women.[15] These were followed by a plethora of political personalities such as Surendranath Banerji, Lala Lajpat Rai, and most famously M. K. Gandhi and Jawaharlal Nehru.

Early Indian-language autobiographies were also written in surprisingly large numbers by women, figures more marginal to the national narrative.[16] In Bengal, a profusion of female authors began to appear

---

[13] Ibid.: 8.
[14] See Hatcher (2001).
[15] Datta (1987): 274–86. For early autobiographies from Kerala, see Kumar (2008).
[16] Tharu and Lalita (1991): 160.

after 1850. Here, the wives of prominent citizens did not, as a rule, write of their lives. Those who initially took to writing were the unheralded women of the inner quarters. Autobiographies were also penned by actresses from the Bengali stage, women like Binodini Dasi who possessed public reputations but received an ambiguous kind of respect. Both groups, Tanika Sarkar argues, wielded the power of self-narration to reverse their low social esteem.[17]

Female autobiographers in Marathi were often associated with men active in politics and reform. Ramabai Ranade, wife of the jurist-nationalist M.G. Ranade, published her autobiography in 1910, focusing on their life together.[18] Kashibai Kanitkar, who pursued a lifelong friendship with the Marathi novelist Hari Narayan Apte, wrote several novels herself as well as an autobiography. Women from privileged families in Parsi society in Bombay also wrote candidly of their achievements. Dosebhai Jessawalla received education in an English school at the early date of 1842. She wrote *The Story of My Life*, a now-forgotten 500-page autobiography, and published it in 1911. Cornelia Sorabji, the first woman to study law at Oxford, wrote two autobiographical works, the first of which has been reissued.[19] For these writing women, personal growth was linked to national progress, as it was for the male intelligentsia. In common with the Bengali housewife and the actress, however, these authors stirringly called for female education, and they broke norms that had placed constraints upon women for generations.

Memoirs written by actors and theatre personnel constitute another significant subset of the early autobiography in India. These accounts have escaped notice until recently. Many were published by small presses with limited circulation, although some have recently been reprinted. Compared to the lives of political leaders or social reformers, these narratives were tangential to the trajectory of India as an emerging nation. Professional entertainers at the turn of the nineteenth century rarely entered politics, unlike film actors today. Their humble circumstances and minimal education placed these autobiographers on par

---

[17] Sarkar (1999): 131.
[18] Tharu and Lalita (1991): 281–90.
[19] Kosambi (2008); Lokuge (2001).

with the self-taught women who first wrote of their lives. Like the secluded wife, the theatre performer was arguably a subaltern subject who rarely spoke in his own voice. In writing of his life, he harnessed the force of self-representation to break the silence, to speak his own existence into being.

Despite a certain similarity, however, a huge disparity in the degree of their visibility separated theatre people from family women. The playhouse was a well-established public arena, unlike the domestic space of the household. Theatrical productions were open to view and comment, and, prior to the act of writing, actors and playwrights were known to society at large. The identities of theatre personalities had already been constructed, in part through their performances and stage personae, in part through the stories and rumors that spectators spread about them, and increasingly through the published reports in newspapers and magazines that formed part of urban folklore.

Theatre Reminiscences and Lives in Print Culture

Biographies of nineteenth-century Parsi theatre personalities featured regularly in the pages of Bombay's newspapers—before theatrical autobiographies as such were composed. The most notable example is the series of sketches written by Dhanjibhai N. Patel. Himself a playwright, actor, poet, and photographer, Patel enjoyed personal friendships with Parsi theatre personalities. He was active on the stage until 1886.[20] Patel penned some 97 essays, each of which was published serially in the Gujarati and English daily *Kaiser-i Hind*, probably in the first decade of the twentieth century. In 1931, 68 of the essays and 150 accompanying photographs were compiled in a 422-page volume, *Parsi Natak Takhtani Tavarikh*. The sketches begin with the first Parsi Theatrical Company in 1853 and extend through the 1890s. This rare volume is an indispensable aid for reconstructing the early phase of the Parsi theatre.

A similar work is the semi-autobiographical *Mahro Nataki Anubhav* (My Experiences in the Theatre) by Jahangir Khambata. This

---

[20] Darukhanawala II (1963): 270–1.

250-page narrative covers the same period as Patel's text and, like it, is a compilation—of 62 essays that were published weekly in the journal *Parsi*. Khambata was a well-known actor and company owner who also penned a number of popular social dramas. He founded the Empress Victoria Theatrical Company, was its managing director, and later performed with several other leading companies. *Mahro Nataki Anubhav* begins with five or six episodes from Khambata's life: his birth, parentage, education, and the onset of his "dramatic mania."[21] Thereafter he describes the dramatic clubs of the day, returning only rarely to his personal role in the remainder of his account.

Theatre biographies were also published in other formats, such as an introduction or preface to a work authored by the subject. The actor and director Amrit Keshav Nayak wrote a novel entitled *M.A. Banake Kyon Meri Mitti Kharab Ki?* (Why did you educate me and destroy my honor?) This book "[exposed] the evils of the social life of Indian graduates of the present time," according to a British Museum catalogue. It was prefaced by a biographical essay written by Nayak's friend Thakkur Narayandas Visanji, and reprinted from the journal *Gujarati*.[22]

Although generally quite brief, these published biographies preserved luminous memories of performers and performances. They created name-recognition for the actors and their companies, celebrating the early days of Parsi theatre. The pieces were published in Gujarati-language newspapers and magazines, and the primary readers would have been men and women literate in Gujarati and affluent enough to purchase newspapers. Because newspapers were read aloud and passed from hand to hand, they may also have reached a large secondary audience. Such "readers" were not necessarily acquainted with the Parsi theatre, but through hearsay they likely gained an interest in it.

Another forum for the telling of theatrical lives was the theatre magazine, a byproduct of the public theatre in Bengal.[23] Bengali-language theatre journals such as *Rangalay* date to 1901, although theatre-related items appeared in ordinary newspapers in Calcutta earlier, as they did in Bombay. These specialized theatre magazines

---

[21] Khambata (1914): 5.
[22] Nayak (1908): 12.
[23] Bhattacharya (1995).

documented the golden era of Bengali theatre, taking a retrospective view on the past century. Alongside historical surveys, the magazines favored scandal, allegations, and diatribes. They prominently featured the lives of theatre personalities, especially actresses; often the actress-stories were fabricated. The first autobiography of the celebrated actress Binodini Dasi (1863–1941) was serialized in one such magazine, *Natya-Mandir*, in 1910. Binodini's second autobiography, *Amar Abhinetri Jiban* (My Life as an Actress), came out in *Roop o Rang* between 1924 and 1925.

In Tamilnadu too, the vernacular theatre was on the threshold of transformation toward the end of the nineteenth century. Pammal Sambanda Mudaliar was the founding figure in the early modern Tamil theatre. A prolific playwright, actor, director, and producer, Mudaliar established a theatre company in 1891, the Suguna Vilasa Sabha, that became a model institution. His theatrical memoirs are a treasure house of information on late-nineteenth and early-twentieth century Tamil theatre. Mudaliar's autobiographical work, subtitled in English *Over 40 Years Before the Footlights*, extends in book form to six volumes.[24] The memoirs were originally serialized each week in the Tamil newspaper *Swadesamitran*, a pioneering venture affiliated to the nationalist movement.

The Marathi stage also produced a number of theatre biographies and autobiographies. The founder of the modern Marathi theatre, Vishnu Amrit Bhave, was the subject of a biography by Vasudev Ganesh Bhave. The playwright Sripad Krishna Kolhatkar wrote of his life in *Atmavrutta*. Govind Tembe, the pioneering musical director, wrote two autobiographical accounts. Another well-known playwright, Mama Varerkar, published his memoirs in two volumes. None of these works has been translated into English, and little is known about them.

Within this body of life-writings from the theatre, the autobiographies contained within this volume are historically significant, representative examples. They belong to two distinct phases. Betab's autobiography is best located within the early stratum of theatrical memoirs. Installments from what became the *Betabcharit* were initially serialized in the magazine *Arya Kumar* in 1924–5. This publication

---

[24] See Mudaliar (1998).

postdated the biographical sketches by Patel and Khambata and overlapped with the publication of Binodini Dasi's second autobiography. The theatrical era evoked, however, was of a more recent time. Patel and Khambata commemorated the Parsi theatre up to 1890; Binodini Dasi's career on the Bengali stage was over by 1887. The early twentieth century was when Betab flourished, and his account engaged with the period of Parsi theatrical history from 1900.

Sundari, Radheshyam, and Fida Husain, on the other hand, were born toward the end of the nineteenth century, their lives continuing well into the second half of the twentieth century. Changes in publishing practices and reading habits made it possible for Radheshyam and Sundari to bring out their autobiographies in book format from the beginning. Both Sundari and Fida Husain became cultural icons in independent India, winning recognition and patronage from the government and cultural elite. Despite these factors, their narratives reveal the preoccupations and patterns of earlier texts. Their years in the Parsi theatre also overlapped to a great extent with Betab's. Despite the age difference, they worked in the same or parallel companies with a common cast of colleagues. For Sundari and Radheshyam, this was possible because they became involved with theatre at a young age. Fida Husain joined the profession somewhat later, but he inherited their world.

The Archives of Autobiography

As historical documents, these autobiographies are a trove for those interested in the institution of theatre and dramatic practice. The texts abound in the names of actors and companies, titles and dates of plays, and other minutiae vital to constructing a factual record of the stage. Equally valuable are the descriptions of audience and patronage, reviews and controversies, which locate theatrical activity within civil society. Several of the texts discuss stagecraft and production techniques, and all of them mention the importance of rehearsals and discipline. The value of these sources within the archive of theatrical history is corroborated by their publication under the auspices of the National School of Drama and Natya Shodh Sansthan.

Theatre-related data does not exhaust the usefulness of these memoirs. The autobiographies may be situated within two additional archives, bracketing the purely theatrical. First, these documents offer unprecedented insights into India's cultural formation in the nationalist era. They comment upon political developments, religious reform, language debates, caste mobilization, changing attitudes toward women, and the spread of education and reading. The texts also belong to the archive of oral performance and the popular performer. The history of orality is ephemeral and elusive, but it can be glimpsed through the systems of knowledge and ground realities of performing communities attested to in these works. The autobiographies document the landscape of performance genres, the locations of performers, and the social environments they were required to negotiate.

In the following section, the contributions of the autobiographies to each of these archives are analyzed in turn. In this reading of the works, their documentary value is separated from their character as accounts of the self. This choice is guided by Francis Hart's differentiation among the three "autobiographical intentions:" memoir, confession, and apology. According to Hart, memoir is not a distinct genre or sub-genre of autobiographical writing, but rather a stance of the author, a way of narrating the self. Memoir is "personal history that seeks to articulate or repossess the historicity of the self . . . [it] places the self relative to time, history, cultural pattern and change."[25] Autobiography is always part memoir. Focusing here on memoir in Hart's sense, I am considering one particular mode of the autobiographer's address to the reader.

The four theatrical memoirs differ in the degree to which they project a chronology of modern Indian history. Betab is virtually silent about events at the national level, whereas the others all mention the struggle for Indian independence and its attainment in 1947. Both Radheshyam and Sundari announce that they became followers of Gandhi, with the former joining the Congress Party. References to the British Raj, on the other hand, are sparse. Where they do occur, the interest is not in colonial governance but in its implications for cultural performance. Fida Husain cites Queen Victoria's Golden Jubilee in 1877 and the Delhi Durbar of 1911 as occasions when performers congregated in expectation of lavish rewards. More obliquely, Betab tells of a meeting with one Shor Saheb, an Englishman who

[25] Hart (1970): 491.

was an accomplished Urdu poet; his occupation or relation to the Raj is uncertain. In regard to colonial censorship, Radheshyam makes note of police surveillance at the time that his play *Prahlad* opened. The charge of sedition had to be dropped, he proudly narrates, because no specifically anti-British sentiments could be found in the performance. Of the three narrators who lived through Partition, only Fida Husain comments upon the Hindu–Muslim riots in Calcutta at the time. His memories of the Japanese bombing attack in 1942 are far more vivid.

If major historical events are infrequently foregrounded in these narratives, the cultural changes that accompanied the spread of nationalism are very evident. The most significant of these was the mobilization of the Hindu majority and its growing identification with the nationalist cause. In the nineteenth century, religious and lay leaders of all communities had begun to re-examine their sacred texts, reform their religious practices, and redefine their identities. The religious debates spilled over into the early twentieth century to a much broader swath of the population. Groups like the Arya Samaj began to proselytize widely, and Betab was attracted to its moralistic program of self-examination. He even adopted a distinctive mode of dress to signal his conversion. The Arya Samaj critique of caste influenced his playwriting as well.

By contrast, followers of the *sanatan dharm* like Radheshyam continued to espouse Brahminical privilege. In his autobiography, Radheshyam stressed his personal purificatory acts, such as going on pilgrimage and preparing his own food. Yet despite their religious divergence, both men embraced the mythological drama as the new vehicle of popular entertainment. The reworking of mythic material within the context of national political awakening had already begun in Indian painting with Raja Ravi Varma, and popular plays based on mythological episodes flourished on the Bengali and Marathi stages in the nineteenth century. The Parsi theatre was a relative latecomer to adopting Hindu religious themes, but when it did the trend was irreversible. By recasting tales of epic heroism and portraying parables of devotional fervor, mythological dramas allegorized anti-colonial resistance and promoted patriotic sentiments.

Closely allied to the hitching of Hinduism, of whatever variety, to nationalism was the shift from Urdu to Hindi. The language debates, like those related to religion, had for decades raged in educational and administrative circles as well as literary production, popular culture, and national politics. Betab and Radheshyam grew up in the composite culture of Uttar Pradesh where Urdu and Hindi coexisted in primary education. In his writing Betab switched from Urdu to Hindi; Radheshyam wrote exclusively in Hindi. The autobiographies announce this preference (which may have been at root economic) with the salvific overtones of sacrifice and service to Hindi literature and the nation. They reflect the growing perception that Urdu poetry was associated with a feudal culture of decadence and self-indulgence, as opposed to the stringent, puritanical norms of nationalism symbolized by Hindi. Among Gujaratis, meanwhile, the Gujarati theatre in Bombay was defining itself on the basis of religious community, ethnicity, and language. Sundari's own trajectory epitomized the shift as he abandoned Urdu and the Parsi theatre for the ascendant Gujarati stage.

Another development in this period was the consolidation of communities identified by caste and subcaste. Associations or *sabhas* increasingly coordinated the collective interests of caste groups around agendas of internal unity, genealogical claims, and reformed social practices. These reconstituted clusters could compete more effectively with one another for upward mobility and even enter the national political arena. The mobilization of middle-caste groups is exemplified by Betab's quest to gain Brahminical status for his subcaste, the Brahmabhatts. Betab was also apparently aware of efforts among low-caste groups such as Chamars to gain remediation for their hereditary "untouchable" status, as witnessed in the interpolation of his crusading Chamar character, Cheta, in his *Mahabharat*. Sundari's narrative provides evidence of upward mobility among the Bhojaks of Gujarat. Outlining his caste's achievements as musicians and bards, Sundari characterizes their hereditary occupation as service in Jain temples and for royalty, rather than the lowly performance of Bhavai. Radheshyam's constant reference to his Brahminhood reinforces the sense that contestation over caste gained momentum in the nationalist era.

A major transformation in the status of women and attitudes toward gender roles also occurred, beginning with the posing of the "women's question" in nineteenth-century Bengal. On the one hand, the autobiographers allude to the older social order in which courtesans provided sophisticated entertainment and enjoyed a privileged position. The figure of the playwright Agha Hashr Kashmiri, with his penchant for wine, women, and song, emerges in these narratives as the epitome of the feudal configuration. The playwrights admire him as a poet and personality, but view his pleasure-loving habits with considerable ambivalence. Similarly, Fida Husain describes the efforts to ban the custom of aristocratic courtesans displaying themselves in public at theatrical events. In order to purge the space occupied by the audience and make it respectable for family women, managers barred women of ill repute, even mistresses of powerful maharajas, from the seating area called Special Class. The rejection of courtesan culture formed part of the basis for the New Alfred imposing its ban on actresses. One effect of its policy was, of course, the revival of the institution of female impersonation.

On the other hand, certain of the autobiographers comment upon changing notions of conjugality, companionate marriage, female education, and widow remarriage. Their remarks suggest the degree to which the high-caste nationalist project of women's reform impinged on the lives and attitudes of *qasba* dwellers. Fida Husain carefully maintains silence about his married life. Nonetheless, he seems compelled to deny having had extramarital liaisons with actresses. The others acknowledge their wives and praise them in conventional terms for their domestic virtues. Betab mentions his first wife selling her ornaments to support his career and his second wife's attempt to revive him when he was near death. At a more theoretical level, he argues against the freedom with which widowers marry again while taboos on widow remarriage remain in place. Sundari relates a series of ill-fated marriages and love affairs, stressing the importance of compatibility for a successful conjugal relationship. Radheshyam hints at a long-lived, stable bond with his wife, who was so devoted to their son Ghanshyam that she went blind with weeping when he died.

The advent of education, or at least the awareness of its possibility, also connects the autobiographies to their historical moment. The presence of primary schools in small towns is confirmed by the accounts of Sundari, Betab, and Radheshyam. Betab poignantly laments his lack of access to formal schooling. Sundari, perhaps with a bit of ornamentation, says that he, his sister, and his brother all started school at the age of 7. Reflecting on pedagogical practices, he questions the emphasis on rote learning and protests the use of corporal punishment. Perceiving the benefits of education and the spread of literacy, they refer to the formation of the reading public in their time. Radheshyam and Sundari describe themselves as readers of prestigious novels, newspapers, and journals. They mention their reading habits and provide details of their contact with literati, establishing a putative bond with the educated and well-informed.

The printing press emerges as a historical agent in these autobiographies. Apprenticing as a compositor in a press was an ideal vocation for young men desirous of advancing themselves. The press provided gainful employment and strengthened knowledge of letters. Since playbills were printed there, it often served as a conduit to the theatre. Betab and Radheshyam became publishers and ran their own presses, employing others in the trade that had given them their start. Small-town popular publishing concerns were important to the flourishing of a multiplicity of literary genres in this period.[26] They were noteworthy for extending the vernacular reading public in uncharted directions, leading to greater political participation.

Situating these autobiographies now within the second archive, that of theatrical history, one notices immediately the many references to names, places, and dates. These details acquire meaning when placed in relation to larger cultural phenomena. One learns, for example, of the heightened visibility of playhouses on the urban skyline and their role in the city's cultural life. These playhouses are now all extinct, although each was associated with a landmark performance or performer: the Gaiety Theatre in Mumbai and the Thanthaniya Theatre in Calcutta (Sundari); the Rama Theatre and the Sangam Theatre in Delhi and the Bradlaugh Hall in Lahore (Betab); the Sangam and Banarsi Krishna theatres in Delhi (Radheshyam); the Minerva and Moonlight in Calcutta (Fida Husain).

Passing across the stage of these autobiographies are countless performers and theatre celebrities, from the scintillating playwright Agha

---

[26] See Orsini (2009).

Hashr to the dictatorial director Sohrab Ogra. The accounts are particularly helpful in identifying actors whose forte was the female part but who otherwise remain hidden behind masculine names: Nisar, Narmada Shankar, Bhogilal, Amritlal, Phulchand Marwari, Master Mohan, Chaube Ramkrishna. Many of them later directed the dance routines of the younger boys and became directors themselves, in the manner of Sundari and Amritlal. The names of actresses are more legible, but their mention is significant insofar as it confirms that actresses and female impersonators worked side by side in the companies. Bijli, Putli, Mary Fenton, Gauhar, Sharifa (who played a male role) and her daughter Husn Bano, Mukhtyar, Kajjan, Patience Cooper, Sita Devi, Sultana, and Munni Bai took to the stage and made history.

The professional theatre company emerges from these accounts as a living organism. It is often compared in positive terms to a nurturing family, or more ambivalently to a school, college, or boot camp. The separate functions performed by painters, musicians, dancers, actors, laborers, managers, and owners come to life. The autobiographies conjure up the collaborative nature of stage production, showing how playwrights worked with directors and actors relaying scenes back and forth, and how songwriters, singers, and tabla players who doubled as choreographers developed new items to please the public. They also tell of the rivalries and rifts that could tear companies apart. Company owners suffered from the perennial anxiety that their best actors would quit or be lured by a rival group. In addition, the narratives document the living conditions in the companies, the structure of rehearsals, and off-stage opportunities for diversion. The far-flung travels of companies, to the west as far as Afghanistan and to the east toward Calcutta, are a recurring narrative motif.

An invaluable component of any theatrical history is the dramatic repertoire. The autobiographers detail the titles, authors, and dates of Parsi theatre plays that were popular in their lifetimes. They provide rare information about sources, such as the inspiration for Betab's *Mahabharat* or the antecedents to Radheshyam's *Vir Abhimanyu*. They document the creation of songs, noting the blend of innovation, adaptation, and parody that produced catchy new tunes. The close connections between the Parsi theatre and the Gujarati theatre companies is made transparent in Sundari's life story. Radheshyam worked for a Gujarati company briefly, and employed actors from the Bhojak community. Sundari acknowledges being influenced by the great Marathi performer Bal Gandharva, and both Radheshyam and Fida Husain mention the influence of Marathi theatre, including a visit of the Kirloskar Company to Kanpur.

Cross-regional trafficking in style, personnel, and dramatic material supports a somewhat different interpretation of the mythological genre in the Parsi theatre. The turn to the epics and Puranas is generally explained as a consequence of growing nationalism and the expansion of the Hindu audience in the North, as well as a play for profits by Parsi company owners. But the evidence suggests a longer trajectory of interest in religio-cultural themes covering an extensive geographic area. Whatever its roots, the advent of the mythological led to a measure of ritualization of the heretofore secular space of the playhouse. Betab recommended that Vedic rites be carried out before the debut of his *Mahabharat*, and he credits the success of the opening to them. Radheshyam notes that a Satyanarayan *katha* was held at the launch of *Vir Abhimanyu* together with Parsi rituals. Fida Husain comments on the performance of *arti* at plays related to saints and gods, observing that gullible viewers thought they were receiving darshan of the divine. The autobiographies also emphasize the purification of the performer's body and mind, whether through yogic personal habits as with Fida Husain, through self-reform as in the case of Betab, or through Brahminical rituals in the case of Radheshyam. These trends toward infusing theatrical discourse and practice with Hindu sacrality coincide with the popularity of the mythological and mark a watershed in the Parsi theatre.

Interestingly, changes moved in the other direction as well, toward dilution of the sacred in the mythological. Comic subplots were routinely added to the Puranic legends when they entered the Parsi theatre repertoire. Although Betab's *Mahabharat* omitted this feature, Radheshyam joined scenes of comedy to his *Vir Abhimanyu* and *Prahlad*. He notes with pleasure how Sohrab Ogra, an otherwise dour presence, carried off his comic roles in these plays with aplomb. The performance of mythic female roles such as Sita and Draupadi by Muslim actresses from a dancing-girl background was another site at which *hindutva* might be disrupted. The famous actress Gauhar played both heroines, provoking occasional outrage, as both Betab and Radheshyam narrate. In general, cross-casting was common, and the utilization of non-Hindu actors and actresses for Hindu roles was not remarked upon. Fida Husain makes no mention of the disparity between his Muslim background and his signature role as the saint Narsi Mehta. Such combinations obviously worked and were accepted, although they may have challenged norms of Hindu purity.

The autobiographies illuminate other debates and contestation that surrounded controversial theatrical productions. Censorship was an ongoing reality, although only one clearcut case of police surveillance is cited, that of Radheshyam's *Prahlad*. Court cases could be launched against theatre companies, as when Betab's early play *Qatl-e Nazir* was cancelled due to allegations that it was libellous. Providing officialdom such as police chiefs and judges with free passes was one way of handling these charges. Another method was to cultivate the political elite, a practice favored by Radheshyam who was drawn to leaders such as Motilal Nehru and Madan Mohan Malviya. He even mentions trying to get Gandhi to come to the Parsi theatre.

These accounts also document new sources of patronage for the theatre in the early twentieth century. Sundari mentions the interest evinced by the maharajas of Mysore and Baroda. Fida Husain lists a plethora of princely states with which he had contact: Bikaner, Patiala, Tonk, Jaipur, Indargarh, Charkhari, Jawara, Ratlam, Rampur. As for fans and acolytes from the audience, Sundari details the diverse attentions of a Bohra *seth*, a Bengali *bhadralok*, and women from prosperous Hindu and Parsi families. All of the autobiographies attest to the patronage and financial involvement of merchants or *seths*, be they of Parsi, Gujarati, or Marwari background.

In regard to the third and final archive, that of oral performance and performers, these documents confirm the popularity of many traditions of poetry at the turn of the century. Sundari cites *rasos*, *prashastis*, the *ashtapadis* of Jayadeva's *Gita Govinda*, and Premanand's *akhyans*; Betab mentions the prevalence of *lavani*, *jhulna*, and ghazal; for Radheshyam the significant genres are *bhajans*, *chaupais* from the Tulsidas *Ramayan*, and tales such as *Rukmini Mangal*. The autobiographies also reveal the impact of rural dramatic forms and their connections to the Parsi theatre. As children the authors witnessed

Svang, Nautanki, Bhavai, puppetry, Ram Lila, Ras Lila, and the drama of *Harishchandra*. These oral traditions were embedded within a calendrical cycle of festivals. Dashera, Holi, Janmasthami, Muharram, and the Nauchandi fair are all remembered as festive occasions for oral performance. Importantly, the latter two give support to the thesis of a North Indian composite culture, being venues for both Hindus and Muslims to congregate for parallel or conjoint celebration.

Throughout childhood, these oral traditions anchored the autobiographers to the rural landscape of North India and Gujarat. Most of their fathers were adept at composing and performing the oral genres. Yet beyond this patrimony of orality, their cultural milieu was provincial and *qasba*-based rather than of the village. Betab, Radheshyam, and Fida Husain were all from towns in UP that had a certain diversity of social groupings but lacked contact with cosmopolitan India and the colonial elite. Education and literacy were available in their home towns, but these boys were not formally schooled very long. Betab documents the poverty of his artisan family and his father's resistance to education. Sundari and Radheshyam too seem to have attended school only briefly.

One deterrent was the reality of child labor, unspoken in the autobiographies yet only thinly veiled. Sundari was sent from home to train as an apprentice at the age of 9. Radheshyam was working and traveling with his father at 12 or 13. Betab began to earn around the age of 14. Radheshyam and Betab were by then married and had the additional burden of providing for a wife. These early responsibilities were not unusual, but what is forgotten or covered up is that hereditary performing families often were obliged for economic reasons to hire out their young. The Parsi theatre companies, in turn, stood ready to exploit the talents of this juvenile labor force.

Despite the absence of formal schooling, the *qasba* offered opportunities for learning even to indigent boys like Betab. His earliest instruction was with a local pandit who tutored him in Hindi prosody. Next he undertook lessons with one Ustad Talib. He mentions studying *Hidayak-ul Balaghat*, suggesting literacy of a fairly high order, and since he committed his poems to paper he clearly knew how to write. Betab's history confirms that Urdu literary culture extended to provincial towns, circulating among Hindu groups of middle or low social rank. Urdu poetry enjoyed higher status than *lavani* and other folk genres, and as Betab matured he rejected the latter. Still, his acquaintance with Urdu poetics relied less on formal study and more upon its dissemination through oral culture and traditional pedagogy.

Betab's arithmetical facility sheds further light on the knowledge systems of artisan groups in the *qasba*. It is likely that he learned arithmetic beside his father in the sweetshop. When he began working in Meerut, he was promoted to accountant and looked after the books. His fondness for numbers and what they represent is evident throughout the autobiography. He recalls salary figures, raises, rents, train fares, lawyers' fees, and business losses—and measures his self-worth against them. Betab's mathematical acumen may also have assisted him in absorbing the Hindustani musical system, especially its rhythmic side. He casually mentions that he played the sitar, and here too he seems to have learned through oral pedagogy; he credits one Barkatullah Khan with teaching him during his sojourn in Bombay.

Education in letters also occurred within the workplace. Betab apprenticed himself to a Sanskrit scholar while working as a compositor at the Kaiser-i Hind Press. Accompanying his father as a *kathavachak*, Radheshyam absorbed the repertoire of Hindu mythology that influenced his writing for the Parsi theatre. When he left for Calcutta, Sundari must have had only a slight acquaintance with Urdu, but he quickly learned the language and became a star pupil of the company owner, Dadabhai Thunthi. The need to compensate for lack of formal education and participate in vernacular literary culture became more pronounced as the boys became successful Parsi theatre actors and playwrights. Sundari reports reading the mammoth Gujarati novel *Sarasvatichandra*, as well as studying the dramatic traditions of English and Sanskrit. Acceptance by Premchand, the leading figure in Hindi literature, was extremely important for Radheshyam. Ultimately, the autobiographies suggest a complex of overlapping literary cultures, showing not only how a poet such as Betab might move from Hindi to Urdu and back again, but how autodidacts could claim a position within literati circles, starting from a foundation of orality.

The autobiographies go beyond demographic indicators—class, caste, education—to assemble pieces of their subjects' emotional lives. The pushes and pulls of surviving as a performer come into focus, suggesting a high degree of psychological resilience. These individuals' interpersonal relationships—with parents and older relatives, womenfolk, children and dependents, patrons and bosses, masters and teachers—were full of ambiguities and not infrequently sources of emotional conflict and distress. For Betab and Fida Husain, adolescence was marred by the objections of family members to their choice of theatre as a profession. Although they needed to leave home to pursue their careers, they recall the moment of departure as involuntary, as exile forced by an evil stepmother or a cruel uncle. With Sundari and Radheshyam, the tension arose not from their decision to perform, but from competition among family members who wished to exercise control over the youths. Radheshyam's father would perhaps have allowed him to sign on with a Parsi company at a tender age, but his widowed aunt insisted he sing bhajans in her temple instead. Sundari tells of a tug-of-war among his relations over which theatre company he should join. His mother seems to have played the dominant role in setting the terms of his contract. Later he recounts the pressures upon him to marry, attributing the difficulties in his relationships with his wives to community control and censure.

Finally, each autobiography may be read as the living transcript of the performer's personal repertoire. All the narratives except Sundari's are studded with verses, passages, songs, and other examples of the theatrical art. Particular incidents are styled as parables, suggesting their origin in oral performance. Above all, the autobiographies attest to the multifaceted talents of their subjects. As performers, they moved easily across the religious/secular divide. Sundari's community, the Bhojaks, served as Jain *pujari*s and genealogists, but were equally comfortable dancing Bhavai or acting on the Parsi stage. Radheshyam was a versatile performer who delivered Vaishnava *kathas* one day and directed Parsi theatre plays the next. Betab played the sitar and penned dramatic verse, and Fida Husain could intone the *azan*, sing *qavvali*, and perform in the Nautanki style. For these dexterous artists, performing was their identity, their way of life. They lent their skills to the Parsi theatre and were handsomely rewarded, but had it not existed they would have stepped into another arena.

Part 2

3

Narayan Prasad Betab, *The Deeds of Betab*

Introduction

The poet-playwright Narayan Prasad "Betab" lived through an extraordinary time. During the course of his days, modernity seeped into the fabric of small-town society through the channels of religious reform, caste mobilization, and public entertainment. The movement for India's independence drew diverse sectors into a common anti-colonial struggle, and increasingly Hindi, not Hindustani or Urdu, became its mouthpiece. Betab's career was punctuated by the large shifts occurring around him. After a brief period composing folk verse, he sought training as a poet of Urdu ghazals. He used that language to compose social melodramas, Shakespearean adaptations, and Indo-Islamic romances in his first decade as a playwright. Coming under the influence of the Arya Samaj, his orientation then switched toward Hindi and the Hindu mythological genre, which culminated in his influential version of the *Mahabharat*. While interpreting the epic within the frames of nationalism and reformist Hinduism, in this drama he also articulated the strivings of low-caste groups and championed untouchables.

Betab's rags-to-riches tale, *The Deeds of Betab*, voices the restless yearning for opportunity that must have seized many a youth from his bleak background. Not only is his the earliest autobiography we have from the Parsi theatre, it sketches the starkest scenes of deprivation. His memoir also documents clearly the rising fortunes of a pushy, provincial writer. Betab's mythological dramas earned huge profits for his employers, the Bombay Parsi theatre's Alfred Company and Madan Theatres of Calcutta. He moved into the film industry in 1931, writing screenplays for Chandulal Shah of Ranjit Studios. His mythological and social films earned handsomely for himself and his employers. He also wrote the song lyrics for over two dozen films of the 1930s. At the time he concluded his autobiography in 1936, his pension was worth Rs 1000 per month. Although Betab showcased his moral progress in life, as did every autobiographer of his time, his celebration of materialistic values makes his narrative an indispensable guide to his age.

Betab was born in 1872 in the town of Aurangabad in Bulandshahr district, Uttar Pradesh. His father was a sweetmaker (*halvai*) of the Brahmabhatt caste. His mother died when he was two and a half, and his father remarried. Betab yearned to attend school but instead was trained in the family occupation. His father, although unlettered, was skilled in composing folk plays (*sang*), and Betab inherited the art of

6. Narayan Prasad Betab

versification from him. When he was an adolescent, he began to recite his poems in public competitions. He attempted to learn the rules of Hindi prosody from a local pandit, but gave up on the complexities of the *matra* system. Next he turned to an Urdu *ustad* and gradually developed his poetic taste and skill. By the time he left home, he had abandoned the folk forms of verse such as *lavani* and *jhulna* and was composing ghazals in the classical style.

Following his marriage, disagreements with his stepmother compelled Betab to move away. He began looking for work and found his way to Delhi, where he apprenticed at the Kaiser-i Hind Press. After being trained, he was given a salaried position as a compositor. He started to frequent the shows of the Jamadar Drama Company on the pretext of delivering their printed handbills. Once, he composed a song for the company, and after that he was always admitted for free. He fell passionately in love with one of the boy actors, but the company moved on to Ludhiana, and in time he forgot about him.

When the New Alfred Company came to Delhi in 1899 or 1900, Betab met the well-known poet Murad. After challenging the accuracy of one of his verses, Betab earned Murad's respect despite his unseemly arrogance. From Murad, Betab derived his fondness for writing drama. Among his earliest efforts in playwriting was *Qatl-e Nazir*, based on a topical incident—the murder of a well-known courtesan.

Betab's wife joined him in Delhi around this time, selling her jewelry to buy a train ticket. In addition to his salary from the press, Betab worked as a copyist for additional income. Then he joined the Jamadar Company as a paid employee. He traveled with the company to Lahore, Karachi, and Allahabad. In 1903 he joined the Parsi Theatrical Company of Bombay, owned by four partners including the Apu brothers. He relocated his family to Bombay, but his wife died shortly thereafter; Betab quickly remarried. He teamed up with the popular actor-director Amritlal Keshav Nayak, achieving renown for his social drama, *Zahri Sanp*.

After Nayak's death, Betab was hired by the prestigious Alfred Company, led by Kavasji Palanji Khatau. He moved to Calcutta with his second wife and rented a cheap room, where the couple almost died of asphyxiation. While on tour with the Alfred Company in Karachi, he was introduced to Arya Samaj teachings and underwent a spiritual

7. Scene from *Zahri Sanp*

conversion. He composed *Gorakhdhandha*, an adaptation of Shakespeare's *Comedy of Errors*, during his stay in Quetta.

In 1913, Betab's momentous *Mahabharat* was staged in Delhi. Khatau specially commissioned it in response to an attempt at mythological writing by the Urdu poet Talib, of the rival Victoria Theatrical Company. The debut of Betab's *Mahabharat* was celebrated with Vedic rituals—for fear that staging the strife-ridden epic could lead to disaster. Betab's initiative established Hindi as a viable language for the Parsi theatre, and it brought into the audience Hindu groups who had not frequented the theatre on moral grounds. Betab's addition of Cheta Chamar, an untouchable character, nonetheless aroused many objections.

Khatau died in 1916 while the Alfred Company was in Lahore. Betab was invited to stay on by Khatau's son Jahangir, but he declined and left the company. He taught for several years in a school in Bulandshahr before rejoining the Alfred Company briefly and then transferring to Madan Theatres. Once more he was writing plays in Calcutta, but not for long. Other interests and business opportunities intervened. He initiated a correspondence course on prosody, ran a printing press in Delhi, and operated a grocery in Ludhiana. As founder of the

Atharva Brahmin Sabha, he pursued a campaign to have Brahmabhatts recognized officially as Brahmins. In 1928, needing money for the dowry of his eldest daughter, he wrote the play *Ganesh Janm* and sold it to Madan Theatres.

Betab built a house in Muzaffarnagar, but when sound films (or "talkies") were introduced he was in demand in Bombay. He met film director Chandulal Shah in 1931 and joined Ranjit Studios as a screenwriter. His first successful film was a mythological, *Devi Devayani*, starring Miss Gohar Mamajiwala. Betab suffered a stroke in 1933 but continued to write screenplays and countless songs. He minted money for Ranjit Studios up to the time of the completion of his autobiography in 1936. His last play was *Shakuntala*, performed by Prithvi Theatres in 1945.

The language of Betab's memoir, like his plays, is rich in the vocabulary of both literary Urdu and Hindi. It is full of metaphorical expressions and clever idiomatic usages, some of which lend themselves more readily to English translation than others. In the first half, Betab's mode of expression is quite compressed. His prose possesses a tension and energy that drive the story forward. These qualities are largely missing in the second part.

The translation follows Betab's text closely, and each of his 37 chapters or "stages" (*manzil*) are represented herein. The dedication and invocation are omitted, as are some digressions in the nature of rejoinders to allegations. Often these concern his reputation as an authority on poetry rather than his activities as a playwright, as when he defends his textbook *Padya-Pariksha* (manzil 2) or his correspondence course on poetics (manzil 31). Several long moralizing discourses have been abridged (manzils 10, 12, 24) and a number of narrative passages tightened. Paragraphing has been added when necessary, and although some lists have been retained, others have been rendered as running text.

In regard to Betab's extensive quotation from his own oeuvre, much of his poetry has been omitted from the translation. Of the epistolary poems, "Correspondence in Verse" in manzil 23 has been reduced by half, and "The Wedding Gift" in manzil 34 has been entirely deleted. Poetic couplets and whole dialogues adorn his text, giving it a performative flair. These dramatic examples provide a metatextual comment on his reputation as a poet, but they have largely disappeared from the translation. In the places where I have retained samples of verse, I have made use of rhythm and rhyme to suggest the rather sing-song quality of the original. It seemed appropriate to suggest, however imperfectly, the demotic character of his verse.

The original Hindi text, titled *Betabcharit*, was published in 1937, but the first edition has not been located. It was reprinted by the National School of Drama (NSD) in Delhi in 2002. Several errors were added to this edition, e.g. Modern Theatres for Madan Theatres. To correct the NSD edition, I turned to the biography of Betab written by his daughter, Vidyavati L. Namra. Namra cited many passages

8. Vidyavati Namra

verbatim from the *Betabcharit*. Whenever the NSD wording seemed in doubt, I consulted her version of Betab's text. However, discrepancies between Namra's citations and straightforward passages in the *Betabcharit* caution against a total reliance on Namra. At times she amends Betab's language to clarify his meaning, and occasionally she alters the original sense. Describing an incident in manzil 2, where the NSD version reads, "I was an irritant in the eye of my newly-arrived stepmother (*navagata mata ki ankhon men khatakne laga*)...a whole world of faults began to appear in me (*duniya-bhar ke durgun mujh men nazar ane lage*)," Namra implies that Betab's father was instigated by his stepmother to see his faults and drive him out of the house.[1]

Despite these shortcomings, Namra provides a useful service, corroborating Betab's account through reference to outside sources. She supplies facts for the period after the 1920s, which is only sketchily covered in the autobiography. She also provides plot summaries, dates of opening, and notes on directors and casting for Betab's plays. I have incorporated some of her research into the editorial apparatus but have adopted her readings of the *Betabcharit* only in the case of obvious errors in the NSD edition.

Betab's text is an example of a serial autobiography, a work written and published in discrete sections.[2] In the book's foreword, Betab explains that he first wrote several installments of his life story in 1923–4. These came out, rather irregularly it seems, in the monthly magazine *Arya-Kumar*, a journal for young men with Arya Samaj leanings. Betab had become an Arya Samaj initiate and preacher some twelve years earlier. The magazine was published by his own Betab Printing Works in Delhi.

The autobiography was apparently elicited by one Pandit Durgaprasad, a leader of the Brahmabhatt community, and owed its serial format to the editor of *Arya-Kumar*, Dr Yuddhvir Singh. The latter was a well-known Gandhian and Arya Samaj member who later became Betab's family doctor. These two "coaxers" or "coercers"—Ken Plummer's terms for those who solicit or provoke others to tell their stories[3]—were undoubtedly familiar with Betab and his celebrity in

[1] Betab (2002): 15; Namra (1972): 141.
[2] Smith and Watson (2001): 203–4.
[3] Ibid.: 50.

the Parsi theatre. Perhaps they prevailed upon Betab out of friendship and respect, but other motives may have been present. Betab likely had a special appeal to youthful readers that these older gentlemen admired and sought to harness. Possibly they wished to publicize his life story to draw adherents to their causes, respectively the advancement of the Brahmabhatts and the promotion of the Arya Samaj. Betab's extended treatment of his Arya Samaj experiences and reflections on caste in the autobiography suggest that his coaxers influenced his narrative.

The text is also notable for its bipartite structure. After Betab brought out the first part in the early 1920s, he abandoned the project. He returned to it over a decade later. In 1935–6 he wrote the second part, and the entire autobiography was published in 1937 by Ramrakha Ram in Patiala. The second part of the autobiography differs markedly from the first. It suggests an inchoate pastiche assembled from pre-existing texts. These include his own verse, both narrative and didactic (23, 34), sermons (26), rebuttals aimed at detractors (27, 36), and testimonials about his accomplishments (29). Overall, it is more tendentious and self-aggrandizing.

The dividing point between the two parts is not clearly indicated. The second part may begin at manzil 21. This chapter, unlike the others, bears a title, "All Days Are Not Alike." It contains the first didactic digression, on the topic of widow remarriage. Another break in the narrative comes between manzils 30 and 31. Here, Betab has resigned from the Parsi theatre and gone back to teach in Bulandshahr. If correct, this division would suggest that Betab's account of the *Mahabharat* production belongs to the first part and was written in the 1920s, when the debates and controversy surrounding it were still fresh.

In manzil 37, the final chapter, Betab says he suffered a stroke in 1933 that left him paralyzed on one side. The fragmentary, discontinuous character of the second part may be due to memory loss suffered as a result of this stroke, or it may indicate urgency, prompting Betab to cobble together an assortment of materials, some extant, others new. Although nothing is known about the publisher Ramrakha Ram, it could be his initiative that finally facilitated the completion of the autobiography despite its imperfections. For this, we must be thankful.

Noted Works

Plays

Qatl-e Nazir, 1901; *Zahri Sanp*, 1906; *Gorakhdhandha*, 1912; *Mahabharat*, 1913; *Ramayan*, 1915; *Krishna Sudama*, 1920; *Kumari Kinnari* or *Mother India*, 1928; *Hamari Bhul*, 1937; *Shakuntala*, 1945.

Screenplays

Devi Devayani, 1931; *Radha Rani*, 1932; *Zahri Sanp*, 1933; *Barrister ki Biwi*, 1935; *Prabhu ka Pyara*, 1936.

The Deeds of Betab

Narayan Prasad Betab

Foreword

No name nor fame, I am as one
Whose life cannot make any claim.
To write a tale that bears no fruit—
Useless the task, pointless the aim.

Beneficial it is when those who have achieved prestige or accomplishment write their life histories. To the contrary, nothing I'm aware of having done has advanced my caste, uplifted my country, served the cause of literature, or provided assistance to others. Of what use will my autobiography be to my readers? Nothing at all. A further question then arises. When this life history is completely devoid of substance, why did I decide all of a sudden to write it down? The answer is simply that Pandit Durgaprasadji, Presiding Officer, Brahmabhatt Sabha, Mathura, prevailed upon me to do so.

Around 1923 or 1924, the monthly *Arya-Kumar*, a journal directed toward young Aryan men of India, was being published at the Betab Printing Works, Delhi. It was edited by Dr Yuddhvir Singh, the benefactor who first published some sections of my life story in its pages. With a dearth of free time, I wrote whenever I feared that I couldn't manufacture further excuses. If I was silent for several months, Dr Singh would spur me on, saying, "Letters are coming in from the Aryan boys, asking for your autobiography. Don't abandon the series." His moral support tied a knot in the broken string. The thread unwound for several more lengths and then ended.

Today, twelve or thirteen years later, I've boiled up the stale curry with fresh enthusiasm and started to write once more. I may have taken pen to paper, yet full well I know:

Neither stealing the heart, nor sacred lore,
Just drivel meant to amuse my friend;
No sweetness here nor brilliant thought,
This offering is but tasteless bread.

Whether it will be done well or not, write it I must, and for that I invoke the blessings of Lord Ganesh.

The events of times gone by: I no longer remember the dates, the months, the calendar years. In asking forgiveness for these lapses, I cite two of my favorite lines from Professor Munshiram Sharma of DAV College, Kanpur:

My goal is to write a chronicle of life,
Not to produce a five-fold almanac.[4]

Life is a compulsory journey, with numerous halting points along the way. One must stop at many way-stations, both good and bad. There are countless destinations that must be traversed. I too have passed through many stages to reach the place I am in. It is the reality of those scenes, whether frightful or charming, that I set down in sequence in this narrative.

Bhanu Bhavan, Plot Number 520   Narayan Prasad "Betab"
Matunga (G.I.P.), Mumbai 19

Beginning the Journey

(1)

Narayan Prasad, blot on the tribe of poets, who am I? The worthless son of Dullaray. I stuck the word "Betab" to my name like a tail, so that people would recognize me as a poet.[5] I was born into a family of

---

[4] The traditional almanac, *panchang*, treated five topics: solar and lunar days, constellations, conjunctures, and actions.

[5] Betab's *nom de plume*, meaning "restless, agitated, uneasy," refers to the psychological state of anxiety of the lover separated from the beloved. It also gestures toward the constant striving and ambition that are hallmarks of Betab's life story.

Brahmabhatt Brahmins in Aurangabad, a small town in the district of Bulandshahr. My date of birth was November 17, 1872.

(2)

After just two and a half years of tender nurture, my respected mother turned her earthly remains over to the goddess Nature and took the road to heaven. Father made a second marriage for himself, and somehow or the other I survived childhood and reached the age of adolescence. Careless upbringing dried me out and made me thin as a thorn. I was an irritant in the eye of my stepmother. Blinded as she was by the collyrium of envy, she saw a whole world of faults in me.

On the other side, my father was not—alas for me—a lover of knowledge. In his opinion, education was the root of the nation's weakness. If fate had bestowed upon me the same temperament, the measure of my rebellion would have been somewhat less. As it was, although I knew nothing of the greatness of letters, I considered them the means to eternal joy.

Our hereditary profession was making sweets. In the way that a child learns his mother tongue, effortlessly on his own, I too learned to be a *halvai* as the family calling. With father's instruction, in spite of my young age and frail physique, I became a good workman.

Years have passed, but it seems that just yesterday I sat making *batasha*s, little sugary puffs, while tears dropped from my eyes, reproducing their shape. I wept because I had been given a ladle instead of an ink-stand, a mallet in place of a pen, a drying cloth instead of a sheet of paper, and I could only wonder why.

Generally one observes that children cry while on their way to school, but I cried because I was not sent to school. In a home with no respect for learning, where was the money for books, where the time for study?

God may not have granted me knowledge, but he provided me with the ability to versify. This wealth, I should say, was my patrimony, my hereditary estate. Although father was uneducated, he was from a line of poets; he composed the verse-dramas called *sang*s and other such things. A scribe wrote down the lines while the goddess Sarasvati sat on his tongue and spoke forth. As the family bequest, perhaps not the goddess Poetry, but certainly the demigod Rhyme, had been gracious to me. I began to compose verse incessantly. When I had accumulated a heap of rhymes, I joined an *akhara* and began to compete. People objected to my cheeky fabrications full of mistakes. In those days, when someone pointed out my errors, I considered in my foolishness that person a fool himself. Seasoned scholars were idiots, the best artists utter simpletons, in my view. I even stooped to abusing them behind their backs.

Finally, unable to resolve my critics' doubts with mere doggerel, I went in search of a guru. With great respect I take the name of Pandit Shleshchandra Vaidya of Aurangabad. He bestowed upon me whatever I learned of *pingal shastra*, the science of prosody. Alas, the effort turned into a calamity. The system of syllabic weights and measures wreaked havoc on me. With just a bit of knowledge under my belt, I abandoned writing verse in Hindi entirely. What I had composed so freely, filling page upon page, now seemed all wrong. In panic, I turned toward Urdu. Blocked gas will seek its own outlet. My teacher advised, "Now look, Narayan. If you're going to write in Urdu, you must show your work to somebody for correction." My intelligence wasn't sufficiently developed for me to understand the value of this suggestion. Quite the opposite: I thought if my verses were pleasing when recited, if listeners swayed to my *jhulnas* and asked to hear more, could my poetry be faulty?

Nevertheless, I began to attend upon Ustad Muhammad Khan "Talib" of Aurangabad and to present my compositions for poetic revision in the tradition of *islah*. He too declared my versification completely opposed to the principles of meter. My stupidity was so great that I ridiculed him within myself and decided he was an ignoramus. Being an *ustad*, he guessed my train of thought. With amazing generosity, he told me that he was no expert in *jhulnas* and *lavanis*. I would have to look after those on my own. If I still wanted to study with him, he was willing to teach me.

Sweetmakers' shops open before those of other trades and close after them. After eighteen hours of stoking the fires, I would call upon my *ustad* at eleven or twelve at night. I studied the lessons of poetics from his own copy of *Hidayak-ul Balaghat*. He took pity on my poverty and passion for verse, ordering me to wake him up if he fell asleep. I will never be able to forget his kindness.

The more I learned, the thinner grew my stack of writing. Every line I examined now seemed defective. I began to burn up what I had already written. Within a few days, I felt a hatred for *jhulna* and *lavani* composition. I avoided those circles and began reciting ghazals in *mushairas*, and in accord with my temperament and capacity, I continued to recite.

(3)

An inviolate law states that without a cause there can be no effect. Yet my life story has convinced me that the discord created by women needs no cause. As far as my stepmother was concerned, the crime of my being born of a different mother was sufficient to produce enmity. On top of that, I sneaked off to study against her wish and command, and that was enough to warrant a life sentence. My wife suffered the stigma of being married to my unlucky self. With the two of us blameworthies in the house together, my stepmother could get no peace.

In Ayodhya, Kaikeyi bristled at the thought of Ram inheriting the entire kingdom. In Aurangabad, my stepmother chafed when she saw me stoking the fire. Back there, king Dasharath was compelled by the boons he had given Kaikeyi on the field of battle. Over here, my father was bound by the vows he took when he remarried. Finally, what Kaikeyi did to Ram, my stepmother did to me. She was not at fault in this. Killing Ravan, vanquishing *rakshasas*, attaining fame— none of this could be accomplished while sitting at home. Destiny alone knew the mystery of this exile. With constant trials and tribulations as provisions for the journey, I departed from home.[6]

(4)

I set out for sure, but with no fixed plan for where I was going. My destination was simply the four directions. Somehow I arrived in Hapur, a small town in Meerut district. When times are hard, one seeks out friends and acquaintances, but wrongheaded as I was, I avoided running into people. I worried lest the couple of acquaintances I had there might notice me.

---

[6] According to his daughter, Betab left home at the age of 14. Namra (1972): 141.

The Ram Lila was at that time under way in Hapur. I reached the enclosure where the performance was taking place, but I couldn't get past the fence and the police. From where I stood, Ram and Lakshman were not visible. I can't say if it was reverence for their godly forms or desire to see the spectacle, but my urge was so great that I slipped inside when the police weren't looking. My filthy clothes and roguish look betrayed me. The guard inside immediately nabbed me and dragged me off to the tent of the Ram Lila organizing committee.

After hearing the guard recite his brave tale, the officer in charge asked me, "Who gave you permission to enter the arena?"

Fearlessly I replied, "Your maladministration."

Everyone chuckled, and the officer seemed embarrassed. One of the men told me to sit down. The officer queried, "What is your business inside?"

"I wish to pay homage to Lord Ramachandra."

"Take him up to the throne," he answered kindly, sending me off with a guard. Hurriedly I touched Lord Ram's feet and bowed my head, thereby fulfilling my heart's desire, if not redeeming the purpose of my life in this birth.

Later that night I left Hapur for Meerut by the cheapest means available—a camel cart. There I took shelter with Lala Sundarlal Saraf for a few days and began to look for work.

(5)

There was an Englishman settled in Meerut who wrote Urdu poetry under the name of "Shor."[7] In the hope of employment, I sought out his bungalow. Expending all my skill, I composed a letter full of elaborate turns of phrase yet devoid of meaning excepting the simple request for an interview. I sent the missive to him through his peon. He accepted the letter as a recommendation and called me in.

Expecting a man of rank, he welcomed me at his doorway joined by his wife. Despite my obvious presence, he asked the *chaprasi*, "Where is the gentleman who wrote the letter?"

---

[7] The Englishman's surname could have been Shore, but more likely he assumed the pen-name *shor*, "noise, outcry; renown."

The servant signalled in my direction. Although I was not worthy of sitting on his chairs, nor even of entering his room, Shor Saheb ushered me in with civility, displaying his high breeding. Conversation commenced. And what is the conversation of poets? The same old pattern: "Please recite something," "Kindly proffer your work," and that sort of thing.

The Saheb had a copybook containing his poems, and I had committed to memory a number of ghazals that had been corrected by my *ustad*. We began to waste time in a mutually agreeable fashion. I was surprised at hearing Urdu spoken so eloquently by an Englishman, and he was amazed at the ease of expression of an oily grain-parcher. After a bit of exchange, I lost my fear of white skin and he his hatred of filthy clothes.

Shor Saheb could not have guessed that I was looking for a job. My letter had merely requested a meeting. Nonetheless, the result of our hour-long poetic assembly was that he politely invited me into his service. False pride, however, caused me to repress my true need and reject his offer outright. I had gone there looking for work, but ill fate accompanied me and silenced my tongue. I returned even more downcast, shutting the door of hope on myself.

(6)

Having forfeited a job pushing a pen, I spent my last three rupees on food and went back to laboring over a hot stove. Lala Nandram hired me to make sweets. I was used to a small town, with small batches of dough and smallish pots, but now I had to contend with huge quantities and enormous vessels. I failed the tests of strength and might, but received passing marks in method and technique. After a few days, Lala Nandram came to know that I had a smattering of knowledge. My education was next to nothing, but in the country of the blind the one-eyed man is king. He took me away from the stove and set me up on the accountant's cushion. I began keeping track of weights and credit accounts, which was worth more than hard cash to him.

(7)

When I vanished from Aurangabad, my father sent the usual notice to all the relatives. My sister had married into a landed family in

Bhatiyana in Meerut district, one of several affluent households in our caste. She heard the news of my disappearance and was grieved greatly. My brother-in-law, Prabhu Dayal, came regularly to Meerut to look after his legal affairs. One day he spotted me at the sweet-shop. He grabbed my hand and pulled me up, urging me in the strongest terms to come with him to the house in Bhatiyana. It must have been due to God's grace that self-reliance remained foremost in my mind. Certainly I had not studied sacred texts or availed myself of the company of holy men. How then was I able to resort to such high-minded thinking?

I was desperately poor, immature and inexperienced, barely eking out a living. Yet my pride would not allow me to live off my relations, and I flatly refused to go to my sister's home. I can only interpret this as the positive *samskaras* inherited from a former lifetime and the fruit of God's infinite grace. Nevertheless, I accepted their offer to set me up in Delhi in a position that would enable me to fulfill my ambitions. This solution pleased me, for I had no ill feelings toward any town. I only disliked freeloading. As I took my leave from Lala Nandram, he added his tears to my salary as final payment.

(8)

I reached Delhi with Prabhu Dayal, and we stayed with Chaudhri Shibbaray, a resident of Bhatiyana who was hosting several other country cousins down on their luck. Shibbaray was by nature a protector of the poor. His residence was an orphanage for the needy, a refuge for the unemployed, a shelter for the homeless, a resting house for the weary, and a hotel for the fasting, of which he himself was the manager. His wife had died, and his family consisted of two nephews and a five-year-old daughter.

The unwritten rules of the ashram required the ability to subsist without food, suffer heat and cold, be detached in deportment, and make one's own bread. I too attached my mental signature to this paperless document. Then the workers' committee unanimously approved Chaudhri's proposal to send Narayan Prasad to apprentice at a printing press. Thus I joined the Kaiser-i Hind Press, managed by the late Lala Devi Sahay Vaishya Agraval.[8] The terms were that I would

---

[8] Referred to as Lalaji in subsequent sections of the narrative.

work for nothing during training, and my salary would be fixed after several months according to my ability. To this I appended my own condition, that I be given five or six days of leave each month so that I might fill my stomach with other sorts of work. Lalaji listened to me attentively, and with a charitable glance approved the arrangement.

The coins in my pocket were running out. It was the festival of Divali, and I took some extra time off to work at making sweets. For three days I did nothing but cook *imarti*s. In exchange for this labor I received three rupees and a bunch of sweets. I distributed the sweets to my co-workers in celebration of the holiday, keeping the three rupees to support myself for the next thirty days.

(9)

By good luck, the foreman at the Kaiser-i Hind Press was one Pandit Balmukund, a distant relation of mine. With his help and affection, I advanced rapidly in my apprenticeship.

According to the rules of the hermitage, there was no "mine" or "thine" among us workers. Regardless of who earned the money, it went toward meals for everyone in equal measure. Nobody had any spending money. Everybody brought home their earnings and turned them over to Chaudhri. Chaudhri himself made ten or twelve annas a day, and that too was always deposited in the common coffer. Living like this in that womb of a house, we all became brothers.

One incident there I still remember as if it happened yesterday. Chaudhri had gone on business to a certain village, saying he would return the next day. Those of us left behind had used up the few annas we'd been given for food. Nobody had any money, everybody was starving. We were forced to fast all day and wait for Chaudhri's return. Somehow the day passed, but the night became long and heavy. For fear of the demoness Hunger, the goddess Sleep would not grant sight of herself.

Finally the day dawned. I got up, performed my ablutions, and went to the press on an empty stomach. Balmukund had upon occasion invited me to share his midday meal, but that day he happened to be ill. The shelf where he kept his tiffin-carrier was empty, like my belly. It was time for lunch, but where could I go? It was better to die than to beg, so I said nothing to Lalaji. Going outside to while away the hour, I sat down beside a well and aimlessly scratched the soil with a scrap of brick.

When suffering lies ahead, the good Lord gives the sick man a little strength to withstand the residue of his misery. As I poked around in the dirt, the very root of life, the cure for ill health, the destroyer of sorrow, the protector of pride, appeared—in the form of a shiny copper penny. I picked it up as if it were a coin of gold and rubbed it off with a piece of cloth. My cloudy view of the world was wiped clean. I visualized the true form of my destiny, and the illusory appearance of external reality was banished. Cashing the coin in, I bought some parched gram. I munched on it, sipped some water from a tap, and went back to work.

(10) My First Step of Progress

To a man immersed in terrible darkness, to one deprived of the sun's rays or a gas lamp, devoid of an electric bulb or a kerosene lantern, the momentary flicker of a match comes as an enormous boon. I lacked the light of knowledge, the brilliance of good company, the illumination of sacred texts, the flame of sound instruction. In this time of blindness, as I stood at the crossroads of heaven and hell, the smidgen of sense that I did possess was like a small oil-lamp. It shone brightly, illuminating for me the heavenly path.

After I had worked for a while at the press, Lala Devi Sahay told me I would receive four rupees per month as salary. The month passed by, pay-day arrived, and along with all the others I put my signature on the receipt sheet. Grasping the substance of life in the palm of my hand, I went back to my work station. When I opened my fist, instead of the four silver pieces I expected, I saw five. Not the purveyors of the four aims of life—duty, wealth, enjoyment, and liberation—but proof of the five-faced lord Shiv Panchanan's mercy, or the blessed sight of the five deities: Vishnu, Shiv, Ganesh, Surya, and Durga. For a hungry, fasting devotee like myself, these could have been the five sacred foods—milk, curds, ghee, sugar, and honey.

Had my step faltered, I would have stumbled at the brink of hell, for indeed I was a disciple of Charvak, not a vessel fit for the five sacred foods. But thanks to the lord, whichever one it was, I recovered my wits. My inner voice said, you earn four rupees a month, and the fifth is a mistake. It's not yours, it belongs to somebody else. Give it back and be content with four.

> Wrap tight your own blanket; touch not the other's shawl.
> This key will open the lock and let good fortune call.

I heard the voice and followed its counsel. This was the moment of my awakening, my first step of progress. I went right back to Lalaji's table and handed him the extra rupee.

"Is there something wrong with the coin? Should I exchange it for another?" he asked.

"No, sir," I replied.

"Do you want change?"

"No, I've been given too much."

Lalaji looked me up and down and said, "It's not a mistake. I gave you an extra rupee on purpose. Go ahead and keep it."

By renouncing my greed for sixteen annas, I earned sixteen annas worth of his trust. I figured out whether that rupee belonged to me or to another, and as a result it opened the gates to a mint containing thousands.

(11)

The twentieth century usurped the place of the nineteenth, just like an upstart removing a king from his throne. Around this time, the Rama Theatre was built in Delhi near the main police station. Jamadar Saheb's drama company started performing there. To get their handbills printed, company employees began visiting the press, and the press's delivery boys visited the company. The drama company issued a few free passes, and Lalaji would hand them out to the workers by turns. I too occasionally got a pass, but my turn came after a very long wait. It was as if:

> Though called the water of life, it left my thirst unquenched.
> Desiring to consume gallons, my cup contained two sips.

All of those splendid things that make the heavens heavenly now began to appear before me in the theatre. Its actors were gods, the boys who played the female companions heavenly nymphs, the singers divine minstrels, the secondary actors sprites and elves.[9] This court of Indra cast such a spell over me that I was smitten by those witches of the day and fairies of the night. For a wretch like me, however, access was difficult. I wanted to grab onto the foot of a throne or dangle from a flying cot to be carried to heaven, but no such prospect presented itself.[10]

Pandit Balmukund used to get the theatre bills printed, and a laborer would deliver them in a bundle. I begged him, "What's the need of a laborer? I'll take them myself." At first he refused, but guessing the reason for my insistence, he agreed. Silently thanking my cousin and exulting at the change in my fortune, I picked up the packet and arrived at heaven's door. It was daytime, and there was no chance of seeing the full court, but I managed to catch sight of King Indra, which was auspicious enough.

When a new day is about to begin, the sun doesn't rise all of a sudden. First, certain preparations must be made. Usha, the goddess of dawn, spreads down a carpet of vermilion in the east. A chorus of sunbeams chants their welcome call to Bhaskar, the sun god. Wearing a crimson costume, Divakar, the day-maker, shows himself somewhere, and a little later he throws off the red mantle for white robes and advances boldly. In the same way, my night of misfortune had passed, daybreak was at hand, and preparations were under way.

The Jamadar Company's dramatist, Babu Dhanpat Ray "Bekas," had gone on leave. In his absence, the company needed someone to write lyrics for a new song. The manager spoke to Balmukund, and he recommended me. "Betab stays up half the night strumming his sitar. He's always going off to recite ghazals in *mushairas*. If he can do the job, you won't have to pay him."

To me he said, "Today is your examination. Go get the question paper from the Rama Theatre."

---

[9] The heavenly creatures are *devta*s, chief among them their king Indra, *apsara*s, *gandharva*s, *yaksha*s, and *kinnara*s.

[10] Indra's court (*indra/indar sabha*) became a popular setting for the romance between a fairy and an earthly prince in nineteenth-century Urdu drama. In some versions, the hero Gulfam, desirous of a glimpse of heaven, is transported there on a flying cot.

I was beside myself with joy. I flew to the manager's side and noted down the song's tune, beat, and placement. I dashed off something that very night. Who knows if the meter scanned correctly, but the higher-ups loved the lines. There were four proprietors in those days—Ibrahim Karim, Abdur Rahim, Rahim Bakhsh, and Harun Taiyab—and they all praised me. When the company director heard the song, he awarded me the ultimate prize: "Come whenever you wish to watch the show." Now I went to the theatre every day, heedless of whether it was my turn for a pass or not.

Within a few days, the measure of my joy increased even further. At first I had only limited rights and sat among the spectators during the performance. Then I was promoted for my creative efforts and became a free agent. With this unprecedented glory, I felt compelled to show off and act the wise guy. I would stand pompously at the entrance to the theatre, fondling my almost nonexistent moustache, hoping a friend would spot me. When one appeared, I made a point of ducking inside on some pretext, just to show him that I could.

No one stopped me entering the abode of the minstrels. I was free to consort with the nymphs. I had no fear of the dark demigods. The result of this independence was that I fell in love with one of those nymph-like boys. The beauty of the entire world seemed to be contained in his face.

A secret pain now settled in my heart. If I went home, I grew restless. If I worked at the press, I was uneasy. In front of him I was tormented, and away from him anxious. There was no peace anywhere, no solace in either separation or union. Rather, if in distance there was the pleasure of yearning, when we were together it was a peculiar joy.

In this time of temptation, my destitution and poverty saved the day. I wanted to buy him items from the bazaar, present him gifts like scarves, silken handkerchiefs, fine stockings, fancy combs. But I had no money, and I had to suppress my urges. Many times I thought of inviting him home to a nice meal, but everyone there was starving. My desperate love could not spring forth and reveal itself. My desires stayed behind the screen, and no one saw them.

> It's just as well, desire, that you too stayed behind.
> Longing lodged in my heart, with no loss to my name.

The company moved on from Delhi to Ludhiana, and I was left behind like a pigeon with clipped wings. It is due to God's grace that while on the one hand I suffered the hardship of penury, on the other I knew that respect and regard were sweeter than hugs and kisses. Thus, in spite of the pain in my heart, as a patient I never wrote to my doctor for a prescription in the form of a love-letter. My self-respect advised me, saying, "Don't start corresponding with these nymphs. King Indra and the four proprietors will not take it kindly. They will rub your reputation in the dust."

When we gain distance from fire, its heat decreases. My love was not like that of a Dhruv or a Prahlad—immortal, immoveable, and timeless. Rather, it was a spark of nature that flared up, blazed in the breeze of beauty, and then fizzled out. The restlessness of my heart had a specific cause. When that cause vanished, the ache subsided.

(12)

A Sanskrit scholar named Pandit Shambhunath worked as a compositor at the press. Unfortunately for him but luckily for me, he had been unable to find work as a lecturer. He was old, lame in one leg, and lagged behind in jobs that required speed. I was young, healthy, and quick in setting type, and I always finished ahead of him. He earned eight rupees a month, I five. Seeing the discrepancy, the boss decided to sack him, but this seemed too harsh to me. I made a deal with the pandit, whether out of friendship or seeing my future advantage, I cannot say. I would help him finish his work, and he would teach me the niceties of spelling and diction in exchange. I placed my wholehearted devotion at his disabled feet, and he sharpened my wits like the blade of a sword, such that I began to edit the sentences of regular writers and even correct the length of pandits' vowels.

With practice, I became so cocky that I tangled with an honorary magistrate, a man who had received dozens of decorations. I hesitate to mention his name lest he file another lawsuit against me. If Lalaji hadn't bailed me out, I would undoubtedly have landed in jail. Panditji had warned me that he was an important man. "You shouldn't have pointed out his errors and humiliated him in front of everyone," he advised. "If you keep doing things like this, it will turn out badly for you."

I became a bit more moderate, but my habit of looking for trouble was alive and well when the New Alfred Theatrical Company arrived in Delhi. Our press was again the one to print its handbills. The drama *Khurshid-e Zarnigar* by Murad Ali Murad was on the boards, and the playwright gave us a splendid poster to print. It featured a line at the top of the sheet praising the heroine's beauty. The poetry contained a mistake in scansion, which I corrected according to the metrical principles I'd learned from my *ustad*. This involved changing the phrase *ik alam men* to *zamane men*.

When the copy went to Murad for proofing, he restored the original words *ik alam*, thinking the change to be an error of the calligrapher. I was the calligrapher, and I wouldn't stand for it. Once the job was finished and Murad saw that the words had been changed back, he stormed into the press in a fury, accusing Lalaji of lack of supervision. I was summoned and interrogated. I explained that the line was now correct. Things went from bad to worse. When my boss too started to abuse me, I rose to my defence, saying, "Lalaji! If we print mistakes, the press will get a bad name. You should be fair. Ask the *munshi* to prove that he's right. If he is, I'll become his absolute slave." I then elaborated on Murad's error and threatened to answer his insults with a shoe beating. Outraged, eyes popping out, lips atremble, muttering imprecations, Murad left at last.

Murad sifted through his entire library looking for an example that would prove his point. Finally he bowed before the truth. That evening, he came with Balmukund to my place while I was practising the sitar. He made a brief but humble confession of his guilt, Balmukund embraced each one of us, and we put the quarrel behind us.

(13)

Munshi Murad departed, first from Delhi and then from the world, but he left me with a passion for play-writing. I immediately began composing the drama *Husn-e Farang*. The famous playwright Agha Hashr Kashmiri attached his endorsement to it. This was the first drama that I penned, and the second of mine to be staged.

In those days, a famous courtesan of Delhi named Nazir had just been murdered. Her story was so hot that wherever four men gathered, nothing else got discussed. *Lavanis, jhulnas,* and novels were composed about her. Even roasted-gram vendors worked her into their dialect. The spectre of drama had taken possession of me. I too dashed off a play entitled *Qatl-e Nazir*, "The Murder of Nazir." Now I had two dramas but no buyer. Then fate spoke to me, "You fool, go to the Jamadar Theatrical Company and cash them in."

(14)

I was a married man, and yet I was worse off than a celibate student. I had a woman of the house but no home. How could I alter that situation on five rupees a month? My wife wrote, asking me to bring her to Delhi. I explained my low salary. She wrote back saying it was enough, she would earn an extra two or three rupees a month grinding grain and spinning cloth. But the cost of transporting her remained. She had a couple of silver hoops in her ears—the sum total of her fortune—which she took off and gave to her brother to exchange for the train fare. As soon as she got the money, she came to Delhi, bringing her auspicious presence with her. Lalaji, satisfied with my work, increased my salary to eight rupees. I earned another three or four rupees a month by hand-copying texts at night. What a golden time it was—we were rich on eleven or twelve rupees a month. Now, in 1936, one can't even make do with eleven or twelve hundred.

(15)

Jamadar Saheb's company had gone to Ludhiana, where he was rehearsing a play called *Rup Sundari*. The staff writer had gone on leave, and some scenes had to be altered. The company manager sent a letter inviting me to come and work for them on a salary.

I was at a fork in the road. I was free to take either path. Along one lay lovely green fields and fragrant flowers, but after a while it turned to thorns. The other was strewn with stones and brambles but later became a beautiful garden. My fate told me to follow the doctrine of contraries. "If my boss agrees," I wrote back, "I'd like to come. Please write directly to him."

Jamadar Saheb wrote to Lalaji, "In your press, there is one Narayan Prasad, a compositor. Please send him to us." What is the difference between requesting and raiding? The same difference as between marriage and rape. The act and its consequence are the same, but one leads to heaven, the other to hell.

Lalaji called me in and asked, "Do you wish to join the theatrical company?"

"If you give me permission, I would like to go."

"Years from now, you'll be making no more than fifteen rupees a month at the press, even if you get promoted. I'll get the company to offer you twenty or twenty-five right now."

Taking my silence for assent, Lalaji wrote back as if he were a trader reluctantly selling his goods at twice the price. He upped the salary to thirty rupees, agreement was reached, and to show his affection he dropped me at the railway station in his cart. The ox-cart, back then, was a sign of great wealth, even more prestigious than a motorcar today. The ride in Lalaji's cart, the good wishes of my fellow employees, and the pomp of this farewell to poor Narayan—all lodged in my heart. If I had made the mistake of sneaking away and had ditched my job at the press, I never would have received that respectful send-off.

(16)

I reached Ludhiana and was greeted kindly. I got a room and settled in. On the face of it, rehearsals for *Rup Sundari* were under way, but actually things were not going very well. By investing a lot of energy and dedication, the company had put together an impressive *svayamvar* scene. Eight thrones had been constructed for the eight kings from various parts of the land, but the playwright had only written six introductions. I was ordered to compose another two couplets to fit the required meter, *dumila savaiya*, and I did so readily.

Then I was asked to revise the garden scene for the same play. I was exhilarated by the work on that scene. Not only that—the company's fancy accommodations, my newfound passion, the force of my temperament, the opportunity to patch up another's play, the language of Delhi, the ingenuity of women's jests and idioms—I was having a great time of it all. But trouble was brewing.

The company owner listened to the new scene being read and declared, "Get the new *munshi* to rewrite the whole play, or leave the scene out! It will ruin all the fun. We don't need one scene to be so good that it makes the other twenty look inferior."

After much discussion, it was decided that this play would be postponed and rehearsals for *Qatl-e Nazir* would start instead. And so they did. Nazir, the heroine of the play, had been murdered at the home of an aristocrat. He belonged to both Delhi and Lahore. In both places he had houses, businesses, and prestige. And in both, *Qatl-e Nazir* was famous. The company, for better or worse, arrived in Lahore. The handbills had barely been printed when a commotion broke out in the city, not on account of Betab but because of Nazir. First there was her beauty, for which she was already renowned, then cohabitation with a high-ranking noble, and finally the fact that she had just been murdered. This was breaking news; there was gossip in every lane. In this climate, one poster would have done the work of a thousand copies, and now there were thousands ready to be distributed.

Wherever four friends congregate, forty enemies spring up. Certain envious gentlemen could not tolerate my advancement. The actor who played the part of the hero went to the aristocrat and spread slander, saying, "This play is an insult to your mother." The nobleman accepted this comment at face value and registered a complaint with the police commissioner.

The company had sold more tickets than for any other play in its history. The public was so eager that we could have sold twice or thrice the number, had there been space. No effort had been spared on the production. Women from the red light district generously provided expensive dresses, jewelry, carpets, bolsters, spittoons, perfume jars—whatever was needed. I was so proud of myself that I was bursting the buttons on my long dress-coat. I was more delighted than a father at his son's wedding.

The ghee-filled lamps were burning brightly, and then a single gust blew them out. The kettledrum overture turned into a funeral dirge. Songs of praise became sounds of mourning. Hearing the news, I grew dizzy. I fainted and fell to the ground like the staff of a blind man who loses his grip.

It was night-time, and no legal work could proceed. Lacking recourse, we were forced to shut down the performance. The tickets were refunded; we were left wringing our hands. Jamadar Saheb's distress was greater than mine. He would have moved heaven and earth, if he could.

The next day Jamadar was up and out before sunrise. A lawsuit had been filed, and the case against us began. There were nine hearings. The writer was summoned, the writing was examined. The plaintiff retained a barrister for five hundred rupees a day, while the company's lawyer worked *pro bono*, fighting the case in exchange for a free pass. Whether there was really anything sensational in the play or not, the courtroom drama blew it completely out of proportion. The whole city was abuzz. Even before, the turnout had been exceptional. Then, when *Qatl-e Nazir* reopened (I hesitate to describe the reaction lest it smack of self-promotion), it played continuously for eleven days. A successful run is normally three days. It all worked out for the best. The pain that I suffered was transformed into pleasure.

(17)

Jamadar Saheb's company left Lahore and returned to its home base in Karachi. It was there that my second play, *Husn-e Farang*, was staged, and it was well received by the spectators. My third play, *Krishna Janm*, was still-born. It was a good thing that it died; a bad son is worse than no son at all. How could there be a serious drama about Lord Krishna's birth with a comic heroine who was a European girl? The foolish dramatist should have known it was ridiculous to introduce a white-skinned female at the time that a Hindu god was born. The reality was that in those days, if a play didn't have a white woman paired with a black man, it didn't stand a chance. My play had both stock characters, but it still flopped. I may have been blind, but the spectators were not. My fourth play, *Mayur Dhvaj*, was an even worse disaster.

When my first two plays passed muster, Jamadar Saheb gave me five rupees extra for each one. After the two flops, the reward was that I didn't lose my job. Three years went by. The company traveled to Allahabad. Profits were down, and salaries were running three or four months behind. Complaints were filed, injunctions issued, property attached. Sometimes somebody got paid something, other times someone ran off. As for me, neither was I paid anything, nor could I run anywhere. My pocket didn't carry even two paisas, let alone two rupees for the train ticket.

The company manager, Abdur Rahim, was very kind to me. He couldn't give me any money, but he gave me some invaluable advice. "Panditji," he said, "quit these quarrels with the Jamadar and go to Bombay, to the partnership company." I took his point. At his urging, I sent my letter of application to the Parsi Theatrical Company of Bombay. The eight days I spent waiting for an answer seemed like eight months. Finally the reply came. I was to report to Bombay for an interview. If I didn't get hired, they would still cover my travel expenses. What could be more courteous?

Now I had to get to Bombay, but the question was how. I had nothing to use for the fare. My wife was exactly like this narrative, devoid of ornament. She had no bangles that could be sold to pay for the ticket. However, she did have a pair of silver anklets, and these she turned over to me, shedding a few tears. I packed up my worries about my wife and son, and I gave them me to worry about in return. Then I got onto the train, the whistle blew, and we were off.

(18)

I arrived in Bombay and presented myself to the *seths* who owned the company. With the brusque manners typical of the big city, they told me to sleep in the foul-smelling hall where the scenery and props were being painted. Keshavlal Manchand Nayak was deputed to welcome me. He took me to the Victoria Gardens for sightseeing but, distracted as I was by the upcoming interview, my heart wasn't in it.

After two days, the *seths* made time to see me. They asked me to recite some samples of my dramatic verse. I regaled them with several select scenes from *Husn-e Farang* and *Qatl-e Nazir*, which they listened to in dead silence. Then they commanded, "Go out and roam around Bombay for a couple of days. On the third day we'll let you know." Keshavlal extricated me from the noxious fumes of the painting hall and took me to stay with Ustad Chiranjilal, a *pakhawaj* player from Mathura. Chiranjilal made every attempt to keep me cheerful as his guest, and I will never forget his hospitality.

(19)

Waiting for the third day was agony. Each twenty-four hours seemed like twenty-four hundred. I was bobbing between hope and despair when eleven o'clock on the third day finally arrived. The *seths* filed into the office, ready to decide my fate. Actually, they had already decided, it was only left for them to tell me.

Seating me at the table opposite, Dadabhai Mistri began to explain, "Look, *munshiji*. We like your writing, but we already have a senior staff writer here. We can't pay you more than his salary. He gets fifty rupees a month. We'll give you the same."

Propping my elbows on the table and bowing my head, I silently gave thanks to God. The *seth* thought I was keeping quiet because I was unhappy with the sum. After consulting with the others in Gujarati, he told me, "Don't worry. You'll be promoted quickly."

I came to my senses and replied, "*Sethji*, I wasn't thinking about the salary. It's the senior writer who could become an obstacle. As long as he doesn't advance, I won't either." The *seths* assured me that in the beginning they would have to adhere to their policy, but later it would depend on how things developed.

Amritlal Keshavlal Nayak was a discerning man of letters. He was the director of the Alfred Theatrical Company and my friend. I told the *seths*, "I'll consult with Amritlal and let you know tomorrow." Amritlal thought that fifty rupees was a huge salary, and that I should accept even twenty-five.

The next day I said to the *seths*, "Housing is very expensive here." They agreed to cover the rent on a room worth seven and a half rupees a month. In other words, the agreement was for Rs 57.50 per month. On top of that, I asked for a month's advance, and then I returned to Allahabad. Abdur Rahim was very happy when he heard the news, and so were my children.

(20)

Within ten or fifteen days I returned to Bombay, bringing my family with me. There I began writing the drama *Kasauti,* an adaptation of the Gujarati play *Dorangi Duniya.* This play was first performed in

9. Amrit Keshav Nayak

the Bradlaugh Hall in Lahore in 1903. The partnership company had sufficient fame and facility for success. Thanks to them, I too was doing well. But a small-time theatrical company had also halted in Lahore, and our rising sun made their moon set. The members of the rival troupe became so jealous that they set fire to our company. It burned and burned until not a rope was left. We returned home to Bombay and began all over again with the production of *Kasauti*. Within a few days of its opening, it had made such a profit that we started to prepare for other plays.

My second play to come out with this company was *Mitha Zahar*. With its success, the senior *munshi* got his comeuppance. The junior one received a raise of twenty rupees a month, as well as a boost to his spirits and courage. Moreover his knowledge was refined, like steel made into gold, by four gurus comparable to the four faces of Brahma. These four savants gave me the wealth that no king can confiscate and no thief steal, which never decreases when given away and is never left behind by mistake. Nizami Saheb taught me the fine points of playwriting, Sakha Saheb imparted some knowledge of jurisprudence, Kaif Saheb tutored me in poetic composition, and Barkatullah Khan inculcated the principles of rhythm on the sitar. I may not have become a good poet despite their blessings, but at least I made an effort, and I began to play the sitar with the best of them.

When God bestows fame, he assembles the ways and means to sustain it. It was my good fortune that Amritlal and the famous actress Gauhar also joined the Parsi Theatrical Company of Bombay. Although Gauhar was a very fine artiste, she could not become an immortal ruby (*amritlal*). But Amritlal was such an expert in stage direction that he could turn whoever he wished into a pearl (*gauhar*). He was short of height, but his knowledge was vast. It was a matter of luck that I found such a complete director and an actress who was a paragon of beauty.

There are hundreds of playwrights in India, but in my opinion only two associated with the contemporary stage are really capable: Agha Hashr Kashmiri and Mehdi Hasan Ahsan Lakhnavi. People have made fun of their style, but both are outstanding in their own way. For years, Amritlal directed the plays of only these two dramatists. He acquired a taste for their sort of writing, and then he discovered that he held Betab's rubbish in his hands.

"Well, my friend," I asked him. "Will it work or not?"

"Judge for yourself," he replied. "I didn't tear up the script, did I?"

My third play was *Zahri Sanp*, and it exceeded all expectations. It brought me another twenty-rupee raise. One day Agha Hashr walked in while Amritlal was studying a scene from my fourth play. As a playwright Hashr was superb, and as a human being guileless and open-hearted. He never felt competitive towards his brothers in the profession, in fact he enjoyed the work of other poets and encouraged them. Of course, his usual conversation employed an ample store of abusive phrases. Amritlal, however, enjoyed a special exemption. Seeing Hashr, Amritlal said, "Come here, you rogue, and listen to this scene."

10. Postcard of Gauhar Jan

He recited some of my lines, and Hashr embraced me, complimenting me on the verse. Tragically, Amritlal died while this fourth play was being written. In his memory, I named it *Amrit*.

The Parsi Theatrical Company had established a ladder of twenty rupees per play, but I knew my value and strength. I wanted to leap bounds and reach the rooftop. Each jump could take me no higher than twenty inches, so I quit my job.

(21) All Days Are Not Alike

How can happiness remain constant? We perform some actions that are good and some that are bad, so why shouldn't hard times follow easy ones? My employment in the Parsi Theatrical Company had brought me name, fame, and fortune, but there was a sore spot too. My wife had died. I spent some time in grief and mourning. Then I married again, ostensibly at my father's insistence but in truth out of my own desire. The wedding took place in Katiyavali village in Bulandshahr district when I was thirty-one years of age.

At the time I did not see the injustice, but today I recognize that selfish men hide behind *dharm* and make rules that are unfair. When the wife dies, the husband has the right to marry a second, third, or fourth time. But if the husband dies, the wife must remain a widow her entire life and suffer the torments of hell. Why is this? Have men received some mark of distinction that they are not debauched by having multiple wives? And does the wife commit the sin of cow slaughter that she is consigned to the prison of widowhood for the rest of her life? Far from taking the name of a second husband, if a widow even contemplates the possibility, she is labelled fallen and promiscuous, but when the husband's better half dies, all he has to do is buy another bride.

I am not in favor of women being given the freedom to marry again and again. However, I think that when men are widowed, they too should remain widowers. Or at least if they are going to remarry, they should marry a widow, not a virgin.

Pardon me, I have strayed far from my subject. As I was saying, even though I was earning Rs 125 per month, I assessed my worth and quit my job.

(22)

Seth Qayyum Mamajiwala, the father of Miss Gohar of Ranjit Film Company fame, was forming a new company. Seeing a fruit fallen from the branch, he picked me up. Not for free or by stealth—he paid the full price. He gave me an advance of Rs 400, but for some reason the company never got off the ground, and I got to keep the money. Not that I wasn't willing to give it back. Gohar's mother, Putlibai, and Qayyum Seth were generous and weren't concerned about the money, so it became mine.

(23)

After quitting, I went without work for eight days. Then Seth Kavasji Palanji Khatau hired me to join his Alfred Theatrical Company at Rs 175 a month. Come the start of 1909, and I was off with the company to Calcutta.

Habituated to largesse, I might have become a spendthrift, but I was careful to save as much as I could. When we reached Calcutta, I rented a single room in a house on the ground floor at Rs 20 a month. Salon, bedroom, kitchen—all were combined. The house was newly built but low-lying, and it got no sunshine. The damp made me ill as soon as I moved in.

There wasn't even a cot in the house. I was lying on a mat on the floor one day, sick as a dog, when I received a letter in verse from my colleague "Vali" of Aurangabad. I wrote a response to him, also in verse, which I copy here word for word, so that others may be forewarned. Poisonous gas released from charcoal can get trapped in a closed room and become life-threatening. The wise would do well to avoid such a place.

> What can I say of my state, Vali?
>   To describe it is impossible, Vali!
> Leaving Bombay, to Calcutta I came.
>   Oh, God help me! Where did I land?
> Soon after I arrived, sickness came on.
>   My body was wracked, my countenance wan.
> How can I speak of that strange plight?
>   My dear wife was in the same straits.
> Both grew ill and both powerless.
>   Who came to nurse us back to health?
> To my own lips came the final breath,
>   It seemed that I stood at the door of death.
> Near to my corpse, my wife was alone.
>   She was weak, naïve, and on her own.
> She called out to me, but no one replied.
>   Then she assumed that Betab had died.

She started at once to wail and to mourn,
   What else could she do but feel forlorn?
My head was resting on someone's thigh,
   My limbs lay low; my body was high.
All of the tears that fell on my face,
   Like smelling salts, were an act of grace.
Those tears in fact had the qualities of Christ;
   The tears were the very water of life.
What do I see then? She too is still.
   Who is this lifeless one, quiet and chill?
Betab's heart was mightily distressed,
   Seeing her stupor, I too was oppressed.
Friends and companions were miles from home,
   In the house were two beings, both broken down.
The night passed off, then daybreak dawned,
   We both arose and managed to stand.
Who knows the pains that torment the heart?
   The suffering ones know, or God, for his part.
There is no path but forbearance,
   What other course or way do we chance?
I beg of you, oh glorious God,
   Patience do grant to those downtrod.

(24)

After that incident, several years passed but nothing memorable happened. Then an event occurred which in some small part gave meaning to my life in this birth as a human being.

The company was touring and had reached Karachi. Pandit Bhavanidatt Sharma was an artist from a company based in Lahore. As it happened, neither of us had our families with us, so we took up residence together. Our house became a veritable Arya Samaj. Every afternoon at four o'clock, I would recite from the *Satyarth Prakash* and expound upon it. Many actors from the company came to listen, full of devotion, and we held question and answer sessions to discuss philosophical issues.

How was it, two of our members asked, that after thousands of years people still revered Lord Ram and celebrated his victory with the festival of Dashera? This was not an ordinary question, but a rare desire to know the inner truth of an extraordinary being. It led to a discussion of the ten traits of *dharm* that Ram embodied, and an analysis of the difficulties we might face if we tried to adopt them ourselves.

1) Steadfastness: very difficult. If our salaries were late by even two days, we lost control of our faculties.
2) Forgiveness: almost impossible. We were like caged tigers. Rendered powerless, we stayed quiet, but once set free we would drink blood.
3) Self-control: a little easier, except for the requirement to rein in the heart. Just the sight of another man's comely wife, and we were beside ourselves.
4) Refraining from stealing. Theft was, thankfully, not in our nature, except when driven by the needs of the body. However, we stole each others' hearts and words shamelessly.
5) Purity. We managed to wash ourselves with soap and water, but we could not cleanse our hearts of the filth of jealousy, greed, and partiality.
6) Subduing the senses. When the heart couldn't be ruled, how could we possibly control the ten sense organs?
7) Sobriety. This too looked straightforward but turned out to be a crooked business.
8) Knowledge. If people behaved in accord with sound knowledge, they could master anything in the world.
9) Truth. Here there was a glimmer of hope, provided that God granted us the capacity to overcome the obstacles.
10) Abandoning anger. We Indians were pretty good at upholding this rule. A merchant would pass the blame for his own error onto his clerk, or an office manager would accuse his subordinate of his mistake, and neither employee showed anger. A kick of the sacred boot might rupture the spleen, but we never objected. We were well practised in passivism. But if we accepted oppression in the name of *dharm*, what was so saintly about that?

Focusing on the ninth trait, truth, our fellowship chose Dashera as the day to begin a program of personal reform. We invited our friends and held a *havan* ceremony before an assembly of some hundred men. A *sannyasi* came and delivered a speech. Four of us were initiated at this *yajna*: Pandit Bhavanidatt Sharma, Purushottam Manchand Nayak, Mahashay Liladhar, and myself. In front of the assembly, we all repeated the vow to never tell a lie, regardless of the insult, financial distress, or marital discord that might result.

The vow was short, but its impact was great. It was easy to pronounce the words, difficult to live up to them. Since I had told lies my whole life, I had a hard time of it. Staying in touch with one's inner self is almost impossible in a householder's existence. There needs to be a watchman who will stand outside the house, on high alert. From that day onward, I adopted two sacred ochre garments, a turban and a shoulder-cloth, to serve as silent reminders of my promise to adhere to the truth. This dress became my permanent wardrobe, like the uniform of a holy warrior.

(25)

Every evening at sunset, we reviewed our daily progress. Sharmaji never lied again, as far as I recall. He maintained a sort of oath of silence, speaking only when absolutely necessary, and that too with great care. I was a real bull-slinger and had been dishonest for thirty or thirty-five years. In spite of the vow, I still told some whoppers over the course of the next few months, although I realized what I had done almost immediately.

Seeing my newfound truthfulness, one of my fibbing friends became my enemy. Another labelled me a schemer. One time, honesty almost cost me my job. I wasn't the old Betab who told fashionable tales and half-truths to advance the company. But then *sethji* realized that my vow was genuine, and he respected me all the more. The other two fellows broke their vows within a week.

With one illness cured, sorry to say, another developed. Having distanced myself from lying, I became arrogant about it.

> By trying out reason, I got addicted to thought.
> I forswore one fault but gained greater guilt.
>
> —Dagh

A member of the Arya Samaj in Karachi told me how he had cured his pride. He reminded me of the nine other vows incumbent upon Arya initiates. Whenever my vow of truthfulness came to mind, he told me to feel ashamed after recalling that I was only 10 per cent pure.

(26)

You may laugh at Betab for being a fool. Who does he think he is, lecturing us on falsehood, a topic we know so well that it runs in our veins? We practice it night and day, and even our children have picked up everything we know.

You may be experts in this art, but you still need to examine it. When the thief steals, he knows he's stealing, just as the adulterer knows when he commits adultery. But we are so accustomed to lying that we don't even recognize it when we lie. Without intending to, lies tumble out of our mouths. Even when no benefit to ourselves is apparent, we still speak untruths.

Examples

1) You are entertaining a small child with a rattle. You hide the rattle behind your back and wave both hands, saying, "I don't have it. A crow took it." Tell me, what do you possibly gain by inventing this make-believe crow?
2) Madanlal arrives at Shyamsundar's house. Shyamsundar says, "The food's ready." Madanlal is hungry, but he says, "I've eaten already." He goes away without eating, swearing a false oath.
3) You are going to fetch vegetables. You run into Seth Motilal. He inquires routinely, "Tell me, sir, where are you headed?" You cannot just say, "To fetch vegetables," lest the lowly nature of the task reduce your status. You lack the nerve to say, "None of your business." You answer tartly, "Just going to see that barrister, Banerjee." Both of you are happy with this lie.
4) On the other hand, if Baldev promises Bihari that he will come over that evening, and then cannot go in spite of his good intentions, this I would not consider a lie.
5) Gaurishankar wants to sell his cow for fifty rupees. The cow is worth fifty, but nobody wants to pay that much. The next day, Gaurishankar is due to leave on a trip. He has no way of taking care of the cow in his absence. He sells her for forty rupees.

The earlier customer says, "You said the price was fifty, you liar!" I would not call this a lie.

Thus excuses, white lies, and big fibs can look quite similar. It is best to avoid them altogether.

(27)

Those who read this autobiography may say it does not acquaint the reader with the reality of my life. It's a whitewash job, tells only one side of the story. I accept this objection, but presenting just the good side seems fitting. Here are the reasons why:

1) What is the main purpose of publishing an autobiography? It is so that people may derive educational value from someone else's life story, so they may shape themselves in another's positive image. The purpose is not to spread evil ways.
2) I am guilty of hiding my vices, but this is not so that I may appear entirely blameless. Why should I make my *Ram-kahani* a *Kam-kahani*? What benefit can that bring the young? They will gain no instruction from it. Mothers, sisters, and daughters should not roam in the garden of obscenity, picking fragrant flowers. Propriety is not defended by painting a picture of the naked truth.
3) There are hundreds of sadhus, saints, and blameless people in the world—but so what? My task is to describe myself, and I know perfectly well that my life is long on evil deeds and short on good ones. If I were to write about them, it would fill another huge book. But what's the use of such a tale of bad deeds?
4) If I retell my wrongdoings myself, what's left for my detractors to write about, those who needlessly envy me?

Lust, anger, intoxication, greed, infatuation, and the sins arising from them—not one have I abandoned, nor has one abandoned me. There—that much I've declared! Now has the duty of an autobiographer been fulfilled?

(28)

After touring here and there, the company reached Quetta in Baluchistan. Nothing special happened there, but times were hard. Income was low, salaries in arrears. I quickly drafted a version of Shakespeare's *Comedy of Errors* in Urdu, calling it *Gorakhdhandha*. This comedy proved so successful that it freed us from financial crisis. What's more, grapes were easy to come by, a whole bunch for a paisa, and the melons were sweeter than sherbet. We gorged on fresh fruit and recouped what we had lost during the three months of penury. Hale and hearty again, we left our mountain retreat and went back to the plains.

(29)

I had been working on my *Mahabharat* for several years, revising and refining it. It was difficult to pare down to four hours an epic whose eighteen books could not even be performed in eighteen months. I couldn't decide what to include and what to cut out.

Urdu plays ruled the stage at that time. The Parsis who ran the theatrical companies were afraid of the Hindi language from a business standpoint. Seth Khurshedji Balivala had commissioned the late Vinayak Prasad "Talib" to compose a play based on the *Ramayan*, the Hindus' favorite tale. Balivala had then staged it, exercising caution so that spectators not notice they were watching a Hindi play, nor sense it belonged to the Hindus. Even the character Sita, who spoke Sanskrit, the language of the gods, appeared before Ram addressing him as *khuda*, the Persian word for God.[11]

What could Talib Saheb do? The times were such that there was no permission for Hindi to be implanted on the stage. But hats off to Seth Khatau! He was a true warrior in this line. Whatever he meant to do, he went ahead and accomplished it.

After numerous difficulties, the moment we had been awaiting finally arrived. A date was fixed for the debut in the Sangam Theatre in Delhi. Just then, a well-wisher approached Seth Khatau and explained that the *Mahabharat* was never recited in an inhabited area. If it was, the consequences were inauspicious. After the initial shock, I came to my senses and responded, "*Sethji*, what people say is true. Wherever the *Mahabharat* is performed, that place becomes Kurukshetra, a field of battle. But if the preliminary rituals prescribed by

---

[11] Betab cites a line from Talib's *Ramayan*, but Gupt gives a different wording. In neither version does Sita address Ram as *khuda*. Gupt (2005): 77.

the *rishis* are scrupulously observed, there is none of that. In fact, the outcome is beneficial and profitable."

Thousands of rupees had already been invested in the production, and there was no way of getting that sum back except by going through with the ritual. I explained the proper procedure to follow. First the playhouse was purified, and then a *havan* ceremony was performed. A special feast was offered to the Brahmins. Once the Brahmins' blessings were secured, Seth Khatau was not the man he had been the day before. Auspicious resolve made his fearful mind strong and firm. The gates of the Alfred Company were decorated with banners, ribbons, and flowers, until the enclosure looked like a marriage canopy. The first performance was held on the night of January 29, 1913.

The drama ran for three or four days in a row. There was much fanfare in the city. The play was truly novel. What's more, a huge amount of money had been spent on the spectacle. One night, a group comprised of aristocrats, leading Hindus, and well-to-do citizens from Delhi left their seats in the playhouse and came onto the stage, bringing garlands and baskets of flowers. *Sethji* was playing Duryodhan, and thus he was on the stage already. I was called upon to join him. The fictitious scene in the drama was interrupted for a few moments, and a real-life scene began to unfold. The foremost dignitaries of the Hindu community gave a series of short speeches, not only praising the drama's originality, but dispensing epithets like "harbinger of a new age," "revolutionary," "reveals Hindu history," and "sacred entertainment." They presented *sethji* with a gold medal and gave me one too, piling flower garlands around my neck.

When this occurrence was publicized in the local newspapers, the excitement spread to the surrounding towns. Letters and telegrams poured in from Meerut, Saharanpur, Muradabad, Aligarh, and Agra, from people wishing to book seats. *Sethji* heard the praise with his own ears and saw the heat rise on the thermometer of his purse. He began praising the efficacy of the ritual. Then a series of events occurred. The *paris* and *devs* vanished, and Gulfam hid in a dark well.[12] The best plays in Urdu started to pack up their bedrolls. Even the late Agha Hashr put down his powerful Urdu pen and began

---

[12] That is, Hindu epics and mythologicals replaced Indo-Islamic romances

11. Gold Medal Given to Betab

writing paeans in Hindi. Respectable gentlemen who had vowed never to see stage-plays out of hatred for obscenity began coming to the theatre and brought their wives along. Ladies had so much respect for the *Mahabharat* that *sethji* had to make special arrangements for women-only shows. Babu Shyam Sundar Das of the Nagari Pracharini Sabha, Kashi, praised Betab's *Mahabharat* for turning people away from ugly, tasteless dramas.

Nevertheless, after a few days the spectators split into two groups. One group gave out gold medals while the other started issuing abuses.

---

full of fairies (*pari*) and devils (*dev*), such as the *Indar Sabha*, in which Gulfam is cast from heaven and imprisoned in a well.

The controversy focused on one scene: that of Cheta Chamar.[13] This quarrel never would have developed if people had viewed drama simply as drama. The problem was that this play brought the past, a period over 5000 years earlier, into the present, or it took spectators back 5000 years into the past. If the audience had considered it a mere show, they could have ridiculed the scene, as they did countless others. But that proved impossible now. One camp considered the Cheta Chamar scene a blot on the moon, the other thought it was life-breath in the body. So many notices were published for and against it that the stack weighed almost two pounds. And why should there not have been objection after objection, fault after fault, complaint after complaint? The *Mahabharat* had, after all, been performed in the city. It was fortunate the preliminary rituals had been performed, otherwise blood would surely have flowed.

Whether authorities or laymen, everybody jumped into the field of battle. Those with no objection dressed up the published critiques in new clothes, claiming to defend society and represent *dharm*. It seemed that with this rebirth of doubts, there were no less than 500 complaints, although in total they amounted to 245.[14] I listed them with my responses and published them as a book from Delhi Printing Works, then included them along with the *Mahabharat* play published by Betab Printing Works, Delhi.[15]

These objections did not trouble me. In spite of the brouhaha, the critics declared that Betab had turned the stage around, produced a revolution in the theatre world, given notice to Urdu plays to vacate the stage, and performed a valuable service for the spread of Hindi. The first three seemed to me to be ordinary achievements, but if there is some substance in the fourth, then I consider my labors to have been fruitful.

---

[13] Cheta Chamar is the central character in Act II, scene 10 of Betab's *Mahabharat*. Cheta, an untouchable, is prevented by Dron and Duryodhan from worshipping God by singing *bhajans*, reciting Vedic mantras, and conducting *puja*. Cheta defends the right to his faith, and the goddess Ganga vindicates him.

[14] The number 245 here may be a misprint for 24, which is the number given by Namra (1972): 207.

[15] Namra lists twelve objections together with their refutation. Ibid.: 207–10.

Oh Hindi, I gave your literature a bad name.
I'm glad I served you, all the same.

(30)

After the *Mahabharat*, the company arrived in Lahore and produced the *Ramayan*. It was a misfortune for the arts that the company owner, Seth Khatau, died there during an operation for kidney stones. With him, my enthusiasm also ended. I was left an orphaned child. I will never forget the date: Thursday, August 16, 1916.

Khatau's heir and son, Seth Jahangir Kavasji Khatau, took up the company reins. The younger *seth* respected me as his father's right-hand man. He insisted that I remain with the company, but my heart was broken. I was no good for anything. Having lost a boss of such refinement, virtue, and courtesy, I was stricken and went back home.

(31)

For some years I led a simple village life in Bulandshahr. Pandit Ram Prasad Sharma, a solicitor, established a DAV school about then, and I offered my services and taught religion there as an unsalaried instructor.

Back in Calcutta, Seth Jahangir Khatau remembered me once more. He lured me to Calcutta on a salary of Rs 500 a month, and there I wrote *Patni Pratap*. I was only able to produce a single play under him before I transferred my allegiance to Madan Theatres Limited at a salary of Rs 750 per month.[16]

This was also the time when I started to teach a correspondence course on poetics, aided by Pandit Ramrakha Ram. Although I had some 340 pupils, this project received only hostile comments from my rivals, and I abandoned it.

(32)

The truth vow had molded me in such a way that falsehood seemed an unnecessary substance. Yet at a certain point the winds of time whispered in my ear that lies were needed again. This happened when

---

[16] Betab apparently wrote *Krishna Sudama* and *Shankh ki Shararat* for Madan Theatres in 1920.

I quit working for the Madan Company and tried my hand at other businesses: running a rickshaw company in Calcutta, buying and selling freight containers, operating a printing press in Delhi, and setting up a wholesale grocery in Ludhiana. Rather than dooming my vow, these ventures themselves were doomed. As they each went belly up, they consumed whatever savings I had amassed. I threw Rs 2500 into the rickshaw pit. The containers took just a small offering. The grocery gobbled up Rs 4000, and the press squeezed Rs 20,000 out of me. In the beginning I thought I would invest, at the most, Rs 10,000 in the press, but I sacrificed much more than that on machinery, ink, paper, and employees' salaries.

(33)

Although I lost a lot of money on the press, it had many advantages too. It was a convenient means of publishing my long-standing sentiments on the uplift of my caste. In Delhi I established the Atharva Brahmin Sabha, whose purpose was to free my caste-fellows from improper deeds and create commitment to actions appropriate to Brahmins. Pandit Ramlalji Bhatt of Kanpur came to my aid in this time of trial, strengthening my position with textual research and proofs of the antiquity of the Atharva caste. In connection with this I also started a monthly magazine called *Utthan*.

Before I founded the Sabha, I had been invited to speak at the All-India Mahasabha session held in Kanpur in December 1924.[17] There I made a proposal and revealed my scheme in public. Which is to say, my views were the same from then until now. If my respected brethren had not bowed to tradition and ignored my proposal, the Mahasabha would not today be obliged to answer the allegations in the Mishra brothers' book, *Hindi Navratna*, nor would I have been compelled to raise my pen against them.[18]

---

[17] Not the Hindu Mahasabha (a national political organization), but a caste organization such as the All-India Brahmin Mahasabha.

[18] Ganesh Bihari Mishra and his two brothers, collectively the *mishrabandhu*, published *Hindi Navratna* in 1910. See Mishrabandhu (1975). With regard to Surdas, the brothers referred to the debate about his caste, making a distinction

One of the terrible problems in our community was that many surnames were in use. According to the period and region, different branches of the Brahmin caste had developed—Saraswat, Gaur, Sanadhya, Shukla, Mishra. Brahmabhatts were a branch like them, but we were not known by one name either. Brahmabhatt, Bhatt, Ray, Rao, Bandi, Tripathi—what was the necessity of so many names? Why so many branches? It unnecessarily spread confusion. If for some genuinely good reason we could not get rid of these branches, then what was wrong with calling ourselves "Atharva"? Where there were 99 names, let there be 100.

My guess is that if one name were to be chosen from those presently in use, one group would be happy and many would be unhappy. The logical solution is to fix on a new name so that there would be no question of satisfaction or dissatisfaction. This proposal appears to some impossible to convert into action, yet in reality, this is not the case.

I remain hopeful. One day soon, a fine young man will advance from studenthood to householdership and find old issues of *Utthan* lying around his house. If he gives them thought, he will water those seeds hidden in the earth's womb and live to taste their fruit.

(34)

In 1928 I was completely broke. My external form looked fine, but the condition inside was destitute. The marriage of my eldest daughter, Richavati, had been arranged, yet I had no funds for the wedding ceremony. Postponing it would have meant disgrace. I gave in and accepted a contract to write a play for Madan Theatres. Searching for a quiet place in which to work, I went to a *dharmshala* in Rishikesh on the banks of the Ganga and began writing *Ganesh Janm*.[19]

---

between Brahmins and *bhat*s, whom they equated with *brahmabhatts* and ranked lower. Betab published a book-length rejoinder, *Mishra Bandhu Pralap*, in 1937. See also Nijhawan (2010): 342–9.

[19] Around this time, Betab also wrote *Kumari Kinnari*, or *Mother India*, *Sita Banvas* (coauthored with Agha Hashr), and *Samaj*. These plays were all performed in Calcutta in 1928–9. His last plays were *Hamari Bhul* (1937) and *Shakuntala* (1945).

I finished the play, got paid, and married my daughter on May 15, 1928. The *rishi* Kanva had nothing other than words with which to honor his daughter, Shakuntala, at the time of her marriage, so he simply gave her advice. Likewise, on the day of my daughter's farewell ceremony, I had no dowry to offer. Instead, I tearfully presented her with the following poem. This gift has pleased many householders, and I publish it here so that whosoever wishes may use it to instruct their daughters.[20]

(35)

My patron Sardar Karam Singhji of Ludhiana district always wanted me to establish an ashram in a peaceful spot where I could teach the Vedic books and be an instrument of uplift for Aryan youths. After losing my entire fortune on the businesses already described, I could not build an ashram, but I managed to construct a house in Muzaffarnagar with a few saved up pennies. It was as if, on the road to salvation, I suddenly took a detour toward engagement.

Just at the auspicious moment when the housewarming rituals were to begin, a letter came from Bhagvandas Nayak in Bombay, asking me to join the Ranjit Film Company immediately. Those were lean times, and I needed the money. The letter was a gift from God, the key to hidden stores of wealth. Taking it as an invitation to revive my fate, I took the next train and headed for Bombay.

(36)

June 30, 1931, too was an auspicious day, for it was then that I met Seth Chandulal J. Shah and his elder brother Seth Dayaram J. Shah. It took only fifteen minutes to come to a decision. I was offered a job writing for the film company at Rs 1500 per film. I took their leave and went back to Muzaffarnagar via Ahmedabad, where Bhagvandas lived. On July 12, I departed with my son Vedbhanu and my dear friend Lalita Prasad for Bombay. With the Shahs' approval, I began writing the screenplay for *Devi Devayani*. Chandulal Shah himself

---

[20] *Vivahopahar*, "The Wedding Gift," consists of thirty six-line stanzas. The poem instructs the young wife to accept fate, be modest, and serve her husband even in the face of infidelity.

directed the film. The role of Devayani, daughter of Shukracharya, was played by Miss Gohar.

This was the same Miss Gohar who is now famous from one corner of India to the other. The most discriminating critics have agreed that she has no equal in expressing the sentiments of the poet and portraying the inner states of her characters. I beg your pardon, I am writing my own story, and her artistry has no need of my humble powers of description. Nevertheless, I wish to clarify just three items about her private life, so that readers may better understand her.

12. Miss Gohar in the Film *Barrister's Wife*

1) I have been an employee of the company since its earliest days, and Miss Gohar is a partner in the company. For several years, I had no idea that she too was one of the company owners. This girl is so selfless, pure, and simple-hearted that words like "actress", "star", and "*abhinetri*" do not fit her.
2) I never saw her use her position or power to remove any employee from the company.
3) In June 1936, the new film *Prabhu ka Pyara* was in rehearsals. In it, Gohar played a respectable daughter whom adversity makes a beggar, and who then makes a life for herself as an actress in the theatre. She had to play the role of a courtesan who serves wine to spectators and entertains them with songs. I wrote a song: *pi lo, pi lo surang lal pani*, "drink, drink the bright red water."

When Gohar was to film this song, she blushed so much that she could not even sing. Her honest heart could not accept the pretence. She tried again and again to satisfy the requirements of art, but she had no breath to sing in opposition to her feelings. I was compelled to change the song to: *pi lo, pi lo, ye ras bhar-bhar pyala*, "drink, drink the cup full of juice." Today this is the very song that is sung in the film.

On September 5, 1931, *Devi Devayani* was screened. In honor of its success, great celebrations were held. The Shah brothers gave the employees gold watches and chains. In addition to these gifts of gold, I received a bonus and was overjoyed.

(37)

On December 28, 1933, I suffered a paralyzing stroke. But God is merciful. Fate threw me into the river, my whole body was drenched, but not a hair of my head got wet. From my topknot to my toenails, my entire right side became useless, yet by God's kindness my mind was saved. After this attack, I wrote a dozen screenplays that pleased the bosses. The humble abode in which I sit writing my autobiography, this very Bhanu Bhavan, is a blessing of the Shri Ranjit Movietone Company.

From *Devayani* up until today, I have earned more from the Ranjit Company than I can put into words. The amount can be estimated from the fact that I pay approximately Rs 1000 every year as income tax. In addition to working for the Ranjit Company, I have permission to write for the Saroj Movietone Company run by Seth Nanubhai B. Desai.

Now, in 1936, the Ranjit owners have set aside a contracted amount of Rs 1000 per month for me. I consider this their pension to an old servant. Put in other words, this is the straw for their old, worn out bullock, tied to the post. May God grant them all the four fruits: duty, wealth, enjoyment, and liberation.

OCTOBER 1, 1936

4

Radheshyam Kathavachak, *My Theatre Days*

Introduction

My Theatre Days is a classic autobiography from the Parsi theatre. Available since 2004 in a modern Hindi edition, it colorfully describes the life and times of Radheshyam Kathavachak, noted playwright and director. The book has enchanted readers with its portrait of commercial drama in North India in the days of Mahatma Gandhi and the Indian independence movement. Radheshyam straddled the great divide between older recitational practices that stressed personal devotion and more modern, public ways of marrying religious emotion and mythic stories to political agendas through theatre. He was by birth and training a reciter-singer in the Vaishnava sectarian tradition of the Hindi heartland. Bringing the poetic finesse and fervor of his background to the Parsi theatre, he created a series of powerful mythological plays. These dramas were performed by the New Alfred Theatrical Company at the very time that the nationalist movement was gaining momentum across North India. Radheshyam's use of Sanskritized Hindi and epic allegory were well matched to political and cultural trends of the 1920s, and he earned the respect of national leaders and literary giants like Premchand.

Radheshyam wore three or four hats, depending on how one counts. Firmly rooted in the world of oral performance, he gave devotional recitals all his life. He founded and operated a publishing house that printed devotional literature for the mass market. For several decades, he composed dramas while on contract with a large Parsi theatre company. And he worked in the film industry fitfully as well. His dramatic works apart, Radheshyam is known for his adaptation of Tulsidas' *Ramcharitmanas* in popular verse, which he published from his Shri Radheshyam Pustakalay in Bareli (Bareilly). The *Radheshyam Ramayan* not only was widely read and adopted for Ram Lila performances, it became one of the core texts utilized in the influential television serial directed by Ramanand Sagar in the 1980s. His legacy endures in regular productions of his plays at the National School of Drama

13. *Radheshyam Ramayan*

and other urban venues, and in the continuing circulation of his devotional verses in the countryside. On a more sinister note, Radheshyam's dramas contributed to the consolidation of Hindu nationalism, and some view him as a harbinger of the divisive Hindutva politics of recent decades.

Radheshyam's story begins with his birth in 1890 into a poor Brahmin family in Bareli. His father was a professional *katha* singer, and Radheshyam often accompanied him. At the age of 8, Radheshyam began playing the harmonium and singing in the Ram Lila. One of the foremost Parsi theatre companies, the New Alfred, frequently came to Bareli, and during one of their visits Radheshyam's father tried to enroll him as a child actor. However, a pious widowed relation persuaded the family to keep Radheshyam at home and hired him to sing hymns in her temple. Influenced by the songs of the New Alfred, Radheshyam began adapting devotional verses to the popular theatre tunes of the day.

Touring with his father for *katha* recitals, Radheshyam stayed in Agra for over a year. There he got married at the age of 13. As an adolescent he also lived for extended periods in Muradabad, Kanpur, and Lucknow. He attended Parsi theatre shows wherever he went. The impact of seeing *Khubsurat Bala*, a play by Agha Hashr, was so great that in 1910 he began to work for the New Albert Company (not to be confused with the New Alfred) in the capacity of song-writer and assistant director. The company's production of Talib's *Ramayan* marked Radheshyam's professional entry into the Parsi theatre and strengthened his resolve to write plays on themes from Hindu mythology.

Shortly after this experience, Radheshyam began writing his first play, *Vir Abhimanyu*, based on an episode from the *Mahabharat*. He went to Bombay in 1912 to expose himself to Marathi and Gujarati dramas and production techniques. After revising *Vir Abhimanyu*, he sold the play to Sohrabji Ogra, and the New Alfred started rehearsing it. After some disagreements over casting, the play opened in 1916. Fearing the public reaction to the Sanskritized Hindi in the play, one company owner predicted it would flop, but *Vir Abhimanyu* was a resounding success.

Radheshyam's initial effort set a precedent for playwriting in Hindi and was quickly followed by other playwrights. His next mythological play was *Shravan Kumar*, written for the Survijay Natak Samaj. Then Radheshyam tried his hand at writing social drama, and the result was *Parivartan*. When his retelling of the story of Prahlad, a devotee of Vishnu, was performed in 1921–2, it was subjected to police surveillance. Although the drama contained rousing speeches against unjust rulership, no evidence of it being seditious could be found. Radheshyam joined the Congress Party in 1919 and attended party meetings as a delegate until 1929.

Tensions between Hindus and Muslims intensified in the 1920s across North India. It was not surprising that the Parsi theatre too was affected by schisms. Radheshyam himself favored the Gujarati Nayaks, a performing subcaste known for their expertise as female impersonators. He also facilitated the hiring of more North Indian Hindus into the New Alfred, including some of his relations. Among those he fostered was the young actor Fida Husain, who played the female lead in *Masharqi Hur*, the only Muslim social that Radheshyam wrote.

In 1926, the New Alfred performed Radheshyam's *Shri Krishna Avatar*. The playwright had now become a director in the company and was responsible for scenery, costumes, music, dance, and casting. This devotional drama proved to be an enduring hit and was quickly followed by a sequel, *Rukmini Mangal*. In 1927, Premchand praised these mythologicals in his magazine *Madhuri*, citing them for their high ideals and educational qualities. Next, Radheshyam wrote *Ishvar Bhakti*, the tale of Ambarish from the *Bhagavat Purana*. This play was inaugurated by Motilal Nehru, then president of the Congress Party. Radheshyam followed this with *Draupadi Svayamvar*, the third part of his Krishna saga. Subsequent to this, he became ill and retired from the company in 1930.

After leaving the New Alfred, Radheshyam earned a living from his *katha* performances and publications. He joined the film world in 1931 and went to Calcutta to work for the Madan Theatres. After composing the dialogues and songs for the film *Shakuntala*, he was commissioned to adapt the screenplay for the stage. He also wrote a philosophical drama, *Maharshi Valmiki*, which debuted in 1932. Radheshyam continued to write for both stage and screen, but his departure from the New Alfred Company marked a turning point in his attitude toward the entertainment world. He could not adjust to the presence of women in the profession and was increasingly drawn to spiritual pursuits, including the service of a personal guru. He also suffered reverses in his family life. His mother died, his son Ghanshyam suffered a serious illness, and his wife too had been unwell. In 1940, he took the decision to cease working for money and began to perform *katha* for free.

Radheshyam's last theatrical success was *Sati Parvati*, which was finally staged in 1944 by the Shahjahan Theatrical Company. At the time of Indian Independence he was working on a film entitled *Ram Janm*, but the project was never completed. His elder son Ghanshyam died later that year, and Radheshyam withdrew from the world in grief. He eventually found his way back to Bombay, to return to Bareli when his wife was dying. Writing his autobiography at the age of 65, Radheshyam was beset by illness and loneliness. However, he remained fixed on the eternal verities he had celebrated in his devotional recitals. Lamenting the decline of the stage in recent times, he harked back to the simplicity of his years in the theatre, when men and women knew their appropriate roles and dramas were educative as well as entertaining.

The style of Radheshyam's autobiography is very much in keeping with his background as an oral performer. His memoir focuses on a series of significant moments arranged in a linear chronology, told with considerable vigor. He is well-practised at elaborating and expounding upon a theme, in the effortless manner learned by entertaining an audience night after night. This oratorical aspect of the art of *kathavachan*, rendered on the printed page, often comes across as verbosity. Of the four autobiographies, this one is the most replete with detail. The translation therefore represents a significant reduction of the original: it has been abridged by about half.

All six of its chapters are represented, but not in proportion to their length in the original, which varies tremendously. The longest, Chapter 3, comprises 50 per cent of the original text; it constitutes rather more than that in the translation. The translation of Chapter 4, on the other hand, is considerably shorter than the original, because most of the testimonials praising Radheshyam have been omitted. In general, I have "translated up" and presented the narrator in a good light by selecting passages where he seems most credible. I have also improved the text at the level of sentence structure and punctuation. Radheshyam's sentences are strewn with dashes, quotation marks, parentheses, and exclamation points. He puts quotes around proper and common nouns, willy-nilly. One sentence should suffice as example:

> Original: *"nayak"—ambarish—bana tha—"chaube ramkrishna" (shrikrishnavatar ka "narad"), uski patni—nayika—(padma) ka "part" tha "narmadashankar" ka.*

> Translation: The "hero"—Ambarish—was played by "Chaube Ramkrishna" ("Narad" in *Shri Krishna Avatar*), with the "part" of his wife—the heroine—(Padma) played by "Narmada Shankar."

The original punctuation turns an entirely factual statement into a melodramatic revelation. The translation reduces the number of quotation marks and dashes and aims for a more tempered tone.

Radheshyam uses many English words from the theatrical trade and other realms of discourse. If the English words in the original were highlighted, this would be the result:

> Whether out of regard or affection, Sohrabji gave Bhogilal, the **assistant director**, the **part** of Abhimanyu, the **hero**. This was the same Bhogilal who had earned a name as a performer of the woman's **part** in **comic** scenes opposite Sohrabji. How could an **actor** who was a female impersonator **fit** in that **part**? Because of such mistakes, the biggest companies have **failed**. **Parts** should be distributed by matching the **nature** of the **part** to the **nature** of the **actor**. (pp. 55–6)

The effect of this code-switching is entirely lost in translation. To summarize, the original text has been flattened in various ways, although the translation may have gained somewhat in elegance and fluidity.

The history of the text is quite straightforward. *Mera Natak Kal* was originally published in 1957 by Radheshyam's own press. A copy of this edition is held in the National School of Drama Library, New Delhi, and a photocopy of it is in my possession. The original has no prefatory material that could explain the circumstances behind the autobiography, nor any reference to its prior publication. The first edition was 304 pages in length. The book was reprinted by the NSD in 2004, after being reformatted to 244 pages.

None of the existing scholarship probes the origin of the autobiography, nor does the author suggest motives for its composition. The questions of how the autobiography was composed, for which readers, and with what intentions are difficult to answer with any authority. Nonetheless, some speculative comments may be in order. Radheshyam was 67 when his autobiography was published, and it is likely that he finished it in the two years prior to this date. In his last chapter, Radheshyam mentions the poor state of his health at age 65. Earlier sections may have been composed previously. The relatively uniform style of the narrative points to a single author, although a careful editor could have achieved the same effect. It may therefore be concluded that Radheshyam wrote his autobiography himself, composing it between the ages of 65 and 67.

Nonetheless, details within the text suggest a more complicated genesis. Radheshyam had two sons, Ghanshyam and Balram. In addition, he adopted his younger brother Madan after his mother died. These three junior kinsmen appear to have been actively involved in the business of editing and publishing the songbooks, devotional texts, and theatrical dramas that Radheshyam authored. Radheshyam makes scattered references throughout the autobiography to these family members. He mentions that his publishing concern, Radheshyam Pustakalay, was handled by Ghanshyam up until 1924. Ghanshyam and a partner purchased the copyrights to all of the New Alfred's plays for the Radheshyam Pustakalay after Radheshyam retired from the New Alfred Company in 1931. Balram was involved in a dispute with another press over a pirated edition of *Vir Abhimanyu* as early as 1916. Both sons joined Radheshyam in Bombay for film projects in the 1930s and 1940s. At Radheshyam's instigation, Madan was put on salary with the New Alfred Company.

Ghanshyam died in 1947, a decade before Radheshyam's autobiography was published. As the elder and favored son, his death profoundly affected Radheshyam and his wife. The incident may have prompted Radheshyam to confront his own mortality and examine himself and his legacy. Ghanshyam may possibly have assisted his father in maintaining the archive of press reviews, clippings, correspondence, and other memorabilia from which the narrative was composed. However, given his early death it is unlikely that he played a role in eliciting or encouraging his father's autobiography.

The surviving heirs, Balram and Madan, would have had a larger stake in publicizing the legacy of Radheshyam and converting it into book format. They were probably involved in assisting Radheshyam in his old age with various aspects of his daily life and work. One or both of them may have suggested the project and assisted as editors or coauthors. Less likely is the hypothesis that they served as scribes, as appears to have been the case with Jayshankar Sundari's son. Radheshyam was an oral performer when he delivered *katha*, but he was also an accomplished writer committing compositions to paper, editing, and publishing them. Unless he was so infirm that he could no longer sit to write, it seems unlikely that he would have dictated his autobiography.

If indeed Balram and Madan had a hand in eliciting, editing, or authoring the work, their motives would not have been very different from what seem to have been Radheshyam's own: to celebrate a career and create a lasting name for the man, to explain the character and practice of the theatre of his time, and to set the record straight and deflect criticism. Incidentally, there may have been a financial motive for bringing out the book, but the autobiography probably did not sell very well. The republication by NSD has attracted a fairly large Hindi readership. Whether the family receives royalties from this edition is doubtful, insofar as there is no mention of the first edition on the copyright page.

Noted Works

Dramas

Vir Abhimanyu, 1916; *Shravan Kumar*, 1916; *Parambhakt Prahlad*, 1921; *Parivartan*, 1925; *Masharqi Hur*, 1926; *Shri Krishna Avtar*, 1926; *Rukmini Mangal*, 1927; *Ishvar Bhakti*, 1929; *Draupadi Svayamvar*, 1929; *Sati Parvati*, 1939.

Other

Radheshyam Ramayan, c.1920; *Radheshyam Vilas*, 1922; *Radheshyam Bhajanmala*, 1930.

My Theatre Days

RADHESHYAM KATHAVACHAK

Chapter 1: Childhood (1890–1902)

I was born Monday, November 25, 1890, at 8 p.m. in Kamarthiyan lane, Biharipur quarter, town of Bareli. The house of my birth was small, with mud walls, a tiled roof, and two thatched verandas. My father, Pandit Banke Lal, had received this house from his maternal grandfather, and it was his only possession at the time.

To the east of this house was a mansion called Raja Chitrakut Mahal. Drama companies that came to Bareli would rent this building and hold their rehearsals in it. The songs and voices from these companies reached me in my little house to the west, and as a four- or five-year-old boy, I listened with rapt attention.

My father was not a lover of drama, but he was fond of singing and knew a number of ragas. His voice was silken, and he was a fine vocalist. When he sang *chaupai*s in the Ram Lila, he was much appreciated. In those days, singing *lavani*s while playing the tambourine was all the rage, and father was very involved in that too. I usually went with him on these occasions. Father taught me how to play the harmonium and sing. By the age of 8, I was earning kudos for my songs in the Ram Lila. When Bareli's leading advocate, Pandit Shaligram, awarded me first prize and gave me his blessings, my joy knew no bounds.

The populace of Bareli was mad about music, especially in the nineteenth century. Every home resounded with drumming on the *dholak*. The *Ramayan* was sung, the story of *Rukmini Mangal* was recited, there were Ras Lilas, Ram Lilas, Svangs, dramas, dances, and *mujra*s. These activities reached their peak during the four months of the monsoon season. In this atmosphere, I not only learned music, I soaked it up and became intoxicated by it.

Of the various traveling troupes, the New Alfred Theatrical Company of Bombay came to Bareli the most frequently, probably every second or third year. Bareli railway station was the first stop on their tour. The town was head-over-heels in love with that company. They say that water-carriers would sell their leather water-bags just to see them perform. The hit plays in those days were *Alauddin, Ali Baba,* and *Chandravali*,[1] and their songs echoed in every lane. There was no electricity at the time, not even gas lamps. The stage was illuminated by flaming torches. Yet all of the seats, from the four-anna class to the three-rupee section, would be jampacked.

The reason that people were so fond of fine arts in those days was that we enjoyed a carefree life. A family's expenses could easily be met on a small income, with a little left over. The food was simple: just one kind of dal with roti. In the winter it was *urad*, in the summer *arhar*, and in the monsoon *mung* dal. The ghee was very pure (no one had even heard of hydrogenated vegetable oil), and most homes had their own cow or buffalo for the daily supply of milk, curd, and butter. We ate whatever vegetable was in season. We hardly ever got sick, and the only illness I heard named was fever. The cure for that was cheap: the *hakim* wrote a prescription for two paisas, and we were made to fast.

Nowadays the streets are full of doctors' offices, and every household suffers from illnesses. Every kind of treatment can be bought in the market. It's not just Ayurvedic, Yunani, or allopathic medicine. There's the electricity cure, the water cure, the mudpack cure. As I see it, the source of all these ills is the lack of simplicity and purity in diet, and the absence of tranquility. Mankind has abandoned morality and become decadent. There is no strength of character or effort made in trying to build it.

Our leaders tell us to raise our standard of living, put more dishes

---

[1] All of these popular plays were written and rewritten several times. *Alauddin* or *Aladin* was composed by Zarif in 1889; later versions were by Talib and Murad. *Ali Baba* exists in versions by Abdullah, Zarif, and Talib. *Chandravali* was written by Ahsan in 1895, as well as by Murad.

on our tables, dress in finer clothes, build fancier homes. They want us to increase the income of the poor and give them a daily wage. But France, England, and other Western countries have not achieved peace by raising their standard of living. They cannot even imagine the spiritual riches that India has always enjoyed, the source of our eternal happiness.

But let me bring my train of thought back to the main line. My father had noticed the New Alfred Company and got the idea that Radheshyam might be enrolled in it. One day he took me to Raja Chitrakut Mahal during rehearsals and had me audition. The director was pleased and invited us to the show that night. *Chandravali* was running, and our seats were in the Special Class. This was the very first time I saw a live drama. The scenes stayed with me all night, even in my dreams. The next night I saw *Alauddin*, and the night after that *Ali Baba*. The company director, Sohrabji Framji Ogra, told us that every time a boy joined the company, his father had to sign a formal agreement. My father obtained the printed contract, but it was in English and he couldn't read it. He told the director he would take it home and think about it.

Our lane was named for my father's maternal grandfather, Mulchand Kamarthi. One of his daughters was my paternal grandmother, Shrimati Kokila Devi, and she had given a house to each of her sons-in-law. Near my house lived one of them, Gangaram Maharaj. He had a daughter named Rukmini Bibi who was a child-widow. Rukmini was a model of refined behavior, self-denial, and devotion to God, just like Mirabai. Her house had been turned into a temple, and my parents were appointed to live there and perform the daily *puja* services. When Rukmini chanted the Tulsidas *Ramayan* every afternoon with her circle of ladies, I was the one who played the harmonium and sang *chaupai*s for her.

Rukmini found out that Lallu (my pet name) was going to join a theatre company, and she objected strenuously. My father was compelled to bow to the wishes of his elders. The next day, he took me along with him to Chandausi where we performed *Rukmini Mangal* for a month. I sang while father explicated the meaning. By the time we returned to Bareli, the New Alfred had left town.

At the age of 8, I could read enough Hindi to make out words, and I knew about the same amount of Urdu. Father sometimes composed poetry for *bhajans*, and as a *lavani* singer he naturally had a taste for Urdu poetry. My temperament inclined that way too. I composed my first song, *karo kripa guru maharaja*, to the metrical scheme of a tune I had heard from the New Alfred.

Every singer of Bareli sang the New Alfred's songs, and I learned each tune by heart. The company sold printed song booklets, and I collected those too. I began to set religious and inspirational lyrics to theatre melodies, a passion that kept growing over the years. Readers may see such songs in my publications, *Shriradheshyam Vilas*, *Shriradheshyam Kirtan*, and my *Ramayan*. Later I began to compose the melodies myself. During those three days of watching plays on the New Alfred stage, I quaffed that *bhang* whose intoxication has never worn off.

The next year a company came from Agra to perform Munshi Nazir's drama, *Shakuntala*. I pleaded with father to go see it, but he wouldn't take me. The New Alfred returned next with *Dil Farosh*, but we were out reciting on tour and missed it. Then Aulad Ali's company arrived with *Gulru Zarina*, and Bareli went wild. Unable to hold me back, father bought two tickets in the four-anna class and we went one night. Those actors were powerful singers who belted it out in a way seldom heard later. The company's style favored plenty of songs without much scenery or stagecraft and lots of encores or "once-mores." Sometimes a song was repeated four or five times. The show lasted till four in the morning.

Muslims were greater fans of drama than Hindus in those days, and the company management, actors, and writers were mostly Muslims too. Plays were written in pure Urdu, with sentiments of romance and beauty dominating. Even the dialogues featured refrains with end-rhymes like *amma jan, mehrban, qadr-dan*. The chief playwrights or *munshis* were Murad, Ahsan, and Nazir. Hindus were mainly interested in forming Ras Lila and Ram Lila troupes, although Svang captured the middle ground—their parties contained both Hindus and Muslims. The Hindi–Urdu or Hindu–Muslim controversy had yet to reach Bareli. Both communities lived in harmony. Bareli's Muharram was famous; all of us kids freely went to watch it. Wealthy Hindus distributed *jalebis* during the *taziya* procession. In the same fashion, during the Hindu festival of Holi, Muslims played with colors and went to greet each other. In our Kamarthi Lane lived a Muslim tailor, Ghuran, and his wife, whom I called uncle and auntie. One day his son captured my kite, and when I went running to auntie, she scolded the boy so sharply that he fell at my feet to ask forgiveness and returned the kite, string and all.

Although I was a Hindu, I went to learn music from Ustad Rahat Ali, and he accepted me lovingly like his own son and taught me the harmonium. Mainly I studied the harmonium with Pandit Bahadur Lal in the Brahmpuri quarter, and father always went with me, carrying the single-reed Mohan Flute harmonium under his arm. He was very proud of my singing and playing, and he dedicated himself to me twenty-four hours a day for years. Not only do I bow my head a hundred times, today I revere him with all my heart and soul.

Later during my youth, when I saw Hindus fighting Muslims, it saddened me greatly. Politics, that evil witch, set Hindus and Muslims against each other and divided India into two parts. Who knows when the time will come for them to reconcile and treat each other like human beings.

Chapter 2: Adolescence (1902–1910)

I began composing poetry in simple language and performed *katha* in a melodious voice. I was good-looking, full of strength and enthusiasm, and ready to take it all in, as if making my father's penance worthwhile. Father now sought programs in one city at a time, where we could rent a house and give a series of recitations. In this way, I came to live in Agra for over a year between the ages of 13 and 14. My marriage took place near Agra in Raiva village. I was 13 and my wife 11. Because my brother-in-law performed priestly rituals for families in the Muradabad–Bareli area, he was in a position to organize *katha*s for us in the households he visited each year. This connection was firmed up when my marriage was arranged. My father-in-law and mother-in-law were already deceased.

Back in Bareli, the New Alfred returned and performed *Bhul Bhulaiyan*. I longed to see it—the songs were big hits—but could not. The drama was by Ahsan, on the model of *Dil Farosh*. It happened that Motilal Nehru came to Bareli to consult a certain lawyer. In the course of business, he mentioned that he was looking for a good *Ramayan* singer to entertain his wife, who was ill. Our names were recommended, and father and I spent over a month in Allahabad, living in Anand Bhavan. Jawaharlal Nehru, who was a year older than me, was present at the time. He gave me a copy of the Tulsidas *Ramayan,* which I have carefully preserved. Vijayalakshmi Pandit was a girl then. Everyone called her Nanhi Bibi. She was particularly fond of one of my songs, *apar teri maya,* and she made me sing it every day after the *Ramayan* recitation. Motilal Nehru was a great lover of drama. Mehbub's Coronation Theatrical Company came to Allahabad while we were living there, and we went with the Nehru family to see the show. Mehbub himself was an excellent dancer, and the plays were like those of Aulad Ali's Jubilee Company, but with better costumes and scenery. I especially enjoyed *Kanak Tara.*

Father had instilled in me the entire *Ramcharitmanas,* the *Ramayan* of Tulsidas, together with commentary, and now I sought other volumes related to the stories I had learned. I began ordering books from the Venkateshwar Press in Bombay and building up a collection. I subscribed to a number of Hindi and Urdu periodicals and gradually expanded my knowledge of literary topics. The writers who most influenced me were Mahavir Prasad Dvivedi, Bal Mukund Gupt, Bharatendu Harischandra, Devakinandan Khatri, Akbar Allahabadi, Ufaq Lakhnavi, and others. My favorite monthlies were *Sarasvati, Kamla, Devnagar, Jasus, Zamana.* The weeklies I liked were *Hindi Bangvasi, Anand, Hindi Kesari,* and *Shrivenkateshvar Samachar*; and my preferred daily newspapers were *Bharat Mitra* (Calcutta) and *Aftab* (Delhi).

In connection with our *katha* recitals, I lived for a year or more in both Muradabad (Moradabad) and Kanpur, and for about two years in Lucknow. Through a friend in the Lucknow railway station, I got a pass to see the Ripon Theatrical Company and was introduced to Mehrji, the director. Mehrji was keen to induct me as both an actor and script writer, but I stuck to my father's principles and maintained my commitment to *katha.* I even began to add the label *kathavachak* to my name.

Mehrji was a proper gentleman, and from him I learned about the various Parsi theatre companies of Bombay. The Balivala Victoria Theatrical Company had brought out *Satyavadi Harishchandra,* and after that they were preparing a new version of the *Ramayan*. The author of both plays was Vinayak Prasad Talib of Banaras. His language was a theatrical mixture of Hindi and Urdu. I heard of another company, the famed Parsi Theatrical Company of Bombay, and learned that the old Alfred Company had split into two branches, the Parsi Alfred of Kavasji Khatau and the New Alfred of Manikji Jivanji Master.

Mehrji's company generally performed its own plays, with Mehrji himself playing the comedian. I saw their *Khun ka Khun* and liked it very much. Seeing these plays, I often wondered why they did not perform Bharatendu's *Bharat Durdasha* or *Nildevi*. Maybe these dramas were not three-acters, maybe they were too short, and that was why. I later realized that the professional drama companies had no custom of performing plays in Sanskritized Hindi. Such Hindi plays were limited to the amateur clubs.

I began writing my first play, based on a novel by Lajjaram Mehta, but lacking knowledge of the stage and scene construction could not complete it. When I was performing *katha* in Jaipur, I heard that the New Alfred had returned to Bareli and this time performed a new play, *Khubsurat Bala*, which was a huge hit. I truly regretted that I had missed it.

Now a flood of theatrical companies appeared, and the peculiar thing was that all of them adopted English names. Moreover, regardless of where they came from, they added the phrase "of Bombay" at the end. The company owners thought that this enhanced their prestige. And in truth the New Alfred and the Parsi Alfred were chief among the companies that spread the name of Bombay throughout the country.

Like a monsoon deluge, in every town local theatre companies stole the dramas of the Bombay companies and performed them. Only one or two of the actors were any good. The rest just earned enough to get by. In one such company—maybe it was the Empire or Edward, I don't really remember, but it was in Bareli—I saw *Khubsurat Bala*. This was the first play that really swept me away. I went to see it twice and still had not had my fill. The drama contained both tragedy and comedy in equal and just measure, with language appropriate to each. I learned that the author's name was Agha Hashr Kashmiri and the director Sohrabji Ogra. Feeling deep respect for both individuals, I felt the urge to go to Bombay to see the play in the New Alfred.

Sohrabji became famous throughout the country for the part of Khairsalla, and Agha Hashr became the most popular playwright. Not only the professional companies, the amateur clubs too started performing *Khubsurat Bala*. It was seeing this performance that inspired me to jump into the torrent of the theatre. My love of Hindi was growing apace, and I decided to clutch Hindi drama to my chest like a gourd to float on. Surely this burning desire came from past influences or *samskaras*, or else my future was speaking to me.

Then I noticed that the list of playwrights was growing—Bekal, Afsun, Zeba, Betab, Shaida, Hasrat, Jauhar—and all of them chose pseudonyms from Urdu. It irked me that none of them used Hindi pen-names. Ufaq Saheb, who was actually Munshi Dvarka Prasad of Lucknow, had published a play called *Ram Lila* which used Urdu poetic tropes to refer to Ram's birth. It was performed by Ram Lila lovers in the Punjab. To counter that trend, I took a tune from the Parsi play *Zahri Sanp*, which was all the rage at the time, and set Hindi words to it, giving birth to my own *Ramayan*.

In 1910, a company from the Punjab came to Bareli—the New Albert Company owned by Nanak Chand Khatri. Khatri was a warm-hearted man who had spent a lot of money to make his company the best. One day he arrived unannounced at my thatched hut with several of his leading actors. After introducing himself, he explained that his company had just performed their *Ramayan* before Maharaja Savai Madhosingh of Jaipur. The maharaja had found some defects in the play, and his secretary, who remembered me from a *katha* performance at the palace, recommended that I be enlisted to revise it. I happily accepted the invitation. Father was ill just then, and we had no plans to go on tour, so I got down to work.

To bolster my knowledge I attended rehearsals every morning at ten and watched the performances at night. Officially, the company director was Rahim Bakhsh, a comic actor, but the actual direction came from the tragedian Abdul Rahman Kabuli. Kabuli was known for stealing plays from other companies, but he was such a good performer that the shows were always hits. The company also had fine singing actors in Rahmat Ali and Nisar.

It was my nature to adopt the dictatorial mode whenever I worked, and by force of will I would push through a task to its completion. Within a month, I not only revised the entire play, I corrected all the songs. Then I was asked to provide stage direction, and the Muslim director did not interfere, thinking that this was a *dharmik* play and whatever Panditji was doing must be correct. The harmonium master rehearsed the singers with my tunes and turns of phrase. The tabla master, Ghulam Husain, was first class, a real *ustad*. He played such spectacular flourishes to announce the entrance of each actor that he earned his own once-mores.

The version of the *Ramayan* that the company had been performing was an amalgam of texts written by Talib, Ufaq, Rameshwar Bhatt, and Tulsidas. When I added my changes, it became a five-part sweet dish. Finally opening night arrived, and I invited father and all my relatives except Rukmini Bibi. Nanak Chand did not stint on free passes, so during the course of a month more than a hundred of my guests got to see the play. The performance was a big success. My fame spread all over Bareli. Master Nisar played the part of Sita and was a crowd-pleaser with his sweet voice, subtle vocal ornaments, and pure pronunciation. Master Prabhu as Ram got the audience to break down and weep with his singing of Tulsidas' *chaupais*.

I had admired the company's new folding harmonium with reeds from Paris, and now Nanak Chand presented it to me with a note: "This is a token of my love and esteem—do not return it." Upon his recommendation, I began writing *Babhruvahan*, but the plot did not prove suitable. In the meantime I read the poem *Jayadrath Vadh* by Maithili Sharan Gupt,[2] which I thought would make a good play, along with Lala Shalagram's drama *Abhimanyu*, which was not stageable but had a fine plot. Finally I ordered the *Mahabharat* translated by Mahavir Prasad Dvivedi from the Indian Press in Allahabad. Adapting its story line, I began to write my *Vir Abhimanyu*.

Chapter 3: Early Adulthood (1911–1931)

After the New Albert's *Ramayan*, my name became known among the community of actors, and I often availed of conversation with

---

[2] Gupt's second major work, the narrative poem *Jayadrath Vadh* (1910)—The Slaying of Jayadrath—derived from the *Mahabharat* and related the slaying of Arjun's son Abhimanyu. Nijhawan (2010): 139–40.

them. While reciting *katha* in various cities, I worked on the first act of *Vir Abhimanyu* in my spare time. In those days I traveled with one or two servants, while father stayed behind at home. As the household had grown, so had its responsibilities.

In 1912 I went to Bombay for the first time, and that magic city cast its charms over its new visitor. I saw the plays of the Marathi and Gujarati theatre companies, as well as *Zahri Sanp* performed by a Parsi company. I learned that its director, Amritlal, had gotten his scriptwriter, Narayan Prasad Betab, to compose this play after much travail. *Zahri Sanp* was a roaring success in Bombay, and tickets were hard to come by. Amritlal was without doubt a fine actor and director. He also composed the lyrics and tunes for the company's songs. He belonged to the Nayak caste. The Nayaks were from around Ahmedabad; many villages were full of them. Their principal occupation was singing, dancing, and acting in plays. Nayak fathers and guardians would fill out an agreement and enroll their boys in the Gujarati and Parsi companies at a young age. There these boys developed into stars like Amritlal, Bhogilal, Mohan, Purushottam, and Narmada Shankar. Nayak youths excelled in performing female roles, which was why most companies—especially the Gujarati companies—did not employ women as actresses. Among the Parsi companies, the New Alfred was the only one that actually had a rule against allowing women to perform; the policy was maintained until 1932.

The Marathi companies did not employ actors from the Nayak caste, as far as I could see. Marathas did the acting for them. Their writers, who were often scholars, would take up social problems and write about them. Marathi actors certainly had their own art, but it seemed to me that they had only a single style. Songs were deemed less important in their plays, although they were usually in the classical mode.

Religious or *dharmik* plays were first introduced to the Bombay stage by Kathiawar Brahmins. Their language was Gujarati, and women did not work in these companies. The playwrights here were prone to emotional excess. They took legends from the Puranas and adapted them to the stage. They used fine scenery in their productions, and I was very impressed by their plays. The companies were generous too: they had whole plays, in Gujarati of course, printed and offered for sale. I bought a number of such published plays and brought them back with me. My eagerness to read them compelled me to learn Gujarati. After *Narsi Mehta*, the most popular Gujarati play was *Bilvamangal* or *Bhakt Surdas* by the court poet of Rajkot, Nathuram Sundar Shukla. Agha Hashr based his Hindi *Surdas* on this Gujarati *Surdas*. In the same manner, a popular Gujarati play titled *Sati Draupadi* was picked up by Kavasji Khatau after he saw it, and Betab turned it into his *Mahabharat*.[3]

When I got back from Bombay I scrapped the scenes of *Vir Abhimanyu* that I had written earlier, excepting a few emotion-packed lines. I rearranged the order, putting the Bhagavad Gita sermon of Krishna to Arjun right at the beginning, after the introduction. Actually, writing *Vir Abhimanyu* was a hobby for me, not a thing to be hurried or constrained. I had hardly any free time, since, in addition to performing *katha*, I had taken on another burden, book publishing. I started in 1908 with the first part of *Radheshyam Vilas*, which was published in Muradabad at Lakshmi Narayan Press. I had to spend thirteen rupees to get the job done, but I earned more than three times as much from it. The copies sold out wherever I performed *katha*. Then I published *Draupadi Lila*, *Sita Haran*, and other books with epic themes. These works turned a profit, and I developed the habit of putting gain ahead of pleasures such as playwriting.

Other difficulties arose having to do with Rukmini Bibi's house and property. Gradually all four sides surrounding the plot of land became involved in court cases. Until then I was unaware that when a person does well, his neighbors often resent it. Father was a plain man, a simple Brahmin. Aside from bathing in the Ganga, singing *bhajans*, and reading the scriptures he took care of the horses and cows, and that was his entire life. What did he know of worldly matters or the law? By good fortune, I made the acquaintance of an advocate who managed my legal affairs and yet maintained the deportment of a member of the family.

Finally, I had composed a sufficient portion of *Vir Abhimanyu* to allow reading scenes from it out loud to my friends. I began to add

---

[3] Premchand, writing in *Madhuri*, appears to be the source of this reference. *Sati Draupadi* was perhaps the version by C.D. Jhaveri.

these dramatic readings to the tail end of my *katha* recitations. Whether one is a *kathavachak* or a poet, the feeling common to all is that wherever one recites, one should be the best. This is a natural inclination. The good part of this feeling is that one constantly strives to improve one's art and perform well, but the drawback is the egotism that results. I did not manage to remain untouched by it, especially given my string of successes. When I turned 50, I began to control the tendency, but the ailment still flairs up like an old itch.

In 1911 or 1912, Pandit Madan Mohan Malviya came to Bareli to raise funds for Banaras Hindu University. He was accompanied by the Raja of Darbhanga and other luminaries of Kashi. Their procession through Bareli was magnificent and has yet to be matched in the town's history. An elegant assembly was held in their honor. Some of my friends organized a program in which I sang a number of topical songs. I had composed these in support of the BHU campaign. Within a couple of days, several thousand rupees accrued from the sale of these songs, and I donated the entire amount to the university fund. This was my first acquaintance with the great Malviyaji, which deepened over the years until I formally became his disciple at the age of 50.

When I first met Pandit Malviya, he asked me my profession, and I told him I was a *kathavachak*. Then he invited me to recite. After I sang some passages from my *Ramayan*, he asked me the difference between the *lavani* and *chaubola* meters. Then he wanted to hear a scene from *Vir Abhimanyu*. Overjoyed, he told me to invite him when the play was performed. "Sanskrit drama is a storehouse," he advised me. "You should make a study of plays written in Sanskrit. In my boyhood, I too was very fond of drama. I played the role of Shakuntala in our club of amateurs." Thus I received a blessing from my future guru at the very start of my career.

In 1913 the New Alfred Company returned to Bareli with Agha Hashr's play *Achhuta Daman*. The trend for *dharmik* plays had been started by the Balivala Victoria Company, and the owners of the New Alfred wanted to follow suit. But no Hindi playwrights were available. I happened to be in Bareli, and the company's assistant director, Bhogilal, called on me and insisted I meet Sohrabji, the director. It goes without saying that it was the *Ramayan* as performed in the New

Albert that had established my fame and brought me to Sohrabji's notice.

Sohrab Ogra was a very intimidating director, but because I was a professional raconteur I was not the least bit shy with him. At his request I recited several scenes from *Vir Abhimanyu* with such bold passion that he was extremely impressed. Bhogilal complimented me on my eloquence, likening me to Agha Hashr. Sohrabji then chose my play for his own company. I said that I had written it for the New Albert. He responded, "The New Albert is breaking up. Nanak Chand is seriously ill. Several actors from the company have written to me, looking for work here." I agreed that if this was the case, I would turn the play over to him within a couple of months. We shook hands and parted.

I was concerned about the ethics of selling my play to a different company than the one that had commissioned it. After I confirmed that Nanak Chand was indeed ill, I went to Ambala to meet him. He happily granted his permission to sign *Vir Abhimanyu* over to the New Alfred. For five days I attended the exhibition in Bulandshahr where the New Alfred was performing and saw five different plays. Sohrabji played the comedian in all of them, dressed simply and without makeup, omitting the usual grimaces and comic antics. His vocal delivery and pronunciation were exemplary. He seemed to drop his sentences into the listener's ears as though blowing a cool breeze through a garden.

Because the company had no Hindi copyist, Bhogilal had my scenes transcribed into the Gujarati alphabet. I read them out line by line, and the scribe took them down. Then Sohrabji read the scenes over several times, carefully analyzed each line, and dictated where the curtain drops should be placed. He favored ending a scene at the height of dramatic tension, right at the spot where the writing was most powerful. He often said that if the scenes of a play were well written, and if the artist delivered his lines correctly and forcefully, the play could not possibly fail. This was the reason why there was no prompter in the New Alfred and no prompt book on stage. The actors had to memorize their lines thoroughly and come onstage prepared to deliver them without assistance. This method persisted in the company up till 1930.

I learned that the company retained two *munshi*s, Bekal on a salary of fifty rupees a month, and Ahsan Saheb on a hundred a month. Agha Hashr had demanded more than that and quit when he didn't get it. You may ask what publishers paid Hindi writers in those days. They got a quarter- or half-rupee per page. Later, Premchand earned a rupee per page. In that setup, when Sohrabji offered me Rs 300 for *Vir Abhimanyu*, I accepted the deal without further negotiation. He gave me Rs 100 as an advance on the spot. We agreed that whenever I needed to travel to the company, they would pay for a round-trip ticket in the second class and another in the third. All the company's actors traveled second class, and a special train transported them from one city to the next. This arrangement too continued up to 1930.

The company had one kitchen for Muslims and Parsis, and another for Hindus (members of the Nayak caste) in which Audichya Brahmins from Bombay prepared the meals. All the same, I was reluctant to eat that food. The young today may think it strange, but the fact is that when in my youth I had to dine out over the midday meal, I cooked my own dal and roti. This was because of my strict Brahmin upbringing—more's the pity! When Sohrabji heard of this, he added two rupees per day as a stipend for my meals, and this provision continued long.

In May 1913 I broke my leg while on the train back to Bareli. It was late at night, and I was asleep with my left foot hanging out the window when a windstorm knocked down a tree, and it fell on me. It took more than a year for the leg to heal. Nothing got done during that time—no *katha*s, no writing. Then Nanak Chand died, and that came as another blow. In Surat the New Alfred's pavilion caught fire, and this too upset me, but who can avert the wrath of fate?

In the winter of 1915, with Sohrabji insisting upon it, I went to Kanpur and handed over the *chakravyuh* scene of *Vir Abhimanyu*. Sohrabji decided that the act would end at this point. It was a long scene, full of fighting and violence, but it was deeply affecting too. In Kanpur I met Agha Hashr for the first time. He had come to sell his drama *Surdas* to the New Alfred Company. When it was being read out loud, Hashr Saheb approached me and spoke with great civility, "I am a Muslim, and Urdu is my language. This is a *dharmik* play full of Hindi. If you find fault anywhere, please don't hesitate to tell me."

I surmised that Hashr was a real expert in marketing his work, because right in front of me Sohrabji offered him Rs 1000 for a single scene. I thought this meant that *Vir Abhimanyu* would be postponed, and the company would perform *Surdas* next. But the next evening I learned that Sohrabji had told Agha Hashr he could only take up *Surdas* after *Vir Abhimanyu*. What good luck, I thought!

I continued working on the play, spending the hot season in Lucknow at my friend's government quarters near the city railway station. I would sit outdoors on a string-cot beneath a tamarind tree, oblivious to the searing winds, utterly engrossed in scene-writing. I mention this for the sake of our delicate young people today—what a contrast between then and now! After receiving the second installment of Rs 100, I said goodbye to Lucknow and sent the last act of the play by registered post from Saharanpur, where I had gone for a *katha* recital. By then, Sohrabji had grown accustomed to reading the Devanagari script. I would write to him in Hindi, and he would write back in Hindi written in the Gujarati script.

After Divali, the company arrived in Delhi and stayed in the Sangam Theatre (now Jagat Talkies), intending to stage *Vir Abhimanyu* there. I was told to report for duty and begin work on the song lyrics. After bathing in the Ganga on Kartik Purnima, I arrived in Delhi and occupied a room in the theatre right in front of Sohrabji. Two actors from the New Albert, Abdul Rahman Kabuli and Nisar, had joined the New Alfred, and from them I learned that Rahim Bakhsh had gone off to Calcutta and Rahmat Ali had started his own company in the Punjab. Ustad Ghulam Husain, the tabla master, had also joined the New Alfred. The senior harmonium master in the company was Nihal Chand. He was an excellent player who also composed the songs. The tradition was that the harmonium master would first establish the tunes, and then the playwright would write lyrics to fit them. I wanted to change this tradition because it did not give priority to the words, and as a *kathavachak* I thought the words were what made the greatest impression on the audience. In the end a compromise was reached. I wrote the lyrics for certain songs first, and for the others I supplied lyrics to match pre-composed melodies. The dance numbers were choreographed in consultation with the dance master, Bhogilal.

In this way we arranged the songs in a month's time. Over this period I observed Sohrabji conduct rehearsals. He was very diligent about instructing correct pronunciation to even the best actors. He asked them to act naturally. The pronunciation rehearsals took place in a special session, with the actors seated. Acting was rehearsed with everyone standing on the stage. When Sohrabji determined that an actor possessed the right degree of naturalness, he finalized or "set" the acting. He eliminated overacting.

Costumes and scenery were less his concern; he left them to Bhogilal. The New Alfred had a practice of designing entirely new sets and costumes—down to the shoes—for each new drama. The dress master or senior tailor was very capable. He was Mohammad Ali from Lucknow, a twelve-month employee. He designed such splendid, showy costumes for *Vir Abhimanyu* that people said they had never seen anything like it. As each scene was presented on stage and each new costume introduced, Sohrabji and I gave it a passing mark. Once or twice I disapproved, but I kept my opinion to myself lest I appear foolish. I was learning about scenery and costuming from this play and was hardly an expert. Nevertheless I objected to the portrayal of Garuda in the Kailas scene. The chief painter was a Punjabi named Harishchandra, and he took my advice without further ado.

There was one major irritant during that month. Whether out of regard or affection, Sohrabji gave the part of Abhimanyu, the hero, to Bhogilal, the assistant director. This was the same Bhogilal who had earned a name as a performer of women's parts in comic scenes opposite Sohrabji. How could an actor who was a female impersonator fit the hero's part? By such mistakes have the biggest companies failed. Parts should be distributed by matching the nature of the part to the nature of the actor. But the owners and directors of drama companies were often blind to this, giving the best roles to their favorites in order to promote them, whether they were appropriate or not.

I did not wish to see my first play weakened, and it was to the advantage of the New Alfred that the play be well staged. I confronted Sohrabji on the casting of Bhogilal, and he agreed with me, yet he felt he could not ask Bhogilal to give up the part. I said I would take care of it. I took Bhogilal to the park in front of the Sangam Theatre and explained the matter. He said he was no longer interested in playing women's roles. So I suggested he perform the role of Lord Krishna.

He wasn't sure he could master the new assignment in the month of rehearsals that was left, but I assured him he could, adding that he would become famous as Krishna, and his photograph would be in every home. In fact this is what happened. Even Sohrabji's room was always adorned with that photo.

Finally, all the casting changes were settled. Ammulal played Abhimanyu, Elizar played Arjun, Abdul Rahman Kabuli played Bhim, Jagannath was Subhadra, and Nisar was Uttara. Another headache for me was the advertising: publishing the notices in Hindi and Urdu, getting publicity in the newspapers, and printing up the song books. If I hadn't tackled all of this, the company would have been in a sorry state.

The opening of the play was set for Vasant Panchami, February 4, 1916, the same day as the ground-breaking for Banaras Hindu University. On the night of February 2, the grand rehearsal was held. In the New Alfred, this meant that the actors were not in costume, but the entire play was staged with all the scenery and props. We sat in the audience and noted down mistakes without interrupting the show. The rehearsal lasted from nine until three in the morning. The play was too long, I decided; it would have to be cut. The company owner, Manikji Jivanji Master, watched the rehearsal and grew depressed. He pronounced the play a total failure, a waste of money.

"How will the public be able to understand so much Hindi?" he asked Sohrabji.

"That's why I had most of the comic scenes written in Urdu," Sohrabji retorted. But he too was worried. When the rehearsal was over, he went straight to his room, shut the door, and went to bed.

The next day I went to see Sohrabji and told him the play needed to be cut. He said we would perform it as it was for the first two nights and then make cuts, depending on which scenes the audience liked. He explained to me his old love of Hindi. It had been implanted by an aged Brahmin from Banaras who had since died. Sohrabji felt that by exhibiting this degree of Hindi on stage, we were performing an experiment and doing a good deed. God alone knew if we would succeed.

On the morning of February 4, as I bathed, I heard a voice inside myself saying, "The play will be a success." I had never had such a premonition before. At 9 a.m. when the bell sounded, I appeared for rehearsal wearing fresh new clothes. I gave my list of corrections to Sohrabji, and Bhogilal gave him his mistake book. There were little defects, problems with scenery, errors in pronunciation, an actor coming out of the wrong wing, or changes like adding a flourish to the end of a song phrase. It took Sohrabji an hour to fix these mistakes. Then it was time to raise the new curtain. This is a special moment, observed with certain rituals by the Parsis. Just like the Hindus, they place incense, camphor, flowers, and sugar-candy on an offertory platter. They bring in sweets like *laddus* and *peras*. Before the curtain is raised, they break open a coconut and smash a bottle of alcoholic spirits. As the curtain goes up, they sing a hymn and then distribute the *prasad*. The proprietor himself performed all these rituals, using the hymn to Ganapati from *Vir Abhimanyu*. After the ceremony, Bhogilal told me that he had arranged a Satyanarayan *katha* for that day too, and a feast of *halua* and *puri*s had been prepared.

In the evening the theatre was full of commotion inside and out, just like a marriage. So many tickets had been sold, not even standing room was available. Sohrabji had reserved a special sofa behind the harmonium for myself and a friend, while my servant waited nearby to fetch *pan*, water, and such. The curtain went up at a quarter to ten, and the first song, *bharat viron ki yad men*, "in memory of the heroes of Bharat," received three once-mores. I wanted to rush backstage and congratulate Sohrabji, but the manager wouldn't let me. I waited until the end of the first act and then went outside. Everyone was praising the play. At the end of the second act, they were saying that they had never seen such a thing. To tell the truth, I too was powerfully affected by the *chakravyuh* scene. When Abhimanyu dies and the gods come down to rain flowers on him, the audience had the curtain raised again and again. In the final scene of the third act, Uttara, played by Nisar, came out in a white *dhoti*, her hair unkempt, wearing a red *tika*, and sang mournfully of her loss. Even I could not restrain my emotions. As I left to go to my room, I saw Sohrabji sitting on a trunk with his head bowed, a stream of tears flowing from his eyes. I said nothing but went to my room, and when the song ended I came back out. Sohrabji said, "Congratulations," and I responded, "Congratulations to you too."

Over the next five or six days, we discussed cutting the play here and there, and once the final cuts were made I collected my salary and traveling expenses and got ready to go. I was given a copyright form in English and signed my rights to the play over to the company without a thought. My lawyer later objected, but I explained I would have no trouble requesting permission to publish the play myself. Sohrab Ogra, though a Parsi from Bombay, was more like kin to me than the lawyer, a Brahmin from UP. Two or three years later, when I decided to publish *Vir Abhimanyu,* Sohrabji immediately sent me the documents with Manik Seth's signature. The first print run was 2000 copies, from Lakshmi Narayan Press, Muradabad. The second printing was 5000 copies, and the third 8000 from Naval Kishore Press, Lucknow. The play continued to sell well, for a total of one lakh copies to date.

Vir Abhimanyu was picked up and performed by drama clubs all over India. When I went to Rameshvaram on a pilgrimage, I saw posters at the Madras railway station announcing *Vir Abhimanyu* along with my name. In Bangalore I met a professor named Shri Jambunathan who was a great fan. He had taken the comic subplot and turned it into a separate piece, publishing it, with my permission, under the title *Bahadur Sundari.* Madan Theatres in Calcutta did the same thing, having Jauhar rewrite it as *Desh ka Lal.* Agha Hashr fought for me there. He made the company acknowledge Pandit Radheshyam and *Vir Abhimanyu* in their publicity for the performance.

The play was also adopted in several academic syllabi. Punjab University put it into their MA course. In UP the published play was chosen as a prize for school competitions and purchased for libraries. It received favorable reviews in such journals as *Sarasvati, Vijay, Bharat Mitra, Brahmachari, Aaj, Sanatandharm Patak, Pratap*, and *Pratibha*. A printing press near Bareli even tried to publish the script under my photograph, using the name "Radheshyam Press," but my son Balram intervened: they apologized and sent all 2000 copies back to us.

Now I describe an event of note, an act of fate. On December 25, 1917, I purchased the building known as Raja Chitrakut Mahal to the east of my little thatched house. After renovating it, I established the Radheshyam Press, which is still extant. When the New Alfred came to Bareli a few years later, I accommodated Bhogilal and his wife in the former "palace" and invited Sohrabji to tea there. I told him how as a boy I would listen intently when the New Albert and New Alfred companies stayed there. Why was I drawn thus toward the theatre? Was it my *samskaras?* Was it divine destiny?

Sohrabji gave his opinion: "Thanks to God's will, you delivered the characters of the *Mahabharat* age to the Parsi stage. You did the job well—and in Hindi. Maybe the Lord approved of your work and rewarded you with this house and name and fame. The Lord is that generous."

"Do you remember?" I continued. "When I was 6 or 7 and your company came here, my father wanted to sign me up as one of the dancing boys. That never happened, but now I've become part of the company as a playwright. It's obviously in the divine plan. Right here in Kamarthi Lane, a poor Brahmin's son with a smidgen of education in Urdu and Hindi has become one of India's most famous *katha* reciters and dramatists."

Sohrabji responded, "I too share this belief. That's why at the top of every sheet of paper or book that belongs to the company, I inscribe, 'In the name of God.'"

The success of *Vir Abhimanyu* awakened writers of Hindi, encouraging hundreds of poets to go down the same road. Each day I saw new authors come to the company with their plays. At first they were mainly Punjabis, then later people came from Delhi and Meerut, followed by residents of Allahabad and Banaras.

One of my friends from Meerut, Vishvambhar Sahay Vyakul, was a schoolteacher by profession. He was quite good at composing *thumris* and ghazals and was popular among the wealthy gentlemen of the town. He took to playwriting with his drama *Buddhadev* and formed the Vyakul Bharat Company Limited. After great expense, his play premiered in Delhi at the Banarsi Krishna Theatre (now Moti Talkies) and received much acclaim. Chunnilal Nayak was impressive in the part of Buddha. Next Vyakulji asked me to write a play for his company, and I began to work on *Prahlad*.

When I went to meet Vyakul in Muradabad, however, all was changed. He had taken seriously ill and left the company for Meerut. At his bedside I learned of his great disillusionment. "Forming a drama company is so expensive. Even when the plays are successful, it's a strain putting up with the constant complaints of the actors. We teach them, we give them good parts and bring them onto the stage before the public. But as soon as they achieve a little fame, they begin to think of leaving the company. Every month they ask for a raise. Or else they pretend a headache or stomach ache and refuse to perform."

Vyakul agreed to let me offer my drama *Prahlad* to the New Alfred. Eventually the Vyakul Bharat Company was liquidated, and I purchased the copyright to its three dramas for my press. I published two of them, *Tegh-e Sitam* and *Chandragupt*, but refrained from publishing *Buddhadev* at the request of Vyakul's son.

The era of Hindi mythological plays was well under way. From Kathiawar, the Survijay Natak Samaj, a company of Brahmins, arrived in Delhi under the proprietors Durlabh Ramji Raval and Lavji Trivedi. Lavji had already earned a name in Bombay performing the part of Surdas in the Gujarati play *Bilvamangal*, and now he brought the company to Delhi to perform the same play in Hindi. The Survijay had spectacular scenery, and its managers were very cordial. It happened that I was in Delhi performing *katha* when they arrived, and they all came to hear me. Thus formed a tie not only of mutual affection, but of Brahminhood. I saw their play *Surdas* the next night and loved it, and at their request I revised its language and song lyrics.

The Sangam Theatre, where *Vir Abhimanyu* had opened, was the venue for *Surdas*. On the opposite side of the street was the Banarsi Krishna Theatre, where the New Alfred was then performing. The New Alfred wanted to outdo the Survijay, but because *Surdas* was such a hit they were having trouble. One evening I went with a friend to see the New Alfred's *Vir Abhimanyu* in the Banarsi Krishna Theatre. The manager seated us on a sofa behind the harmonium, but half an hour later the same man told me the sofa was reserved and made us move further back. This upset me, and I got up and left for the Sangam Theatre. I've always been able to endure an insult, but I cannot tolerate a slight to a friend. The Survijay manager not only seated us on the first sofa, he offered us *pan* and water.

The next day the Survijay proprietors came and met me, and I accepted an offer to write *Shravan Kumar* for their company. I finished the job in just eighteen days. As each scene was completed, it went directly into rehearsals. The costumes, scenery, and songs were prepared in great haste. A date was set for the performance while the New Alfred was still in town. Throughout this, I never set foot in the New Alfred. One day Bhogilal came to find out what had happened, and I told him about the foul-up with his manager. Bhogilal relayed the story to Sohrabji, and Sohrabji fired the manager. He even apologized to me himself.

I invited Sohrabji to the opening night of *Shravan Kumar*. Sohrabji agreed to come and arranged for an Urdu play in the New Alfred that did not require his presence. I reserved the first sofa for him and Bhogilal, and the Survijay management welcomed them with garlands and tea. After the performance, Sohrab praised the play wholeheartedly, adding, "What a shame I couldn't direct this one." *Shravan Kumar* was a big hit in Delhi, and the New Alfred was defeated. One night their house had only fifty people in it.

I informed Sohrabji that associating with theatre folk had made me temperamental and arrogant. It would be better if I left this line of work and went back to *katha*. He responded, "How can you be satisfied with *Vir Abhimanyu* and *Shravan Kumar*? These are *dharmik* plays, an easy job for a *kathavachak*. If you were to write a social drama, that would be the real test of your mettle." Although this was meant as praise, I felt the sting in his remark. I began to write *Parivartan*. Though a difficult task, the play came out well. The next season, when the New Alfred was in Bombay, I went to Sohrabji and regaled him with scenes from *Parivartan* in his house on Grant Road.

Sohrabji liked *Parivartan*. "It really is good," he said. "Now you are a proper playwright." He took the original copy of the play from me and locked it in a box. I had no idea why he did that at the time. Later I realized he didn't want any other company to get their hands on the play.

The New Alfred was rehearsing *Chalta Purza* in those days. Bhogilal had taken the plot from a Gujarati novel, and Munshi Ahsan had adapted it for the stage. Sohrabji was very excited because he was to perform the principal role of Sikandar. When I saw *Chalta Purza*, I recognized that Sohrab was not only a great director, he was India's greatest actor. I have seen many famous actors on stage, and I've been powerfully affected by them too: Kavasji Khatau as Duryodhan in

Mahabharat, Chunnilal Nayak as Buddha in *Buddhadev*, Sohrabji Katrik and Purushottam in the Gujarati plays of the Royal Drama Company, Gauhar in the Parsi Theatrical Company. Then later I saw Sharifa in the Madans' production of *Ankh ka Nasha*, Shishir Kumar Bhaduri on the Bengali stage, Bal Gandharva on the Marathi stage, and Lavji in the Survijay Company. But my heartfelt verdict is that Sohrabji Ogra outshone them all.

When I got back to Delhi, I saw that the Survijay Company was still in the Sangam Theatre. It seemed they were going to make Delhi their base. I wrote a play, *Balkrishna*, for them and offered to help with revisions and the editing of future plays if they hired a regular staff writer. Finally the Survijay retained Kishanchand Zeba from the Punjab, and I worked with him on *Sita Vanvas, Gangavataran*, and *Mahatma Vidur*.

Durgadatt Pant, the founder of the Rishikul Brahmacharya Ashram and Ayurvedic College in Hardwar and a respected lecturer, showed me a play he had written, *Usha Aniruddh*. The play had some good points but lacked theatricality, as one would expect—he was not in that line. With the help of two assistants, I rewrote the play from scratch. Suddenly the Survijay Company showed up in Bareli. There was no time to lose. The production was readied within a few days, and *Usha Aniruddh* opened in Bareli and passed muster. The Survijay made Bareli its second home, after Delhi.

The Kirloskar Company of Maharashtra also came our way. I saw one of their plays in Kanpur. The music was praiseworthy, but the Hindi translation of their Marathi drama was atrocious. Maybe that company never found a proper Hindi playwright. I for one told them I was not available.

Earlier I had begun work on *Prahlad* for my friend Vyakul, but because of his illness I hadn't shown it to anyone else. Then, one day in Aligarh, I read the first act to Sohrabji. He was overjoyed and offered me Rs 1000 for it. He copied down the first act in the Gujarati script, and I sent him the next two acts in Hindi by registered post. I kept waiting for his invitation to come and revise the play, but that didn't happen this time. He started rehearsing the play just as it was. Then I got a call from Ahmedabad to come and compose the songs. Ghulam Husain, Nihal Chand, and I sat down for a music session, and Sohrabji approved on the spot all that we composed.

I did not get to Ahmedabad for the debut, but I heard *Prahlad* did very well. It would have been better if I had gone. I could have taken Bapu with me on the opening night. By then I was well acquainted with him, having joined the Congress Party in 1919. For ten years, I attended most of the annual Congress meetings as a delegate. Until today I've never belonged to any other political party or institution. As far as I recall, I began writing *Prahlad* in 1917, and the play opened in 1921.

Finally, I visited Ahmedabad while on my way to a *katha* program in Bombay. There I made a distressing discovery. Sohrabji had suffered a heart attack one night while playing the part of Lobhilal, the comic character in *Prahlad,* and given up acting. I was left with an unfulfilled desire to see Sohrabji, the one who had played Raja Bahadur in *Vir Abhimanyu*, perform the part of Lobhilal in *Prahlad*. If I had come for *Prahlad*'s opening night, this desire would have been fulfilled.

Nonetheless, the beauty of Sohrabji's direction was manifest in every character. Prahlad was played by Purushottam, Pramod and Shyamlata by Phulchand, and Hiranyakashipu by Shakir. Their enunciation was magnificent, as was Vasudev Divakar's scenery and Bhogilal's choreography. Even though the run was in its fourth month, the house was packed and all of the upper-class tickets were sold far in advance.

One of the managers, Manikshah Balsara, told me that a senior officer from the secret police had been watching *Prahlad*. He was looking for evidence of sedition so that he could shut it down. But the police had not been successful. The drama had plenty of explicit speeches by Prahlad and Pramod against "the ruler," but which ruler? Against Hiranyakashipu—who had declared himself lord of the world and deceived the people. Once more, I regretted not having brought Bapu to see the play. I stayed on another day, but he was not at Sabarmati Ashram. Later, Pandit Madan Mohan Malviya came to see *Prahlad*; he saw it twice.

At the time the company traveled to Kanpur, Sohrabji was getting medical treatment in Bombay, and Bhogilal took over as director. *Prahlad*'s fame swept through every home in Kanpur. Vishvambharnath Kaushik, a friend of Bhogilal's, invited Ganesh Shankar Vidyarthi and Balkrishna Sharma Navin to see the play. I was still a newcomer to Hindi literary circles. Mahavir Prasad Dvivedi alone had become a supporter of mine. But this time I made firm plans to attend on Vidyarthi, the well-known editor of *Pratap*. When I went to see him, he greeted me, recited a song from *Prahlad*, and pronounced the play a harbinger of the new India. He became my backer, and as long as he was alive copies of *Pratap* arrived free at my doorstep. Where else could one find such a godly personage, immersed in love of country and the Hindi language?

Sohrabji was ailing, and I decided to go to Bombay to pay him my regards. After all, he was the one who had encouraged me and promoted me in the drama world. I was also worried about the fate of my manuscript of *Parivartan*, which lay locked in his trunk. When I met him, he refused to hand over the play. He said he wished to stage it and play the comic role of Ramzani himself. He offered me Rs 2000.

That night the set painter Dinshah Irani accosted me at a Marathi play: he suggested I sell the script of *Parivartan* to the Parsi Alfred Company. It was his view that Sohrabji would never return to the stage, and without him the New Alfred would collapse. Jahangir, the son of Kavasji Khatau, was now in charge of the Parsi Alfred, and business was booming. Dinshah assured me I could earn double the amount that Sohrabji had offered.

I lay awake that night, debating whether it was right to get my play back and sell it to a higher bidder. The next morning I went to Sohrabji and placed the entire matter before him. Touched by my truthfulness, he returned the copy of *Parivartan*. But he warned me against the tactics of Bombay's businessmen. Dinshah was a fine painter, he said, but he was egotistical. And the other company had no money in its accounts. I listened to my elder like an innocent child, and then left for Surat to meet Dinshah.

In Surat I was warmly greeted with sweets and a full feast. My host then took me to a performance of *Asir-e Hirs*. There I observed that the Parsi Alfred Company employed not a single boy from the Nayak caste. Instead they used a large number of professional female dancers. Ammulal, who had played Abhimanyu in the New Alfred, was now with this company, perhaps as director. So was the actress Sharifa Bai, performing a male role, which I found artistically rather pleasing.

The next morning I recited the first act of *Parivartan*. They liked it and wanted to make a deal. I demanded an advance of Rs 2000, to which the company replied that they could only pay me after fifteen days. The negotiations broke down. Ammulal tried to reassure me that he would send the check directly to Bareli, but having been forewarned by Sohrabji I rejected the deal.

A year or two later, Ammulal and Sharifa formed a new company and came to Bareli. Needless to say, the Surat company had dissolved completely. Ammulal and Sharifa importuned me for *Parivartan*, but I refused. Their company did not last long either. New companies were formed at the drop of a hat in those days, and they folded just as quickly. Every successful actor considered himself a writer and director and lay in wait for a rich patron to come along, become proprietor of his company, and squander all his money on him.

At the end of 1922 the New Alfred brought *Prahlad* to Delhi, and even though Sohrabji was ill and could no longer direct or perform, he came along for the production. I had written him the details of the Surat episode in a letter, and he thought the time was ripe to begin rehearsals of *Parivartan*. Bhogilal was not pleased. The reason was obvious: there was no part for him in the play. He could have been Lakshmi, but he had stopped playing female roles a couple of years before.

The next thing Bhogilal came up with was that he would provide the plots, and I would turn them into scripts. I rejected the idea. I made it clear that I was primarily a *kathavachak* who wrote scenes as a hobby. I did not want any binding arrangement. Sohrabji asked me to find a Hindi playwright who could be hired on a regular salary so that Bhogilal could dictate his plots. The man had to be reliable. There were too many dishonest operators stealing songs and scenes from their employers and selling them to other companies.

For a while I was unable to comply with Sohrabji's request. Finally, I sent him Gopivallabh Upadhyay, who had been my assistant in the Radheshyam Press. It was my hope that he might increase his income and at the same time serve Hindi and society by writing dramas.

The truth is that man, his ideas, and his activities are finite. Call it the cycle of fate, planetary influence, or God's will, but an invisible force controls our destinies. Manik Jivan Master, the proprietor of the New Alfred, had grown addicted to gambling on the stock market. It is one thing to pay cash for the shares of a successful, strong company so that one can hold them in one's own name—that's called investment. It's another thing to trade on the increased or decreased value of shares in the futures market—that is speculation. Mr Manik suffered major losses. He was forced to relinquish the land he had mortgaged for the Master Theatre in Ahmedabad. And finally his position became so weak that he had to sell off his stake in the New Alfred. He gave up the proprietorship, and three of the company's old managers took his place: Framroz Karanjiya, Mehrbanji Kapariya, and Manikshah Balsara. Sohrabji Ogra announced his retirement, and Bhogilal became the director. I went back to book publishing in Bareli, taking up the reins from my eldest son Ghanshyam.

In the winter of 1924 the new owners called me back to the theatre company. Sohrabji was worried lest the standard of the New Alfred decline. He urged me to reconsider, praising me in the highest terms. I departed for Peshawar, where the company was in residence. I presented my conditions. First, the company would hold the right to perform my plays, but I had the right to publish them. Second, I would continue with my *katha*s, writing dramas only in my spare time. As salary, I agreed to Rs 300 per month plus expenses. Readers, witness the wheel of fortune. Where my first drama, *Vir Abhimanyu*, had altogether fetched only Rs 300, now that was to be my monthly wage.

The only drama I had to hand was *Parivartan,* and the owners started rehearsals for it immediately. Bhogilal had quit the company, and in his place the Jewish director Daniel Dada had been appointed. A humble fellow, he considered everyone in the company his friend. He made a Gujarati copy of *Parivartan* in his own hand. Another young man, Narmada Shankar Tribhuvan Nayak, worked with him as dance master and stage manager.

I spent some time in Peshawar, performing *katha* as well as working on the play. The company owners took us sightseeing to the Khyber Pass. I even set one foot on the soil of Afghanistan before being ordered back by the border guards; such were the pranks I pulled from time to time.

Rehearsals moved to Delhi in January 1925. Imagine my surprise when I attended upon Daniel Dada the first day, and he said, "Now that you are here, I want you to run the rehearsals." Considering this request a mere courtesy, I refused. Every day I watched rehearsals for half an hour and then went to the dressing room, which doubled as the music room. There I worked on the songs with Nihal Chand and Ghulam Husain. I felt uncomfortable watching Daniel, who was not a Hindi speaker, trying to direct rehearsals. It was troubling to see his disregard for the exact pronunciation that Sohrabji had always demanded. Mehrban noticed it too, and one evening he brought Daniel to my room. Again he asked me to conduct the rehearsals, saying he hoped to learn from me, and this time I agreed.

Within two days, I determined that the parts had been distributed incorrectly. Mehrban announced to the actors that I was now the person in charge. I became very diplomatic, treating everyone even-handedly. Narmada Shankar I appointed as assistant director and liaison to Mehrban. Pravasi Lal Varma, who knew Hindi, Gujarati, and Marathi, I hired to handle the copy work. Gujaratis would get their parts in the Gujarati script, the Hindi speakers in Hindi. The hero's role, earlier assigned to a Parsi, now went to Shakir, a Muslim. He was too tall for the part, but he spoke correctly and was intelligent. This move virtually eliminated the resistance to me among the Muslims. I never found the perfect youth for the part of Chanda, the heroine, but Narmada Shankar was fine for the role of Lakshmi. When the play opened in the second week of March 1925, it was repeated for nine consecutive days by popular demand. In April, my salary went up to Rs 500 a month.

Several other things happened around the time of *Parivartan*. Agha Hashr's play *Ankh ka Nasha* opened in Calcutta in the Madan Theatres and was very successful. Sharifa, who had wanted the role of Chanda in *Parivartan*, performed the part of a courtesan so well that she broke all records. A huge part of Agha Hashr's life was focused on women and wine, and his writing on these subjects was without equal. For me, it was a big problem to treat such things on stage. As a last resort I was compelled to spend time in the company of a certain courtesan to learn her culture. She was a Hindu woman from a hill community, a very high-minded person, and because of her the character of Chanda acquired noble ideals. At the end of the play, when Chanda became an ascetic and departed to serve the nation, the audience's joy knew no bounds.

Manikshah Balsara, the second proprietor of the company, had some Muslim friends in Delhi, and they objected to a comic phrase in *Parivartan* that mentioned the name of Allah. Both Mehrban and I decided to ignore this complaint. We were of the opinion that Allah belonged to everyone. The objection was actually to the fact that a Hindu had become a director in the New Alfred. (In the salary register, my name was the first on the list, followed by the title "director," beginning on April 1, 1925.) To calm the tense atmosphere, I announced the appointment of two assistant directors: Ibrahim Bhai for Urdu plays and Narmada Shankar for Hindi plays.

Manikshah Balsara employed a servant boy from Muradabad named Fida Husain who made his tea and such. I asked if I could enroll him as an actor and went to a great deal of effort to train him. He turned out so well that he reached the first rank of performers in the company. After he left the New Alfred, he earned much fame playing the part of Narsi Mehta, and the public began calling him Fida Husain Narsi. He is now the director of a theatrical company in Calcutta.

I have written of these matters to show that I made no distinction between Hindus and Muslims. My sole interest was the success of the stage. Nonetheless, Hindu–Muslim tensions continued to mount. Mehrbanji preferred Hindus, or perhaps he was influenced by the reality that the company was advancing because of its Hindi plays and Hindu audiences. It is a known fact that once a Hindu approves of a drama, the next day he brings his entire family—wife, children, and all—to watch. Even veiled women turned out in large numbers to see the Ram Lila, Ras Lila, or any religious play. This was one reason for the success of my mythological plays. Nowadays women roam about with their heads uncovered and attend cinema shows, but twenty-five years ago they would join their hands and bow respectfully when they received darshan of Lord Krishna in a stage play.

At any rate, because Mehrbanji took cognizance of the Hindus, the number of Hindu actors in the company began to increase. From

Gujarat, it was mostly the Nayaks who joined. From North India, I promoted fine actors and singers like Nand Kishor, Bhagvat Kishor Vyakul, Girija Shankar, and Gangaprasad Gavaiya. After the company went to Bombay to perform *Parivartan*, Daniel Dada quit and remained there. Muslims and Parsis slowly began to drift away too. Muslims from outside the company raised the objection that the New Alfred was becoming a "Hindu company," just like the Survijay. It was in this atmosphere that I wrote and staged the Urdu Muslim drama *Masharqi Hur*, at the behest of the company owners. They were surprised to learn that I could also write in Urdu. They didn't know that this *kathavachak* had cut his teeth on Urdu in the district school in Bareli, advanced to the *Dastan of Amir Hamza*, *Fasana-e Azad*, and Khushtar and Farhat's *Ramayan*s, and then gone crazy over the *divans* of Ghalib and Nasikh.

The success of *Masharqi Hur* was in large part due to Fida Husain, who played the heroine Roshanara and earned many once-mores for his ghazals. Ghulam Husain's tunes and Narmada Shankar's dance number were big hits too. But Manikshah was worried that the Muslim press would condemn my Urdu play. One had to be wary of journalists who wrote critical reviews for the newspapers in those days. Kavas Khatau and his Parsi Alfred Company had been seriously weakened because of negative press comments, and after that the company was sold off to Madan Theatres. Kavasji's demise was even precipitated by these sad events.

A Lahore journalist named Lalchand Falak had attacked the Parsi Alfred Company's productions of the *Mahabharat* and *Ramayan*. The campaign started because the actress Gauhar played Draupadi and Sita, and this was not warranted from the standpoint of the Hindus. Then there were objections to the addition of the character of Cheta Chamar to the *Mahabharat*, to the song about Sita in the *Ramayan* that praised her fair cheeks, and other such matters. Incensed, Betabji, the author of both plays, published his rejoinder, but this only increased the storms of protest. As a result, the company and its owner suffered considerably.

None of this had been forgotten by the proprietors of the New Alfred. To reassure them, I called on Hasrat Mohani, the famous leader and poet of Kanpur. I asked his opinion of *Masharqi Hur* from the Muslim point of view and in regard to its Urdu. He endorsed the play and wrote his approval right on the handwritten manuscript. Publicizing his views served to put out the religious fire surrounding the play.

Next, Manikshah proposed to stage *Sati Parvati*, but there was no suitable female impersonator available for the title role. I wanted to cast Phulchand Marwari, but he had joined Madan Theatres. Although I explained the situation to Manikshah, he thought I was keeping the play locked up, away from him. Just then Betab approached me in private. He needed money for his daughter's marriage, and I agreed to relinquish the story so that he could adapt it, if he changed the title. I put Manikshah off for a while, but finally I had to sign a document attesting to the New Alfred's ownership of the play. I didn't like Manik's behavior, and I regretted that I was on salary and writing on contract. But what could I do? I was helpless to change things. Meanwhile Hashr, Betab, and I maintained our friendship even while writing for separate companies. How could I turn Betab away over a trifling request?

In short, *Sati Parvati* was delayed and Betab's *Ganesh Janm* opened instead in Calcutta. Dinshah Irani's scenery alone was marvelous enough to make it successful. I chose *Shri Krishna Avatar* for my next play and completely immersed myself in its production. I was no longer a mere playwright or director who rehearsed the actors. I was now the dictator, and everything was done to my taste—scenery, costumes, and casting. I worked so hard that I succumbed to malaria, but I kept at it through the grand rehearsal. Then I went home to Bareli to recuperate. The play opened in Amritsar on Dashera in 1926, played there for several months, and traveled to Lahore where it was even more popular.

Shri Krishna Avatar earned many kudos. The film producer Raghupati Ray later told me that he saw the play in Lahore after living for many years in England, where he had lost contact with Hinduism. On the very next day he brought his wife, and on the third day all his relatives; he saw it a total of seventeen times. His home acquired a picture of Shri Krishna, a copy of the *Gita*, and the family began offering *arti*. The great Sanskrit scholar Giridhar Sharma

14. *Krishna Avatar* Handbill

Chaturvedi gave it as his opinion that the drama was a mobile unit of the *sanatan dharm*. The Hindu actors of the New Alfred were so moved by the production that they installed an image of Shri Krishna on a small throne and worshiped him every morning before rehearsals.

In spite of all this I still had deep misgivings about working in the theatre as a salaried employee. Because of my personal distaste, after recovering from malaria I stayed away from the company for six or seven months. During those months of absence I formed the opinion that no artist could flourish in bondage, or in a state of greed, or by flattering others; rather, these led to one's downfall. The artist needed independence—complete independence.

I was visiting the stationmaster in Hardoi in the summer of 1927 when I heard that the New Alfred's special train was coming through. The train stopped right in front of me, and Mehrbanji pulled me into his first-class compartment and took me along with him to Lucknow. Showering hospitality on me, he tried to overcome my diffidence, and when we reached Lucknow he paid me my entire back salary. He wanted to bring out a sequel to *Shri Krishna Avatar*, copying Madan Theatres' series of *balak* dramas: *Vir Balak, Premi Balak, Dharmi Balak*, etc. I quickly wrote three acts in time for Dashera, titling the play *Rukmini Mangal*.

This time the reviews were more mixed. The Hindi author Ugra attacked the play, saying mythological dramas were not needed. A monthly journal from Kanpur praised Jaishankar Prasad's dramas and declared Radheshyam's weak. Where indeed was the competition between Prasadji's literary dramas, which were taught to students in their college courses, and my plays, which were meant to be performed on the Parsi stage? It may be that the poverty-stricken Hindi writers were jealous of me because I had become wealthy. However, I found support from noted literary figures like Vidyarthi, the editor of *Pratap*, and the famous story writer and novelist Premchand, then editor of *Madhuri*. He published an article on the Parsi theatre illustrated with photographs of the actors, giving special attention to my Krishna plays. It was signed, "A Theatre Lover." Similar articles also came out in *Chitrapat*, a Gujarati weekly, and the Hindi magazine *Chand* around the same time.

Here is a verbatim copy of Premchand's essay, which was published in *Madhuri*, vol. 8, no. 6, from Lucknow.

The Hindi Stage

There was once a time when the art of drama was very advanced in India. We are speaking of the age when Sanskrit spread throughout the country, when plays like *Uttararamacharita* and *Shakuntala* were performed. Many historians go so far as to claim that drama, like the other arts, was born on Indian soil. Some say the first teacher of drama was Bharata Muni, some Lava and Kusha. Shankara, Narada, and Hanuman have been unanimously acclaimed for their contributions to drama. At any event, during the last several centuries this literature began to decline along with other areas. Leaving aside Sanskrit, even in Hindi no drama worthy of mention emerged from the time of Chand Bardai onward. When Muslim rule ended and the East India Company's dominion began, a new wave came from across the seas. It is India's misfortune that it is still divided by regional languages, and it was in these languages that dramas began to be performed. Maharashtrians and Bengalis made good progress in drama, but the impact was only on the Marathi and Bengali stages, not on Hindi. Gujarati playwrights also produced a good many plays, which are now being adapted by Hindi playwrights.

The Parsi community took the initial steps toward forming professional touring companies and ventured to northern India. In those days, there were neither dramas nor dramatists here. Songs dominated, as did romantic plays in clumsy Urdu, like the *Indar Sabha* and *Hava'i Majlis*. Lest we forget, the initial activity in Hindi drama must be credited to Bharatendu Babu Harishchandra. But his plays were only performed by amateur clubs; they never reached the stage of a professional company. Fortunately, Munshi Vinayak Prasad Talib Banarsi wrote Hindi plays like *Harishchandra, Ramayan, Kanak Tara,* and *Bhartrihari* for performance by the famous Balivala Victoria Company. Talib's virtue was that he used Hindi mixed with Urdu, giving drama lovers the pleasure of tasting Hindi, and the plays themselves were popular too. Then after a few years, Betab's *Mahabharat* and Hashr's *Surdas* appeared on stage. Although the language of these plays was also mixed Hindi–Urdu, and their plots were adaptations of the Gujarati dramas *Sati Draupadi* and *Bilvamangal*, there is no doubt that they were highly regarded, and Parsi company owners felt they should bring out more plays in Hindi. When we look at the Urdu plays of that period, such as *Zahri Sanp* and *Khubsurat Bala*, we can say without hesitation that most of the songs of these dramas were written and sung in the Hindi language. It is not understood why this was so. Either it was the weakness of the song writers, or else the Hindi lyrics forcibly claimed this position on account of their sweetness.

Then Radheshyam's *Vir Abhimanyu* appeared. I believe that, prior to this, such a degree of Hindiness had not appeared on the Parsi stage. The comic subplot of this drama was also very educational and devoid of obscenity. This was the age when so many Urdu playwrights were presenting vulgar comic scenes on stage. One felt shame bringing mothers and sisters to the theatre. It seemed the sacred duty of some Urdu playwrights to call mother "woman," and woman "mother." In any case, *Vir Abhimanyu* was very successful, and even Pandit Malviya saw and praised the drama. Not only that, the public appreciated it more than they had any previous drama of the Parsi companies. Punjab University chose this play for their Hindi Bhushan and Intermediate Class textbooks.

Now began the adolescence of Hindi in the theatrical companies. Harikrishna Jauhar's *Pati Bhakti* and *Vir Bharat*, *Nal Damayanti* by Shaida, and other plays were staged. The enthusiasm was such that in Meerut a limited company called Vyakul Bharat was formed to showcase the pre-eminence of Hindi drama. Undoubtedly, this company's *Buddhadev* was both beautiful and well conceived. It is regrettable that because of poor management the company went into liquidation, and its most expert and learned playwright, Vyakul, died prematurely. If he were still alive, much would be expected of him in the Hindi world. While associated with the Vyakul Bharat company, the *Varmala*'s famous author Pantji took an interest in writing plays, but unfortunately he wrote closet dramas instead of stageable plays. I request that he now write for the stage; he has the experience, and we have high hopes of him.

In the same period, a company from Kathiawar, the Survijay, came north and performed its entire repertoire in Hindi. After completing *Vir Abhimanyu*, Radheshyam wrote *Shravan Kumar* and several more plays for this company. Alas, the Survijay is not alive today. The notable companies that are now performing Hindi plays, and from whom Hindi lovers can expect even better work, are the Corinthian of Calcutta owned by the Maharaja of Charkhari, whose staff playwright is Agha Hashr; the Parsi Alfred of Madan Theatres owned by the late Kavasji, whose current playwrights are Jauhar and Shaida (it is said that Betab is also writing Hindi plays for this company); and the New Alfred, running for thirty-five years, whose director and actor of all-India fame is Mr Sohrabji Ogra. Although Ogra is now retired, he has enhanced the fame of this company and given it a prestigious name. In this essay I have specially discussed the plays of this company and offered pictures of them as well. This company's proprietors are Mehrbanji, Manikshah, and Framroz. There is a fourth company, said to belong to Hashr. A little while back, its name was the Great Shakespeare Company, but for the last few months the name has been changed to the Great Alfred. God alone knows why there are three Alfred companies. At least the immortal soul of Mr Alfred must be pleased by this, if no one else.

I myself have seen many plays of the New Alfred Company, and I consider this company to be ideal, not only from the standpoint of plays written in Hindi but in terms of stagecraft as well. Radheshyamji, whose dramas are performed in this company, and who, after Sohrab Ogra's retirement, is staging his own dramas himself, is doubtless achieving success. *Vir Abhimanyu* has already been mentioned; in addition, Radheshyam's *Prahlad, Parivartan,* and *Masharqi Hur* are all outstanding. These plays contain ideals, education, sanctity, and brilliance. Now I shall discuss Radheshyam's *Shri Krishna Avatar* and its second part, *Rukmini Mangal*.

The playwright begins *Shri Krishna Avatar* with the earth trembling under Kamsa's atrocities, the universe crying out for help, and the royal sage Narad prevailing upon Lord Vishnu in the sea of milk to reincarnate in order to protect *dharm*. Narad's conversation with Vishnu is effective, moving, and full of fervor. On one side, Narad insists that Vishnu take form as an avatar, while on the other he goads Kamsa on to greater misdeeds, thinking this will accelerate the lord's descent to the mortal world. Meanwhile, the residents of Mathura grow more and more agitated, and Narad preaches to them to remain calm. These three aspects of his character are shown in a unique way. The gentleman who plays Narad does an excellent job. Next there is the role of Yogmaya, created by assembling all the elements of the hidden world. This character too is natural, and her songs are enchanting and well sung. Just see the pictures of Narad and Yogmaya, how natural they are. The first act ends with the birth of Lord Krishna.

In the second act the boy Krishna appears, and his various *lilas* are shown in sequence: the tending of cows, the killing of Kaliya, the lifting up of Govardhan, and the Ras Mandal. The playwright has beautifully expressed the essence and purpose of each of these *lilas*. Some thirty boys perform in this act, among whom the parts of Shri Krishna, Mansukha, and Shridama are praiseworthy. The purity of the love relationship between Radha and Krishna is shown without the slightest hint of obscenity or opportunity for offense. To the contrary, a spotless image of their supreme love comes before our eyes. Please look at the picture of the youthful pair in act two, scene two, standing beneath the *kadam* tree with the cowherds and cowgirls, which in my opinion is the finest scene in the play.

In the third act, Kamsa is killed. If the first act is full of politics, the second makes the current of *bhakti* flow through every vein, and the third presents a living portrait of heroic valor. The roles of Vasudev, Balram, Devaki, and Ugrasen are performed very well. The scenery is so fine that the audience says it has never seen its equal. Here the company's painter, Mr Vasudev Divakar, must be congratulated. At a young age he has achieved extraordinary command of his art. The dances at their different places are also well done. The dance master, Narmada Shankar, has really worked hard in preparing them. The costumes are also correct. All told, the stage is so well decorated that the spectator just stares at it endlessly. I myself have never seen a better play on this theme.

Rukmini Mangal exceeds its predecessor in every sense. Those who have not yet seen it should see *Shri Krishna Avatar* first. Here the main events are the fight with Jarasandh, the burning of the Kalay forest, the romance between Rukmini and Krishna, and finally the abduction of Rukmini, the defeat of Shambarasur by Pradyumna, and the arrival in Dvaraka. The true nature of the relationship between Radha and Krishna is depicted in the final scene in a jocular way. Just as the characterization of Narad stands out in *Shri Krishna Avatar*, here the character of Rukmini's sister-in-law, that is, Rukma's wife Sulekha, is most impressive, thanks to the poet's imagination, talent, and originality. But in fact each character is well portrayed by the author. The best performances are by the actors who play Rukma, Shri Krishna, Rukmini, Sulekha, and Rukmini's mother Prabha. The same actors as in *Shri Krishna Avatar* play the parts of Narad, Yogmaya, and Radha.

Here too the scenery is outstanding, with excellent and appropriate costumes. The dances too are quite good. The best dance, and a first in the theatre world, is the one set to rhythmic syllables from Sanskrit. Twenty-four boys perform this dance. The songs are also much better than those in the first part, and their melodies are very pleasing. In my view, no company and no play has contained such songs before.

Pandit Radheshyam himself is a fine actor, in that he has spent his entire life in *katha* recitation. He would be the equal of Girish Chandra Ghosh, Shishir Babu, or Dani Babu if he were ever to take to the stage.[4] He is an expert in writing songs and lyrics, and he also created a revolution in the world of Urdu drama with his *Masharqi Hur*. With great respect, I have included Panditji's picture in this essay. He intends now to stage the entire Krishna epic in sequence. May Lord Krishna grant him success in this endeavor. It is also said that for three or four years he has been at

---

[4] Three famous actors of the turn-of-the-century Bengali stage.

work on another drama, *Sati Parvati*, now more than half finished, which is going to surpass anything written or staged thus far.

Working from the play I had dashed off hurriedly for the Survijay Company, I next revised *Shravan Kumar* for the New Alfred stage. The Survijay had folded after the death of its owner, Durlabhram Raval. Running a theatre company was a heavy burden. In addition to making proper arrangements for the stage, humoring the actors, and getting good plays written, it was a big job to deal with the external organization, handle publicity, keep track of the properties, prevent fires, safeguard the box office, and hire honest gatekeepers. The manager could not be prone to lining his pockets and seating spectators wherever he pleased. When Lavji Bhai, the leading actor, was left on his own after Raval's death, he could not manage both the inside and outside work, and he became ill. The company dissolved, and Lavji became a brass merchant in Bankaner, Saurashtra.

I had *Shravan Kumar* staged in Delhi in a tin shed theatre, which had been erected by the New Alfred in the Lajpat Ray market around that time. The stage was 70 feet wide including the wings, and 60 feet deep. The dressing room was in a separate area. The house was 115 feet long and 60 feet wide. In the middle of the stage was a well that connected to an underground tunnel with its own lighting, through which the gods appeared or disappeared. There was also an aerial machine to raise or lower actors from above the stage. The stage manager sat near the drop-scene, controlling a creaky reel that activated the scene transfer. He also rang a bell to signal to the men on the scaffolding overhead as to when to lower or raise the curtain. When he pressed a button, a faint light went on in front of the harmonium master, telling him to begin a song or supply an encore.

The stage manager reviewed the costume, hair, and makeup of every actor before he went on stage. Next to the stage manager sat an employee who noted each flaw in a mistake book. The director would correct these mistakes during daytime rehearsals before the next performance. The stage manager knew the entire play by heart; no copy of the manuscript was kept in the theatre, nor were prompts given. If an actor had a bad slip of memory, the stage manager would provide a prompt, but after that the actor would lose his part or have to beg the director's forgiveness. All these stage manager jobs were performed by Bhogilal during Sohrabji's tenure, and by Narmada Shankar in my time. This position enjoyed prestige in the company. All the stage hands were under the stage manager's control. Next in the hierarchy was the director position, and above that the proprietor. Sohrabji's reputation was such that he was considered equal to a proprietor. The attitudes he imparted served me well. The proprietors did not meddle in my work. They carried out my requests without a whimper.

Once, Pandit Malviya came to see *Prahlad*, and I was seated next to him. Several times I had to call out to Mehrbanji to order items of hospitality. Malviya asked me, "Are you his servant or is he yours?" I laughed and replied, "We don't think of each other as master and servant. Our relationship is like brothers." My sincere dedication and service to the company earned me the respect of the owners. Plus they were worried that as a *kathavachak* I had plenty of money, and if they offended me I'd up and away and cause them big losses. Mehrbanji in particular had this fear. Moreover, Narmada Shankar, who shared their room, was learning the theatrical art under me and making good progress.

Shravan Kumar opened in May 1928. At my request, it was inaugurated by the Arya Samaj leader Indra Vidyavachaspati. The Delhi newspapers all praised my play, and I collected a trunkful of press cuttings. This revised version of the earlier Survijay production illustrated the ideal of devotion to mother and father. However, a personal tragedy occurred during the play's run. The plague swept through Bareli, and my mother, Shrimati Rampyari Devi, fell victim. Her last remains had been cremated before I could get back to Bareli. When I arrived home, I told my father how much remorse I felt at being unable to care for her as I had truly wished.

Several years earlier, my wife had quarreled with my mother. At her insistence, I set my wife up in the Chitrakut Mahal building while my parents remained in the Bibi Rukmini temple. I sent Rs 60 a month to my mother, Rs 100 to my father, and Rs 150 to my wife for their expenses, since I was seldom at home. I arranged the marriage of my younger brother Madan, and he lived with his wife in the Rukmini temple along with my parents. After my mother died, my father looked to me to help Madan get on his feet. Although I had already taught him poetry and got him a paid position at Rs 100 per month in the New Alfred, I promised to look after him and treat him as my son for the rest of my life. This was the root of much discord in my family. My wife was unhappy with my decision, and the issue remained a source of tension to the bitter end.

That year, when the New Alfred Company was in Peshawar, I went along for the fun of it. *Shravan Kumar* was a huge hit, and the company made so much money that they recouped their losses and had enough left over to purchase a motor car. I had a great time touring up to Kohat and the Khyber Pass. Those were the days!

The company returned to Delhi in the beginning of 1929, and I began to work on a new production, *Ishvar Bhakti*, based on the tale of Ambarish from the *Bhagavat Purana*. This time I decided to give more scope to the role of the villain and the villain's wife. The cast included Chaube Ramkrishna as the hero, Narmada Shankar as his wife Padma, Nand Kishor as the villain, and Fida Husain as Uma, the villain's wife. Motilal Nehru, then president of the Congress Party, agreed to conduct the opening ceremonies, bringing much favorable publicity to the show.

In true Allahabadi style, the respected Motilalji came to the theatre with ten or twelve companions, including Sarojini Naidu. We reserved the whole front row of sofas for them. Outside, thousands of spectators had congregated, and Motilal had to stop for a while to give darshan. When he entered, the company owners greeted him with flowers. Then he came onto the stage and performed *puja* to the drop-scene with *roli*, rice, and other items in the Parsi fashion. After that he touched the curtain as if to say, "Ready." The bell rang and the invocatory hymn to Ganesh echoed as the curtain was raised. During the initial scene, the song, *bharat valo, phir bharat men lahraye ishvarbhakti*, received several once-mores: "Oh residents of Bharat, may devotion to God flourish once more in your land." Although Nehru had intended to stay only half an hour, he and his party remained seated until 2 a.m.

After the essay in *Madhuri*, my admiration for Premchand increased tremendously. He came to Bareli on three occasions, and we spent long evenings together talking. He too wished that he could come before the public as a playwright, but he was a man of noble ideals. After he saw *Ishvar Bhakti*, he was pleased for the most part, but he asked, "Why all the miracles?"

"The public is not yet as sophisticated as you are," I replied. "This play is being put on by a professional company, and if it flops, the company will be in danger of folding. Ninety per cent of our income comes from the kind of audience that goes wild over miracles and illusions."

After *Ishvar Bhakti*, my monthly salary was raised to Rs 600, but this did not particularly please me. By then I was being invited by royalty such as the Maharaja of Alvar and earning Rs 500 a day for my *katha* performances. I earned even more from the publication of my *Ramayan*, which is still in print. I used to go on a pilgrimage after each new play. I took my mother and wife with me to Jagannath Puri after the performance of *Parivartan*. When *Ishvar Bhakti* concluded, I went with my wife to take darshan of Omkareshwar in Malwa. People in the drama companies could avail of concessions from the railways, and as a director I took advantage of that privilege. I would buy a second class ticket and travel with my wife in the first class.

The New Alfred owners were always wary about competition from the Madan Theatres of Calcutta. Master Mohan, a famous actor from that company, came to Delhi to see *Ishvar Bhakti*, raising the fear that he was going to lure me away to Calcutta. This had happened before with Phulchand Marwari, the female impersonator, as well as with two young Nayak boys. Not only had the Parsi Alfred been absorbed by the Madan Company in Lahore, when the Imperial Company of Bombay weakened, the Madans bought it too. I urged the New Alfred owners to go to Calcutta and challenge the Madans on their own turf, but they remained apprehensive. As a result, although the New Alfred company performed in cities all over India, it never ventured into Calcutta.

After *Ishvar Bhakti* I was tired, and I persuaded the Urdu playwright Ahsan to compose a drama for the New Alfred. Ahsan's play on the life of Nero was rejected, however, as being behind the times. Instead, I wrote the third part of my Krishna cycle, entitled *Draupadi Svayamvar*, but with a depressed spirit. Not only was I growing weary of life in the theatre, my elder son Ghanshyam, whom I dearly loved, had contracted a fever that would not go away. The new play again featured

Fida Husain in a major singing role. The play was first performed in 1929, and I was honored by the Nawab of Rampur's warm reception when the company toured that princely state.

Coming back to Bareli, with difficulty I got Ghanshyam cured through water therapy. When the company went to Delhi for the winter, I had to go and teach Nisar his new roles. Suddenly I came down with a cold and bad cough. I took various medicines, but to no avail. The whole night I would sit up, coughing. After several days in this state, I had to tell the company owners, "This time, I really must take care of my health. You can run the New Alfred as you like." They were disheartened, but they had no choice. And thus I said farewell to my dear New Alfred on February 11, 1930.

While I was in the theatre line, I would become entirely absorbed when writing each new play. One evening in Bombay, I turned off the dal and rice I had prepared, left them on the stove, and went off to see a silent movie. The film affected me so powerfully that when I returned at ten o'clock, I immediately picked up pen and paper and began revising a scene of *Masharqi Hur*. I scribbled and cut, scribbled and cut, until I heard a sound outdoors. The tram had started up; it was already morning. By a happy chance the scene had just a few lines left. I finished them off and called my servant. While the rest of the world awoke and attended to its morning rituals, I asked him for water, opened the cooking pots, and ate my dal and rice. Then sleep overwhelmed me and I went to bed.

I was very strict about conduct during rehearsals. Chewing *pan* and smoking cigarettes weren't allowed, nor the reading of novels or newspapers. Rehearsals began promptly at 9 a.m. The first bell rang at 8:30, the second at 8:45, and I entered the theatre at 9:00. If an actor was late, I made a point of starting with a scene in which he appeared. He would be humiliated in front of the other actors and have to grovel before Mehrbanji. This kept everybody punctual and enhanced my authority. On that Monday morning, after I had stayed up all night and eaten my dinner at 6 a.m., it was essential for me to show up for the rehearsal. Narmada Shankar woke me at the correct time and asked if he should ring the 9:00 bell. I said yes, threw on my kurta and shawl, and ran off. The rehearsal didn't last long that day, but that was up to me, after all.

Ordinarily, the company had two harmonium players—the main

one who was the music director, and the assistant who provided accompaniment after the first act. It happened during *Rukmini Mangal* in Lahore that only one harmonium player was on the staff. He was threatening to quit if he didn't get a raise. One night he came to the theatre with a bandage around his head, complaining of a headache. I told him flatly, "Go and get some rest." He was perplexed, and when I repeated the command he went to Mehrbanji. Mehrbanji couldn't work out who would take his place. I said I would play the harmonium, and that is what I did. After that, there was no more nonsense about a raise.

Another incident occurred in Lucknow when *Parivartan* was playing. Nand Kishor, the actor who was to play Shambhu Dada, was arrogant about his abilities, and that put me off. I told him to fetch his costume and wig, and dabbing a little powder on my moustache and eyebrows, I went on stage as Shambhu. The actors crowded in the wings, curious to see me perform. The three company owners watched my scenes intently. At one point, Shakir was supposed to kick Shambhu, but he held back out of respect and fear of his Panditji. I was compelled to improvise, "Master, you tried to raise your foot, but you were too drunk." When the first act ended, Mehrbanji placed a huge garland of flowers around my neck. After the second act, Nand Kishor fell at my feet. Then he offered me the intoxicant *sulfa* to give me strength for the third act. Framroz Karanjiya, the third proprietor, embraced me at the end of the play, saying this was the high point of his life in the theatre world. Thus for one night—only once—was I required to play a part. If I had so desired, I could have become an actor and earned Rs 1500–2000 a month from the New Alfred. But I simply wished to remain a *kathavachak*.

Chapter 4: Later Adulthood (1931–1940)

I left Delhi on February 21, 1930, went back to Bareli, and was examined by Dr Shyam Swarup. He explained that the stress of hard work, late hours, irregular mealtimes, and loud singing of *katha*s had ruined my health. He prescribed various tonics and injections, and I went up to the mountains to recover. I returned much improved, but I never completely got rid of my cough and excess wind.

In August 1930, I submitted my letter of resignation to the company owners. I also published a notice explaining the reasons for my departure.

My Farewell to the New Alfred

It is with regret that I must say good-bye to my dear New Alfred Company, due to a sudden bout of illness. Because of the difficulty of writing separately to my many friends, I deemed it appropriate to send word to them all through this document. My relationship with the New Alfred began in 1914. My first play, *Vir Abhimanyu*, was staged then, followed by *Parambhakt Prahlad*. In those days, the respected Mr Sohrabji Framji Ogra was company director. On November 15, 1924, I became a salaried employee, and now for reasons of health I have had to terminate our relationship.

I will forever be grateful for the friendship and respect shown to me by the company ownership. I doubt whether any drama company in India has ever been as civil in their dealings with a playwright as the New Alfred has been with me. At most, I was required to stay three or four months a year with the company when a new play was being produced. For the rest I was completely free to go where I wished. I was always given second class railfare for travel with a servant, and all my expenses were covered. I retained the right to publish all the plays I wrote through my own concern, Radheshyam Pustakalay. The owners were generous in their salary arrangements as well, and my younger brother Madan Mohan Lal was made assistant dramatist. In five and a half years of service, I staged seven original plays in the company. In addition to writing new plays and rehearsing them, I also operated my press and went on tour to recite *kathas*. No doubt the overwork contributed to my failing condition. But I considered it to be my duty, and I pray that God will come to my aid and restore my health.

The right honorable Pandit Madan Mohan Malviya had never seen a play performed by a professional drama company, but I brought him twice to the theatre, for two different dramas. Brother Indra, son of the late Swami Shraddhanand, performed the opening ceremony for my play *Shravan Kumar*. At my request, India's great leader Motilal Nehru inaugurated *Ishvar Bhakti,* and that too in the year in which he was president of the Indian National Congress. Numerous political figures, religious personages, scholars and pandits, princes and kings also attended from time to time, and to them all I am deeply grateful.

It is a source of delight that by means of these dramas I have been able to perform a service to the Hindi language, as well as advance the cause of Hindutva and promote religious feeling. One extra amenity throughout was the fact that prostitutes never entered the New Alfred. The *dharmik* roles were always played by Brahmin boys.

Today the company contains many well-known actors, but in my time there were few. If the company has nonetheless achieved fame and respect, we—the company owners, my loyal disciples who are today the chief actors, and myself—all should offer our heartfelt thanks to God. With these few words, I bid farewell to my dear New Alfred.

Bareli, August 21, 1930   Radheshyam Kathavachak

The newspapers published this announcement in their "letters to the editor" section. My intention had been to dissociate myself from the New Alfred, so that in case the company grew weak in my absence I would not be blamed or suffer ill repute. But the owners thought that publishing the notice could have a negative effect in itself. They felt that when the public learned that Radheshyam was no longer attached to the company, its image would suffer. Under this illusion, they withdrew the rights I had been granted to publish my plays and sent me a notice to this effect. Eventually, my son Ghanshyam and a partner purchased the full copyright to all of the New Alfred's plays, even those written by other playwrights, paying the company whatever they demanded. After this, they could no longer print those plays or ever stage them again.

In 1931 when the company was in Nauchandi, they called me back to revise a play called *Hindu Vidhva*. Vishvambharnath Kaushik had written the dialogues and songs, but the plot that a Muslim actor had constructed was lame, and the performance had been a flop. In Delhi, religious conservatives had also expressed objections to the drama. I cut out some parts and changed the name to *Sudhara Zamana*, but the play was beyond repair. The main reason was that not one character remained on stage throughout the play. Each one died after a few scenes, or simply vanished. No plot can succeed that does not have a distinct Ram and Ravan from beginning to end.

Another time when the company was in trouble I was called to Hardwar. One by one, all the company's gems had quit. Vasudev, the scene painter; Mohammad Ali, the costume designer; Nihal Chand, harmonium master; and Ghulam Husain, tabla player, as well as the best actors were gone. In three days, I rehearsed my edited version of *Gangavataran* and staged its debut. Rather than accepting payment, I donated the income from opening night to the Rishikul Brahmacharya Ashram. Then I bathed in the Ganga and returned to Bareli.

The company started employing women to act the female roles, and after this the famous female impersonators Chaube Ramkrishna, Fida Husain (aka Prem Shankar), and even Narmada Shankar departed. Professional Muslim actors took over for a while and performed plays like *Laila Majnun* and *Shirin Farhad*. That great company, whose sacred dramas had been patronized as family entertainment by the wealthy Hindu public, became a third-rate outfit. How could the impoverished lower classes keep this huge company afloat? Finally, the company went into debt. It was mortgaged off, and in the end it closed down.

In 1927, at the insistence of some friends, I made a trip to Calcutta. It had often occurred to me that the New Alfred should venture to Calcutta and confront Madan Theatres head on. The Madan Company collected the best Hindi- and Urdu-speaking actors from all over India. When the top theatrical companies of Bombay fell on hard times, the Madans bought them out. They wanted to establish a monopoly in the theatre world.

I was warmly welcomed by the literary community in Calcutta and expounded *katha*s in various places around the city. In the evenings, I went to the Madans' Corinthian Theatre whenever I was free. There I observed innumerable female performers, even white women. At the Urdu dramas, it was mainly Calcutta's Muslims who were in attendance, while the Hindi plays were frequented by Marwari youths. I cannot say how much pleasure these people took in the art of drama, but they were completely beguiled by the beauty of those young actresses. This particular fact threw me into a dilemma. Could the New Alfred, with no women in it, possibly compete with this company?

Agha Hashr was the company's most respected playwright. Harikrishna Jauhar and Tulsidatt Shaida were also employed in that capacity. Hashr was a very sociable and friendly person. On two occasions he brought his companies, the Shakespeare Theatrical Company and later the Great Alfred, to Bareli and stayed with me. However, he was no good at running a company. The leisurely life of a poet was one thing, being a businessman was another. When Agha Hashr realized that he could not combine the two, he devoted himself entirely to playwriting. Once he told me that he and I should write dramas on every single subject so that there would be nothing left for future playwrights. He was very ambitious and never married. Utterly dedicated to the theatre, he was extremely successful at it. He was such a spendthrift that the Rs 4000–5000 he received for a new play would be squandered in less than four or five months. He usually did not write the whole play. He composed the most important scenes, and the rest was written by his disciples. Nevertheless, the scenes that he did write were masterful, without equal, from the point of view of poetics as well as stagecraft.

When my *Shravan Kumar* was sharply criticized in one of the Agra weeklies, Hashr said, "Why do you publish your plays? Drama is a thing to be performed, not read. Hindi has still not come up the way that English has in the West. *Khichri* language will prevail in the theatre for some time to come. The Hindi elites want a high standard of language spoken on stage so that they can bring their families to the theatre. But they wouldn't be able to understand that kind of Hindi. The company would go bankrupt the very first night. These critics have no knowledge of the stage or its realities."

To write further of my reception in Calcutta would be self-congratulatory. Instead I offer a published newspaper article from the daily *Vishvamitra*, January 3, 1927:

Felicitation for Poet

On January 2, 1927, the local Hindi Natya Parishad offered a certificate of felicitation to Bareli's eminent poet, Pandit Radheshyamji. The attendance was good. Presiding over the session was the editor of *Matvala*, Navjadik Lal Shrivastav. First Vijaykrishna Shukla sang an invocatory hymn. Then the editor of *Hindu Panch*, Ishvari Prasad Sharma, and the editor of *Narayan*, Narottam Vyas, introduced the poet and praised his efforts to spread Hindi through his *Ramayan* discourses and theatrical art. After that the Parishad's chairman, Madhav Shukla, read out the felicitation and presented the certificate, inscribed in gold, to Panditji. Giving his thanks in return, Panditji eloquently analyzed the relationship between the Hindi language and the Parsi stage, and called for the establishment of an all-India Hindi-language theatre. The speech, although to the point, was deeply moving. At the insistence of the audience, Pandit Radheshyam then enchanted the guests with a recitation from the *Ramayan*. The meeting was adjourned after the presiding officer was given a vote of thanks.[5]

I have expanded on the earlier Calcutta visit because after I left the New Alfred's employ, I too established a connection with Madan Theatres. By October 1931, my health was restored, and I went to Calcutta to present my *katha* of the "Complete Ramayan" in the old post office near Bara Bazar. The large crowd included journalist friends, actors, and notables, and my picture appeared on the front page of the *Hindu Panch*.

This was the beginning of the talkies era. Elizar, the actor who had played Arjun in the New Alfred's *Vir Abhimanyu*, was the star of India's first sound picture, *Alam Ara*. Hashr wrote the ghazals for *Shirin Farhad*, the Madans' first talkie starring Kajjan and Nisar, another veteran of *Vir Abhimanyu*. The contest was on in Bombay and Calcutta to make the next movie as quickly as possible. In Calcutta, Mr Bhavnani started working on *Shakuntala*. Jahangirji (J.J. Madan), the managing director of the Madan Theatres, devised the scheme of beating Bhavnani to the punch with his own *Shakuntala*. The roles of Shakuntala and Dushyant would be played by Kajjan and Nisar who had just headlined in *Shirin Farhad*. The scenery and costumes would be taken from the theatre, the studio was already there in Tollygunge, so what could stop him? Dadabhai Sarkari intervened and asked me to write the dialogue and songs, which I agreed to do. But then I got into a fix. Jahangirji wanted the songs to be shot each day, as soon as they were written, and he wanted large numbers of them in the film, since that had been the formula for success in *Shirin Farhad*.

That month passed with great difficulty. It was a good thing that I had already finished my *katha* performance, else I would have fallen

---

[5] Omitted here is a second felicitation, almost identical to the first, published in *Bharat Mitra*, January 7, 1927. It was offered by the Bajrang Parishad, and the guests included the Hindi poet Suryakant Tripathi Nirala.

ill. I spent every night writing. In the morning I traveled the eight or ten miles to Tollygunge and presented myself in time for the shooting. My midday *parathas* were delivered from home by a servant. I rehearsed the parts with the actors using a chalk board, writing sometimes in Urdu, sometimes in Hindi, so that they could read the words from a distance. I worked on the song lyrics even at night when I took the tram home. It's true that Jahangirji loaned me his own automobile, and I received a pass for the Special Class in all of Calcutta's theatres and cinema halls. But I had no free time for any of that.

One day, in the rush of production Jahangirji even asked me to shoot a scene. For the first time in my life I looked into the face of the machine that swallowed songs. Luckily the cameraman Raj Hans and sound engineer Marconi were right at my side, helping out.[6] Or maybe it was that foreign lady, who always held the "scenario" book in her hand, who sat with me while Jahangir told her to list this section as a long shot, or that one as a close-up. Without doubt that lady, that foreign beauty, was very sophisticated, clever, and dutiful. Whenever I started to cough, she straightaway reached into her pocket and gave me a cough drop. That cough stayed with me forever like a blessing from the New Alfred.

Somehow we finished *Shakuntala*, and not at great cost. The actors, costumes, and scenery were all from the theatre, thus the only real outlay was for film stock, yet the film was sold to the distributors for between one and two lakhs. Opening night was truly exciting. Severe critics attacked the large number of songs, but music lovers were entranced. The review in the *Hindu Panch* singled out Radheshyam for praise:

Kathavachak's Skill

In the field of drama, Pandit Radheshyam has vast experience. He fills his works with the attractions of romance and magical effects. His skill is evident in this instance as well. The plot is carefully constructed, and although it is predominantly a love story, nowhere does it stray into obscenity. The songs are charming and sweet, almost excessively so. This

---

[6] Radheshyam confuses the specialties of the Madan crew. T. Marconi was the Italian cameraman who joined the Madan film company in the 1920s.

film is undoubtedly the most beautiful and appealing of those made by Madan Theatres Limited. The Madan management and Kathavachakji are to be heartily congratulated.

Suddenly Jahangirji decided that *Shakuntala* should be converted into a play and be ready to open in the Corinthian Theatre in nine days. He told me to revise the script and rehearse the actors, relying on prompts for the performance. I was stunned by his haste, but he insisted it was the season and no other new play was available. Every day I would sit in the room full of beauties, teaching the actresses pronunciation. Although I was a man, I was as shy as a young girl. I kept my eyes firmly planted on the script book, as though I were giving instruction to it.

One of the girls complained to Jahangir that she had never seen such an odd director, and word of his displeasure got back to me through another actor. I explained my position clearly. It was my passion for theatre that brought me to the playhouse. My true occupation was that of a *kathavachak*. In order to maintain my reputation, I had to protect the purity of my character, whether in private or in public. I would lose my calling as India's most beloved reciter if I became debauched. It was this feeling, and the devotion to Ram behind it, that saved me from the foul atmosphere in that room full of collyrium-adorned women.

Still, I had to attend rehearsals, no matter what. Around this time Hashr's *Dil ki Pyas* had begun its run. Backstage, the actors and actresses were smoking, chewing *pan*, even drinking alcohol. The rooms they slept in adjoined the theatre, and they met there freely. One Sunday afternoon, I saw the leading actresses and dancing girls surrounding a maharaja from Rajputana, entertaining him with liquor. The scene struck me as so debased that I returned directly to my quarters. I cursed myself, wondering why I did not abandon this addiction to the theatre. I sent my son Ghanshyam a letter, explaining that I felt as though I were living in a lavatory.

Kings and princes would visit the New Alfred in large numbers, but they paid for their tickets like everyone else and left after the show. Once in Kanpur a maharaja wanted to present gold medals to two boys, but the company management refused. It was a principle of the New Alfred not to accept medals for actors. This was the era when maharajas were operating their own theatre companies—whether from motives of art or business, one cannot say. The Maharaja of Charkhari owned the Corinthian Company for a brief while. Sharifa and Agha Hashr were in it, and it was managed by Madan Theatres Limited.

Shakuntala, the play, opened in July 1932 with Miss Mukhtyar of Lahore in the singing lead and Master Mohan as comedian. Despite these attractions, it bombed and was never published. Meanwhile, I had written *Maharshi Valmiki*, a philosophical play with long speeches, imitating a type of drama found in Marathi and Bengali. I attempted a composition entirely in Hindi, without the couplets and end-rhymes of Urdu. The actors were terrified of the long passages, being unused to so much Hindi. I chose Abdul Rahman Kabuli for the part of Valmiki and asked him to direct. The play was successfully staged in 1932, and a Bengali newspaper hailed it as "the first and possibly last spiritual drama." But I missed seeing my own play performed, because my wife had come down with dysentery and beseeched me to return to Bareli.

This experience left me with the deeply satisfying feeling that the Parsi theatre, which had begun with the *Indar Sabha*, had now reached the point of *Maharshi Valmiki*. My period of activity had been a link between the obscenity of the Urdu stage and the purity of the Hindi stage. It was the duty of the playwrights of the future to build on this ideal.

In his textbook *Rupak Rahasya*, which was used in the Hindi MA course, Shyam Sundar Das wrote:

> Pandit Radheshyam "Kaviratna" and Narayanprasad "Betab" are renowned for their *pauranik* plays, as is Harikrishna Jauhar for his social dramas. These three playwrights have completely transformed the Parsi theatre and replaced Urdu plays with Hindi plays. Of the three, Pandit Radheshyam's language is the most refined and well-honed. Their dramas have been well received on the stage and have altered the general public's mentality. Their most famous works are Radheshyam's *Vir Abhimanyu, Parambhakt Prahlad, Shri Krishna Avatar* and *Rukmini Mangal*, Betab's *Mahabharat* and *Ramayan*, and Jauhar's *Pati Bhakti*.

Gopivallabh Upadhyay published a series of reviews of my dramas in his journal, *Tyagbhumi*. Because he was a man of the stage himself, I include some excerpts from volume two of his magazine:

> For the past fifteen years, the dramas of Bareli's treasury of *kirtan* art, Pandit Radheshyam Kathavachak, have been performed in all the large cities of India by the New Alfred Theatrical Company. Whoever has seen these plays cannot forget their fine qualities. They contain great characters, high ideals, and serious and touching amusement mixed with topicality, such that no thoughtful viewer cannot be won over by their effectiveness.
> Panditji's first drama, *Vir Abhimanyu*, amazed the populace of Delhi with its emotionalism, language, and costumes. Before this, only Urdu plays had held sway. In *Parambhakt Prahlad*, he has interwoven the story of Prahlad with the events of the 1920 Satyagraha and Non-Cooperation movement so neatly that the viewer is deceived into thinking he is seeing before his eyes the recent Non-Cooperation campaign.
> *Usha Aniruddh* was composed in 1924–5 at the height of the pro-Hindu agitation. It is the chief goal of Radheshyam's plays to link every contemporary event to its historical antecedent. Thus in this play he beautifully illustrates the conflict between Hindus and non-Hindus through the conflict between the Shaivas and Vaishnavas. In *Parivartan*, the character of Chanda demonstrates a new ideal of service to society, just as in *Masharqi Hur* the heroine Hamida's role displays extremely heroic qualities.

My wife recovered in 1933, and I left Calcutta for good. I busied myself with the Radheshyam Press, bought some land, planted an orchard, and built a house. Every morning I went bright and early with my wife to sow flower beds, plant fruit trees, bathe, and sing *bhajan*s. Sometimes we made *dal bhati* and ate it right there. Following this program, both of us became much healthier. On June 1, 1934, my first grandson Vishvanath was born, Ghanshyam's son. My father Banke Lal was still alive, just as my grandfather Nannu Mal had been at Ghanshyam's birth.

Drama companies and film people kept sending me offers, and finally I accepted a proposal and wrote the screenplay *Shri Satyanarayan*. When I went to Ahmedabad to deliver it, I met a saint called Bapji; his full name was Nityanand Maharaj. I spent most of my time between 1936 and 1940 in his service, and a more joyful soul I have never known. On the Badayun Road beyond Bareli Station I bought a plot for Rs 40,000 and built two houses, with kitchen, *yajnashala*, and garage. There I arranged for *katha, kirtan, yajna*, and holy feasts, inviting *shankaracharyas* and *babas* to visit and sanctify the site. Even now, sometimes I organize religious functions there.

When the film *Shri Satyanarayan* went into production, I took my younger son Balram with me to Bombay, hoping to introduce him to the film line. I had already taught him *katha* and provided him with education through the MA and LL.B degrees. He was intelligent and a smooth talker.

In Bombay, whenever someone begins to discuss making a movie, the ordinary class of directors, actors, and crew descend upon him like a bunch of touts at a pilgrimage site. If the filmmaker has limited funds or is inclined to keep expenses down, he chooses his favorites from among those hovering around, or falls for the clever fellows who overwhelm him with their verbosity and flattery. The true artists do not call upon film producers themselves. They will go if invited, and if they are available they'll make a contract for a stipulated amount and stick to it. Motilal Mistri, the producer of *Shri Satyanarayan*, was not able to engage this better class of people, so he cancelled the program in Bombay and decided on Dada Torney's Sarasvati Cinetone in Poona. Drupad Ray was appointed director, and I worked with him to develop the dialogues and songs. Nowadays the story, dialogues, and songs are written by three separate individuals, but at that time they were the responsibility of one person. This was the way it had been in the theatre, and it remained the practice in the film world for a while.

One night I told Balram to consider seriously the role of Sadhuram, one of the leading parts in the film. But after several days, I abandoned this idea; in fact, we left the company entirely. Madan Theatres was full of prostitutes who had illicit relations with the actors, but the women in the film line were even worse. We found the atmosphere impossible to deal with and made a plan to return to Bareli. Nevertheless, we stayed for the *muhurat*, which was conducted by the famous director Shantaram. The picture was released within a year, under Torney's supervision, and although I never saw it I heard from my son that the dialogues came out brilliantly.

I have one more regret from those days. Himanshu Rai of Bombay Talkies tried to engage me on several occasions to become a writer in his studio. I was interested in working with him, but we could not come to an agreement. My head was full of the monthly salary and privileges I had enjoyed in the New Alfred, whereas Himanshu Rai was just starting up and had a limited budget. If I had come around to his side, I could have become a successful screenwriter and made a lot of money. But now, when I reflect on it, I arrive at the conclusion that it was not in the nature of things for my earnings to increase. This was amply borne out by my experiences investing in the stock market. Casting aside the recommendations of my advisers, I sold all of my shares before I realized a profit. I was the son of a Brahmin, not a Bania—how could it be otherwise?

At the age of 50, I decided to stop trying to make money. I would no longer take up a collection at my *katha* performances but rather offer them for free. My two sons were adults, and it was time to end conjugal relations with my wife. I would devote myself to social service and singing the praise of Ram. My wife was already an ardent believer in *bhajan* and *puja*, and she gladly acceded to my plan. We received spiritual initiation from Pandit Madan Mohan Malviya and at his command traveled throughout Bihar, Rajasthan, Malwa, and Uttar Pradesh performing good works. I chaired the annual function of the Nagari Pracharini Sabha in Banaras. Then I went to the Punjab with Ram Narayan Mishra to campaign for the use of Hindi. Such were those delightful years, which even today gladden my soul when I recall them.

Chapter 5: Middle Age (1941–1955)

The first few years of this period were among the happiest in my life. My health was excellent, and I received plenty of spiritual food, bathing in the Ganga and serving holy men. The pleasure I received by giving free performances of *katha* was unparalleled. A Brahmin's livelihood brings honor as well as food, clothing, and other necessities, but Brahmins must fulfill their Brahminhood by adhering to simplicity. Many a preacher or pandit has fallen in the eyes of the public because of his addiction to expensive goods: *pan*, cigarettes, cinema, cosmetics. He ruins his health and then goes running to doctors and *vaidyas* for prescriptions.

Attending a *yajna*, I found myself in Delhi in 1944, and there I ran into the Shahjahan Theatrical Company of Manik Lal Dangi, whose director was my disciple Chaube Ramkrishna. He insisted that his company be allowed to perform *Sati Parvati*. Although this drama of mine had been published, it had never been staged. I told him I was no longer interested in that line, I was leading a sadhu's life. After much resistance, however, I gave in, and the play was mounted and first performed in my presence. The house was packed on opening night, and even I had to admit that this play, like my others, was a hit in terms of its stageability. Chaube played Shiv beautifully, and an actress did a creditable job of the role of Parvati. Manik Lal acted the part of Narad; he had been with Madan Theatres and was a fine actor and singer. Then I set out on my pilgrimage to Badrinath in the Himalayas.

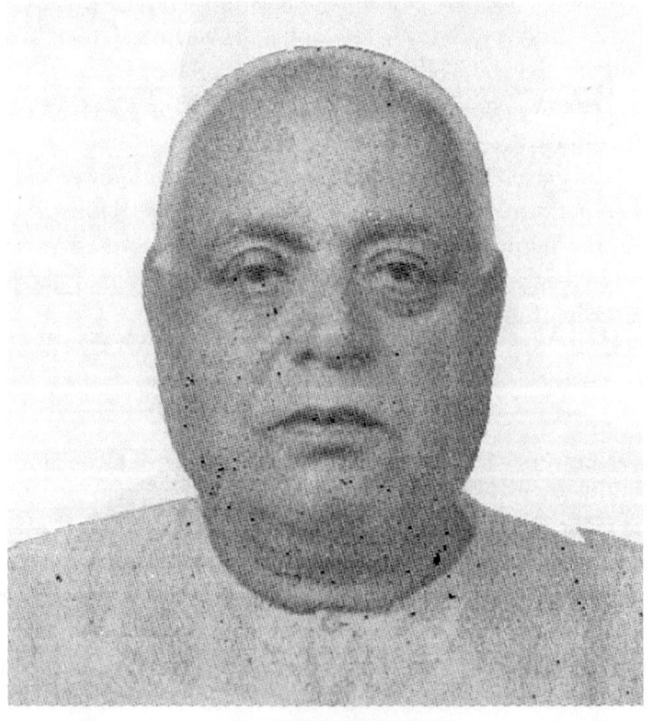

15. Radheshyam Kathavachak

When I returned to Bareli, I found that my son Ghanshyam had taken seriously ill with diabetes. After attending to him, I resumed my roamings in the service of religion. In Ranchi, I gave a sterling performance of the Ram and Bharat episode of the *Ramayan* and was approached by Radha Babu, a businessman who wanted to turn the epic into a series of films. We decided that since I had abandoned the pursuit of profit, I would donate my earnings from the film to religious causes. The producer too agreed that he would donate his profits to charity. Then Ghanshyam and I traveled to Bombay to assess the financial climate for the first of the films, *Ram Janm*. All of the budget estimates came in much higher than expected, and the producer suggested we look at studios in Calcutta instead.

After Bombay, Ghanshyam's health once more deteriorated, and I postponed my trip to Calcutta. Coming back from a religious function in Hyderabad, I stopped in Kolhapur and Poona and visited several well-known studios to discuss the film. Hindi-speaking actors would have to be brought in from Bombay, and it would be difficult to find a director immersed in Ram-*bhakti*. I rejected this plan, desirous of avoiding a tone of Marathiness in this very North Indian story.

In early 1947 I worked on developing the story-line of *Ram Janm* and wrote some dialogues with my colleagues. Then in April we left for Calcutta. I took along Fida Husain, who was at that time the director of a theatrical company in Calcutta. He was familiar with all the artists in Calcutta. I was referred to a director, Rameshwar Sharma, whom I judged suitable, and we looked at possible studios. Finally, we were ready to get in touch with the producer to arrange the financing and begin production.

Then, one day, my cough returned with a vengeance. This time there was blood in the sputum, and I suffered repeated fits of coughing. At the same time, Hindu–Muslim riots broke out in Calcutta. For the first night, Fida Husain was compelled to hide with us for his own survival, and the next day we all went back to Bareli. Enthusiasm for the play was still strong, but Ghanshyam was severely ill, and I commenced a naturopathic cure for my cough. We called in various medical specialists. My wife and I repaired to the bank of the Ganga, where she embarked on a course of prayer to save Ghanshyam's life. His condition continued to worsen, and we returned to Bareli.

The day of August 15, 1947, arrived. On one side, there was our sadness for Ghanshyam; on the other, joy at India's independence. For a few hours I forgot my pain and composed a song, *jay jay nav bharat nirmata*, which I sent to Gandhiji. Finally came that inauspicious day, October 3. Ghanshyam died in the morning, but I remained in bed, immobilized by grief. My heart was in such pain that I attended none of the death rituals. For an entire year, I took refuge in a thatched hut near the Ganga, going back and forth to my house in a tonga.

All of a sudden, word arrived that Rameshwar Sharma, the director, had also died. And following this, from Ranchi came news that Radha Babu too had passed away. The plans for the film were scrapped. The whole matter was over. What was meant to be was more powerful than our earthly plans.

Chapter 6: Old Age (1955–)

Separated from her son, my wife went blind with weeping. She wept so much that she developed cataracts and had to have an operation. I did not go blind, but I had to don glasses to be able to read again. Truly a son is the light of one's eyes.

Leaving my wife in the care of my son Balram, I went to Bombay to try to forget Ghanshyam's death. My colleagues assumed I was there to start another film project, but the fact was that I could not tolerate our dwelling in Bareli. Those large rooms and verandahs seemed enormous, as though they were going to eat me up.

The main reason for returning from Bombay was my wife's illness. It proved to be a lengthy one. In the end she died, and this second blow was so devastating that I never fully recovered my health. At the age of sixty-five, I accepted that old age had come. Illness and mental anguish were ever-present. I might have done some further work, but all of my dear companions had departed: my wife, son, sister, friends from Bareli. Solitude and loneliness overwhelmed me. I was reduced to a blank page.

In this darkness, a thin ray of light, the light of knowledge from the study of scripture kept me company, no matter where I was. I owe this to the blessings of holy men. In the flood of 1956, our boat at Garh Mukteshwar sank; two years before, the little dinghy had capsized. Transient objects will perish, after all. One day this body too will perish. Wherefore then this deluded enchantment with material things? Our attachment should be to the imperishable force that exists both within the body and without, in every atom, in every particle of the universe. This force, which is called Brahma, is truth. It alone is immortal.

The all-encompassing Brahma is composed of three parts—truth, mind, and joy—and thus it is called *sacchidanand*. The momentary pleasure that we find in women, offspring, wealth, and sensual enjoyment is a signal, an indicator of the bliss within us. It tempts us with perishable things, trying to awaken us to the reality of that joy which is within. Change this dream of joy into true enlightenment, it tells us. Meditate in solitude, concentrate your awareness within yourself. This is the fulfillment of human birth. This is the ultimate peace available to human beings. Each adept who arrives at this destination attains the final blessing, the eternal happiness of the Lord Ram.

Now I return to the subject of this book. It was my desire to reform the cinema world in some small way, but I found myself too weak to achieve that end. Man is the slave of wealth and sensual pleasure. India's perennial faith has always respected conjugal fidelity, has operated on that basis for thousands of years. But in foreign countries, relations between the sexes take the form of mere infatuation. Foreign films laden with that infatuation came to India, and financially they were very successful. Bombay's film impresarios also embraced that mode out of financial motives, and they profited. The result however was that young men and women—even college students—became dyed in that color. Beautiful looks, splendid clothing, acting that lights up lustful fires, poses, and so on were introduced. That was all it took—India's perennial faith let out a wail, and foreign civilization sounded the victory cry.

Half-educated and uneducated shopkeepers, laborers, rickshaw pullers, and tonga drivers drowned in that stream. The streets and markets were full of girls with two plaits and alluring outfits, the hotels filled with merrymakers and drinkers. Not that I am in favor of long veils or burqas. Indian women should take a middle course between full purdah and the bareheaded display of two plaits. The sari should be used to cover the head, in the manner of Gujarati women, but with the face revealed. Letting the sari slip from the head shows loss of modesty in Indian culture. When Draupadi's sari slipped from her head, Lord Krishna himself had to appear to defend her. Today's young women deliberately lower the sari from their heads, and this is not a good thing.

This autobiography of mine is the memory of a bygone era. Now even the form of drama has changed. One-act plays with only a single set, or plays without songs and dances are popular these days. Only the skill of acting is given importance, and this too is a Western trend. Otherwise our dramas were always full of music, and this made them entertaining and educational.

In the altered theatrical conditions today, women play the women's roles, and this practice has completely caught on. Quite the contrary, at the beginning of this century women's parts were performed by men even in the amateur clubs. The great Malviyaji himself played the part of Shakuntala in Kalidasa's play, while his son Shyamsundar played Dushyant.

In my time too, Kavasji Khatau brought actresses into his Parsi Alfred Theatrical Company, as did Madan Theatres in the Corinthian Theatre in Calcutta. This was out of a desire for profit. But in the same period, the New Alfred and Survijay drama companies remained firm in not allowing actresses, and even flaunted their policy. These companies molded the public to their taste, and the public stayed with them. That is why families rushed to see their plays. Brother and sister sat side by side and watched those dramas. The Vyakul Bharat Company which performed *Buddhadev* operated along the same lines. Actresses were not permitted in it.

Men and women, when they play the hero and heroine, in a manner of speaking become husband and wife. In the cinema, they appear on the screen and remain there, but in a play they speak directly to each other on stage, they meet, they perform their roles in person. What the effect is on them, as well as on the public, is for both the male and female readership to determine.

Now I present some thoughts to my fellow writers. A playwright requires a thorough knowledge of the stage. He needs familiarity with pronunciation, music, and poetics. After studying several languages, he must read as many books as possible in those languages. One ought not become a playwright out of lust for lucre. Writing a play demands a great deal of thought. First one must immerse in fashioning a story, and that story must be grand in order to be successful. In a two- or three-act play, each scene should have its own interest, and the settings should vary so that the spectator isn't bored. It is essential to avoid obscenity while maintaining amusement. Characterization must be natural, but such that the public derives an educational message. The playwright has a grave responsibility to choose social problems and represent them on stage in such a manner that the public recognizes them as flaws.

The world we come into at birth is itself a playhouse. To become a good actor here, we have to love the art of drama, we have to master it, comprehend it, and then translate it into our personal behavior. Our knowledge of this art brings all manner of success into our lives, enabling us to exert our influence on other people readily.

Finally, I offer my prayer to the all-powerful Ultimate Being. May this ancient art once more flourish nobly in India in accordance with our civilizational values, and may it show to Indians the true path. Om Shanti.

5

Jayshankar Sundari, *Some Blossoms, Some Tears*

Introduction

In the next two autobiographies, the memoirs of poet-playwrights give way to those of actors. Both Jayshankar Sundari and Fida Husain enjoyed sustained, successful careers on the professional stage. Sundari entertained fans for over three decades, while Fida Husain performed and directed plays for half a century. Sundari was formally attached to the Parsi theatre for only a few years. His apprenticeship with the Calcutta-based company of Dadabhai Thunthi created the foundation for his meteoric success once he began to perform in Bombay. The close connections between the worlds of Parsi theatre and Gujarati theatre toward the end of the nineteenth century make it logical to include Sundari's autobiography in this volume. The two theatres shared a pool of actors and musicians, and worked in the same playhouses. They both employed the Gujarati language, although by Sundari's time plays in Urdu dominated the Parsi theatre. The chief difference was in the owners, who tended to be Parsi merchants on the one hand and Gujarati Hindu merchants on the other.

In the early twentieth century, leading Parsi and Gujarati companies still hired men to perform women's roles. All the autobiographies mention this practice as routine, just as they refer to the employment of women as actresses, which had begun in some companies, as problematic. None of the other autobiographies, however, describes how it felt for a man to play a woman's role. Sundari's autobiography is extraordinary in documenting his experience as a female impersonator. No other "lady actor," as such performers were sometimes called, has left such an insightful account of the process of transformation from man to woman. Sundari was a female impersonator of the highest order. Through his method of total identification with women, he created idealized feminine characters that were widely imitated. Sundari's stage movements, attire, and speech became models for women offstage. He was second only to the great Bal Gandharva in bringing about changes that led, paradoxically, to greater freedom for women.[1]

Jayshankar was the son of Bhudhar Das Bhojak and his wife Krishna. He was born in 1889 in the town of Visnagar, Gujarat. His grandfather had been a court singer, and his father performed rituals and sang in Jain temples and households. Jayshankar grew up in a musical atmosphere and, like his elder siblings, he started school at the age of 7. A rather timid child, he was terrified of the schoolmaster, who had a penchant for corporal punishment. He was less drawn to studies than to the Ram Lila and Bhavai performances around him. Identifying emotionally with dramatized scenarios, from an early age he readily memorized poems, songs, and stories. By the time he turned 9, he was already disinclined toward formal schooling; his true education occurred while watching rehearsals and performances.

In 1898 Jayshankar was recruited by a Parsi theatrical company from Calcutta. With his family's consent he left home and undertook the long train journey. Under Dadabhai Thunthi's direction he began learning Urdu theatre songs and training for *sakhi* roles, female companions to the heroine, typically enacted by young boys. The rehearsal regimen was strict and the boys were vigilantly watched, but the company provided a comfortable existence. Jayshankar began to play the heroine in Urdu dramas in the Thanthaniya Theatre: Chatra in *Chatra Bakavali*, Mehnigar in *Haman*, Aban in *Khudadad*. His sole effort to play a man resulted in ridicule.

After Thunthi's retirement, Jayshankar returned to Gujarat. He was again enrolled in school but quickly fell in with theatre fans who made frequent trips to Ahmedabad. Many of the actors in the Gujarati companies were of the same caste as Jayshankar, Nayak-Bhojaks. His

---

[1] See Hansen (1999).

talents came to the attention of Bapulal Nayak, an established actor and director. After negotiations with his family, Jayshankar once more left home, this time for Bombay. He joined the Mumbai Gujarati Natak Mandali and appeared regularly on the boards of the Gaiety Theatre. In 1901 he made his debut in *Saubhagya Sundari*, playing the heroine Sundari opposite Bapulal as hero. Following this triumph, *sundari,* beautiful or lovely lady, was attached to his name for the rest of his life.

Over the next few years, Jayshankar was coached in Gujarati, classical music, and the realistic style of acting. Offstage he enjoyed special living arrangements with the family of the company owner, a prosperous businessman. With the help of private tutors and interested patrons he furthered his education, learning about English drama and Gujarati literature; later he briefly studied Sanskrit. His method of preparing for his female roles involved close observation of actual women from respected families. The result of his skillful interpretation of feminine gestures, speech, and sentiments was that women in society copied his gestures and look. He embodied the glorious, self-sacrificing woman of Gujarat. His theatrical portrayals were produced at the very time that this womanly image appeared in works of Gujarati literature, such as in the great novel *Sarasvatichandra*.

After *Saubhagya Sundari,* Jayshankar played Rambha in *Vikram Charitra*. Costumed as a milkmaid, he sang a song that became an immediate hit. The lyrics were even printed on the borders of cloth pieces manufactured in Bombay's mills. Next he played Shirin in a version of the famous Urdu romance *Shirin Farhad.* The social drama *Jugal Jugari,* about the evils of gambling, was also a popular vehicle for Jayshankar; he played a long-suffering wife and mother, Lalita. Jayshankar developed the role through his acquaintance with a young girl named Gulab from a well-off family.

In 1903, at the age of 14, Jayshankar was married to a girl of 11. She developed several infirmities and was never sent to join Jayshankar in Bombay. His family arranged a second marriage, and this time his wife came to live with him, but she was uneducated and he rejected her. His third marriage, performed in 1917, proved to be compatible, and his wife Champa bore three sons and a daughter. Outside of matrimony, Jayshankar encouraged the hopes of several girls and women who fell in love with him through his stage performances. These affairs of the heart often took a painful and tragic course, comparable to portrayals in fiction and drama of the period.

The Gaiety Theatre was renovated in 1906, and, while construction was going on, Sundari's company went to Karachi. *Saubhagya Sundari* and *Shirin Farhad* were very popular there. However, rumors reached Bombay that Sundari had been abducted by Pathans. The story enhanced his reputation, and when the company returned to Bombay another run of hits ensued: *Nand Battisi, Sangat ke Rang, Chandrabhaga*. The company began producing mythological plays around 1910, including *Devkanya* and *Krishna Charitra*, both written by Mulani. Next, several plays by Vibhakar on patriotic themes were mounted. In *Sneh Sarita* Jayshankar played an English-educated girl who fights for India's independence. He was still performing opposite Bapulal. *Sudhachandra* (1916) and *Madhu Bansari* (1917) again treated the independence movement, whereas Vibhakar's *Meghmalini* (1918) dealt with issues of labor and management.

In 1922, the owners of the Mumbai Gujarati Natak Mandali sold the company to Bapulal Nayak. For several years, Jayshankar was estranged from Bapulal. While Bapulal shifted the operations of the company to the interior of Gujarat, Jayshankar remained in Bombay, acting and directing for the Lakshmikant Natak Samaj and the Subodh Gujarati Natak Mandali. In 1925 Jayshankar and Bapulal joined together again under the aegis of the Mumbai Gujarati Natak Mandali at its new headquarters in Baroda. Jayshankar was increasingly engaged in directing junior actors, but he also performed female roles in plays such as *Nurjahan, College ni Kanya*, and *Swami Bhakti*. In 1932 he retired from the professional stage and returned to Visnagar.

In Jayshankar's later years, his theatrical activities took a new turn. Between 1932 and 1949 he had little to do with his former career. Then he regained the limelight as codirector with Jasvant Thakar of *Rai no Parvat* for the centenary celebration of the Gujarat Vidya Sabha. This event launched the final stage of his life, wherein he experimented with middle-class directors and actors, incorporating traditional theatre and folklore into productions for modern, socially conscious audiences. He formed Nat Mandal, a training institute and amateur company in Ahmedabad, achieving national acclaim for *Mena Gurjari*,

16. Bapulal Nayak and Jayshankar Sundari in *Sneh Sarita*

a folkloric pageant starring Dina Pathak. Other collaborative efforts to revive traditional forms included *Mithyabhiman*, Dalpatram's play performed in the Bhavai style, and *Sharvilak*, an adaptation of the Sanskrit drama *Mricchakatika*. These activities drew attention to Jayshankar's directorial talents, and in 1957 he was awarded the Sangeet Natak Akademi prize for direction. In 1971 he received the Padmabhushan, a high honor of the Government of India, for his rich contributions to the Gujarati stage, old and new. Four years later he died, at the age of 86.

17. Jayshankar Sundari Receives Padma Bhushan

Jayshankar Sundari's autobiography was first published in Gujarati in 1976 as *Thodan Ansu: Thodan Phul*. It was reprinted in 1989 in an expanded edition. The earlier edition was translated into Hindi by Dinesh Khanna and published in 2002 by the National School of Drama. In Hindi, the autobiography has attracted a new generation of readers and resurrected the reputation of Sundari. This translation is based on it. I have compared the two at length and found a close correspondence. The prefatory material is different, but this does not limit the utility of the Hindi version. For this translation, the Gujarati original was consulted whenever a typographical error was suspected or the wording seemed unclear.

Of the original twelve chapters, the first eight are presented here. The narrative halts in 1922 at the end of Jayshankar's tenure in the Gaiety Theatre. This decision is warranted by the structural break in the 1976 text. Chapter 9 consists of an account of the Gujarati stage told in the third person with no mention of Jayshankar until the final two paragraphs. The first-person narrative resumes in chapters 10 and 11, and chapter 12 presents a summing up. These chapters lack the verve of the earlier part and are less important historically.

The style of Jayshankar's autobiography is generally sincere, self-reflective, and even-handed. Variations occur at points where theatrical history takes over and the text becomes quite dry, or where Jayshankar explores his emotional responses with poetic ebullience and lyricism. The translation process was relatively clearcut, the main issue being that of abridgement. The original has been compressed by 25 per cent to 50 per cent, depending on the passage. In general, rather than eliminate incidents or personages entirely, I have tightened the telling of long anecdotes.

The publication history of the autobiography is rather complex. Attached to the three published editions are various prefatory essays. Close perusal of this matter and the main text led to a surprising discovery. Jayshankar's autobiography was ghostwritten. It is an unambiguous example of collaborative autobiography, an "autobiography of those who do not write," following Philippe Lejeune.[2] Jayshankar's story is told almost entirely in the first person. It is labelled *atmakatha* on the title page and published under his name. Yet both Gujarati editions credit two ghostwriters under the rubric *sankalan*, "compilation." Their names are given as Dinkar Bhojak and Somabhai Patel in the 1976 version, with the order reversed in 1989. These credits are absent from the title page of the Hindi version.

The question of authorship is important for the interpretation of the autobiography and the persona of its subject. The main text briefly

---

[2] See Lejeune (1989): 185–215.

mentions the two helpers near the very end: "It is the morning of October 27, 1969. Sitting beside me, my spiritual son Somabhai Patel, inscriber of my memoirs, and my son Dinkar Bhojak are silent today."[3] Patel is termed *manasputr*, the offspring of one's heart, and *sansmarano shabdasth karta*, the one who puts memories into words. No descriptors are attached to Jayshankar's son, but his mention indicates his participation in the project.

Dinkar Bhojak provides further information in *Nepathye* (Behind the Scenes), the sole preface to the 1976 edition. He relates that Somabhai Patel approached him with the idea of writing his father's autobiography in 1964. Jayshankar was 75 years old and beginning to withdraw from the world. After first expressing reluctance, Jayshankar agreed to work with Patel. The project began in 1964 and lasted four years. At first Patel transcribed Jayshankar's remarks by himself, but then Bhojak joined in and the sessions acquired more depth. It seems the manuscript was left in an unfinished state.

Patel gives his account of the collaboration in a preface to the 1989 edition. In 1964 he became a Gujarati lecturer at a college in Patan after completing his MA. On a visit to Visnagar, he was seized with the idea of writing Jayshankar Sundari's biography. First he met Dinkar Bhojak, who enthusiastically supported the proposal, and then he approached Jayshankar. Jayshankar suggested that Patel use an autobiographical fragment he had already written, 25–30 pages in length, as the foundation for the narrative. After immersing himself in this sketch, Patel discarded the question-answer format and began to transcribe what Jayshankar dictated. To research the project, he sorted through newspaper cuttings, letters, diaries, notebooks, magazines, and other papers. With the assistance of Jayshankar and his son, he assembled the memoir in four years.[4]

In both accounts, Patel's initiative was central to the production of the memoir. Patel had earned a Master's degree in Gujarati, and his literary preferences and skills must have played a role in shaping the narrative. Bhojak's influence is more elusive. From what is known, it seems his investment in his father's autobiography was both personal and professional. He likely served as a go-between, providing access

---

[3] Sundari (1976): 300.
[4] Sundari (1989): 13–15.

to his aging father and authorizing the selection of Patel as ghostwriter. He would have been interested in publicizing his father's legacy as his son and heir. Moreover, Bhojak eventually became a scholar. He published at least ten books on the history of the Gujarati theatre, most relating to his father's period. It is not known whether he had begun his academic career when Patel approached him in 1964. If so, he must have been desirous of securing his father's place in Gujarati literary and theatrical history, a striking feature of the autobiography.

Bhojak's second preface, published as *Nepathye* in the 1989 edition, is quite different from the 1976 preface. Here he presents a relatively objective retrospective of the Gujarati theatre, rather than lauding his father's accomplishments. He credits a number of scholars and theatre practitioners for their help in preparing the edition. The 1989 version includes several additional prefaces. It also contains four new chapters, adding background on the history of the theatre in Gujarat and stressing the contribution of Jayshankar to post-Independence cultural development. Perhaps Bhojak had the work enlarged to strengthen his father's position in official culture circles. As for the four new chapters, it is unknown whether they were based on material elicited from Jayshankar while he was alive or composed anew for this edition, although circumstances favor the latter.

In the Hindi translation, the role of Somabhai Patel and Dinkar Bhojak as co-creators of the original is effectively erased. None of the earlier prefaces is reprinted, and the narrative includes only the twelve chapters of the 1976 edition. Notably, Bhojak is still attached to the project, as are several scholars from the National School of Drama, the publisher. In a new preface, Bhojak hails the memoir as a classic of the autobiographical genre in Gujarati. Theatre scholar and NSD professor Anuradha Kapur elaborates on this theme, tracing the history of the genre in Europe and India. Jayshankar's narrative is repositioned by these prefaces within a global history of autobiography that promises access to the authenticity of individual experience. The memoir is assimilated within eurocentric norms of autobiography, with the accent upon the singularity of the authorial voice. This new reading of Jayshankar's text and persona collides with the evidence of multiple authorship present in the earlier editions. The question is whether the suppression of the compilers' names and their part in the collaboration was deliberate or accidental.

In any event, the engagement with Jayshankar's story explicitly shifts to another plane. Kapur observes that she was first introduced to the autobiography while developing an adaptation of the actor's life for the stage, a process that resulted in her production, *Sundari: An Actor Prepares*.[5] Bhojak was a colleague in that effort, and he is credited by both Kapur and Khanna with facilitating the translation and providing photographs. Central to Kapur's performance piece was the gender transformation at the heart of Jayshankar's theatrical experience and the larger questions it posed about self and identity. The celebrated actor, now a visual icon, offered a means to explore gendered categories within a postmodern representational mode. Kapur and her team's interest lay in performatively recasting Jayshankar's life to accent gender ambiguity. The blurring of father and son, author and scribe, self and other, thrown into relief by the collaborative process that produced the original text, was seemingly of little concern.

Yet in translating the autobiography into Hindi, another collaborative act occurred. Khanna acknowledges the work of several colleagues, beginning with Amritgangar who transcribed the Gujarati into an "English [romanized?] manuscript, which became the foundation for the first phase of the Hindi translation." He credits Aruna Patel with translating "a number of chapters" from the original into "easy Hindi." He also acknowledges the translation assistance of Hemant Kher. Khanna emerges as the coordinator of a translation by committee, prompting additional questions about authorship, translation, and collaboration.

This discussion would be incomplete without mention of the English-language biography, *Jayashankar Sundari and Abhinayakala* by B.B. Panchotia. Panchotia identifies himself as Jayshankar's sister's (Muliben's) son; his educational qualifications include a BA in English literature and a law degree. In his preface he explains that he first thought of writing his uncle's biography in 1932 just after his retirement from the professional stage. In reality, he began the project in 1944, returned to it at different points in 1961 and 1966, and completed it in 1973.[6] The book was published in 1987, after a gap of fourteen years. Panchotia's biography in draft form would have been

---

[5] See Shodhan (1999).
[6] Panchotia (1987): xiv.

finished after the completion of the draft of Jayshankar's autobiography in 1969, but before its publication in 1976.

There are striking similarities in the two accounts, especially in the opening chapters. Given this fact, several possibilities emerge. Panchotia could have borrowed material from the autobiography. Bhojak and Patel, or later editors, could have had access to the unpublished biography by Panchotia and borrowed from it. And both could have used common sources such as newspaper accounts, magazine articles, and family archives. The direction of influence cannot be determined, and a mutual synergy may well have existed. It may be best to view the four life histories (two in Gujarati, one in Hindi, and one in English) as a palimpsest, a manuscript on which more than one text is written with earlier versions only partially erased. To these is now added a fifth, this translation. Taken together these texts, none of which was penned by Jayshankar himself, suggest not only an intricately layered composition, but an expanding reading public for his life story, beginning with the Padmabhushan award in 1971 and extending through the discovery of the actor by new generations who had not known the old Gujarati theatre at all.

Noted Performances

1901	*Saubhagya Sundari* (Mulani)	– played Sundari
1901	*Vikram Charitra* (Mulani)	– played Rambha
1901	*Dagh-e Hasrat/Shirin Farhad* (unknown)	– played Shirin
1902	*Jugal Jugari* (Mulani)	– played Lalita
1904	*Kamlata* (Mulani)	– played Kamlata
1907	*Nand Battisi* (Mulani)	– played Padmini
1915	*Sneh Sarita* (Vibhakar)	– played Sarita

Some Blossoms, Some Tears

JAYSHANKAR SUNDARI

Chapter 1: At the Dawn of Life

In the year 1853, before I was born, the Gujarati stage came into being. I was meant to be an actor, and who knows why, whether from family influences or some unknown source, I was attracted to the profession from childhood. The Gujarati stage was established in Bombay by educated Parsis, and I was, it seems, destined to inherit its great legacy.

Playwriting in the Indian languages started in Bengal in 1826, in Maharashtra in 1843, and in Hindi in 1853. The Nawab of Lucknow, Wajid Ali Shah, commissioned the writing of an operatic drama in Urdu, and the *Indar Sabha* was performed in his palace compound in 1853. Gujarat's drama lovers were not far behind. In 1868 they formed the first professional drama company.[7] In 1870–1 pure Urdu drama companies emerged.[8] When Master Narottam was insulted by his Parsi bosses, he established the Gujarati Natak Mandali in 1870.

Many professional drama companies traveled to Gujarat and Kathiawar. Urdu drama companies roamed as far as North India, Punjab, Bengal, Madras, Rangoon, Africa, Java, and Sumatra. The actors of those days were primarily Parsi, Brahmin, Nayak-Bhojak, Muslim, and Irani. The famous artists were Amrit Keshav Nayak, Vallabh Keshav Nayak, Sohrabji Ogra, Dayashankar Vasanji Girnara.

---

[7] Possible reference to the Victoria Theatrical Company, founded in Bombay in 1868.

[8] In 1871 *Sone ke Mol ki Khurshed*, often considered the first Urdu drama, appeared. "Pure Urdu drama companies," however, would be a later development.

Ranchhodbhai was the founder of Gujarati drama. Among the actresses there was Miss Fenton, and following in her footsteps Gauhar, Moti Jan, Agha Jan, Gulab, and Ganga. Balivala was an expert actor and director.

As if passing on the magnificent tradition of these leading artists, the Mumbai Gujarati Natak Mandali was born on May 3, 1889. It might have been the rule of fate or a mere coincidence, but my birth occurred in the same year, on January 30, 1889. I was born into a family of Shrimali Bhojaks in Visnagar, Gujarat. My parents were Bhudhar Das, the son of the famous singer Tribhuvan Das, and his wife Krishna. At that exact time, Dayashankar's troupe was winning the hearts of the public with the drama *Kanta*. Simultaneously, my inner actor was imbibing grandfather's music and being nurtured by the atmosphere at home.

As far as I recall, the now crowded Station Road was virtually empty then. Our little house stood beside a neem tree, and nearby were the houses of Patidars, Nayak-Bhojaks, and other castes. Outer display was little, money too was scarce, but inner peace was abundant. In one corner of our house sat my grandfather Tribhuvan Das singing, his notes dissolving into the *tanpura*'s hum.

Among the Bhojaks of Visnagar, our family had been quite prosperous for three generations. My grandfather had found fame through his music, and in our caste and especially among the Jains he was a well-known singer. He had studied music in Jodhpur with Chhote Fakhruddin Khan, himself a celebrated figure among the 150 singers at the court of Raja Ram Singh in Jaipur. His reputation extended to the wealthy houses of Ahmedabad, a connection that my elders considered their patrimony. His father Mansukh Thakor, his grandfather Bhaichand Thakor, and his great-grandfather Jagannath Thakor were all famous singers in their day.

Tribhuvan had also studied the Jain scriptures and was a singer and composer of Jain tales and *raso*s. He was a hereditary musician at the house of Hemabhai Bakhatchand. When Hemabhai took a large entourage to Palitan, Bhaichand Thakor wrote a *prashasti* in his honor in 1834. Later Tribhuvan Das was a singer for many years in the household of Jesang Bhai, a lover of the arts.

When I was born, there were eight people at home: grandfather, grandmother, mother and father, my nephew Chhotelal, my elder brother Motilal, my elder sister Muliben, and myself. The household was thriving and happy. I was told later that owing to my robust health I was much petted and loved as a child.

At the age of 5 or 6, I spent my mornings listening to grandfather singing Anandaghan's *padas* or the *ashtapadis* of the *Gita Govinda*. Sometimes father accompanied him on the *tanpura*. Listening to grandfather practice every day, we all learned to tell good music from bad. The musical tones echoing in my ears created ever new shapes and waves. Other influences and *samskaras* similarly shaped my childhood being, giving me a definite identity.

In our family there was a natural affection for the Jain religion. We were familiar with the Jain calendar, festival days, and rituals, and had faith in them. Our auspicious ceremonies were fixed according to astrological calculations as to the correct time for starting and ending.

The most superstitious one in the household was my sister Muliben. She was afraid of all sorts of ghosts and spirits, and she worried that they might torment me too. Whenever anyone fell ill, she took vows, burned lamps of coconut oil and ghee, and performed all sorts of rites. The menfolk never bothered their heads with this nonsense. My father condemned black magic. He believed in the principle of karma and opposed all these superstitions. In fact, he would go roaming around the graveyard on the nights when spirits were said to be at large, challenging them to appear. He said that up till his death he never encountered a single one. He was a simple-hearted, honest person. He served his father and took pity on all beings, including animals. One time he even risked his life to return a young monkey separated from its mother.

I was a real coward as a child. Who knows why, but I was mortally afraid of ghosts and spirits. My father often sat beside me and tried to bolster my courage, explaining that they were imaginary beings. When I was 6 or 7, I saw my first ghost. My grandfather used to call me *jambu beti*, Plum Girl, because I was so fond of the fruits of the rose-apple tree. He slept with me at night because I was the youngest child. One night he put me to sleep as usual, telling me to wake him up if I needed a drink of water. Feeling thirsty around midnight, I got up and went into the courtyard. There I saw a dreadful apparition. I trembled with fright, my chest pounded, my whole body broke out in a sweat. I couldn't even cry out, I was so terrified. I ran back to bed and crawled under the covers, sobbing.

Grandfather woke up, asked me what was wrong, and began to soothe me. "There's a ghost in the courtyard," I wailed. He went to the wall, removed his shirt and turban that were hanging there, and the ghost vanished. He turned on the light and hung the shirt and turban back up. Now I realized that the shadow of his clothes had created the appearance of a ghost. The next day he chided everyone, "Don't talk about ghosts and goblins in front of my flower of a child. Last night he got badly frightened."

Every day a vegetable-seller came to our lane, and I had the habit of always buying something—guavas, berries, plums, sugarcane. My mother or sister would trade for these fruits with grain, and my sister would divide the treats among us kids. I was never satisfied with getting an equal share, however, and always wanted more. My brother Motilal was a sickly child and, because of that, he often got special things to eat. This was too much for me. One day I stole a coin from my sister's box, went to the market, and bought a bunch of berries. When she found out, she dragged me outside the house, sat me down, and warned me not to move. No one was allowed to speak to me.

As the hours passed, I began to feel ashamed. When my mother didn't call me in for dinner, I felt even worse. Then it began to rain, and I got thoroughly drenched. I began bawling. Finally, my sister came and took me back into the house. She explained the whole matter to my grandfather. Very calmly he explained, "Listen, sweetie plum, I'll give you whatever you want. But you mustn't do this again." He lovingly brushed his beard against my cheeks and began to tell me a story.

Once upon a time there was a boy. He stole something for the first time, and then he stole again, and finally he became such a dangerous thief that he tried to steal from the king. This time he got caught, and the king sentenced him to hang. The boy said he wished to meet his mother before his death. The king called his mother and let them meet in private. The son shamed his mother, saying, "If you had stopped me the first time, I wouldn't have reached this point today."

Grandfather guessed my feelings and went on, "When you take something without asking, it is stealing. Now go to your sister and say you will never do that again." I ran to her, embraced her, and she forgave me. I promised never to steal again, and I kept that promise except for a couple of times. The first was in 1903 at the time of my marriage, and the other was in 1915 when I lifted a toothbrush from a shop.

The third occasion happened in childhood when I found a coin near the temple. The Jains used to celebrate a big festival called Paryushan, which lasted eight days. They went to the temple twice a day, performed circumambulations, and listened to religious discourses. For the Bhojaks, this was a time of performing *puja* and receiving the annual *dakshina*, which is given on Bhagvan Mahavir's birthday. On this important day, I went with my father to the house of worship. When the service was over, a crowd of devotees rushed to touch the feet of the chief sadhu. Working my way out, I headed for home. Just then, I found a one-paisa coin lying on the ground. I picked it up and began to look for its owner. I asked around but nobody paid any attention. I climbed up on the balcony of a big house and shouted, "Has anybody lost a coin? I've found one, it's brand new."

A striking young man came out of the house. Putting his hand on my shoulder, he said, "Listen, this isn't the way to go about it. You should hide the coin in your fist and ask if anyone has lost anything. If someone sees the coin in your hand, he'll lie and say that it is his."

"Now what should I do with the coin?" I asked.

"Look, you found it near the temple, and nobody claimed it. Go drop it in the donation box," he suggested, and he took me back through the crowd. Little did I know at the age of 7 that this youth was Mahasukhbhai Seth, and that years later after I left the theatre he would become my patron and support the establishment of the Sahitya Kala Mandal in Visnagar.[9]

No one had studied English in our family. A distant relation used to teach English in the girls' school in Visnagar. He was the first in our clan to earn a "Matric Pass" degree. Seeing his example, my father

---

[9] After retiring from the commercial stage in 1932, Jayshankar returned to Visnagar and performed in two literary plays, *Shankit Hriday* by Ramanlal Vasantlal Desai and *Rupiyanun Jhad* by Rasiklal Parikh, under the auspices of the Sahitya Kala Mandal.

wanted to educate us children. Muliben was admitted to the girls' school in 1891 when she was 7, a first for our caste. She was a very bright student and passed with good marks, winning books and silk clothes as prizes. After passing the seventh class, social pressures forced her to leave school. She got married and continued to study a little Sanskrit and Hindi, as well as Jain religion and Vedanta, on her own.

My elder brother Motilal began school in 1893, at the age of 7. He was fond of learning, did well, and was admitted to the MBBS course at Grant Medical College, Bombay. I too started school at 7, in 1896. The teacher was Hargovind Mehta, a person of distinct talents. He was world-famous for his beatings, a believer in "spare the rod and spoil the child." He kept an eagle eye on his 75 to 100 students, seated in four rows. If he saw a student talking or slacking off, he threw a small ball at him, which was a call to come up front to be beaten. He had a number of different punishments which instilled great fear in me. A strict disciplinarian, he actually wished the best for his students. If his students progressed, he was very happy, and when someone won a prize he was always proud. These things I understood only later. At the time, his application of the cane on me simply did not work.

Seeing that I was making little progress in school, my parents became somewhat displeased. I didn't understand the multiplication tables, and as a result I had no interest in them. When I had to recite the tables with the other students, I felt like I was in a dark cave. Out of fear of the beatings, I cut school. Father found out and forced me to go back. Somehow I learned my alphabets and began to read, and thus I managed to pass the first grade.

School seemed like a prison. The education imparted in that atmosphere, locked up within four walls, could produce no awakening in me. I would bunk school and go watch the sadhus perform their daily rituals near the temple. When they recited from the *Ramayan*, I approached and listened from nearby. I thought it would be great to be a sadhu.

I was very fond of listening to stories and tales. Dramas, plays, and especially Bhavai attracted me. Although I had no knowledge of music yet, I enjoyed listening and was more readily affected by music than other children my age. However, the people in my family had no notion of this.

In our neighborhood musical evenings were common. The house of Mohanlal Vaidya, a fellow Bhojak, was near ours, and whenever an artist from our caste came home on leave from the drama companies, he invited everyone for a session of music and dance. We also had frequent Bhavai performances in one part of the town. When the Ram Lila came from the city, my happiness knew no bounds. The palaces, jungles, mountains, rivers, and natural scenes painted on the stage curtains, and the kings, queens, and princes in their makeup and costumes—all seemed real to me. As the jester announced the night's performance by beating on a drum, something happened to me. I excused myself, saying I needed a drink of water, escaped from school, and roamed around following him. Then I took my seat in front of the Ram Lila canopy. I forgot school, home, hunger, thirst, everything, and just waited for nightfall when the performance would begin.

Grandfather had an acquaintance in the Ram Lila troupe, and he allowed me to see three or four plays. Then I went into the neighbor's courtyard and made a miniature stage, draping some clothes for curtains and making cutouts of a king and queen from paper. Standing in front of the curtain, I manipulated the cutouts and imitated the performance. I myself was the producer, director, and spectator.

Other important contributors to the molding of my inner actor were the skits of the Bahurupiyas, the tale of Nal and Damayanti, the picture-story of Ilachi Kumar, and the drama *Raja Harishchandra*. Bahurupiyas would come to our town, wearing unusual costumes and bringing new characters to life. When I saw them, I wanted to mimic their doings. Their method of mime was very effective, and I stared at them with awe and pleasure.

Today, when I recall those bygone stories, it seems that compared to other children my age, I was particularly susceptible to them. They washed me away in a sea of emotion. Once, at my maternal grandfather's, my father gave a recitation from Premanand's *Nalakhyan*. In the story, Nal grows suspicious of Damayanti and abandons her. Damayanti laments pitifully in the forest. Hearing her poetic appeal, I lost all emotional control. The incident came alive before my very eyes, and I let out a cry. My mother hugged me and asked, "What's the matter?" I was sobbing convulsively, everyone was worried. My uncle wondered if something had bitten me. Imagining a poisonous sting, my mother lost her wits. Finally, when I calmed down, I said nothing had bitten me, I was simply weeping with sorrow at Nal's desertion of Damayanti.

My father's gestures and expressions, his emotion-laden singing, his absorption in relating the incidents, and his expressive style—all must have affected me. I could hardly have understood the pain that Damayanti felt at this separation, but hearing her pitiful cry, "Oh Nal, oh Nal!" and seeing my father's eyes fill with tears, I was overcome. The power that an actor needs must have come from such events, or so it seems to me today.

Another deep reaction occurred when I witnessed a picture-story performance: a painted scene from the story of Ilachi Kumar that I saw in a Jain temple.[10] Father used to go there to conduct *puja* with the other Bhojaks. One time, I brought him up to the second storey and asked him about the painting. Who was this acrobat balancing on a bamboo pole? For some reason, father started to recite the entire episode in song, in a manner full of feeling, as though he were planting a seed on the soil of my boyhood. The story and its hero left a very strong impression on me. Lacking maturity, I couldn't fathom the meaning of infatuation, nor had I any notion of detachment, but I did comprehend the hero's attraction toward the acting life and what it meant to leave one's home and family and become a *nat*.

My enthusiasm for storytelling was matched by my memory. Through listening, I learned by heart many *chhappay*s and *chhand*s. We had a relative, Hathiram, who worked in Bombay, and when he came home to visit, a famous storyteller from Kutch named Haribhai Nayak was invited to our relative's to recite. He narrated the story of Padmini of Chittor or some other Rajput queen, joining all manner of subplots and discourses to the main tale. He interpolated Hindi *kavitt*s and *chhappay*s, expounding on the duties of marriage and religion. If he selected a *kavitt* from high literature, his next *chhappay*

---

[10] Ilachi Kumar is the story of a boy who falls in love with a *natni*, a female acrobat. Against the wishes of his parents, he marries her and himself becomes a *nat*. His particular act is to balance himself on a bamboo pole and perform in the air. Once, while he is performing before the king, the king gets attracted to his wife. He realizes that whereas he wants the king's money, the king, desirous of his wife, is wishing his death. At this moment he sees a monk, realizes the impermanence of all desire, and achieves a state of detachment.

would be full of wondrous miracles. The day's telling always ended on a moment of suspense, so that we had to come back to find out what happened. These *katha*s went on for approximately a month.

As a child I had the opportunity to see the dramas *Harishchandra, Mantuk Manvati,* and *Sangit Lilavati. Harishchandra* left an indelible mark on me. I will never be able to forget one particularly pathos-charged scene. Harishchandra's son Rohit, bitten by a snake, falls into a swoon; his friends weep pitifully; Rohit's mother Taramati grieves at the funeral pyre; Harishchandra, although Rohit's father, demands the death tax from Taramati. Then Rohit is lifted onto the pyre and the cremation begins. Seated in the audience, I let out a shriek and started to cry. My grandfather said this was only a play, the boy was actually alive. He took me backstage and there I saw that same Rohit laughing and changing his clothes. My grandfather introduced me to the child-actor, and to resolve my doubts the boy himself said it was all a performance. Then I was shown the pyre constructed on the stage. Subsequently the boy became my friend.

Thus, by the time I turned 9, under the influence of such incidents I spent most of my daylight hours sitting in front of drama canopies, watching rehearsals. The actors' costumes, mannerisms, and images enchanted my young mind. This must be the reason that, even before I completed the second grade, my interest in school had begun to wane.

Chapter 2: The Road to Calcutta

In the rainy season of 1898, a Parsi theatre company manager named Sakharam came to Bombay from Calcutta in search of boys. My caste fellow Balmiya Durlabhram, whom we called *kaka* or Uncle, brought him to Visnagar. Uncle must have heard about me. He summoned me in private, introduced me to Sakharam, and told me to sing. Sakharam liked my voice and asked if I wanted to work in the theatre. I said I did, but my parents would never approve. Sakharam glared at me with experienced eyes, as if sizing me up.

"Son, you say you want to work in the theatre, but you'll have to travel very far," he explained, testing my resolve. "Your parents won't be around, and you won't be able to go back home for a long time."

"Never mind," I replied decisively. "But who will explain to father?"

"Don't worry about him," Durlabh Uncle spoke up. "He'll gladly let you go."

So they met my father and told him who knows what. Perhaps they sowed the apprehension in him that I would run off. At any rate, he gave his consent, and within three or four days, at an auspicious hour, he bade me farewell and I left for Calcutta.

On the way we stopped in Bombay for a few days. For the first time ever I beheld a big city. Gas lamps on the streets, men and women from different parts, their diverse costumes—all these astounded me. The enormous harbor was fascinating. Sitting in trams running here and there, I wanted to travel forever. To my tireless eyes there could be no end to these enchanting sights.

In Bombay, Sakharam gave all of us boys an Urdu song to memorize. Because of the language, I had a hard time of it. The lyrics were something like: *kya josh men hai bari tohri yeh gulkari*. I was unable to get it completely by heart, so Sakharam dealt me two slaps, saying, "You'll get more of that from my hand if you don't learn properly." Then he showed me the bamboo cane, and I remembered my school days. I was afraid: beatings were written on my forehead, it seemed. My enthusiasm waned. However, the next day we went on a tour of the Mumbadevi temple. The natural vista of the sea coast combined with darshan of the goddess awakened a new awareness in me.

A few days later it was decided we would proceed to Calcutta. We took our seats in a big train leaving from the splendid Boribandar Station. The train was headed to Poona, and on the way were a number of tunnels. One big tunnel came along and, taking advantage of the darkness, I went and slapped Sakharam, in memory of the slap he had given me.

"Who did that? Who did that?" he jumped up, yelling. I was sitting three rows away from him. He rebuked the boy sitting in front of me, and the fellow began whimpering. Everyone fell silent. I felt bad about someone else getting the blame, but I didn't have the guts to admit my guilt.

At one station I noticed a gentleman the same height as my grandfather, wearing the same kind of turban. I started crying but Durlabh Uncle hushed me, saying it was someone else. At the next station we were told to get off the train because of an outbreak of plague in the region ahead. For a week we had to stay in local inns. I was dejected because, being curious about Calcutta, I wanted to reach it quickly.

After several more days of travel someone said we were arriving at Calcutta, and I grew happy again. Captivated, I gazed at the distant sights from the train window. Large mansions and mills with chimneys appeared as we sped rapidly toward Howrah. We disembarked at the station and were taken into the city. The enormous Howrah Bridge, its length, breadth, and magnificence, the trains running over it, the Bengali men and women—these scenes seemed uniquely pleasurable to me.

We arrived at the house we were to stay in and occupied our respective places. Setting foot in that strange building, I felt an intense longing for my parents and home. I was restless to return, in part because of those two Sakharam slaps. But now I had been thrown into captivity for years, or so I thought.

After a day of rest our examinations began. The director of the theatre company, Dadabhai Ratanji Thunthi, called each of us boy-actors to sing for him. His son Ardeshar and Sakharam were there too. When my turn came I sang a composition of my grandfather's. Dadabhai gazed at me intently as he listened, but I couldn't tell if he was pleased or not. Still, he tapped the rhythm along with the song.

After the audition he called me over, wanted my name, and asked, "So you want to learn Urdu?"

"Of course I do, if you'll teach me," I replied. That very evening he took me to see the drama *Jam-e Jahanuma* performed by his company, the Thanthaniya Natak Mandali, in Machhua Bazar.

Thus I began to learn Urdu theatre songs from the harmonium master and his disciple, the tabla player. Thunthi placed special emphasis on the original versions with the authentic ragas and *talas*. He had no compunction making us repeat a particular phrase fifty times. Early on he got very angry; he had a harsh temper. Beating was his way of teaching as though that were the only method. Sometimes the corporal punishment was very severe, unrestrained. Our raw voices did get properly trained, but we had to endure much punishment for our mistakes.

In the thirty-two months I spent in Calcutta, I learned the female companion roles within all the old dramas. Fortunately, certain Bengali actresses had just left the company, and I inherited their parts. Dadabhai coached me every afternoon, making me memorize their speeches in poetry and prose. I was fortunate to be the first of the boys to learn Urdu. My guru himself taught me the proper mode of speaking and pronouncing letters like *ain, ghain,* and *qaf,* the pinnacle of education and culture. Six months after my arrival, Dadabhai told the other boys, "See what nice Urdu Jayshankar speaks? You should all speak Urdu with him so your Urdu improves."

Dadabhai was happy with me and paid a lot of attention to my different roles. In the beginning I played bit parts as a *sakhi*. Nobody congratulated me, but if I didn't get beaten I figured I'd done well enough.

Once, I had to perform a woman's role in one of the farces. Dadabhai was delighted when he saw me dressed up as a woman and said, "You're really going to strut your stuff, aren't you?"

"Baba," I replied, "I can do a good job if you go away. With you right in front, I'll get nervous."

"Oh lord!" he laughed. "This scrap of a boy is putting me out of the theatre! Okay son, I'll leave. You'll perform then, right?" And leave he did, or at least he hid in the third-class section and watched from there. I learned this when he came backstage and complimented me at the end of the play.

Thunthi's company was strict at maintaining the rules of rehearsal. If you were five minutes late for an actual performance, you were sent back and excused, but if you missed a rehearsal, your salary was docked. Thunthi gave priority to rehearsals, and all the companies respected him for it.

Thunthi made reforms in several drama companies to maintain discipline and improve continuity on stage. He was meticulous about details—such as when to start a song, which phrases to repeat and which to perform only once, how to introduce the refrain, which patterns to use on the tabla and when. As a result, all the boys sang in complete unison, down to each trill, turn, glide, and melisma. This made a great impact on the spectators.

Rehearsals went something like this. First you learned how to speak the part, then how to sing, then how to move and use gestures and facial expressions. This was a practical method of teaching, but why was it done this way? What was the purpose behind all of this? The logic was never explained. I had to figure out the system of knowledge by myself. Thrown into the water you learn to swim; so we were taught to move our limbs, but there was no opportunity to learn the science behind it. Our training was in a way very useful, but the instruction remained incomplete.

As I developed my acting skills, my primary source of inspiration was the pleasure I felt in merging with the character. In the drama *Sitamgar*, I played Nur Alam, Sitamgar's wife.[11] This character's moment of trial comes when Sitamgar takes her to be sacrificed to the goddess, and out of love for him she silently climbs the altar. What would pass through the mind of an ideal wife at such a time? Doubtless, she would fulfill her duty and without saying a word tolerate the affront. At the time I played the role, however, it seemed that this sorry affair was happening to me, that I was becoming the victim of the knife. Such absorption in the character was my first step in the art of acting.

I began to perform on the Calcutta stage at the age of 9. Chatra and Chapla in *Chatra Bakavali*, Mehnigar in *Haman*, Aban in *Khudadad*, and Padhani in *Jam-e Jahan*—these were my first roles.[12] Here I recall one small but noteworthy incident. In *Haman* one time I played the male part of Muzaffar, but I was unable to carry off a masculine gait, and people hooted me off the stage.

In Calcutta most of the actors were Muslims, and the actresses were Bengali dancing girls. They were a very amiable lot. Subhashini, who was my age, performed with me in the companion role. These actresses all had their mothers and servants to look after them. Ascharya's mother Lakkhi Auntie was very kind-hearted. Charmed

---

[11] *Sitamgar* was commissioned by Thunthi when he became director of the Elphinstone Dramatic Club in 1874. Edalji Khori was contracted to compose the drama, and Thunthi played the part of Sitamgar himself. Khori's play was in Gujarati; presumably the play had been translated into Urdu for the Calcutta performance.

[12] Since Murad had been hired by Thunthi and they worked together in the 1880s, it is likely that the versions of these plays in which Jayshankar performed were Murad's.

by my innocent face and pretty voice, she would put me in her lap and say to Ascharya in Bengali, "Look at him, such a nice boy! How could his mother bear to send him alone all the way to Calcutta?" She brought sweets for me and fed me in private. Though I lived far from my mother, I still received maternal love.

It had been several months since I left my parents, and I missed them a great deal. Every caning following little mistakes made me want to run back home. With my childlike wisdom I figured that I could flee Calcutta and walk along the railway track, reaching Visnagar in a month or two. I would rest at night in huts along the rail line, beg for food, and walk all day. This was my fantasy, but I never carried out the plan.

Sunday was our day off, and we went on outings to the Dharmatolla *maidan* with Durlabhram Uncle. It was about three-quarters of a mile from our Machhua Bazar playhouse. Late at night after a performance, we would stroll under the fragrant *maulsiri* trees. I was fond of flowers and gathered fallen blossoms in my *dhoti*. An old Jewish gentleman was a regular at the shows, and he always presented a garland of roses to the leading actor. One time I had the lead, and I got a rose garland too. I loved the red, yellow, and pink roses, and took them home to scatter on my bedding.

The house had three storeys with a little garden in front. There were two rooms on the ground floor and a large courtyard with a small tank in the middle. Beyond the courtyard were two more rooms. Then came the stairs to the upper floors. The first floor was for the directors, on the third floor was the kitchen, and in front of it a terrace. We newly arrived boy-actors stayed on the lowest level. Six or seven of us had our bedding spread out in one room. Attached to that was our kitchen. In front to the right was the room where Sakharam stayed with his family.

Our food arrangements were managed by Durlabhram Uncle. He made our tea and breakfast in the morning, rice, dal, sabzi, and roti for lunch, and *bhakri* and sabzi at night. Sometimes on festival days he made sweets for us kids. We had to wash the cooking vessels ourselves. The days were divided among us; whoever had his turn had to sweep the room and wash up the lunch and supper dishes. I don't know why, but I truly hated this work. For a few months I did my chores, and then I saved up from my salary and paid the other boys to do my chores for me.

Our salaries were very low. At most, a boy received ten or twelve rupees a month. My salary was fixed at six rupees. Our company mainly performed second-run dramas, and that's why profits were not very good. Nevertheless, we got our pay on the designated date. Aside from salary, each boy received a year's supply of clothing—three kurta sets, three underwear sets, a velvet Parsi cap, three dhotis, and an umbrella, plus a warm blanket or cotton quilt, mattress, and pillows.

In Calcutta plays were performed even during the monsoon and winter months. The daily routine of us boys was as follows. We got up at 7:00, had tea and breakfast, bathed, washed our clothes, and at 8:30 or 9:00 went to rehearsal. At 12:30 we had lunch and then we got two hours to rest. At 3:00 or 3:30, Dadabhai set up an armchair in front of the house and had us all sit around him. There we discussed matters related to the drama, rehearsals, and training. In the evening at 6:00 or 6:30, we had dinner. After that, we spent the night from 8:30 till 2:00 a.m. in the playhouse. We came back home at 2:30 or 3:00 and went to bed.

Our house was quite far from the playhouse. For this reason, the company took a second house in a lane in Machhua Bazar, and we shifted there. This too was a three-storey building with arrangements like the first, but with an open, green backyard where we enjoyed playing. After moving in there we got an opportunity to attend the Minerva, Star, and other theatres.

In those days actors and actresses had their separate dressing rooms, each with three or four large mirrors illuminated by lamps. A wide-mouthed water vessel and four separate cups of color were kept nearby: white zinc powder with a little red and yellow mixed in; pure red; pure yellow; in the fourth black, and next to that a tube of red lipstick. These were the primary ingredients of our makeup. Each actor started by mixing water with the whitish powder in the palm of his left hand, then applying it to his face and neck. Similarly he rubbed a red paste onto his cheeks and then shaded the area around his eyes with a mixture of black, red, and yellow. He accented his lips with lipstick and applied *kajal* (kohl) to his eyebrows and eyelids. As needed he colored his hands and feet too. Then he put on his costume, wig, and jewelry. The actresses dressed their hair and adorned it with flowers. These preparations took an hour or two.

Later oil-based makeup was introduced. This paint was relatively expensive but more natural in appearance. The Maharashtrian drama companies kept skin-colored oil paint in a little kit. All the actors and actresses applied it and then touched up with a powder puff. They used more yellow than the Gujarati companies, so it made their skin tone appear more Indian.

The lighting system in the Thanthaniya Theatre was very simple. Electric lights and petromax lanterns had not yet been invented. As in all the theatres in Calcutta, we used ordinary gas lamps. An iron pipe stretched across the apron of the stage with five or six holes at intervals. At one end of the pipe a switch started the flow of gas, and lights were lit at the various holes. There was another thin pipe with four or five holes which was used for dimly lit scenes. When bright light was needed, the big pipe was suddenly switched on and the whole stage illuminated. Metal mesh covered each light to prevent accidents, and a tin barrier that stretched across the stage shielded the audience from the glare. A similar pipe was attached at the upper part of the stage to light up the faces of the actors. Caution was essential to make sure that the curtains did not catch fire. Sometimes colored lamps were used for special effects.

The auditorium had four seating areas with ticket prices of Rs 1.5, 1.0, 0.75, and 0.25. There was a little open space between the hall and the stage where the musicians sat. Below the stage was a deep tunnel or basement; here, all the scenery and props were kept. The stage floor was made of equal-sized wooden platforms covered with a dark, thick jute carpet. The ceiling over the stage was supported by four columns on each side extending from the basement to the roof. The size of the stage varied but it was a rectangle, formed by the space in between these columns. Side wings were used to block the view of the columns, and fringes at the top of the stage hid the bamboo scaffolding and lighting pipes.

The entire stage was divided into four zones. Each had a painted backdrop curtain which was raised or drawn aside to show the scene behind it. Depending upon the episode, painted columns, flower pots, trees, fountains, scenes of palaces, staircases, thrones were added to construct the scenes. In all the dramas, while one scene was playing another scene was being set up behind the curtain.

During my stay in Calcutta I hardly saw another Gujarati person, and this made me even more homesick. I was always on the lookout for Gujaratis and longed to see my family members. One Sunday I spotted an old turbaned gentleman with a walking stick. I ran up to him and wrapped my arms around him. Startled, he asked me who I was and what I wanted. I explained where I was from and what I was doing, and he took me to a sweetshop where he bought me some treats. I never learned who he was, but perhaps he felt the same pull toward me as a Gujarati that I felt toward him.

It so happened that a shopkeeper in our neighborhood found a telegram addressed to me. Reading it, I was shocked and saddened. My father had taken ill and wanted me to return to Visnagar immediately. The theatre bosses hadn't conveyed this news, in fact they had torn up the telegram, and the shopkeeper had found the scraps. I was very angry with them and my feelings were hurt by this incident, but I couldn't say anything.

Meanwhile our company management had changed. Dadabhai grew old and turned the company over to Ardeshar, Sakharam, and his partner Jamshed Kapadia. Then he retired to Bombay. Several times during our lessons, he had mentioned his intentions as if to prepare me for the future. He had given me much advice and honed my talents as a developing actor. "Son, for your own good, I've thrashed you now and then," he said as he hugged me. "You'll understand the benefit of that when you become a famous artist. I'm not a wealthy man. What can I give you as a farewell present? Take this ten rupees as a reward and think of it as ten thousand or ten lakhs. This is Dadabhai's word: go, my son, and flourish." Then he left Calcutta and went to Bombay.

The new boss, Jamshed Kapadia, liked me a lot too. Out of affection he called me his son Jahangir and after dinner always accepted *pan* from my hand. I told him about the telegram and requested permission to visit my father. He explained it to the other partners and granted me leave, but he made me promise to come back to Calcutta within a month. I promised to return without in the least wanting to.

Years later when I ran into Kapadia at Churchgate in Bombay, I regretted breaking my promise. By that time I had been given the title "Sundari" by the Gujarati Natak Mandali. Approaching him I paid my respects, then asked about his drama company. With a sad heart but chuckling he replied, "Jayshankar, that Ardeshar didn't treat me right. I left the company long back. Now I live here in Bombay."

"I'm still your son Jahangir," I said. "I'm sorry I couldn't fulfill my promise to you."

"Never mind, son, never mind. Those are old matters, let's forget them. Everything is forgiven." I will always remember his generosity.

In that way, I left Calcutta for Visnagar. My father's health, it turned out, was all right. When I returned home, my mother organized a big celebration, went on a fast, and did a *puja*. Father offered a special cloth-piece to the goddess Amba. He could hardly contain himself: his son had returned after more than two years. All the while I was in Calcutta, father had fasted on Ekadashi and mother on Ashtami. Their days of separation from their son had been spent in penance.

Chapter 3: Sundari of the Gaiety

When I returned to Visnagar, my spoken language had acquired a Parsi accent. I looked different from my family with my pants, long coat, and velvet cap. Back home I felt a new interest in studying. I pleaded with my father to admit me to the second class, and Master Hiralal of the Golvad school started teaching me.

Bapulal Amritlal Bhojak was the son of a distant uncle of mine.[13] He was a little older than me and worked in the theatre. He had developed good relations with the music aficionados of Visnagar. A harmonium player lived near the municipality building, and we would all congregate at his place in the mornings and evenings to practice together. Because I had just arrived they wanted to hear me sing the latest songs, and we had good sessions together.

These enthusiasts would all go to Ahmedabad to see the plays of the Shri Desi Natak Samaj, the troupe of Dahyabhai Dholshaji. They started taking me along. I had to give some excuse to my father in

---

[13] Bapulal Amritlal Bhojak is apparently not the same person as Bapulal Nayak, the older actor whom Jayshankar meets later in the chapter.

order to get away, so we developed a code. I would get a letter from Ahmedabad saying, "Dhotis with lace borders have arrived from the mill; come if you want to buy them." This meant that a new play had opened in the Desi Natak Samaj.

I went to Ahmedabad regularly, and my friends bought my ticket. One time I went backstage to meet my relation from Umta, Pransukh Harichand Nayak. He was playing the main role, and when he saw me he insisted on refunding the price of my ticket. This recognition benefited my friends too. Now they had somebody to reserve their seats for them. Pransukh, also known as Eddie Polo, was quite a famous artist. His glowing face was large and fair, and he had a unique talent for putting on makeup.

Keshavlal Shivram Adhyapak, the original founder of the Desi Natak Samaj and the author of the drama *Sangit Lilavati*, was related to me as a *phupha*, the husband of my father's sister.[14] He found out that I was coming to Ahmedabad and frequenting the theatre. He was of the opinion that I should get admitted to some good drama company since I was not likely to go far in school. When he saw me roaming around Ahmedabad, he threatened to tell my father. This made me devote myself once more to my studies, but only for a short while. Soon I resumed going to Ahmedabad to watch plays. Dahyabhai Dholshaji invited me to attend a rehearsal, and then asked me to audition. Pleased with my voice, he offered me a salary of twenty rupees per month.

Meanwhile, without my knowledge, Keshavlal Phupha wrote to several Bombay companies on my behalf, and a couple of the Parsi ones wrote back with offers. Keshavlal went to Visnagar without telling me and got my parents' consent to enroll me in the Mumbai Gujarati Natak Mandali. He chose this company after due consideration, although I didn't fully appreciate it at the time. He and Dahyabhai were partners in the Desi Natak Samaj, and he didn't want me in it.

I left Ahmedabad for Visnagar. A few days later Phupha came to Visnagar and took my mother and me back with him to Ahmedabad. The whole way in the train he talked about my brilliant future. His

---

[14] It is not clear whether Keshavlal was a true *phupha* or a distant "uncle" like so many older caste-fellows in Jayshankar's narrative.

main theme was how artists should protect their character and maintain their modesty, and how those who did not created so much trouble. The whole speech was illustrated with names and details, as if he were explaining everything to a bride going to her in-laws for the first time.

The next morning Phupha took me to meet someone special. As I entered the house, I saw a radiant personage whose large, sensitive eyes seemed to be appraising me. The gentleman asked me to sing and I complied. Then he passed his hand over my throat to see how many years were left before my voice changed. He requested that I recite an Urdu dialogue, and when I did it made him very happy. The one who was testing me was none other than Bapulal Nayak. Who knew that in the coming years Bapulal and I were to become a famous team.

Bapulal fixed my salary at twenty-five rupees and relayed this news to my mother. For her part, she demanded special conditions for my maintenance. "*Bhai* Bapulal,[15] the boy must take his meals with the management, and you'll have to lodge him separately from the other boys in the company. You must also make arrangements for his education. Even if you reduce his salary by five rupees, these terms must be met," she insisted.

That very night we left by train for Bombay. Shri Bapulal traveled second class, and I went with my caste brothers in the third. The time in the train passed pleasantly in joking and fooling around. Then it became night, and I was asleep before I knew it. The next morning Bapulal Mama came and got me off the train. He hired a porter to carry my luggage, and we departed for the Gaiety Theatre.

It was May 18, 1901, when I first set foot in the Gaiety. This was the same Gaiety that would prove to be a milestone in my life. Just walking into it filled me with excitement. The joy and delight that arise on seeing a familiar place welled up in me at first sight, and I was ecstatic. When I spotted the stage my feet wanted to dance, the desire to act surged in every limb. A vision of times to come swam before my eyes. The magnificent stage, the rumbling of applause, the

---

[15] Jayshankar's mother addresses Bapulal as her "brother," and in the rest of this passage Jayshankar refers to Bapulal as his *mama*, mother's brother or maternal uncle.

18. Gaiety Theatre, now Capitol Cinema

form of a woman taking shape! My soul was yearning to take on the features of a Gujarati lady.

What is this that happened without my knowledge? What was the nature of the spontaneous pleasure my actor-soul felt? The Gaiety would bring me fame, the Gaiety would bring me gold medals. The Gaiety would satisfy the hearts of thousands of Gujaratis, and one day I would have to leave the Gaiety. Here in the Gaiety, one role I enacted would be joined to me forever.

May 18, 1901: on that day there was a lunar eclipse. After morning ablutions, we arrived in the sitting room of the second partner-owner, Patel Maganlal Mulchand Seth.[16] Dayashankar Vasanji Girnara, the founding partner of the company, then entered the room. When he saw me he asked, "Is this boy willing to work?"

Bapulal Mama said that I was. Then a harmonium was sent for,

---

[16] Maganlal's colleague in financing the company, and the "first partner-owner" implied in this passage, was Patel Chhotalal Mulchand Kapadia, with whose family Jayshankar boarded for many years. In ch. 8, the two are called brothers.

19. Dayashankar Girnara

and I sang some lyrics from Thunthi's drama *Haman*: *mera gham ka tarana suniye*. Dayashankar praised my clear language and voice. "When this drama *Haman* opened, I was working for Dadabhai Thunthi," he explained. "I used to play the part of Hammala, and I still remember all the songs. Is it true you're a disciple of Dadabhai? If so then we're *gurubhai*s. That's good!"

Bapulal Mama scolded me, saying, "You'll have to work hard on your Gujarati. Your Calcutta Urdu won't get you very far here. Are you going to put in the effort?"

I nodded. Dayashankar, using gestures I didn't understand, asked Mama about my salary. Mama held both palms up and showed ten fingers four times and then two more, indicating forty-two rupees. Dayashankar however decided on twenty rupees.

In the middle of all this, while Bapulal Mama was bringing me to Bombay, Phupha Keshavlal was gently remonstrating with his old partner Dahyabhai. "What's wrong with you? For five rupees you let a talented boy slip away. Bapulal is taking him to Bombay tonight." In truth it was Keshavlal who didn't want me there in Ahmedabad.

Dahyabhai deeply regretted his decision, or so I learned later. Just as the Mumbai Gujarati Natak Mandali premiered its drama *Saubhagya Sundari*, the Desi Natak Samaj Mandali arrived in Bombay with a new play, and Dahyabhai sent me a message. "There's still a place for you in our company. If you come and join us, I'll be very pleased."

I didn't like the idea of leaving one company for another right after joining it. That would be a breach of promise, and the Mumbai Gujarati Natak Mandali people were treating me well. We all lived as one family. My food and lodging were arranged at the home of the bosses. I was kept separate from the other boys. When I thought about it later, I realized that the terms my mother had fixed were a blessing for the management. This way no outside person could meet me, tempt me with an offer of a higher salary, and take me away to another company. Thus I was raised with the *seth*'s family and his nephews.

Following company rules, I went to rehearsals in the morning at 8:30. All the actors sat on benches onstage in a semi-circle with their backs toward the audience. In the middle sat our instructor, Bapulal, on a chair. Just as in Dadabhai's rehearsals, here too all the actors had to beat the rhythm with the singing. Each actor had to memorize every role, so that if one of them was absent another could play his part. After an hour and a half of rehearsal there was a break for ten minutes. Rehearsals went on till 12:00 or 12:30.

The prompter for each play kept a mistake book in which all the errors as well as the stage cues were written down: whose costume was torn or dirty, whose buttons were open, where changes in the scenery were required, where lights had to be lit, when to sound a loud crack. On the next day during the break the mistake book was read out loud in front of everyone. Whoever had made a mistake received direction or punishment right then. The result was that the next day, the error was corrected. Dadabhai and the Parsis had started this form of discipline, and all the Urdu and Gujarati companies observed it.

I had already worked in Dadabhai's company so I didn't need much guidance. In a very disciplined manner I sat as told next to Bapulal's chair. One advantage of this was I got a chance to comprehend the subtlety of the realistic acting style he imparted. Later, this system of seating was changed. Some actors went and sat on chairs in the hall, and one by one they came on stage to play their parts.

An old drama, *Saubhagya Sundari* by the poet Nathuram Sundar Shukla, was then playing. After I joined the company Mulshankar Mulani began to revise this drama along the lines of *Vikram Charitra*, his successful first drama. He was also thinking how I would represent this new character of Sundari. As the scenes were rewritten one by one, they were sent to us and Bapulal directed them.

The music department was led by another of my distant uncles, Pandit Vadilal Shivram Nayak, who was a disciple of Bhatkhande. I had no way of knowing that Vadilal Mama would become my music guru and a well-wisher of our family. Vadilal Mama taught me the songs for the role of Sundari and rehearsed me in the pure pronunciation of Gujarati. During rehearsals my teachers corrected the slightest traces of Urdu and Parsi Gujarati evident in my speech. If the meanings of the words had also been explained to me, I would have advanced rapidly, but as it had been in the Urdu company, here too the parts were rehearsed in an artificial way emphasizing only rote learning. At least in comparison with the Urdu company, the acting technique was clearer and more effective.

I attended all the old dramas, observing the actors in minute detail. This enabled me to develop my own tastes, likes, and dislikes. Among the younger actors Govind Nayak Lakhvadvala's portrayal of Indumati in *Vikram Charitra* most affected me. Samant Kalani's performance of the milkmaid Rambha did not impress me at all.

During this time I developed a relationship with another artist, Mohan Lala. He was always with Maganlal, one of the partners. They used to pass time together in a room on the second floor, and I often went to join them. For some reason they welcomed me from the start. They understood that I had been chosen as the artist to replace Samant Kalani, and they wanted to befriend me. Mohan Lala was playing the part of Madhav alongside me in *Saubhagya Sundari*. We were thus the two main performers in this famous drama. Even after we parted, our bonds of affection remained until his death.

Some time later my parents and brother left Visnagar because of the plague and came to Bombay to stay with me. Their meals were prepared in the company's kitchen, and they lived in a separate room. Father used to perform *puja* at a Jain temple in the city. One day, he encountered my old boss's son, Ardeshar Thunthi. Ardeshar tried to inveigle him, and a hefty sum of money must have been involved. Thunthi probably argued that I had eaten his salt and apprenticed with his company, and I owed it to him to return. This must have convinced father to take his side. He went straight to the owners of the Mumbai Gujarati Natak Mandali and said, "I'm being offered Rs 2000. Why should I keep my son with you?"

When I heard this I was extremely irritated. I had no desire whatsoever to return to the old company. I was receiving much better instruction in acting now, and the Gujarati bosses were treating me very well. My lack of willingness to leave the Mumbai company presented an obstacle to my father's desires. He did however get my bosses to promise that they would give me the Rs 2000 in some form or another.

Nevertheless father was not content to leave this direct benefit until some future time. In the tug-of-war, my health deteriorated. My bosses sent me to some very good doctors and took proper care of me, and I quickly improved.

Meanwhile, father had consulted a prosperous merchant, Gokalbhai Mulchand, who was thoughtful and practical. He posed an appropriate question, "What does the boy want?"

Father replied, "He refuses to go to Calcutta."

Emphasizing this fact, the *seth* advised, "You will lose your son in this struggle if you're not careful. This company of vegetarian Gujarati businessmen is better than that non-vegetarian Parsi one. I know Seth Chhotalal; he has a cloth shop in Jetha Bazaar. Why don't you have the company owners promise me that they'll pay up at the time of your son's marriage. Because I'm a businessman, they won't forfeit their promise."

My father liked this idea. Seth Chhotalal met Seth Gokalbhai Mulchand, and they discussed the amount offered as an incentive by the Parsis. Chhotalal promised that he would give Rs 2000 at my *lagan* ceremony, and Gokalbhai told my father, "Look, Seth Chhotalal is a businessman and a gentleman. He won't renege on his word. I'm the one responsible for the Rs 2000. If he doesn't pay it, I will." In this way Gokalbhai resolved the difficulty, and I was immensely relieved.

A few days before the opening of *Saubhagya Sundari* the company's expert artist, Louis, was painting the curtains while I kept close watch. The curtain for the first act depicted a fair that appeared to be taking place for miles around. In the foreground a person was running toward the fair. My childlike mentality didn't like the eyes of this person, so, taking advantage of the painter's absence I took a brush, dabbed it with yellow paint, and added two spots for the pupils. Now I considered the picture complete.

The capable Louis immediately noticed and scolding his helper asked, "Who made this change?"

"That boy who roams around here—he did it," came the reply.

Louis came over to me, smoking his cheroot, and asked, "Are you a painter? Where did you learn to paint? Do you know anything about it?"

"No," I replied.

"Then why did you change this curtain?" he asked. In my panic no words came out, but before I could confess my error he patted me on the shoulder and said, "Don't do these childish things any more. Look, I'll explain it to you."

Saying this he took me and stood at a little distance from the painting, remarking, "If these eyes looked a little brighter, they would pull the viewer's attention away from the rest of the picture, right? But we want to show all parts of the picture equally. That's why I painted this man's pupils in a pale color." Thus Louis Saheb gave me my first lesson in art.

After Louis's death I witnessed the artistry of several painters, including Dinshah Irani, who became my good friend. He spent a large portion of his salary on art books, and showing them to me he explained the conventions of painting. Dinshah painted two color portraits of me, one of which is still in my living room, keeping his memory alive.

The owners planned the debut of *Saubhagya Sundari* for Deepavali, and the first show therefore occurred on October 19, 1901. I was nervous before I went on stage. My costume was entirely different from the ones I had worn in Calcutta. The sari-end kept slipping from my head, making me halt and lose my concentration. I had to keep the sari in place in order to express the character's traits, and I was torn between fixing the head-cover and delivering my dialogue. My head began to spin, my body was burning. I was very worried about how the role was going.

When everyone clapped after the first song, my fear began to fade. After a few more dialogues it vanished completely. From then on I was swept away in the flow of the drama, and the audience too wanted to drown in the delight of it all. When the performance ended I stayed for three-quarters of an hour to listen to congratulations showered on me by the audience and the owners.

This was the first victory of the instruction I had received. Some of the fame was due to the songs and my musical training, and the rest to my voice and appearance. My intelligence played no part whatsoever. I had no idea what the role was to which people were reacting so positively. I kept wondering about the fundamental reason for their praise. Slowly I awakened to the realization that I had a responsibility, that I could obtain the power of comprehension. But how could I fulfill this obligation? I became engrossed in absorbing knowledge from whatever sources I could discover.

One day a Bohra *seth* named Fazal Husain Kunthavala presented Bapulal and me each with a pair of binoculars. Binoculars were very expensive at the time, and highly valued. I was surprised to see my name engraved on a pair. Fazal Husain said he'd specially ordered them from England so that I could view the subtle nuances on the actors' faces and bring them into my own acting. Fazal Husain also ordered picture books to help me train for the stage. Two books showed the different provinces of India, the famous places, and the characteristic attitudes of women. He also ordered subscriptions to *The Tatler* and *The Sketch* containing reviews of Shakespeare and other European playwrights, pictures of actors in various poses, and details of lighting systems and stage production. However, all this was in English, and I needed someone to interpret them. The binoculars by contrast I could fully utilize. I used them to look out my window at faraway scenes. Men and women on the street, modes of transportation—all this I examined and thus made good use of my free time.

A Bengali gentleman, Narendranath Ghosh, also came to see me in the Gaiety. With emotion he praised my performance and described the plots of various Bengali dramas. He told me I should learn English, that it was necessary for advancement in the world and for my personal development. I had no time to enroll in school to learn English, therefore he appointed a tutor and paid his fees. I asked the tutor to read from English plays and explain their meaning, and I started to make progress with English drama. Gradually I began to understand something of Shakespeare's classics, *Romeo and Juliet, The Merchant of Venice, Hamlet, Othello,* and *King Lear*. I ordered some Gujarati translations of Shakespeare and got hold of a Marathi translation of *Hamlet*. And what was the reason behind that Bengali gentleman's affection for me? I learned later that Sundari's facial features, her voice, her love-filled eyes, her bodily perfection—in all of these he saw his own beloved. Sundari's face was just like hers.

During this time my relations with my music teacher were also deepening. I was inspired by Pandit Vadilal to learn the techniques of creating *rasa* in a musical drama. About half the songs in *Saubhagya Sundari* were sung by me. I called on my teacher every morning and evening, and my voice gradually developed a greater capacity and tunefulness. Enchanted by his vocal style and way of joining words to tune, I made every attempt to imitate him.

One morning, Bapulal and I went for a walk along Chowpatty. He told me he had stayed up all night reading the fourth installment of

Sarasvatichandra, which had just come out. He agreed to loan me the first part, and I started reading the novel. I read the entire work seven times, such was its magic. The lofty diction, intimate love relationships, pain of separation, political and social conditions, and secondary stories woven into the larger tale—countless scenes of Gujarati life were painted before my eyes.

I was extremely influenced by the character of Kumud Sundari, although in fact all the female characters left an indelible imprint on my mind. The image of these characters' femininity penetrated deep into my being. It seemed as if the Sundari I was in search of was portrayed in every page of this novel. I developed a new method of studying the book. Standing in front of a mirror I read out loud the descriptions of the characters and tried to bring their moods and expressions to life.

During this practice I felt a deep urge to portray Kumud Sundari. Our company requested Govardhanram, the novel's author, to produce a stage adaptation. Photographs of Bapulal as Sarasvatichandra and myself as Kumud Sundari were requested for the novel's cover, but our bosses did not comply. A little while later we received the first part of Govardhan's adaptation. For some unknown reason our company owners felt that it would not go over well with the Bombay audience. They didn't encourage the development of this drama, and my ambition to play Kumud remained unfulfilled.

In the time I had, I read short novels, poems, essays, and literary books in Gujarati. I gradually became more educated and was better able to resolve the problems that arose in my acting. To make the role of *Saubhagya Sundari* more vivid, I practised the parts of Shakespeare's Desdemona and Bhavabhuti's Malati, and within six months I began to play the role of Sundari with greater understanding.

Women in society imitated Sundari—this is absolutely true. But how did it happen? I learned to construct my art from my sisters whom I read about in novels and saw in society. I attached a bit of my own knowledge and then presented their picture before the public. People considered the image of Sundari an artistic reproduction and accepted it. Women would be strolling on Chowpatty while I walked by or drove in a car with my friends, and one would blurt out, "Look, look! There goes Sundari." Consuming me with their eyes, they would try to get their fill of me while laughing irrepressibly. I too would smile a bit. They would talk with their friends and try, usually unsuccessfully, to imitate the gestures of Sundari. Then I would chuckle politely, feeling satisfaction and a little charge inside. This is the victory of the stage, I often told myself.

When *Saubhagya Sundari* opened, many spectators came to congratulate me and present awards. I sensed that people were admiring the womanly sentiments that I portrayed rather than praising me alone. They came again and again to see those fine emotions. Behind my success there may also have been something of divine favor. At the moment when Jayshankar first attired himself in a *choli* and *lahanga*, he was transformed into a woman, or rather into the artistic form that expresses the feminine sensibility. A beautiful young female revealed herself inside me. Her shapely, intoxicating youth sparkled. Her feminine charm radiated fragrance. She had an easy grace in her eyes, and in her gait was the glory of Gujarat. She was not a man, she was a woman. An image such as this was the one I saw in the mirror.

My inner voice seemed to be asking, who is this, who am I seeing? Was it Saubhagya Sundari or Kumud Sundari or a reflection of what lay within me? It was not Jayshankar, it was a modest, proud Gujaratin. Her manner, her gestures, her sensuality shone in every limb of my body. A sweet tingling arose for a moment and then vanished, and for that instant I felt as though I was not a man. Initially, I felt some hesitation, but now it seemed to me that I truly was a woman. In this process of impersonating women, my experience as an actor would not have been possible without my spectators. My thousands of viewers made me Sundari, I say this today with pride. Without my appreciative audience, I would only be a lone Jayshankar.

A report providing evidence of the success of *Saubhagya Sundari* was published in Volume 1, Number 1 of the late Vibhakar's quarterly magazine, *Rangbhumi*. Not to praise myself but as a factual document I quote it herewith:

> At that time, all of Bombay was infatuated with Sundari. This Sundari threw female society into a commotion. Women's gait was altered, their style of dressing changed. Makeup and ornamentation, gestures, mannerisms, and tastes changed. The alluring poses of young girls changed. In brief the dress and image of Bombay women changed. If

anyone taught women how to move, to perform, to show off, to flirt, it was first and foremost our shining Sundari. But let me say something more personal. Many puritanical moralists here complain that it was Sundari of the Gaiety who spoiled the climate of Bombay and led people to their ruin. And yet there is no dearth of such moralists eagerly going off to watch Sundari, who don't miss a play of his, and who would not dream of passing up a chance to see him.

Chapter 4: The Seductive Milkmaid

The theatre company made a good profit from *Saubhagya Sundari*, and Bapulal planned to revive the company's earlier dramas with myself in the main roles. Seth Gopaldas took us to Matheran for a break, and there Bapulal rehearsed me for the part of Rambha, the milkmaid in *Vikram Charitra*. The drama was presented before the Bombay public on November 12, 1901.

I had been watching the old dramas since I joined the company: *Vikram Charitra, Jayraj, Rajbij, Mulraj Solanki*. Bapulal's direction and the acting of Tribhuvan Kothari and Govind Lakhvadvala seemed powerful and heart-rending in each. When I got the opportunity to play Rambha, I tried to join my own viewpoint to the role. I became a coy seductress when I approached my husband, Rajratan, in the guise of a milkmaid. First with womanly gestures I charmed him, and when he was charmed I rejected him. Then I charmed him some more and rejected him some more, until he was distraught. In the end I became helpless and overcome by attraction. Behaving as if without recourse, I submitted to Rajratan's demands and surrendered. These blandishments I placed in ascending order and wove them into my acting.

Some people who saw the drama called it obscene or excessively erotic. If I were to refute that comment today, I would simply ask: what is the harm if the actor, staying within propriety, acts out the degree of eroticism introduced by the playwright himself? After all, drama is a picture of the world as it is. I propose that rather than showing false arrogance and acting moralistic, it is better to display what's real in its artistic form.

After attracting prince Rajratan with her youthful beauty, Rambha seduces him and then has a son. When Raja Vikram hears this, he wants to know the truth and calls Rambha to his court. As Rambha I made a grand entry, putting the other actors on the sidelines. To show that Vikram held the status of a father-in-law, I answered his questions with due formality.

Rambha interrogates Rajratan, "My lord, tell the truth, am I guilty?"

Rajratan answers, "A million times guilty." Using facial gestures, I let my thoughts be known, namely, that first he made love to me, and now he refuses to admit the truth. The spectators laughed out loud. The secret of the prince's untruthfulness was thereby exposed. As Rambha I released my anger, and the prince bowed his head with shame. Then a song began: *nazar karo nath zara pahchan lo nari ko.* In this way, Raja Vikram realized that Rambha was innocent. Another song from this drama, *koi dudh liyo dilrangi,* became very famous and was on everyone's tongue. Many cloth mills printed the lyrics on the borders of their saris and dhotis.

Next, Bapulal Nayak gave me the role of Shirin in the company's *Dagh-e Hasrat* or *Shirin Farhad.* This time he retained the old mannerisms in order to take full advantage of my melodious voice. Certain new songs were added. My high level of Urdu helped the drama to succeed. The play was so popular that every Monday the playhouse was sold out. We performed *Saubhagya Sundari* on Saturday, *Vikram Charitra* on Sunday, and *Dagh-e Hasrat* on Monday. These three plays earned a good profit for the company. *Dagh-e Hasrat* opened in the Gaiety on December 16, 1901.

In the romance of Shirin and Farhad, earthly love is transfigured into spiritual love. The role of Farhad is central, and Bapulal performed it most effectively. The heroine Shirin is a passive character who subjects herself to the desires and ambitions of others. There are only two situations in which Shirin acts to fulfill her own objectives. The first is when she takes on the guise of a faqir and goes to meet Farhad on the mountain. The second is when she hears of the death of Farhad, goes to his tomb, and prays to God to enter it. As I was performing this role, it was not enough to simply follow the wishes of others, rather I had to imagine the sequence of events. Should I bow my head before the king? Or go meet Farhad according to my own wishes? I followed my conscience in this choice. Shirin was attracted by the splendor of the king, but when she felt the force of Farhad's sacrifice, true love blossomed in her. As an actor, I kept in mind the difference between these two situations when performing.

After this, Bapulal proposed introducing the drama *Jugal Jugari*. We rehearsed it even as Mulshankar Mulani was writing new scenes. My acting ability was increasing in ways both intellectual and practical. I was powerfully affected by the heroine Lalita, my mind saturated with her role. In the play the husband, who once dearly loved Lalita, becomes so addicted to gambling that he doesn't even want to look at his wife. Not only that, he tricks her and gets her to sign over the money saved for their child. Thinking about this story, during rehearsals my eyes welled up on their own. By the end of the scene it was difficult for me to utter a word. I stopped reciting and sat down on a chair in a fit of emotion. Bapulal encouraged me to try to communicate my intense feelings to the audience. It was the duty of the actor, he explained, to produce an emotional effect upon the spectator.

I got the opportunity to interact with elite families and observe them first-hand in the company of Babubhai Seth. I visited him often when he stayed in Andheri. Through this I learned the difference between highly educated and ordinary people. One day, I found the ideal model for the role of Lalita in *Jugal Jugari*. A girl who was about to be married to a close relative came to meet Babubhai. Babubhai and his wife Krishnaben welcomed her with the appropriate hospitality. Accepting their greeting, modesty rippled across the girl's face. She continued to smile, yet restrained herself in accord with etiquette. This situation seemed to present a model for the scene of the first meeting between Jugal and Lalita.

I was extremely impressed by this girl's attire and elegant manner of dressing, but above all by her behavior. I wanted to talk with her, get to know her. I needed to learn many things. After a couple of days, we grew bold enough to converse. One afternoon, in the drawing room, she was fastening the sleeve-band of her blouse. I happened to enter just then and asked, "Sister, where do you get your blouses stitched? Will you tell me your tailor's name? This color of ribbon suits your blouse wonderfully. You have excellent taste." At this she smiled and, without further ado, wrote down the name and address of her tailor.

She couldn't imagine even in her dreams that I was inspecting her for my performance on stage. Her smiling face, her modesty, her open manner of replying—I was going to put all of this precisely into the character of Lalita. Over a couple of days of observation I learned a great deal about how to formulate the role.

After rehearsals were over, *Jugal Jugari* opened on July 26, 1902. Shri Babubhai sat in the front row with his family and friends. When the play ended, he stayed behind to give Bapulal and me his opinion. The drama had made a profound impact on him. Krishnaben said, "This Lalita is exactly like our Gulab—the same laugh, the same way of speaking, and the same manner of dress. I was under the illusion that our Gulab had somehow made it to the stage."

Educated Parsis and Hindus were especially affected by *Jugal Jugari*. The newspaper *Sanjh Vartaman* praised it, suggesting that Parsi company owners should see it and learn what acting was really all about. This advice was taken to heart by the leading actors and managers. The late Seth Kavasji Khatau, Seth Balivala, Hormasji Tantra, and the Jewish actress Miss Gauhar—all saw the play several times and admired it.

I'll give an example of the large-heartedness of the late Kavasji Khatau. Once I went to see him in the Empire Theatre after one of his shows. He gave me a warm embrace and said, "Come, Baba Jayshankar," and he took me by the hand into the dressing room. He introduced me to the actresses and told them, "You must go see his performance when you have time. You will learn a lot from it."

Mulani, the poet who wrote *Jugal Jugari*, was called the Shakespeare of Gujarati. During one performance, the great Urdu playwright Agha Hashr was seated in the audience. Affected by a tender moment between Lalita and her son, he stood up and shouted, "*Subhan allah! Vah! Vah! Bahut khub, Lalitabai, bahut khub.*" All the spectators were startled and turned to stare at him.

At the end of the scene he came backstage, patted me on the back, and said, "*Bhai* Jayshankar, tell me the truth, who taught you to let out such a sorrowful sigh?"

I immediately pointed to my guru Bapulal, but Bapulal said, "No, these sighs come out of him all on their own. I didn't teach him this."

Hashr Saheb said, "Then, truly, you are a sensitive performer."

Jugal Jugari had a profound effect, making people convinced of the damage caused by gambling. Horse racing at the Mahalakshmi

Jayshankar Sundari, Some Blossoms, Some Tears 215

Racecourse was a big thing in those days. Many scions of wealthy Hindu families squandered their parents' fortunes there. I remember an old acquaintance who was addicted to betting on horses. He would offer everyone cigarettes from a special case with a picture of a naked woman on it. After he saw *Jugal Jugari*, this wayward youth came to me with tears in his eyes and swore off gambling. I didn't believe he would fulfill his vow, but he changed his life, quit horses, and settled down with his family in a bungalow in Baleshwar.

The Maharaja of Mysore, Krishnarao Wodeyar, was staying at the home of Seth Narottam Morarji. He had seen our plays, *Saubhagya Sundari* and *Vikram Charitra*. When leaving for Mysore, he presented us with flower garlands. He gave Bapulal a diamond ring and me a gold-embroidered turban. The date was July 10, 1902. Here is how he was introduced to us. Every year kings and princes came to Bombay to entertain themselves with silent films, theatre, and dancing girls. The Maharaja of Mysore had an attendant, a doctor, who wanted to see some plays. Narottam Seth recommended our company; the doctor saw *Saubhagya Sundari* and enjoyed it. Taking along an interpreter, he went to meet Bapulal and expressed his pleasure. He also said that if we artists were to invite the maharaja, he would come to see our performance.

"We'll most certainly invite His Highness, but the princely states have their own protocols. You must tell us how to present the invitation and how to pay our respects correctly."

Doctor Saheb then described the procedure. Each person who wished to meet the king had to prepare a small silver platter, carefully arranged with *pan* leaves, betel nut, cloves, cardamom, and covered with a cloth. It had to be offered by hand near the king's feet. All these preparations would be made in advance for us. We were to bring three or four men and come the next morning between 8:30 and 9:00.

Bapulal, Maganlal, Dayashankar and I arrived at Morarji's bungalow the next morning. The Doctor Saheb was waiting for us. He ushered us in a friendly way into the living room where the silver platters had been prepared, and gave us each one to carry in. Saying, "His Highness will call you shortly," he left the room in a hurry.

After some time a servant appeared and said, "His Highness is remembering you." One by one we entered, offered our gifts at the maharaja's feet, and stood in an attitude of respect. He asked us some questions in English through his interpreter. It was decided that on the coming Saturday or Sunday a special show would be organized just for his entourage. Arrangements were made for the ladies—the Maharani of Mysore, the Rajmata, and their maidservants—to be seated upstairs on mattresses and pillows, while the king with his chief ministers and courtiers sat downstairs. Between 100 and 125 people came to see *Saubhagya Sundari* that day. Interpreters sat next to the king and his ministers. We surpassed ourselves performing the play, and everyone was pleased.

I remember other command performances for royalty, although I never liked performing for these occasions. The actor is deprived of the reaction of hundreds of spectators, and his performance is lackluster as a result. The pinnacle of acting, its ability to pierce the spectator, cannot come about. And what of all the *rasas*—the comic, the romantic, the heroic, the pathetic? Can they be explained by an interpreter? If the audience is ignorant of Gujarati, an interpreter can never clearly communicate such things. The response is always muted, and if the actor does not gain a proper response, he grows dejected.

In 1902 the Maharaja of Baroda, Sayajirao Gaekwad, came to see *Saubhagya Sundari*, and Dayashankar introduced him after the first act. "His Highness, these are your subjects, two Nayak caste brothers." Indicating Bapulal, he mentioned he was from Undhai village and said I was from Visnagar.

"Then you are indeed my subjects. I come to Visnagar District often, and I've passed through Undhai several times. I'm very pleased to meet you." At the end of the performance, we presented him with flower garlands. He told us he was going back to Baroda by the mail train on Sunday evening. Bapulal took the opportunity to mention my upcoming wedding and told His Highness that we would also be leaving for Visnagar on the same date.

The maharaja was pleased at this news and proposed that we meet at the Grant Road Station. Bapulal was thrilled at the thought that I was about to receive a fine gift. That Sunday after the performance, we went to meet the maharaja in the railway lounge. The Nawab of Palanpur was with His Highness, and they talked for a long time. Seeing no end to their conversation, we finally took leave to board the train. His Highness nodded his permission and dismissed us. We saluted him with a *namaskar*, entered the compartment, and went to sleep. The fine gift remained a dream.

Once, I was sitting on a bench near Colaba Causeway with my music guru Pandit Vadilal. Seeing the maharaja approach, I said, "Look, our king is coming, let's stand up and pay our respects." As he walked by, we bowed and performed *salaam*.

The maharaja recognized me and asked, "How are your plays going?" Then to his minister he said, "This is my subject, a very fine actor. Explain our scheme to him."

The minister told us of the Gaekwad government's philanthropic program, by which artists like Bapulal and myself would be sent to England for theatrical training. Our round-trip travel, accommodation, tuition, and examinations would all be paid out of the royal treasury. Gratefully I thanked him, but because I didn't know English I couldn't take advantage of the scheme. This was always a source of regret.

Chapter 5: Married Life

At the age of 14 or 15, the very mention of matrimony caused me to panic. Every time I was introduced to a girl, I felt shy and tongue-tied. One reason for my fear was that I had read *Sarasvatichandra*, and I was worried about the inequality that pervaded the relationship between Kumud and Pramadadhan.[17]

Near our building lived a girl who had come to the city to pursue private studies. Had I been wedded to an educated girl like her, I reflected, the marriage would have been incompatible, but even if my bride were uneducated the result would have been the same. Though

---

[17] The inequality in the novel is moral rather than social. Both Kumud and Pramadadhan are the offspring of men who achieve high ministerial positions in their respective princely states. However, Kumud is virtuous and self-sacrificing whereas Pramadadhan, counterposed to the hero Sarasvatichandra, is a dissolute libertine. Kumud and Sarasvatichandra had been engaged and were in love with each other, but Kumud agreed to marry Pramadadhan when Sarasvatichandra became a renunciant. Sundari appears to compare the high-minded Kumud with his female acquaintances and the libertine Pramadadhan to his socially inferior self.

I had little formal schooling, I was self-taught and had gained exposure to educated society.

Meanwhile, my father was to receive Rs 2000 whenever I married, so he was eager to push ahead. He may also have feared a loss of prestige if I was not married young. Thus my *lagan* ceremony was held on February 4, 1903. My bosses had been informed several months in advance, and they dispatched Bapulal to Visnagar with the Rs 2000.

I hadn't seen my prospective bride and was in a state of mental confusion. It was difficult to spurn the proposal outright, yet in my heart I couldn't accept it. Girls were not educated in our community in those days, and I felt suffocated, assuming my bride would be rustic and illiterate. I couldn't reveal these feelings.

Moreover, I wished to marry someone else. One day, not long before going to Bapulal's room to borrow some hair-oil, I'd seen a beautiful girl.

"Isn't Auntie here?" I asked, referring to Bapulal's wife.

"No, she's gone out," she replied. "Do you need something?"

"I need some oil for my hair."

She insisted on applying the oil herself. She sat me on a chair and began to anoint my tresses, as women often do for each other. Embarrassed and trying to avoid being seen, I told her to hurry up. But she seemed to have her own agenda.

"Haven't your parents arranged your marriage yet?" she asked.

"They're in the middle of it," I answered.

"If you don't find a suitable girl, may I suggest someone? Will your parents agree?"

"Which girl are you referring to?"

She laughed and gazed into my eyes. Then a bit reticently, she said, "Shall I tell you her name? I am the one. Will your parents agree? Perhaps you don't know this, but a few years ago my parents sent a proposal for my two sisters to marry your brothers, but they refused. If you wish to marry me, then propose the matter to them again. I'll talk to my parents, but they'll definitely go along with it."

This was the first I'd ever spoken of marriage. I thought for a moment, then responded, "Look, I can't speak to my parents directly about this, but a friend is going to Visnagar tomorrow and I'll send a message through him." That was the extent of our conversation.

Some days later the friend returned to Bombay from Visnagar, and the answer he brought from my parents was "no." I was very sorry to hear it. My parents' point of view was that the girl was a child-widow. Since this was to be my first marriage, they were unhappy with her as my choice. With difficulty I restrained myself and went along with their desires. Heavy-hearted, I explained the outcome to the girl and we parted tearfully.

When I went to Visnagar for the marriage that had been arranged for me, the first person I saw was that very girl. She smiled in her familiar way and said, "I especially wanted to be present at your wedding. My parents are here too." I could see how much sadness was suppressed behind her natural ease. The shadow of her grief fell on me too, and so my wedding was not the occasion for joy but rather for dejection.

On March 4, 1903, my wedding procession left Visnagar for Umta in a caravan of oxcarts. When we passed through a forest, the girl sat inside the canopy with me, singing wedding songs with everyone else. She pretended to cover her head to avoid the sun and sobbed under the mantle, deepening the shade of sorrow that had fallen over me. Avoiding the other girls who were in the cart, I went and whispered softly in her ear, "Don't cry. Seeing your tears, the bridegroom will weep too. My mother will see us and figure it out."

She stopped crying and said, "All right, I won't cry, don't be depressed. Why weep on this happy occasion?" Nevertheless she couldn't stop herself, and was again soon lost in the singing of wedding songs and weeping.

"If you don't stop crying, I'll start weeping aloud too," I told her. "It would be better if I got off the cart right now. I'm suffocating sitting here."

"Why should the groom get off? I'll get off the cart myself," and she stopped the oxcart and stepped down. She fell behind and joined her father, who was following on foot.

I didn't see her again during those three days of wedding rituals. I was anxious and worried about my future. What would become of my life? Would this marriage be happy or unhappy? My future seemed to depend on whether my bride understood the nature of the sacrament. Would she be sitting there all night, pondering as I was? If so, it would soon be tested. I waited restlessly in the marriage pavilion. The village priests began the rites, reciting Sanskrit *shlokas* with an impure pronunciation. The bride appeared. She was dozing off. From this I guessed that our future as a couple would be soporific.

I had studied up beforehand on the meaning of the marriage rituals and their importance. I understood the significance of the seven steps and the mutual rights and responsibilities they symbolized. I was entirely aware that I was bound in a relation of indebtedness to my ancestors, the sages, and the gods. So it was that the incorrect recitation by the pandits upset me so much and I blurted out, "Why don't you stop slaughtering the *shlokas* and explain the meaning of the rites instead?" But those godly bumpkins didn't understand what I was going on about, nor did the bride. From the minute she stepped into the canopy, I knew her heart wasn't in the marriage.

My mother was quite sharp-witted. She had guessed that I was upset, and so she made me swear an oath in front of the goddess. I had to recite certain mantras and swear that I would never kill a cow, a child, or a woman, or take a second wife while my bride was alive. I protested, saying no one knew what was written as their fate. But she blessed me and wished me well, and in the end I felt gratitude for the vow. It eased my confusion and gave me some peace. I was going to have one wife, and I would educate her, no matter what. I decided that as soon as we reached Bombay, I would order books for her.

The other girl, the child-widow, got married soon after. One time I went to her home with Bapulal. Finding her alone for a moment, I approached her and asked, "Are you happy?"

"You should not be asking me that," she said, removing her sari from her head and gazing intently into my eyes. "If someone else asks that question, I can tolerate it, but not from you." Her eyes brimmed over with tears, and she brushed them away.

"Forgive me," I said. "I told you long ago I would not be able to disrespect my parents. That's why we are in this position now. But you aren't the only one suffering. My grief is greater than yours. I try to get busy with studies to forget everything. Take care of yourself and do the same. Our lives will pass like this; there's no other way." I left that evening for Visnagar. I sent some religious books and the four parts of *Sarasvatichandra* to her husband, so that he too could read them and benefit.

A few years later I met her again at a wedding. We were all boarding with the groom's party. Staying within the bounds of propriety, I found out about her. When I went to bathe, I asked Bapulal's wife to look after my ring and keys. She said, "I'm busy. Give them to her, she's right here."

I gave the things to the girl and went off to bathe. When I came back, she was alone. Her eyes were full of tears. Worried, I asked, "What's the matter? Why are you crying?"

"My husband came, and when he saw I had your ring and keys, he got angry. He kept asking me, 'Whose ring is this?' He grabbed the ring and keys, threw them down, and slapped me hard. He warned me never to keep any item of yours, and never to speak with you again."

It pained me to hear of her husband's suspicious nature. Taking control of myself, I explained, "Listen to me. Don't be sad if I don't speak to you again. Forgive me. I can see that in your world, your acquaintance with me can create obstacles later. You should treat me as if I'm no longer alive, as though my very existence is wiped out. I'll try to behave the same toward you." I picked up my ring and keys and left the room.

Some years passed. She became a mother and had several children. Then she contracted a serious illness. She was brought to Bombay for treatment, and she stayed in the same building as I. I'd avoided meeting her until then, but she found me alone and beseeched me to come sit with her. "Read something to me, do something that will help me pass the time. Who can have any doubts about a woman who is on the brink of death, lying on her sickbed?"

I was moved by this appeal and, taking permission from my guardians, went to read to her. I read a few chapters from the *Gita*, trying not to select passages that would connect with times past. Her health declined day by day. She was admitted to a hospital, then she died. I could never forget this episode and the entire story has remained a painful memory through my life.

There was one other incident between 1908 and 1909, when we were rehearsing *Chandrabhaga*. One evening, as I was coming down the stairs in the Gaiety, Mr Clement the ticket master said to me, "A woman wants to meet you. She's sitting outside in her carriage."

I went to the door of the orchestra section and saw a beautiful young Parsi lady. I approached her carriage and asked, "Did you wish to see me?"

She smiled modestly and said, "Do you have a copy of the drama *Lalita Dukhdarshak*?[18] I saw the play last week and enjoyed it very much."

"Some books are on sale in the auditorium," I said. "Maybe the ticket master has it. I'll ask him to arrange a copy for you."

The ticket master came up and said the book was sold out. He recommended that she go to a certain bookseller.

"Mister Jayshankar," the Parsi lady retorted. "How can I go there, being a woman? Can't you order the book through the ticket master? I'll come and get it next time."

I did just that. But she couldn't come the next day, and several days later a letter arrived from Matheran in elegant handwriting. It read, "My dear Jayshankar, I cannot forget you. You have inhabited my heart. You are such a gentleman—this I realized from our first meeting. And seeing the Theosophy ring on your finger made me very happy. I want to open my heart and tell you so many things."

It was obvious from the handwriting that the letter was from a woman, but the mode of address struck me as odd. There was no signature, and I wondered who the woman might be. Suddenly I remembered the Parsi lady from a few days earlier. Still, I couldn't be sure it was she.

All my incoming letters were first read by my bosses before being handed over: it was how they kept me under surveillance. They were always alert lest another theatre company lured me away. So they were abreast of everything in my life, and this had two consequences. First, I bridled at these restrictions and was angry, and second I had to constantly bottle up my desires. But like it or not, my life was the target of their moral rescue, and I was powerless to oppose it.

---

[18] *Lalita Dukhdarshak Natak* was the source of several other plays titled *dukhdarshak*, "spectacles of suffering." The play depicts an incompatible marriage between Lalita, the epitome of feminine virtue, and Nanda Kumar or Nandan, an imbecile of low morals.

A few days later a parcel arrived from Matheran containing two bottles of honey, a basket of fresh fruits and vegetables, and a packet of saffron-scented incense. Again there was no sender's name. From this I deduced that the letter-writer and parcel-sender were one and the same.

What was I to do with all these things? I kept the honey and incense and sent the foodstuffs to Auntie. When I opened the incense packet, I saw it was wrapped in a *sadra*, the cloth worn by Parsis as a sacred waist-band. This suggested to me that it must be the Parsi lady who called herself a Theosophist. Then another letter arrived. Both letters were in a woman's hand, and both used the same form of address. Without giving away her name, the writer indicated that she was an admirer. This confirmed my belief that it was the Theosophist lady.

My bosses had read these incoming letters. They called me in and interrogated me, "Who is this? Where does she live? Where did she meet you and what did you say to her?" I replied that I did not know, but that she could be a young Parsi lady who had come once to buy a play-book. There the matter ended.

The Parsi lady came to meet me once more. Again she requested the book, saying she had gone out of the city, so hadn't been able to pick it up earlier. Our conversation went something like this:

Parsi lady: "Mister Jayshankar, why are you so good? I am grateful to you for this book. I love the role of Lalita. She is so tolerant of her unhappy marriage, it makes me want to cry. If you have a photograph of yourself acting, please give it to me. I have a hobby of collecting photos of actors and actresses. Your acting is wonderful, do give me a photo."

Me: "All my old photos are gone. I don't have a single photo left right now. You can inquire at Messrs Tarapur in Dhobi Talao. You'll get many photos of actors there."

Our conversation should have stopped there. My bosses insisted that if a woman came to meet me, it was strictly forbidden for me to receive her. But instead I spoke, "Lady, may I ask you something? An unknown woman sent me two letters. She expressed her desire to open her heart, but I don't know who she was, and I couldn't send her a reply."

She listened carefully and looking into my eyes asked, "Were they love letters? What were you going to reply, can you tell me?"

"I'll tell that to the woman who wrote me," I answered, "not to any other."

"If that woman confesses that she wrote the letters, will you tell her then?"

I laughed and said, "First say whether it was you or not."

My hand was on the door of the carriage. She put her hand on top of mine and in a sweet voice, smiling at me, she said, "I wrote those letters, Jayshankar. I love you, and I want to marry you. Will you accept me and save me from ruin? I'm my parents' only child, and they have lakhs of rupees. Even if I have to leave all of that, I'm ready to do so. I'm a Theosophist and so are you."

Her voice thickened with emotion. Gazing at me, she waited for my reply with great agitation. My heart was full of compassion for her. My own dissatisfaction with my married life cast a pall on my heart, and for a moment I was about to say yes. But the next moment, I caught myself and woke up. "My lady, perhaps you don't know that I am a married man. I cannot deceive my wife, and I know that you would not advise me to do so. There is no question of marrying you. It would be an intercaste marriage, and how do you know that I would be faithful to you to the end? I beseech you, rid your mind of this thought. Get hold of yourself and don't go against society's strictures. Let's decide to be each other's well-wishers and always look out for each others' interests. I too am my parents' only child, and this intercaste marriage would cause them pain. I would not be able to bear it. This is the reason I do not wish to marry you. My answer may seem harsh, but later you'll remember my words with pleasure. If our desires are not fulfilled in this birth, they will be in the next."

Her eyes filled with tears. She rested her chin on her hands with her elbows on her knees, and looked straight into my eyes sobbing. Warning her I said, "Don't cry. If people see you in this condition and spot me standing near you, they'll get the wrong idea. Not only that, the Parsis in the square in front will see you with an actor, and you'll get a bad reputation. Be calm, dry your tears, and for God's sake forget me forever. Better yet, become my friend and well-wisher."

"All right. I'll try to contain my heart. My last wish is that you give me your photo. I don't believe that you don't have any left. I'll hide it in the folds of my clothing and always feel happy when I look at it.

Show me at least that little pity. I'm giving you my address. Send it by mail. One last word. If I write news of myself, you'll answer, won't you?" I gave her my promise, and we parted with heavy hearts.

Our dialogue continued through correspondence. She sent her address but the name she gave was her nurse's. I bought the four parts of *Sarasvatichandra*, inserted my photo between the pages, and sent them to her. Barely a month later the ticket master called me once more, saying the book woman wished to see me. I was shocked to see her wearing a black blouse and sari, without her diamond earrings and ring, seemingly sunk in grief. She told me that she had just been married to a Parsi boy whom she disliked. Her eyes were red and puffy from constant weeping. I felt great remorse and invited her into the playhouse, away from the gaze of the Parsis in the square.

I ordered a soda for her, and she seemed to compose herself. Then she told me that her father had promised her in marriage and put pressure on her, threatening to cut off her inheritance. Her fate had turned out to be the same as Lalita's. I told her to read the books I had sent, they would give her mental strength. She should try to be like Kumud in *Sarasvatichandra*. We said farewell.

This episode troubled me for days. The pain of it tortured me. We corresponded for three or four years after that. With heart-rending expression she told me about her life, her troubles great and small. I consoled her, tried to urge forbearance, and became firmer in my own resolve to live life day by day. These letters long remained in my personal files, but when I retired my family members inadvertently destroyed them.

Now I will describe how I developed an intimate connection with a famous Hindu family and how its members became my lifelong benefactors. After 1910 I got married for the second time, to a girl of my caste. My life became extremely difficult as a result of this marriage. I rented rooms for twenty rupees a month in Bazar Gate in the Fort area of Bombay and lived there with my wife. One day, I received a letter inviting me to come to a particular house at seven in the evening. The letter was written by a woman, and from the handwriting and expression I could tell that this woman was ready to immolate herself like a moth circling a flame. I sent no reply. Another letter arrived from the same address. I didn't answer that one either. When the third arrived I finally answered, telling her that I was married and couldn't deceive my wife. I threatened to inform the police and have a report sent to her family if she didn't stop writing to me. I signed the letter, writing "your well-wisher" followed by my name.

Little did I know that in my absence this woman had come into my house with a neighbor and praised photographs of me that hung on the wall to my wife. I forgot about the occurrence until, one day, I was chatting with a friend: he said he knew I had written to a woman, he had seen the letter. I denied that I had written a love letter and pressed him to tell me how he knew her.

It seems she was from a well-to-do family. Her husband was a big businessman. He had read my letter too. "He wants to meet you. Maybe you'll get a message from someone in the family. If you do, go and meet them, don't be perplexed about it."

I laughed. "So you want me to go and get beaten up by that Seth? Forget it, I'm not going there!"

Then my friend laughed and said, "The *seth* was happy when he read your letter. He wants to see you in person. There's no harm in going. If it's possible, I'll join you and we'll go together."

Sure enough, I was invited for Sunday dinner at the *seth's* bungalow with the whole family. I dined with them and answered his questions. How much schooling did I have? What was I reading these days? Did I like books? He went to his cupboard and gave me a stack of fine books, saying, "Actors like you should read a lot. You should become a moral exemplar. That is how the stage will be strengthened."

He made arrangements to teach me Sanskrit, and a tutor started coming to the theatre to coach me. After completing half of *Margopadeshika*, I asked him to teach me Sanskrit dramas, as that would be professionally more useful. He recited from *Abhijnanashakuntalam, Uttararamacaritam*, and other plays and expounded upon them, increasing my knowledge of the stage. In truth, I have to thank that "moth" for her letter. It established my relationship with an affectionate, honorable family who always gave thought to my well being.

Now I will return to the days after my first marriage. I returned to Bombay and bought a number of books useful to women—on home management, cooking, sewing, and religion. I always felt that by studying one may learn anything, and if one puts into practice what has been studied, one can become a complete human being. But not everyone learns from books, nor do all become complete—this I can say from my own life.

The girl I had been married to had not been old enough to live with her in-laws. She was 11 years old at the time, and it would be a few more years before she joined our household. In this period, she developed several unfortunate diseases which spread slowly through her body. As soon as I received news of this from my family, I consulted a doctor and told him about my wife's condition. He recommended that I bring her to Bombay for treatment.

For some reason, my mother-in-law would not agree to send her daughter to Bombay. For months, I pleaded with my in-laws but was unsuccessful. Finally, they sent word that if their daughter survived she would come, otherwise I should perform her last rites and make an end of it. If I felt so inclined I should get married again: they had no objection. After that my mother-in-law consulted a doctor and had the girl's leg amputated at the knee. Because of the disease, her palate had developed a hole and she couldn't speak beyond emitting a hoarse croak.

My mother felt it was impossible to establish a household with this woman, and she urged me to marry again. Other family members put pressure on me. I had no free time from the theatre, yet mother's letters were pouring in. Somehow, I kept putting off the second marriage. While en route to Bargaon to attend a wedding, I stopped at Visnagar. That very night, my parents took the advice of a relative and located a suitable child-widow. The next day I was married in great haste. Because I was an actor, my mother was continually worried that I would go astray. Once more, I was unable to resist my parents. I was married against my will for the second time and had to bear the sorry consequences of this undesired match.

I established my household in Bombay after this second marriage. My wife was completely unlettered, so I retained a Parsi lady teacher to instruct her. After a year, my wife was able to read only in a broken fashion. The teacher came to me and said, "You're paying me for nothing. I can't teach your wife a thing. She's a total dunce—it's no use."

Cursing fate I smacked my forehead and said, "If even you have lost hope, there's no point." I gave her the money I owed and dismissed her.

I never walked the streets of Bombay with that woman. I never went to a festival, fair, or temple with her. She made no attempt to understand me. Even with a wife, my household was empty. I kept myself busy with the drama night and day, and for the rest passed my time reading. She lacked all capacity for discussion, nor could I read to her or seek her advice on important problems. It was impossible for us to be compatible.

I spent eighteen hours a day out of home and six hours in. This became intolerable. My life became entirely concentrated on the theatre—it was everything I had. On the stage I attempted to display an image of the wife I desired. It became the primary inspiration for my acting. I forgot the tensions in my everyday world, experiencing this otherworldly pleasure in the theatre. Nevertheless my desires, my goals, my ambitions remained unsatisfied, there was a deep disquiet in my heart. As for domestic life, it was torment. To liberate myself from all of this, I tried several times to commit suicide.

A friend took me to the beach one day. Quickly I undressed and ran into the waves until the water came up to my chest. My friend was startled and called out to me to come back. I replied, "This is my final *salaam*. I'm going now." He understood, jumped into the water, and holding me by the neck dragged me back to shore.

"What were you doing, you fool?" he asked angrily.

"My life has no flavor," I replied. He took me to his house, talked to me for three days, and calmed me down. After that I never thought of suicide.

Some people may be surprised to learn that, today, I lead an extremely happy and harmonious married life. I am grateful to my third wife, Champa, for this. My first two wives' names were Ichha and Mani, and even while both were alive I had to marry a third time. My third wife was the daughter of the writer Dahya Lal Nayak, who served the Maharaja of Bhavnagar as a music master. When my mother proposed the marriage, there were negotiations over dowry, but after my future mother-in-law came to Visnagar and saw our affluence, she agreed to my mother's terms. Thus I was married in 1917 and began to live with Champa in Girgaon. After this marriage, my financial position and social prestige began to improve. I told my wife she could never come to see me perform in the theatre. Behind this was the obvious thought that I might be inhibited playing the female role in my wife's presence.

A few days after this marriage, my father-in-law fell ill. When I went to meet him, he said, "Jayshankar, you are my nearest relative. You are influential, a gentleman. I must make a request of you. My daughter has a very tender temperament, but she is intelligent. You must never pain her heart." As he said this, I recalled my two failed marriages.

I still had no children, and perhaps he suspected that I would make a fourth marriage to beget a child. I took water in the palm of my hand and made a vow, saying, "Respected Dahya Lal Thakor, if in the future I marry again even when your daughter is no longer alive, I will incur the guilt of killing a Brahmin."

He quickly tried to prevent me. "Oh dear! What are you saying? Do not speak such words." But in the corner of his eye I caught a glimmer of satisfaction that remains a source of pride.

My first son Prabhakar was born in 1918. Today I have a full family—three sons and a daughter—and I owe it all to my wife, who is like the goddess Lakshmi. She has always shown hospitality to everyone who comes to my home. For many years, she has lived in this large joint family and treated each member of it with love, generosity, and humanity. I consider this my good fortune.

Chapter 6: Sundari's Abduction

Now I return to the main story. After *Jugal Jugari*, Bapulal decided to take advantage of Jayshankar's beautiful voice. He revived the old drama *Shakuntala* under the name of *Kamlata*, and it opened on October 18, 1904. To prepare myself for the role, I read Ubhiyashankar Yajnik's translation of Kalidasa's original. I studied the paintings of famous artists like Ravi Varma, especially the picture of Shakuntala with her friend Priyamvada writing a letter to her beloved.

Bapulal had helped me with every aspect of the first four productions, and his absence during *Kamlata* was troublesome. A further problem was that he fell sick a week before the opening, took to his bed, and showed up only on the day of the performance. Seth Chhotalal meanwhile interfered with the songs, insisting they be sung with extra emphasis on the words. He was present at every rehearsal to make sure each word was pronounced separately, without regard to the rhythm, phrasing, or meaning. This was how it had been done in the old days in the Urdu and Gujarati dramas composed by Dayashankar. Because of these conditions, I couldn't do justice to my role. The first two nights of the show were lackluster. The stage direction was full of problems and uncertainties.

After *Kamlata*, the playwright Mulani left the company and formed the Kathiawari Natak Mandali. Our company sued him because he had broken the written contract that bound him to the company for ten years. Mulani was annoyed by Seth Chhotalal's demand for a simpler language and alterations to the songs. A number of other artists left with him. Bapulal Punjiram, the harmonium master, got Rs 10,000 when he relinquished his share in the company, and Mulani got Rs 15,000.

In 1906 the City Improvement Trust ruled that the Gaiety Theatre, which was constructed of wood, had to be demolished and a new theatre constructed. While the work got underway, the company prepared to leave for Karachi. We were traveling out of the city for only the third time, unlike other theatre companies that toured frequently.

After making inquiries in Karachi, we rented the Parsi Theatre at the Garikhana crossing, built by the late Navrojji Dhanji Pari. His company had disbanded, but his nephew was running the playhouse, and he agreed to rent it to us for Rs 600 per month, plus ten free passes for each show. His lawyer Vadhumal and their friends wanted to make use of these free passes, but we had already heard they were a bunch of trouble-makers. We rejected the condition of issuing free passes and agreed to pay a higher rent instead.

We left for Karachi on April 24, 1906. For security purposes, we took along Vikaji, an experienced stick-fighter from Khambat, and Sheru Miyan, a coachman adept with a sword. At Karachi station we were welcomed with flowers by a number of fans and businessmen. Accommodation for us actors was arranged in a large residence where I was treated like one of the family.

We inaugurated our Karachi run with the auspicious drama *Saubhagya Sundari*. On the first night, the house was jampacked. Just as in Bombay, here too the play received special favor. We invited certain merchants of our acquaintance for free, but the rest of the cultured crowd had to pay their own way, including the lawyer Vadhumal. We had heard he was such a great drama-lover that he never missed a show. Because he was the lawyer attached to the theatre, he was used to coming on a free pass. This time he had to spend his own money, yet we found no bitterness in his behavior.

Two months passed. We had performed all our famous plays at least a couple of times, earning much money and popularity from our fans. Our supposed enemy Vadhumal was at every play. One time he came to see *Dagh-e Hasrat*. Two acts were over and the third was just beginning when four men entered the back of the auditorium without tickets. Fisticuffs broke out, and the audience stood up to watch. We actors were intent on the drama, shouting our lines to drown out the uproar, but our efforts came to naught.

At that moment the company's two guards, Vikaji and Sheru Miyan, arrived on the scene. They grabbed a thug each under their arms, lifted the other two on their shoulders, and threw them out. Meanwhile Vadhumal had vanished. Outside the hall, Vikaji and Sheru Miyan were pelted with soda bottles, but this only enraged them further. Vikaji started flailing his stick, and Sheru beat up whoever he could get his hands on. The thugs began to panic. Some ran back into the hall and hid in the orchestra pit, some faced off against us on the stage.

Bapulal became the commanding officer and started issuing orders. First he had the curtain dropped. Then he told the actors to grab swords, staves, daggers, and whatever stage weapons were to hand. We formed a line in front of the curtain, as though taking a position in battle. Revolvers were fired into the air from both sides of the stage. Then suddenly everything came under control. Our assailants turned tail and ran.

Maganbhai, the company manager, had figured out the situation and informed the police commissioner at the start of the incident. The police arrived at the scene of the crime and arrested several fugitives. The calm restored, we invited the audience back to the hall, offering to refund those who wished to leave. The playhouse returned to normal, and the third act of *Dagh-e Hasrat* began.

The next day the company took extra precautions to safeguard the performance. The attack of the previous night put us on the alert.

The enemy had turned out to be stronger than expected. Vikaji's stick had wounded quite a number of them, and they might seek revenge any time. We filed a court case against the miscreants who had been caught, and they filed one against us in exchange. News of the episode spread through Karachi and was on every tongue. These accounts stressed that the target of the trouble-makers was the female impersonator Jayshankar, whom the gang wished to abduct. This rumor flew with the speed of the wind back to Bombay. In its most distorted version it was so convincing that people began to believe that Jayshankar Sundari had actually been kidnapped by Pathans who thought he was a woman.

Many times I was asked about this piece of gossip, and always by people who sympathized with me and were my admirers. Some were satisfied when I told them that the story was false. Some asked in a manner that prevented me from concealing my amusement. They seemed to want confirmation that I really had been abducted in Karachi. Who knows why abduction should be the touchstone of female impersonation. It was as if abduction represented the pinnacle of my skill as an actor, as if it were a huge event in my career, an accomplishment. Adopting a serious tone, I explained that it was all gossip and hearsay, without any truth whatsoever.

On another occasion a fight broke out during *Dagh-e Hasrat*. Around this time my father received a letter from Karachi, written by some rascal who had found out his address. "What a heartless father you are," the letter read. "Your son has been injured and you take no notice. Some mischief-makers kidnapped him and slashed his face. Now he is in the hospital and wants to see you for the last time. Come quickly to Karachi. Your well-wisher."

Fortunately, a letter from me arrived at the same time, in which I reported on the fight and said that no one had been injured. My father compared the two letters and figured out the so-called well-wisher's was fake. A similar letter was sent to the Bombay drama company. I learned about it later. The abduction story was based on this false letter and the rumors circulating about us.

Another incident occurred that appeared to confirm this legend about me. One night we were returning from an outing to the harbor. As our carriage passed another standing in the street, the other driver suddenly whipped up his horses and chased after us. Four men inside the coach began pelting us with rocks—for no reason. A few hit our wheels, some fell at our feet, and one or two hit our horses and driver, Sheru Miyan. Luckily none of them hit me.

"Catch them, catch them!" we shouted. Sheru Miyan pursued the other carriage. It vanished into a side street. Sheru followed in hot pursuit. Sheru cornered them, and all of us jumped off and fell upon the attackers. Hearing shouts and cries, a crowd gathered. The attackers were apprehended and handed over to the police.

Sethji told me to take the coach and go back home. Mohan Lala took the place of the coachman, grabbed the reins, and delivered me back safely. We gave everybody the news of the incident and arrived at the theatre on time. In this fashion one crisis followed the next, and we became disenchanted with the land of Sind. Therefore we decided to leave Karachi.

Chapter 7: Return to the Gaiety

Our company returned to the renovated Gaiety Theatre in early October, 1906. Bapulal began to give new shape to the drama *Nand Battisi*. Mulani had left and was being sued for breach of contract, but the bosses were not content to leave the revisions to Bapulal. They were of the view that whether one was a partner or an actor, one should stick to one's job and not interfere in the work of others. Bapulal was not supposed to do anything besides direct and act. Two young playwrights and a lyricist were hired, and Bapulal had them rework the play. *Nand Battisi* opened on November 23, 1907, and became very popular.

The good-looking Mohan Lala had been playing women's and men's roles in the company for ten years. We had been good friends, and we respected each other till the end. He used to stay with Maganbhai, and I stayed with Seth Chhotalal, the company's principal owner. Who knows what came over him, but he decided to quit the company and go to work for Nakubhai Seth. One time I went to see him perform over there. He was playing Shambhaji, the son of Shivaji. I was very disappointed to see him carelessly introducing slapstick in a serious scene. I tried to explain afterwards that Shambhaji was Shivaji's heir, and his character needed the dignity appropriate to a future king. I berated him, saying that actors as capable as himself shouldn't abandon their principles and turn the stage into a joke. His behavior was at odds with the noble traditions of the Gujarati company that had trained him.

On another visit, I ran into the playwright Najhi Saheb. It was early morning, but he was already dead drunk. We exchanged greetings, and I asked to see Mohan Lala. "All right, Jayshankar Saheb," he said. "How much does Mohan get per month? He makes over five hundred rupees. And how much does he spend on liquor? Only a hundred and fifty. Forgive my impudence, but if I got five hundred rupees a month, I'd spend every penny on booze."

I laughed and replied, "Najhi Saheb, you're a man of pleasure-loving habits. Just mind your health a little too." Mohan Lala joined us and we swapped stories for a while, but the whole time he was in a drunken stupor and kept his eyes averted. Mohan Lala had the chance to perform in many plays with various companies, something given only to a few actors. He had a kind of creative genius and in every situation he gathered applause, whether in his role as Madhav in *Saubhagya Sundari* or in his final drama *Pravasi*. If this extraordinary artist had not taken to drink, who knows what he might not have achieved.

Before my debut in 1901, other accomplished actors had earned a name on the Bombay stage. Amrit Keshav Nayak was famous for his acting and stage direction. Few artists in our country had his passionate devotion. He beautifully executed the role of the queen in *Khun-e Nahaq*, an adaptation of Shakespeare's *Hamlet*. Between 1898 and 1904 he presented a number of dramas, such as *Murid-e Shak, Bazm-e Fani (Romeo and Juliet)*, and *Asir-e Hirs* (Sheridan's *Pizarro*), and he popularized the practice of casting English plays in Urdu guise. Amrit Keshav had a good grasp of Urdu literature. His famous book, *M.A. Banake Kyon Meri Mitti Kharab Ki*,[19] was an expression of his personal sensibility. After Dayashankar Girnara, he deserves credit as the most capable director of the Gujarati stage.

I always respected Amritbhai for his acting talent, but eventually I learned some things about his personal life that made me inwardly

---

[19] Why Did You Educate Me and Defile My Honor?

angry. One time we ran into each other in Khatau's Alfred Natak Mandali. I looked at him and then walked right past, snubbing him. He came up to me and explained affectionately, "Jayshankar, I can imagine why you might be angry with me, but I'm really helpless. Can't you see anything good in Amrit?" I said I was sorry and forswore my anger, but it seemed that the Bombay theatre was more colorful even than the Arabian nights of yore. How many artists have fallen into the clutches of beauty and died at an unripe age! Amrit's painful story teaches us a great deal.[20]

After *Nand Battisi*, in 1908 we presented a farce entitled *Sangat ke Rang* by Dayashankar Girnara. This was not a particularly noteworthy drama. I was given the part of Chameli, a singing and dancing girl, which required performing three or four songs in Kathak style. It was easy for me to adopt that style because during my childhood I had seen artists perform it in my hometown. I paid special attention to the divisions in the rhythm, enacted the gestures and expressions, and performed the rapid turns and twists with great delicacy.

Next Bapulal took a drama written by a Parsi called *Kala Dev*, "Black Demon," and began to make improvements to it. First he changed the Parsi Gujarati into pure Gujarati. He wrote some songs for the heroine, created scenes for new boys in the company, and premiered the play on May 22, 1909, under the title *Chandrabhaga*. This drama was different from the ones we had done before. The heroine, Chandrabhaga, was a fanatic follower of the Black Demon. In the course of propitiating him with sacrifices, she murders a number of people. I had never performed such a role before. Many spectators were unhappy that a female character was shown committing heinous crimes. What's more, they were not keen that Jayshankar should play such a role. They wanted to see me only as a devoted wife who sacrificed herself for her husband, was always patient and tender. That all of this would make the drama even more profitable seemed lost on them.

Around this time a tragic incident occurred. On November 27, 1909, Dayashankar Girnara, the founder of the Mumbai Gujarati Natak Mandali, died. He was one of the pioneers of performing plays in pure Gujarati. He began directing plays in 1889 when the company

---

[20] Sundari appears to allude to Amritlal's romance with the actress Gauhar.

was established, and in 1896 he took over the entire running of the company. He enrolled many new actors, winning their loyalty by offering them gifts. During his time, the company became a small fiefdom. Many artists and musicians were beholden to him for instruction in their various specialties. Whenever he was pleased with someone he'd say, "Go and look in my pocket, take whatever there is. That's your reward." One time Mulshankar Mulani got Rs 2000 for a single poem, releasing him from his debts. Happy with my work, he always gave me *pan* and some small change, but I refused to accept his tips, and he blessed me for that.

I remember a day in 1909 when I was approached by a well-dressed gentleman from Kutch. The ticket master introduced him, and the man said, "Our king, Rao Khengarji of Kutch, is visiting Bombay. We businessmen want to hold a welcome function for him, and if you would agree to sing, we would be very pleased. We will pay you whatever you like."

"My Rao of Kutch is upstairs on the third floor," I replied. "I can't go without his permission. Besides, I don't sing anything but theatre songs. Please excuse me, I can't come." He tried to dissuade me, but in the end he left, disappointed.

I forgot about the matter, but a little later the *seth's* daughter called me upstairs. *Sethji* was in a very serious mood, and he began interrogating me. "So, I'm your Rao of Kutch, am I?"

When I confirmed this, he was pleased and continued, "Never hold your hand out before anyone but me."

"So far I never have," I replied. "But if you throw me out, I may have to."

He placed his hand on my shoulder and said, "Look, I'm the son of a Patidar. By next year, I promise you will have your own money. If I die before you've received your Rs 20,000, you will be paid out of my sons' inheritance." Following his order, I never revealed this to anyone.

Dr Trilokikar, a famous surgeon, was a friend of Seth Chhotalal and one of the company's benefactors. He was very fond of classical music and loved to hear me sing classical songs. Once, back from London, he brought me pictures of Ellen Terry the actress, and her partner Sir Henry Irving, along with their biography.

That was the time when Bal Gandharva, the famous actor from Maharashtra, had set up his own theatre company. Doctor Saheb invited me to his clinic. Three attractive young men were sitting in it. One was dressed like a prince in his white *churidar*-pajama, aristocratic long coat, pink shirt, and pretty chiffon turban. When we were introduced, I realized this was the supreme female impersonator himself.

Bal Gandharva often came to see our plays. I would usher him into the theatre myself and introduce the characters and plot in my broken Marathi. I also went to see his plays—*Subhadraharan, Man Apman, Ekach Pyala*—and we became close friends. Although he credited me later in life, I never taught him anything. Whatever he liked about my acting he simply absorbed through his own artistic discrimination. In some things I considered him my guru, such as the broad arm motions of a singer to demarcate *sam*. Gandharva would wrap his fingers over the edge of his sari when he sang a particularly beautiful *tan* or became swept away by the music. I too imitated this gesture to express heights of emotion. Gandharva's walk, his costume, and delivery of dialogue were truly captivating. In this way, every actor learns from another, and each one becomes the guru of some other.

Chapter 8: Farewell to the Gaiety

The Kathiawari Natak Mandali, which had been established by Mulshankar Mulani when he left the Mumbai Gujarati Natak Mandali, was in serious debt. In 1909 Mulani sold it and returned to our company. He completely revised a drama that Bapulal had commissioned, and we performed it under the name of *Vasantprabha* on December 17, 1910. This drama was very popular and ran for several months, earning the company a goodly profit.

In 1908 the Kathiawari company had produced Mulani's *Devkanya* in Ahmedabad. By this time *dharmik* or mythological plays had come into fashion, and almost all the Gujarati companies were performing them. *Devkanya* was adopted by our company with some new songs and scenes added. Its subject matter was retained, complete with spectacular effects based on feats of yoga and tantric knowledge. We opened *Devkanya* in 1911. The title role, with its spiritual orientation, was a new experience for me. The heroine, a daughter of the gods, devotes herself to her husband and obtains the powers that a yogi acquires through practice and meditation. I read a few religious texts and books on yoga to prepare for the part.

Krishna Charitra had been written by Mulani for the Kathiawari company and performed in Ahmedabad in 1906. Our company presented this mythological too, with some changes, in 1912. This drama gave me an opportunity to play the part of Radha and exhibit the supremacy of devotion configured as love. In order to bring life to the role, I read the *Bhagavat Purana* and other books, attempting to understand the path of *bhakti*.

I had been enchanted by reading Manilal Dvivedi's *Gulab Singh*, and I urged Mulani to transform it for the stage. In 1914, he rewrote it as *Pratap Lakshmi* and we performed the play, but it was only a shadow of the original story. The drama had an overabundance of miraculous scenes which hindered the impact of the character of Lakshmi, and I was not pleased with it.

The poet Mulshankar Mulani stands in the front row in the history of our stage. His writing wandered in the gardens of the nine *rasa*s. Because of his focus on development of character, I consider him the Shakespeare of Gujarat. His depiction of romance never strayed into obscenity. His works were full of the principles of dramaturgy, and his thought was vast. Along with the famous poets of our time, the late Dahyabhai Dholshaji and Vaghji Asharam Oza, Mulani's pure social dramas made a major contribution to the life of the Gujarati people. His plays were important in mitigating the prejudices of the literati and diminishing their hatred of the professional stage.

History has been unjust to this Shakespeare of Gujarat. The company managers did not publish his works, nor did Mulani have even two books of theatre songs to his credit. Newspaper reviewers also overlooked him. After 1901, all of Gujarat knew the names of Jayshankar Sundari and Bapulal, but few recognized Mulshankar Mulani or knew that he had penned *Saubhagya Sundari* and *Vikram Charitra*. The situation in Maharashtra is entirely different. Plenty of plays for the professional stage have been published there. As a result, the gap between professional playwrights and litterateurs is not nearly as great as it is among us.

Mulani's staged plays numbered approximately twenty-five, and he wrote four more which were not staged. In addition, he amended and adapted another fourteen plays. Only the Morbi Natak Company published Oza's plays; no other company did so. When a play is published, ticket sales decline and earnings drop. The printed play sells, but the grip of the company owners loosens. Other companies can get permission from the playwright and stage the printed play. For all these reasons, our dramas were, unfortunately, never published. The damage this has done to the entire stage is worth pondering.

In 1915, Mulshankar Mulani once more departed from our company, and Bapulal hired Nrusingh Vibhakar to write a new play. This was the time of national awakening, of movements inspired by Gandhiji, of women's education, social reform, and sympathy for the workers. Vibhakar effectively raised these issues in his drama *Sneh Sarita*, which opened on September 15, 1915. In this play the heroine and hero, Sarita Kumari and Snehchandra, wage a struggle to realize their mutual goals and finally are victorious. Sarita Kumari was a completely different type of role, a modern girl who has been to England. She fights for female liberation and works to establish a women's union. To perform this role, I had to understand contemporary trends, but I had already been seriously affected by national events.

Between 1903 and 1912, I had been influenced by Lokamanya Tilak's movement, and I was a regular reader of his newspaper *Kesari*. I was constantly reading about Gandhiji's campaign in South Africa for the rights of the Hindus. This was how gradually I became a Gandhian. As a result, I was able to absorb the sentiments for women's independence voiced by the character Sarita. I became engrossed in her patriotic and feminist yearnings, and through acting her part I expressed my own feelings. The only difference was that up till now I had not played an English-educated woman. Thus I began to practise the particular behavior and family attitudes of this type of female. Luckily I was acquainted with several well-educated families, and I remembered a number of such women, so it was easy for me to portray Sarita.

I also had the job of rehearsing the secondary actors, the hero and heroine of the subplot, whom the playwright had characterized in some detail. Earlier, my directorial work had been to rehearse the boys in the old dramas, but now I was rehearsing a new play. This was key in my life on the stage. The one who explains a role to others must have a much better understanding than the one who simply learns the part. It has been my experience that my own practice has advanced effortlessly through teaching others.

Bapulal played the part of Snehchandra magnificently. He was an expert at understanding every sort of difficult role. He used his keen intelligence to analyze Vibhakar's dramas related to self-rule, and he brilliantly carried off the parts. Vibhakar brought new values and ideas, a new atmosphere, departing from the old plays. To give rhythm to the atmosphere of the independence struggle, Pandit Vadilal created the music for this play. The teamwork among the hero, heroine, and all the characters was excellent, and the play was so popular that the house was full every Saturday and Sunday.

After *Sneh Sarita*, Vibhakar began writing *Sudhachandra*, in which the next several decades were imagined. The play opened on August 5, 1916, and was even more successful than *Sneh Sarita*. Our company was ahead of other companies in treating the independence movement, and this drama strengthened our position. No company could surpass us in music, acting, costumes, or scenery. Toward the end of this play, I choreographed a dance that created an impressive effect through the use of different musical instruments.

Next, Vibhakar's *Madhu Bansari* opened on July 28, 1917. I had to appear in male dress in one scene, which took a lot of effort. Nevertheless, those who saw me said I performed the masculine part with natural delicacy. Because I was well acquainted with the nationalist movement, I had no difficulty performing the heroine's role in this play.

These three plays of Vibhakar's were quite long and full of varying characters and incidents. Sometimes the plot was not entirely clear. Bapulal, an experienced director, told the playwright to abridge these plays and eliminate some characters. Vibhakar hesitated, but in the end he accepted Bapulal's advice. The dramas became tighter and gained in momentum as a result.

Opinions on Vibhakar's dramas varied. Some preferred *Sneh Sarita*, some *Sudhachandra*. Some appreciated his romantic scenes, others liked the comedy in his plays. Some felt that his female characters strayed beyond the boundaries of Aryan womanhood. The primary theme of his plays was that woman is not a mere slave or an object of enjoyment. She is no less than man in her mind, heart, upbringing, and experience. He projected his female characters keeping foremost their fundamental equality.

The drama companies considered the theatre a business. But Vibhakar's approach to writing drama turned the stage into an educational institution. His work was concerned with social issues. He was inclined more toward psychology than traditional aesthetics. A man ahead of his time, he was both an optimist and a revolutionary playwright.

Vibhakar's next play, *Meghmalini*, dealt with the question of labor and management. It opened on November 23, 1918. A superfluity of incidents and faulty construction made it less successful than expected. Moreover, Bapulal fell sick in the middle of rehearsals. It was left to me to handle most of the direction, but I purposely did not rehearse the senior actors since I did not wish to clash with the main director. Bapulal could not play his role properly because of his poor health. The weekend turnout was poor, and amidst these problems Vibhakar was asking for extra money for his next play.

Finally Bapulal's grand desire to become a playwright was fulfilled, and with the *seth's* grudging approval he began to compose *Anandlahari* himself. Eager to make some money, the *seth* rented out the playhouse to European dancing girls, English theatre parties, and film people. *Anandlahari* debuted on August 23, 1919, but it was unsuccessful.

The heir to the British throne came to India around this time. Gandhi's Non-Cooperation Movement was gaining strength, and two groups formed on the issue of whether to welcome the royal party. Bombay's enlightened citizens, mainly Maharashtrians and Gujaratis, were firmly opposed to the welcome, but some Parsis wanted to honor the guests. Riots started up between the Parsis and the Hindus, with rioters attacking Parsi shops on the one hand, while in Parsi neighborhoods Parsis went on the rampage. I was living with my wife Champa in Girgaon, the scene of much fighting. We decided to lock our windows and doors and hole up inside, until a Parsi sister came peering through our third-storey window, saying, "Please help me, Jayshankar and Champa-ben. If rioters break into my house, they'll kill my little boy and girl. But if they think they're your children, no one will bother them. My husband and I will take care of ourselves somehow." My heart melted, and I gave her my word that if necessary we would shelter her children. Luckily the situation never arose, but I formed a close bond with that Parsi family.

Despite the failure of *Anandlahari*, Bapulal was not daunted. He presented *Vishvalila* in September 1920, but that too flopped. The company's debts were mounting. The *seth* decided to invite Mulani back again, and he wrote *Dharmvir*, a drama that very effectively depicted Gandhi's Home Rule campaign. When we began rehearsing it, the play went out to the censors. Within a few days, word came back that they refused to pass the play because of several scenes that criticized the government. Mulani began writing a new play based on Alexander Dumas's *The Count of Monte Cristo*, but before it was complete a sharp rift occurred between the company's two partners, the brothers Chhotalal and Maganlal.

On one side, Seth Chhotalal was expanding his income. He had entered the shares market and was making a lot of money. He sold the ancestral home and started building a new house on land near the Bhangvadi Theatre. Somebody offered him eighteen lakhs for the theatre he owned, and gradually the *seth* got him to increase the price, until the final offer was thirty lakhs. As their possessions increased, the two brothers fought over their respective portions. Mealtimes were full of violent arguments and an atmosphere of conflict prevailed, which saddened me.

Meanwhile Bapulal was making his own plans and preparations. He spoke secretly to a number of actors about forming a new company, offering them three-year contracts, and many were won over. Only Vadilal and I held back. Bapulal presented many arguments for why we should join him. He reminded me that my mother was his sister. He said I would receive even more fame and fortune than I already had. He offered to turn the directorial work over to me in due course, as he got older. But I had already given my word to Mulchand Mama. I had promised to join him in his Lakshmikant Natak Samaj if the Mumbai Gujarati Natak Mandali folded. I told this to Bapulal, explaining that he should have asked me earlier. Now it was simply too late.

As it happened, the *seth* sold the Mumbai Gujarati Natak Mandali to Bapulal Nayak for Rs 40,000. Mulchand Mama and the Lakshmikant company's owner, Seth Chandulal Hargovandas Shah, came with a platter full of garlands, put flowers around the necks of Vadilal and myself, and settled our salaries. My salary was fixed at Rs 551, but because I was a partner in the old company I was given a bonus of Rs 4000. Vadilal would receive Rs 300 per month and a reward for each new song.

Finally, at the end of April 1922, the owners shut down the Mumbai Gujarati Natak Mandali. That entire month the playhouse was filled with spectators. Not a single day in the week could we rest. The company announced a series that included all four of Vibhakar's plays and our other dramas, and the audience flocked to see them. We performers were excited too about these final performances, and we tried to outdo each other for the last time.

The Mumbai Gujarati Natak Mandali had a style its very own. An artistic tradition developed out of the combination of talented playwrights, experienced directors, reputed musicians, understanding actors, and expert stage hands. The owners treated everyone like family, and this was an important part of the tradition. Our spectators were mature and wise as well. The dramas this company performed put special emphasis on acting and less on scenes full of commotion. The atmosphere in the company exuded refinement. This unique legacy made its mark on the development of my personality.

The history of the Gujarati stage is not the history of one caste or one class, nor is it divided between Gujarati and Urdu. It is the history of dedication, worship, and collaboration among those devoted to the arts. It was the Mumbai Gujarati Natak Mandali, the main link in this history, that I saw breaking apart at this time. I was a silent witness to its demise. Nevertheless, just like Arjun I stood by helplessly, unable to save that institution, that temple of talent. The dejection was so great that my entire person felt crushed. I had seen those splendid towers of achievement. Now the time had come to gaze at the terrible chasm of their collapse.

I remembered my first entrance into the Gaiety: the surge of feeling, the waterfall of emotions, which now was turning into an arid desert.

The partnership of Jayshankar and Bapulal was after all these years disbanding, and even to think of it destroyed my ambition to embody that imaginary daughter of Gujarat. It was as if the flow of sap within me dried up. A strange detachment hovered over me, created by uncertainty. Would that moment come again in the future or not, in which I presented the artistic image of those overheated sentiments?

For years I had faithfully served that company, which like the goddess Lakshmi had nurtured me with fame, fortune, and maternal affection. Now the final moment was at hand. On April 1, 1922, a

20. Jayshankar Sundari

heavy-hearted Seth Chhotalal gave everyone their final salary. My eyes brimmed over, not with tear drops, with drops of blood. My throat was hoarse. With great difficulty, I thanked the *seth* in a gruff voice. "Brother, we are parting in this manner, and that makes me extremely sad. I will never forget your kindness, the way you cared for me like a child and brought me up, and then made me a partner. My feet refuse to carry me down the stairs of this theatre."

"God must wish it to be so," answered the *seth* with great self-control. "Look at me, am I unhappy? Not a bit." I felt guilty when I heard him say this, for I had been unable to take up the reins of the company myself. In my heart, I saluted him and departed.

In this fashion, a company that began in 1889 flourished in the hands of Seth Chhotalal until 1922. From 1922 till 1939 it was run by Bapulal. Then, from 1944 to 1945 Messrs Shantilal and Company became the managers. In 1946 it came under the ownership of Rajnagar Theatres Limited, and in 1948 it was taken over by Chandrahas Manilal Jhaveri. Later it was renamed the Mumbai Subodh Gujarati Natak Mandali. Nowadays it is run by Dahyabhai Patel, as far as I am aware.

6

Fida Husain, *Fifty Years in the Parsi Theatre*

Introduction

The final autobiography in this volume is unusual in several ways. First, it was published as an oral history rather than a conventional autobiography. Fida Husain's *Fifty Years in the Parsi Theatre,* although told mainly in the first person, was published under the authorship of Pratibha Agraval, a theatre scholar who interviewed and recorded the actor. Second, its subject had an extraordinarily long life-span and outlasted all of his contemporaries who were active in the Parsi theatre. Indeed, Fida Husain lived for three decades beyond the last extant Parsi theatre company. He remained active at the helm of the Moonlight Theatre of Calcutta until his retirement in 1968. Late in his life, as a celebrated exponent of the "old Parsi theatre," he created greater understanding of the form among the urban educated class. He taught seminars in acting, direction, and elocution at the National School of Drama throughout the 1990s. With his deep voice, artful enunciation, and commanding physical presence, Fida Husain gained respect for his personal talents and for the erstwhile tradition that fostered them.

These final accomplishments are outside the scope of his memoir, published in 1986. It focuses on his heyday between 1918, when he joined the New Alfred, and 1968 when he shut down the Moonlight. Fida Husain performed in hundreds of plays, first in female roles and then in male ones. His most famous part was that of the devotee Narsi. It was one of many portrayals of Hindu gods and saints for which he was known. He made over 200 recordings for His Master's Voice and appeared in a series of films in the 1930s. He received the Uttar Pradesh Sangeet Natak Akademi award in 1978 and in 1985 the central government's Sangeet Natak Akademi award for acting.

Fida Husain's account begins with his teenage years when his attraction to theatre bloomed. Born in Muradabad, UP, in 1899, he grew up with a tremendous fondness for singing. His conservative family was strictly opposed to his interest in music. His father was kindhearted, but his uncle thrashed him every time he was caught attending music sessions. His sister-in-law once tried to ruin his voice by feeding him abrasive vermilion (*sindur*) hidden in *pan*. In 1917 he joined the theatre club of Ray Dayal and played his first female role in *Shahi Faqir*. With the collusion of the club's director, he ran away from home to join the New Alfred Theatrical Company. Since he had just married, his sudden departure aggravated his already difficult position within the family. His in-laws ostracized his father and uncle from the *biradari*, but eventually Fida Husain patched up the quarrel.

The traditionalist New Alfred under Sohrabji Ogra pursued a policy of prohibiting actresses from appearing onstage. As Fida Husain recalls, rehearsal time was sacred, and the rules of decorum were strictly enforced. Ogra himself was a dominating personality who kept everyone in line. The twenty-odd boys who danced and dressed up as girls were only allowed out for an hour or two per week, accompanied by guards. When Fida Husain joined the company, he signed a contract with a policeman as witness. The salary was regular; meals, lodging, and travel were well organized. Entire trains of seventeen cars were booked to carry stage equipment, furniture for seating, costumes, props, and personnel from city to city.

For almost his entire time in the New Alfred, Fida Husain worked as a female impersonator. He was called "Master Fida Husain" in recognition of his youth and expertise in cross-dressed roles. He achieved particular popularity as the melodious heroine in *Parivartan*, a social drama by Radheshyam Kathavachak. He assumed the male part in *Laila Majnun* in 1930, and shortly thereafter his employment with the company ended when it closed permanently.[1]

---

[1] Fida Husain's long tenure as a female impersonator casts doubt on his

In the 1930s and 1940s Fida Husain was associated with a number of theatrical ventures. He joined the Alfred Company, then owned by the Madans, and toured Madhya Pradesh and Uttar Pradesh. He worked with the actress Jahanara Kajjan, becoming her director and leading man. As a member of the Shahjahan Company, he toured as far west as Karachi. When Calcutta was threatened by the Japanese in 1942, he formed the Narsi Theatrical Company, took a number of actors and properties from the Moonlight Theatre, and shifted to Kanpur for eight months. Next he spent three years in Delhi with the Babu Roshan Lal Company. His signature performance in both Kanpur and Delhi was as the poet-saint in *Bhakt Narsi Mehta*. He was also invited by the Raja of Indargarh to lead the Shri Mohan Theatrical Company. This company was known for its production of *Bharat Milap*, an episode from the *Ramayan*. Fida Husain worked in the cinema industry in Bombay and Calcutta as well.

Around 1946 he met a young Bengali actress named Sita Devi. With her strong musical support, he revived his role as Narsi Mehta at the Minerva Theatre in Calcutta. During the riots before Partition, he fled and became engaged in several businesses. He returned in 1948 to take up the reins of the Moonlight Theatre. The company was owned by four Marwari brothers whose interests were entirely profit-oriented. The Moonlight offered two dramas each day, with a film screening sandwiched in between. The middle-class Hindi-speaking audience, many of whom were Marwaris, showed interest in this format. The most popular shows continued to be mythologicals like *Krishna Lila* and the old *Narsi Mehta* in shortened form, plus patriotic dramas like *Desh ki Laj* at the time of the war with China in 1962. Husain maintained a live orchestra of twelve members, and every play featured ten to twelve songs, mostly based on film hits.

In 1964 Fida Husain and his troupe performed *Sita Banvas* before Anamika, a theatre group in Calcutta. Here he met Pratibha Agraval and other figures in modern Indian theatre. In 1968 he retired and

---

birthdate. If he was born in 1899, he would have been 19 when he entered the New Alfred for training with other boys, and 31 by the time he began to appear in male roles. It is possible that his birthdate was pushed back to enhance the image of his longevity.

returned to his family home in Muradabad. With his departure, the last professional Parsi theatre company shut down. Fascination with the older style continued among the cultural elite. After receiving several awards, Husain regularly taught at the National School of Drama in Delhi. One of his favorite sayings was, "An artist, a prostitute, and a race horse all come to a bad end in old age." His own story defied the adage. At the time of his death, his reputation was perhaps greater than it had ever been.

The Hindi text is written in colloquial language relatively free of bookish Sanskritic vocabulary. In the parts that record conversation between Agraval and Husain, the tone fluctuates between a more formal level of courtesy appropriate between strangers and the informal tone of colleagues. In the main body of the narrative, Husain takes on a raconteur's manner, regaling his audience with spicy anecdotes. He improvises, using verbal witticisms, barbs directed at others, and amusing asides.

This translation attempts to convey the humor that is such an intrinsic part of Fida Husain's vignettes. I have compressed his stories to lessen their rambling, repetitive quality, reducing the text overall by about 20 per cent. Incidents not germane to the main narrative have been omitted, such as Husain's dealings with Mr Yardley, the British agent in Jhansi, and the ups and downs of his relationship with the actress Kajjan.

There are no chapters or chapter titles in the original. The 78-page text is divided into sections, and the translation preserves these blocks of text. It also adheres to the alternation between the two speaking "I's," which are indicated by different fonts. I have broken long unparagraphed passages into shorter paragraphs and applied standard indentation and punctuation to conversations. The songs that Fida Husain sang during the interview are mostly deleted, despite their interest to the folklore scholar. The nine-page appendix contains entries on approximately fifty individuals mentioned in the autobiography. Relevant portions have been incorporated into the appendices compiled for this volume.

The book's compositional history is straightforward. Husain's life history was elicited and recorded by Agraval, a theatre scholar and archivist born in 1930. She conducted extensive interviews while he

21. *Mastar Fida Husain* Book Cover

was staying as her guest in Calcutta for two weeks in 1982. To this she added material from earlier interviews held in 1978 in Lucknow. Agraval was then and is at the time of writing the director of the Natya Shodh Sansthan in Calcutta. The audiotapes of her interviews presumably were transcribed at her institute and edited for print publication. The resulting book was published by the NSS with financial support from the Ford Foundation.

Questions remain about the process of transcription and editing. Agraval makes no comment about how the tapes were converted into print. Nor does she specify which comments she added, although it is obvious that she includes reflections that were not part of the original exchange. Judging from the published version, Husain's narrative wandered in time as he spoke. The incidents between his departure from the New Alfred in 1930 and his engagement at the Moonlight in 1968 are presented in two broad narrative arcs (pp. 30–45, and 45–51). The latter seems to tell of events that preceded the earlier one, but the sequential relationships are difficult to untangle. Agraval apparently allowed the non-linearity of Husain's account to stand, a laudable editorial decision. The life-story retains an improvisational, associative structure, rather than having a fixed notion of autobiographical time superimposed upon it.

This text is constructed as a dialogue, the speaking "I" shifting back and forth between the interviewer (Agraval) and the interviewee (Husain). In the opening pages, the interviewer describes her previous encounters with Husain. On those occasions, she posed questions and he provided answers. Agraval then adopts the manner of a biographer, using the third person. Quite soon, she relinquishes the job of storytelling. Husain's voice takes over, narrating in the first person. Although Agraval intervenes occasionally to sum up, for long stretches she disappears entirely. Toward the end of the book, she recapitulates Husain's achievement and provides a benedictory note of closure.

The interview format thus operates as a framing device, punctuating the beginning and ending of the story, rather than being sustained throughout. The omission of the question–answer protocol for most of the book allows the reader to forget about the interviewer's presence. The autobiographical subject appears to speak forth without mediation, creating a sense of immediacy. This is a defensible decision, in conformity with the promise of autobiography to fully disclose the truth about its subject. Nonetheless it obscures to some extent the conscious crafting of the narrative by the interviewer-author.

The fact that this autobiography is elicited within the constraints of an ethnographic encounter bears some scrutiny. In most interviews, one party directs the exchange, and the respondent is obliged to answer questions; a certain answer is often expected. In the ethnographic encounter, the situation is more fraught because the two parties are not equals. Classically, an "outsider" anthropologist questions a "native" informant, using linguistic and epistemological dominance along with material inducements to create compliance. In the case of Agraval and Husain, significant social distance separates the interviewer and her subject. Despite an underlying affinity through theatre, the two are separated by differences of class, education, religion, and gender. Agraval is a well-educated intellectual in the urban theatre establishment; she is also Hindu and female. Husain comes from a Muslim working-class background with minimal formal education. His inferior status makes him dependent upon the social acceptance and economic patronage of benefactors, a condition reinforced through his line of work.

As a result of this dynamic, certain transactions are more obvious in this text than in ghostwritten autobiographies such as Sundari's. The construction of the life history in the ethnographic encounter involves a conditional exchange. The interviewer will honor and respect the actor as a national treasure, an expert in his art, if he makes a reciprocal gift, a guarantee to uphold establishment values and morality. Despite the mutuality of this bargain, the onus falls upon the informant. He must explain the mysterious folkways of his subculture and put them into an orderly system. Through subtle and not so subtle cues, Agraval makes Husain accountable for his world. He in return complies with the class- and gender-based preferences of his interlocutor by delivering an image of himself and the Parsi theatre as fundamentally clean and sober.

This particular memoir, despite being presented as a friendly dialogue, lays bare the disdain of the Indian intellectual for commercial theatre. Agraval serves as the mouthpiece for those who shun it as an aesthetic failure and site of disorder. She repeatedly draws attention to the flawed artistry of the Parsi stage—its loud vocal delivery, visual excess, cheap tunes, and the limited creative role of the actor. From the very beginning, she invokes stereotypes that must have dogged her subject for most of his life: "Educated, respectable people were told to stay away from the Parsi theatre, with its penchant for deluding spectators with poetic flights of fancy, songs and dances, exaggerated melodramatic situations, and abundance of miracles aimed at the lowest common denominator. It was best to avoid even the shadow of theatre people, given their defective character." (pp. 1–2)

As if to defuse the moral reservations held by her Hindi-language readers, Agraval queries Husain about his health and dietary habits. This early dialogue, which may register as overly personal or even offensive in English, is more than small talk. Husain's attestations of moderation serve as an index to his self-control and enable him to pass the test of character. As he shares details of his oral and anal self-mastery, he establishes his own yogi-like restraint. Throughout the autobiography, he paints a picture of personal and company discipline as utterly foundational. In response to accusations against the commercial theatre, he underscores the theatrical life as one lived in service to a public whose tastes required the very kind of entertainment he and his colleagues provided.

If Agraval attempts to shape Husain's story by her questions, he brings to the interview his skills and strategies as a storyteller. Adept at anticipating the expectations of others, he also demonstrates an uncanny ability to thwart them. As if in rejoinder to Agraval's alternately solicitous or censorious presence, Husain composes anecdotes that one minute challenge authority and the next embrace it. He pulls out a battery of weapons of the weak as he deflects the probing of his interlocutor. Sometimes he gives the anticipated information or agrees with the answer inherent in the question. More often, he evades the issue by starting another story. At times he takes complete control by going off on a long tangent that never reconnects to the point of origin. Other times, he circles around in narrative loops.

In all probability, the tailoring of Husain's story to fit Agraval's norms and expectations is not a novel event, but an iteration of the prior construction of his public image. His life narrative would already have been formed through encounters with the media, government, education, and civil society. Newspaper interviews conducted with Fida Husain, archived in the Natya Shodh Sansthan, reveal a story and self-image in close conformity to the autobiography, although details sometimes differ. Agraval's role as elicitor and editor, then, was business as usual for Husain. Its effect was merely to trigger a version of self and history that were already honed through repeated performance. The need to tell a story that works, to provide answers that are accepted, had for long led Husain to his own set of elisions and omissions.

Noted Performances

1922	*Parivartan* (Radheshyam) – female lead
n.d.	*Vir Abhimanyu* (Radheshyam) – played Uttara
n.d.	*Parambhakt Prahlad* (Radheshyam) – played Prahlad's mother
1924–5	*Shri Krishna Avatar* (Radheshyam)
1928	*Ishvar Bhakti* (Radheshyam) – female role
1930	*Laila Majnun* (Raunaq, Abdullah, Dil) – male lead
n.d.	*Nal Damayanti* (Talib)
n.d.	*Yahudi ki Larki* (Hashr)
n.d.	*Khubsurat Bala* (Hashr)
n.d.	*Sita Banvas* (Hashr)
n.d.	*Chalta Purza* (Ahsan)
1939	*Narsi Mehta* (unknown)
1946	*Bharat Milap, Sardar Bhagat Singh*

Master Fida Husain: Fifty Years in the Parsi Theatre

Pratibha Agraval

Winter 1978. A sudden trip to Lucknow. The awards ceremony of the Uttar Pradesh Sangeet Natak Akademi was that evening. One of the guests being honored at Rabindra Bhavan was a good friend, Dr Suresh Awasthi. The face of the other man looked familiar, but I couldn't quite place him. Then someone handed me the program. I flipped through the pages and gasped when I recognized Fida Husain Saheb. How fortunate I felt to be attending this event in his honor and paying my respects.

I was introduced to Fida Husain fourteen years earlier, in a festival organized by the theatre group Anamika. Fida Husain and his Moonlight Theatre Company had been invited to present Agha Hashr's *Sita Banvas* in the Parsi style. My office was right near the theatre. One evening I went there to speak with him. He was a tall man with a deep voice and eyes full of feeling. We finished discussing the details of the production, and a boy entered with tea. Fida Husain courteously refused. Seeing my look of surprise, he smiled and explained, "I don't take tea, and I have no interest in *pan, bidi*, cigarettes. An artist has to control his habits, or he can't maintain his voice and his health. I wouldn't be performing otherwise at the age of 65."

I slowly relaxed as a sense of respect welled up for this man. Imagine: not just a life in theatre, but the commercial theatre and Parsi theatre at that! The stereotype was all too obvious. Educated, respectable people were told to stay away from the Parsi theatre, with its penchant for deluding spectators with poetic flights of fancy, songs and dances, exaggerated melodramatic situations, and abundance of miracles aimed at the lowest common denominator. It was best to avoid even the shadow of theatre people, given their defective character. Thus the jolt: was it possible that this actor and director, who had been involved with the Parsi theatre for the last forty years, was abstemious, was speaking of self-control?

These thoughts recurred when I saw him at age 79, looking fit as a fiddle. In his suit and tie, he didn't look a day older than 60. Asked to speak at the Lucknow function, he delivered a segment from a play in that booming voice of old. It seemed he wanted to get past the microphone in front of him, but he restrained himself and tried not to embarrass the organizers.

Afterwards we exchanged gossip from Calcutta for a while, until we realized where we were and came back to the present. When we met the next day, Fida Husain was restless to hear all the news, asking about everyone he knew. I inquired if he was still keeping to the same routine. "Absolutely!" he said. "No *pan*, no cigarettes, no tea. I go to bed at nine-thirty regardless of whether there's a poetry recitation, a cultural program, or a wedding. I dine only at home. I get up at four-thirty in the morning and immediately head to the latrine, take care of my business for twenty-four hours. My whole life, I've never needed to go twice. Then I step outside, walk four miles, and attend morning prayers. Next I feed and wash my cow, Sarojini. She's a sweetheart, 5 or 6 years old, gives eight kilos of milk a day. At seven-thirty I eat breakfast: two slices of toast with butter, *panir*, a glass of milk. No snacking in between, just water a couple of times a day. I eat lunch at one and dinner at seven-thirty or eight. After dinner, I stroll outdoors for a while and go to bed at nine-thirty. That is the law I still follow, and everything is fine. The machine is still running."

He continued, "On March 11, I'll turn 79. I was born in 1899. The organizers printed 1901, that's incorrect." He hesitated a moment, then went on, "Health is the most important thing. If you are healthy, you have everything. And health comes from self-control. I have always paid attention to that, whether I was at work or resting at home. If you don't take good care of your health, you really suffer in old age. That's when the going gets tough. When you are young, you just think of yourself. You live a life of pleasure, get lost in sensual pursuits. Don't give a thought for family or anyone else. It's especially true of the professional actor. But when old age arrives, you realize the need for all that. Those whom you've neglected your whole life, those whom you've abandoned or ignored, why should they pay attention to you when you are old? I always stayed in touch with my family and fulfilled my responsibilities toward them. Whenever I got the chance, I went home, at least a couple of times a year. I sent money regularly. And I tried to take care of my health so that I wouldn't become a burden on others. I lived an ordinary life, but I always saved something. Whether it was five rupees or a hundred a month, I made a point of putting money aside. That way I never felt the need to beg from anyone. My sole desire is that I will always be able to look after myself, and whenever possible, that I may serve others as well."

"You spent a long time away, living in a completely different world. How do you find the atmosphere at home now, the bustle of children, the relatively quiet life?" I asked.

Fida Husain's eyes brightened. "I love it," he replied. "I have two sons and their wives, and I have two daughters. They're all married and have children. And now it turns out that I'm a great-grandfather on both sides of the family. My granddaughter has a baby, and my eldest grandson has a son. I'm the owner of the family brassware business, Bharat Art Enterprises, but I don't really know anything about it. My sons handle everything. One is studying in Hindu College, Muradabad (Moradabad), and the other in Ugrasen College. In addition to getting an education, they're learning the business. So this is the life I lead after quitting the Moonlight Theatre. Solitude suits me, I've always been fond of it. But things have been a little different, because the younger grandchildren don't see me as an authority figure, don't know I was a director. They run things themselves, and I have to follow their direction. I've fallen for their charms, and truly, they are very cute.

"As far as making a living, all of them are standing on their own feet. Luckily my daughters are very happy too. Both sons-in-law have jobs in the brassware factory. I have two companies, the one I mentioned, and Ansar and Company. Ansar is my eldest son's name, and the younger one is Ayub. They both run that company. The division is because of income tax regulations. There's no worry about income. Worry will eat a man up. When I was in the Moonlight Theatre, it was a constant anxiety. Whenever I held a salaried job, there was worry, especially in the theatre line. You'll be surprised to learn that in the fifty years I've been working, I've never spent a single day unemployed. As soon as I left one position, I found another. That's how it's been."

Four years later I met Fida Husain again, and this time we spent fifteen days together. The Natya Shodh Sansthan was founded in 1981, and in April 1982 we sponsored his visit to Calcutta. He had not been back to the city since his departure in 1968. This time he seemed quite changed. He was bent at the waist and supported himself with a cane. His boils would not allow him to go out to walk, but he paced in his room at five every morning. When I went in at six to offer him tea, he was delighted. Now he took tea twice a day, in the morning and the afternoon, but he still ate a simple breakfast of milk and toast, and had dal, roti, and vegetables for his midday and evening meal. Even when I insisted, he never took anything in between.

The Sansthan held a morning session with Fida Husain and Sita Devi, the actress who was long associated with the Moonlight Theatre. Unequalled in looks, voice, and acting ability, Sita Devi was delighted to see her Masterji, and she touched his feet and reluctantly sat next to him. Fida Husain was asked to speak about the circumstances in which he was raised, grew up, and entered the theatre. Effortlessly, he went back into the past and spoke in public about his life, as though leafing through an open book. Based upon that conversation and the many hours we spent later in discussion, I present the story of a true artist and the history of an important chapter in the Parsi theatre, some in his words and some in mine.

Fida Husain had been fond of singing since childhood. Any time he heard a tune, he could barely control himself. And yet he had been born into a traditional Muslim family in which music was strictly forbidden. Daily, there were incidents. He would run off, avoiding the eyes of the family, as soon as he heard the sounds of singing or playing, but then he was found out and soundly thrashed. After the beating he would swear off music, but then again his ears were beset by the sounds of music and he would forget everything else.

In 1911, the Durbar of George V took place, and artists from all over the country flocked to Delhi to display their talents. When the

Durbar was over, some of them stopped to perform in various places on their way back home. A group of performers came to Muradabad and put on a puppet show in Fida Husain's neighborhood. They propped up a cot on its side, hung a sheet over it, and presented a play. The story was about a king, his minister, the head of the guard, and a general. They clashed over something or the other, picked a fight, and drew their swords. Fida Husain liked it. The play had a story, and that story stayed with him, so when he went back home he began imitating it. This was how his love for acting and drama began.

The occasion passed, but the fondness for music persisted. Every day he was lured somewhere to listen, then beaten when the family found out. His mother had passed away by that time, but his father and elder brother were at home. His elder brother was already married. Once the elder brother, annoyed by Fida's antics, had his wife poison Fida to ruin his voice. Here is the story as told by Fida Husain:

When I refused to give up singing, *bhai saheb* prevailed upon *bhabhi*—my *bhabhi* who was so very fond of me—to destroy my voice. With her own hands, she offered me *pan* with vermilion powder in it, and that made me lose my voice for four or five months. I could only make a wheezing sound when I spoke. I tried every kind of medicine, to no effect. Yet my attachment to music continued. I sobbed in solitude and prayed to God, saying I wanted nothing in the world, just please restore my voice. Then the festival of Janmasthami, Lord Krishna's birthday, came around. In Muradabad there's a temple where all the Ras Lila troupes congregate, and holy men come there too. I was on the lookout for someone who could cure me, and when I visited the place I spotted an enormous figure with a white beard sitting on a cot while a man massaged his feet. I wanted to enter the temple compound, but a guard stopped me. Although the white-bearded sadhu was at a distance, he saw me and told the gatekeepers to let me in. He knew they were holding me back because I was a Muslim. I approached him, caught hold of his feet, and began to weep.

People standing around were saying, "Stop, get him out of here."

But the sadhu said, "No, let him weep. It will ease his mind."

I cried for two or three minutes, and then a *shaikh* standing nearby said, "Saheb, his voice has gone bad. He had a very fine voice, he used to sing *bhajans* sometimes."

Then the sadhu asked me what had happened. After I explained, he said, "I can't prescribe any specific medicine, but I'll teach you a discipline that may be of benefit. First, you must have the person who fed you the vermilion give you ripe bananas fried in ghee for three days. Then practise this: lie over a well, dangle your head over the water, and sing 'ah-ah' until your voice becomes clear."

I went home. There was a well outside, but I was not able to practise there, so I went to a deserted place nearby famous for a ghost that lived in a date-palm tree. This didn't bother me; I wasn't a believer in ghosts. Every afternoon I went there and practised singing "ah-ah." I continued this for twenty days without result. I also followed the banana therapy, and nothing happened with that either, but I was not daunted. The saint had told me to continue indefinitely, and on the twenty-first day my voice began to return. Within twenty-six days, I had my voice back entirely, just as it had been.

After this his craze for music only increased. He attended all the *mehfils*, *qavvalis*, and Nautankis. The beatings too continued; someone was always complaining about him. His father was a kind-hearted man who loved him dearly. His elder brother had died without offspring. Fida Husain was now the eldest son, with two younger brothers and a sister. His father was very indulgent and never beat him, but his uncle would throttle him viciously every time he found out that Fida had gone off to hear someone sing. Two years passed like this.

In those days there were several drama clubs in Muradabad. Ray Dayal's club was the most famous in 1917, during the war. All the best people were in it. Fida trained there for six months and learned his part backwards and forwards. From the first, he took on a female role. Regarding his stage debut, he recounts:

The club was putting on *Shahi Faqir* in a big hall. It was a free program, no question of tickets. The first day I was to go on stage, I got so terrified of the audience that I was stricken with fever. I forgot my part. A couple of prompters from backstage were shouting, "Speak up, you dolt, speak up," but I couldn't get a word out. Finally the audience booed me off the stage. One of the prompters, Madin Khan Saheb, tore up the Urdu script book and abused me. The other one, the manager Ram Bihari, explained that the huge crowd would have made even an experienced actor nervous. He urged that I be given another chance. On my second try I was successful, and that was that.

In this way, the path toward the theatre opened for Fida Husain. When he left Muradabad for the first time, it was to join the New Alfred Company. The company was in Delhi performing the Hindi play *Vir Abhimanyu*. Pandit Madan Mohan Malviya had presided at the inauguration of this drama in 1916. The notable fact about the New Alfred was that the company contained no women. Female performers were hard to come by in those days, and those available were professional performing women. Mahatma Gandhi, Motilal Nehru, Guru Shankaracharya, Malviya, and others could only consider attending the New Alfred because their plays had a conservative Hindu religious outlook, and because the company was pure and untainted.

What happened was that the president of Fida Husain's club, Sahu Maharaj Narayan, was good friends with Manik Shah Balsara, one of the owners of the New Alfred. He arranged for Fida to go to Delhi. Without telling his family, Fida Husain ran away from home on January 12, 1918. That day he had been beaten badly, so badly that his thumb had broken. His hands had been tied, he was hung from a tree and was caned until he promised to give up the theatre. A year earlier, Fida Husain's wedding had been celebrated. It was anathema for a married man to pursue the theatre line. A storm broke out in the *biradari*: the boy had gone bad, turned into a vagabond. His character had no other flaw. He was a hard worker, helped his father in the printing press. But a passion was a passion.

That day, when he was so severely beaten, Fida Husain decided it was now or never. Either he would give up his life, or he would run away from home. Chance presented him the opportunity. His father asked him to go off and borrow two rupees from a man in the neighborhood. Fida went to the man and took the money. But he didn't return home. He went straight to the club, where it had already been decided that Fida needed to get away from his family.

After joining the New Alfred Company, Fida Husain went on tour with them. Before long the company arrived in Meerut to perform at the Nauchandi fair. A boy from Fida Husain's neighborhood back home happened to see him on stage. He reported this to Fida's father, saying, "Fida Husain is having a great time in Meerut with a theatre company. He's got a big following." Fida's father approached the magistrate in Muradabad, a friend of his, and wept copious tears. The magistrate took care of the matter. He issued a warrant for Fida's arrest and sent his father to Meerut, to the police station. Accompanied by the head constable and a policeman, Fida's father arrived at the fair to take custody of his son. Now the details of Fida's capture:

The company had two Pathans who served as doormen, Sayyid Akbar and Nasarulla. Father reached Meerut early in the morning, well ahead of time. He stopped in the mosque first, to pray. During his entreaty for blessings, he broke down. The butchers praying nearby wanted to know what the matter was.

"My son," he blubbered, "... joined that company..."

"To hell with the company," they said. "We'll get your son back."

"No," he said. "If he leaves again and runs away, it will be the death of me."

When the policemen took him to the camp where the company was staying, they said to one of the Pathans, "Tell Fida Husain his father is here."

The Pathan came into the tent and relayed the news. As soon as I heard it, I felt wretched. I wasn't afraid of my father, it wasn't that. The fact was, my mother had died, my elder brother had died, and my father had already suffered so much. When I saw his face, I didn't feel pity—on account of my addiction. Still, as I looked more closely I could see that his eyes were sore and swollen with weeping. There he stood in his *shervani*, an elderly gentleman.

It occurred to me deep inside, if he has to die, so be it. At least I'll be able to continue with the theatre. This was my state of mind. I said to Nasarulla, "Take him out. Don't let him come back in."

Just then the company owner, Manik Lal,[2] came up to me from behind. "What's the matter?" he asked. Then he saw my father.

Immediately, Manik Seth commanded me to get up. "Go on out there. Your father is here."

I stepped forward. My father, seeing me for the first time after more than two months, collapsed with a cry. The Pathan and the *seth* took him inside the tent and turned the electric fan on him.

When he came out of his faint, father was given a lot of reassurance and support. "Whatever your wish, it will be done. Don't worry, your son has come to a good place. He's among decent people."

The sad truth was that it was my father-in-law who had lodged a complaint with the *panchayat* and had my father and uncle banished from the *biradari*. This was the worst sort of blow. A man simply cannot tolerate it. My father said to me, "I've been thrown out of the community, and I'm not going back without you. I'll give up my life right here if I have to."

"If you take me away," I said, "it will be the death of me. I want to work in the theatre. I'll do whatever else you say, just let me work."

---

[2] Manik Lal and Manik Seth are alternate forms of address for Manik Shah.

We talked in private for a while. He explained to me what he thought of the theatre as a profession. He actually had no idea about what went on in that company. In reality, it was less a theatre company and more a college or a university. The wayward were reformed in it. Boot camp, you could call it.

Finally, when I refused to go along, he explained very patiently, "All right. We'll work it out. You can stay, but you must not forget us."

That was when my attitude changed. The fantasy about him dying and all of that ended.

He said, "Don't forget us. There's your sister, and you have your brothers. They are still quite young."

I said, "You can count on me, I won't do anything wrong."

He said, "Okay, but I have certain conditions."

"Tell me what they are."

"I have five conditions. If you follow them, it will be of help to you, not me. They are for your own good."

"I swear that I will carry them out and make every attempt to honor them."

His first condition was that I should observe chastity, avoid lechery, and keep my character strong. The second was to avoid alcohol, never drink or indulge in any form of intoxication. Third, no gambling; fourth, no lying; and fifth, no coveting another's possessions.

Of those five conditions, some I observed, some I didn't. But this much I can say. As long as he was alive, from the time I was 18 till the day I turned 50, I did everything I could to make sure that my father never felt distant from me or alienated. When the drama *Nal Damayanti* opened here in Calcutta in the Moonlight Theatre right before he died, he prayed for me, read *namaz*, and the show turned out successfully. I never let my wife, my brother, or any friend come between us. I was loyal to him and obeyed his orders. And I gave him whatever happiness was possible in his old age.

Thus in 1918 the pattern of Fida Husain's life was set. At first, he traveled about with the theatre companies. Whenever it was convenient, he set up a separate household and invited his wife to join him. For the rest, he lived with the other artists. He always maintained relations with his family, visiting for a week, two weeks, or a month whenever he got leave. In 1968, when his family members told him to quit the Moonlight Theatre and return home, he did. Referring to that event, Fida Husain said:

It's been fifteen years since I left the theatre. My family pressured me to quit, and I too wanted this, because who knows what might happen in old age. An artist, a prostitute, and a race horse all come to a bad end eventually. This is my experience. No one to look after them, no place to go. It was a good thing to leave the stage while the public still valued me. And after all, I worked for fifty years, from 1918 to 1967.

22. Fida Husain

Fida Husain, Fifty Years in the Parsi Theatre

Fida Husain's remarks touched my heart. He had such a clear vision of reality, such an easy acceptance of it. In spite of working in the commercial Parsi theatre his entire life, he had managed to keep at bay all pretence, illusion, and luxurious living, and he had a good understanding of himself and others. I was eager to learn more about his experiences and about the operations of the Parsi theatre companies, their strengths and weaknesses. I provoked him, "I never saw the Parsi theatre, but I've heard that it was full of exaggerated acting, poetry, trick scenes, and dialogues delivered in loud voices. Certainly these traits cannot be considered positive. Our generation of theatre people wish to stay miles away from such tendencies. What do you think?" Fida Husain hesitated a moment as though collecting himself. The gist of what he said here follows.

In the early days before the Parsi theatre, touring drama companies came from England, landed up in Bombay, and performed their plays. Some Parsis went to see those plays and, inspired by them, started their own theatre companies. The acting in these new companies was modeled on the style of Shakespeare's plays. In that period of the English theatre the intonation was loud, actors had powerful voices. Imitating their manner, the tradition of forceful delivery was picked up by the Parsi theatre. The Parsi theatre pioneers were not steeped in Indian civilization and culture; they were heavily influenced by English ways. Thus they gave little scope in their theatre to the ordinary features of Indian life. Moreover, the actors were mostly uneducated, and they just did whatever they were told, without contributing anything of their own.

Among the directors of that early period, Jahangirji Khambata and Khurshedji Balivala were the most famous. To show the high calibre of these artists, Fida Husain related this incident:

Once, Jahangir was performing in Gujarati, the language of the Parsis. Some elderly Parsi gentlemen were sitting right in front of him. The scene in the play was about an atrocity being inflicted upon a woman. The acting was so convincing that one of the spectators took off his boot and hurled it at the stage, hitting Khambata. It was a full-sized boot. Khambata raised the boot and touched it to his eyes in reverence, saying, "Today I have achieved the ultimate success in my work." That's the kind of large-hearted actor he was. Later Khurshedji split off from him. The company was called the

Balivala Company at first. After they came back from England, it became the Victoria Company. They went to England to perform on the occasion of Queen Victoria's jubilee.

I was startled to learn that a Parsi company had gone to England. Who would have wanted to watch an Urdu drama in those days? Or was the performance in English? Who invited them, the government? In fact, the company went on its own, and they performed in Urdu. The few Indians who lived there came to watch, as did some English people, but the play was not successful. The company returned home, having suffered a financial loss.

Another question came to mind. Given that the Parsi companies were imitating Shakespeare's plays, how did they handle the musical element?

The element of music is Indian. From the very beginning, Indian drama was predominantly musical. As far as I know, regardless of language, the musical format prevailed, and even later when the number of songs was reduced, the plays remained musical. Prithvi Theatres, founded by Prithviraj Kapoor, did not give much importance to music. But if Saigal had formed a company, his plays would definitely have featured music.

In the beginning, in 1854 when the *Indar Sabha* was performed in Qaisar Bagh, all of the musicians were Khan Sahebs and experts in music. They started with the classical ragas and set the lyrics to them, not the other way around. When a particular fairy was coming on stage to sing a particular raga, the verses were written to fit that tune. The early plays like *Alauddin, Gul Bakavali, Fasana-e Azad, Laila Majnun* all had lots of songs, and 80 percent of the tunes were composed first, with the lyrics written afterward. Music was dominant; the words followed the music. Then when Agha Hashr came along, and Munshi Betab and Harikrishna Jauhar, they wrote the lyrics first, and the tunes were composed afterward. Because the dramas featured music so prominently, they had to find performers who could sing well. In the *Indar Sabha* Raja Indar has to sing at least sixteen songs. Gulfam and the Sabz Pari have fifty songs between them.

The *Indar Sabha* was an invented story, but the public adored it. They fell over themselves to get there, even committed petty crimes. People had no means, no resources in those days. Households were poor; where was the money? And tickets were at least four annas. When films began to be exhibited, a ticket cost five paise, but theatre tickets were never less than four annas—twenty-five paise. Do you know what I did? One time, I took the copper base off a hookah and pawned it for five annas. It was worth at least one rupee four annas, as it was quite heavy. But I sold it for five annas and bought a ticket for four annas. I got some peanuts for two paise and sat and enjoyed the drama.

The result of all of this was that adults with children got very worried whenever a drama company came to town. One time, things got really out of hand. The Manik Chand Company came to Muradabad.[3] They put on some excellent plays, and the audience was going wild. The townsfolk were afraid that their boys were going to be ruined, so they called a meeting and petitioned the government to send the drama company away. There was no law that could be applied, however. Nothing happened.

Spectacle was a particular feature of the Parsi theatre, and it was used to attract the public. You can get control over anybody, even those with the highest status, by showing them miracles. The spectacle in the Parsi theatre was indigenous; it had nothing to do with the Shakespearean theatre. The first ones to exhibit special visual effects were the painters, like Dinshah Irani. He lived in Calcutta and was very famous. He was fond of reading books about magic tricks and had a number of disciples who were good magicians, like Meenu and Kallan.

I'll describe for you an illusion scene from *Ganesh Janm*. A mirror was used to show that Parvati was taking a bath. She forms a lump of clay and places it on the altar, and then Ganesh is born from it. This illusion involved two mirrors, one with the image of the lump, the other showing a boy. The light was adjusted in such a way that Ganesh seemed to be taking birth from the lump of clay. In the same play, there was another scene in which Ganesh is beheaded. The average man's height is about five feet, but for this scene a boy three and a half feet tall was found. He was fitted with an artificial head, and a false body was painted so that he looked normal. A bunch of rags were dyed red and stuffed into the neck cavity, and he was kept out of sight in the wings. When the main actor playing Ganesh gets into an argument with Shankar, Shankar shoves Ganesh backstage several times. On the third occasion the boy with the artificial head comes out. No one in the audience can tell the difference, because he wears the same costume and crown as Ganesh. This time when Shankar hits him with his trident, his head is cut off and the boy falls down, writhing on the ground. The red rags are revealed and give the look of blood.

You wouldn't believe how incredibly innocent the people of Bihar once

---

[3] Probably a misprint for Nanak Chand Company, otherwise known as the New Albert, an early-twentieth-century company owned by the Punjabi businessman Nanak Chand Khatri.

were. Raja Indar comes into court at the beginning of the *Indar Sabha*, and all the courtiers sing an *amad* for him. When the song is half over, the king goes to sit on the throne. Then an *arti* ceremony is performed and an offering plate is circulated for donations. This was not in the original. It was all the company director's scheme to take advantage of the audience. They had no idea that this was the king of the fairies, and the king of heaven was somebody different. They all paid homage to Indar and offered money. Whatever they had in their pockets, they donated. The income from ticket sales usually amounted to Rs 700, but from the *arti* the company earned another Rs 900 on top of that.

Whenever there was a play about Lord Krishna, womenfolk came to the theatre bearing sweets. They would touch Krishna's feet and put down the plates of sweets. It was fun for the company, because everybody got to eat a lot of sugary goodies. A huge quantity of sweetmeats were presented in those days as offerings. That too was an amazing era!

I'll tell you another story. In *Rani of Jhansi*, they used to bring a horse out onto the stage. In certain other dramas, they would bring a chariot. Well, in this play they made a life-size cutout of a horse and painted it, then attached it to the top of a platform. The platform had little wheels on the bottom, and the horse was fitted onto those at an angle. In front it was like a mountain, about ten feet tall. During the scene, the horse was pulled from a cable backstage, and it looked just like the horse was trotting.

In *Vir Abhimanyu,* Lord Krishna comes on stage in a chariot with his Panchajanya conch. The chariot had genuine wheels, but the horse was the fake one on the platform. Actually there were two horses. They were manipulated so that it looked like they were pulling the chariot.

Now imagine a boat scene. These days the technique has changed a lot, but at that time they did it like this. The idea was to display a river. They would take a large screen made out of long *chik* reeds and fit lights inside it. Above and below were two rollers, and the screen was slowly spooled across those. When lit up, it looked like ripples of water. The point is that all these arrangements had to be perfect, and the movements had to happen at exactly the right time. Otherwise the effect was lost. If the moment was missed or somebody screwed up, there was hell to pay!

Fida Husain's description was so vivid that it seemed the entire scene was floating before our eyes. I recalled similar effects in the modern productions of *Setu* and *Angar*. In both, illusions were created principally through light and sound. In *Setu*, a train rumbles onto the stage and heads directly for the audience, and then with a big clatter it changes lines. In *Angar*, light and music are employed to create the unusual sight of water slowly filling up a coal mine. The lighting was designed by Tapas Sen, and the music was directed by Ravi Shankar. Tapas Sen was in charge of lighting in *Setu* as well. Doubtless a large part of the audience came to the theatre to witness these kinds of spectacles, and the same formula for attracting the public is still used today, when necessary.

The next day, the conversation turned toward the rules and regulations of the Parsi companies. The company bosses were staunch believers in discipline. They knew it would have been impossible to manage so many people without it. The New Alfred Company was especially harsh. No one could chew *pan*, and although smoking wasn't forbidden, it was not allowed in the dressing room or during rehearsals. There was a ten-minute break during rehearsals when those who wanted to smoke could step out. During rehearsals, all the actors had to sit for hours at a stretch with full attention to the training given on stage. No talking or looking around were allowed, and both feet had to be firmly planted on the floor. On their day off, only the senior artists were allowed to go out into the city, not the boys. The boys got one or two chances per week, but when they went out they were accompanied by two guardians and two doormen. Sometimes they took an excursion to a park for an hour. The two dozen boys had to wear a uniform and march in a line. When the older actors wanted to go out, they had to report to the director who made sure their caps were on correctly and their coats properly buttoned. Speaking of discipline, Fida Husain recounted:

Once, the company went to Lahore. Abdul Rahman Kabuli was at that time one of the best-known actors in India. He had a voice like a lion and was unequaled in delivering his lines. The drama was *Dasharath*. Three days were left before opening night, and the stage properties and scenery were being assembled. Kabuli donned his best suit, tipped his cap at an angle, and went to the director, Sohrabji Ogra, to get permission to go out. You should have seen that man's face! He made an intimidating sight—moustache out to his ears, long bushy hair. If he so much as glanced at a boy, the boy would wet his pants in terror. Kabuli's cap was a little too crooked. All the director had to say was, "Look, mister," and Kabuli straightened up the cap and left. The next evening Kabuli presented himself again, and this time the director rebuked him, "If you show yourself to the public before the drama opens, who will come to me and pay five rupees for a ticket?" No one could say a word in front of him, not even the top actors.

Another time, a quarrel started up at the railway station. Master Nisar was playing the part of Uttara, the heroine in *Vir Abhimanyu*. The Jewish actor Elijar, who was the main character in the film *Alam Ara*, was playing the part of Arjun. It was a select cast. Master Nisar was well known for his singing. When the note on the harmonium ended, his voice would linger and soar even higher. The audience went crazy over him. Anyway, the company was taking this play to Amritsar, traveling out from Delhi. Each year the company went on tour for a couple of months. A special train would be booked. It took seventeen cars to carry all the equipment to build a stage, along with furniture for the seats, the costumes, stage props, and so forth. Two electric generators were included for the lighting, because electricity wasn't available in the cities in those days.

Nisar's father traveled with the troupe as his guardian. Nisar was a very handsome youth, with a good voice and excellent reputation. But his father was an alcoholic, and he took cocaine as well. He wasted all Nisar's earnings on his habits. He had been given an upper berth in the second class. Master Nisar had the lower berth, so he asked that his father be given a berth down below with him. The request was conveyed to Sohrabji Ogra by the manager, since he was the one who decided everything.

When Sohrabji refused the request, Nisar went off to speak with him. Sohrabji responded, "Look, Nisar, there are other boys too who have their guardians along. I can't break the rules for just one of you. Why don't you give your seat to your father and sit on the upper berth yourself?"

"No, sir," he replied.

When he heard this, Sohrabji's countenance darkened. His tone grew harsh. "What do you want then?"

"I can't travel like this," Nisar answered.

Sohrabji gave him a look and called Mohanlal Mehta, the company's accountant. "Pay him what we owe him."

Bidding him *salaam*, Nisar departed with his father in a rage.

The company was distraught. The drama booked for Amritsar had been advertised with Nisar's name. Tickets had been sold, the public expected to see him. The opening date was postponed by eight or ten days. There was one Raghubir Sahukar in those days. He ran a Marathi theatrical company for a long time. Raghubir had no equal for playing the flirtatious female, and no woman could match him in looks. He was a colleague of Shantaram, who also acted as a female impersonator in Marathi plays. Sohrabji trained

Raghubir in just eight days, and he rehearsed him so well that the audience didn't even ask what had happened to Nisar. They were entirely satisfied.

Ogra was so domineering that no one dared approach him. If an actor became seriously ill, however, he would look after him, even clean his waste with his own hands. Otherwise he was a tyrant who brooked no disobedience. He laid down the law. Without the law, the company would collapse—that's what he said.

The rule was that salaries were to be paid on the sixteenth of each month. One time the company was going straight from Bombay to Amritsar on a special train. The sixteenth fell during the journey, so Sohrab told the manager to take the salary money along.

"We can pay them on the fifteenth," the manager replied.

"No, we always pay on the sixteenth," Sohrab responded. "Get the money and bring it along."

All the station masters and railway officials were on good terms with the company, as were the city officials, district magistrates, commissioners, and so on. When the sixteenth arrived, the special train got delayed by four hours while the salaries were being paid out.

Once in Bombay a fire broke out in the theatre. Everything was destroyed. Preparations were started, the stage was rebuilt. Salaries were still paid out on the sixteenth of the month. Not a single artist quit.

The employment contract was for three years and was firmly backed by the Bombay High Court. Sir Firoz Shah Seth was the company's legal advisor. Even the most popular actor was not allowed to go work for another company until the three years were up.

And yet, Madan doublecrossed us.[4] He saw that the New Alfred Company was advancing in the competition, even though it lacked women performers. This was due to its popularity with the conservative Hindu public. Madan lured eight actors away from the New Alfred, including the main characters. After that, the company should have fallen apart, but it remained just as it was. The eight actors who left came to no good. They didn't amount to anything, and their lives were ruined. I saw this with my own eyes.

I was listening to Fida Husain, but my mind was rushing in another direction. Fine, the artist was an employee of the company, he had to observe its rules and regulations. But was he not suffocated as an

---

[4] Probably Jamshedji Framji Madan.

artist by the severity of the discipline? Fida Husain immediately grasped my point and explained:

It was hard sometimes, but there were many comforts too. The salary was always on time, which was not the case in the other companies. Meals, boarding, lodging, and travel were all well organized. Everybody got first and second class tickets. Special trains were booked even for short distances. All the actors in India knew it was difficult to work under Sohrabji, but even the most famous ones came to learn from him.

I'll tell you a story about the painter Husain Bakhsh. In 1911, actors from all over the world came for the Delhi Durbar. Many artworks and handicrafts were brought to the exhibition. The company owners asked Husain Bakhsh Painter to make something and submit it so that the company would become famous. This artist was uneducated, but he was an expert in his field. He had a number of disciples in Bengal. He said he would give it a try. He painted two still lifes, one of a slice of watermelon with black seeds, and the other of a brass pitcher. Then he placed them in the sun to dry. Within two minutes, a crow was pecking at the watermelon. This painting won first prize.

Company discipline was not just for the actors, it was for the spectators too. They couldn't put their feet up on the sofas or sit with their legs splayed or knees apart. Students would come to the shows in Aligarh and elsewhere. The manager would tell them how to sit properly, explaining it was a question of his livelihood. They had to mind him.

There was a ticket for five rupees called the Special Class, printed on green paper. On the first line at the top, it read in English, "Pros. not allowed for this class." Just see the rule: prostitutes were not allowed to sit there. Once, when the company went to Delhi, there was an incident—I can't resist mentioning it. The Raja of Bharatpur had a concubine named Shyama Bai. She was very wealthy, always came loaded down with jewelry. She employed an Englishwoman as her secretary. She had reserved the entire sofa for the show, and when the audience started to arrive, she came in wearing a turquoise sari, accompanied by her secretary. They sat down together on the sofa. An absolute fairy she was!

The audience included some rich Hindus, building contractors from Delhi, and they began commenting among themselves that a prostitute was sitting right there, in the front row. One of the jewelers spoke to the *seth*, who was in front of the special class with the other company owners.

"*Sethji*," the jeweller began

The *seth* got up. "Welcome, Lalaji."

"Your rules have changed a little today," he said.

"Why no, what do you mean?"

"Today a prostitute is sitting in the special class."

The *seth* was flustered. "A prostitute? At our show?"

"Yes, sir. Shyama Bai is here, on the sofa in front."

The *seth* needed to hear nothing more. He sent a message to the hands backstage not to raise the curtain until he said so. Normally, everything happened like clockwork in the theatre. It was time for the show to begin. Mehrbanji parted the curtain and announced that due to unforeseen circumstances, the play would start five or six minutes late. This was extraordinary. The show always began on time, whether there were two people in the audience or it was house-full.

Amritlal Mehta was the man in charge. He came up to Shyama Bai and asked her very politely if she would come outside for a few minutes. She understood what was happening and said to him in English, "Get out!" The poor chap left and went backstage, whining.

Mr Sindhi, the manager, had fought in the Great War and was a retired army officer. He was an Anglo-Indian. When he went to talk with Shyama Bai, she refused to budge, saying, "I bought a ticket, and I'm not going to leave."

It so happened that the Deputy Superintendent of Police, Mallik Devi Dayal, was sitting with the owners. He was my friend. When I signed the employment contract in Delhi, he served as my witness. He suggested a way out of the dilemma, hinting that he would not take action against the company. Four strong stage hands and two Pathans were rounded up, and Dayal escorted them to the sofa. The six burly men surrounded it and lifted it up. The English lady was cursing and shouting, "Damn it! Damn it!" but no one paid heed. They brought the sofa outside and set it down at the gate. Shyama Bai was threatening, "I'll bring this company down! You'll be sorry. I'll send you all to jail!" But nothing ever happened. The rule was upheld.

Everything was systematic, fixed. Whether it was eating and drinking, or rehearsals and show times, it was the same attitude. We all got our meals from the company, and they were first-class, of excellent quality. Cooked food was first presented to the bosses to taste. It was not like nowadays, where there are gradations for different people. It was the same food for everybody. In the morning, two eggs. You could have them fried or however you wanted, that was permitted. But two chapatis, two eggs, and tea for breakfast. One, two, even three cups of tea, it didn't matter. The time for breakfast was fixed; the bell rang at 8 a.m. If the rehearsal was at 9:30, the first bell would ring at 8:30, so that anyone that had not eaten could finish. After the second bell at 9 a.m., breakfast was over. No matter how famous the artist, if he arrived after that it was too late. These rules were strictly observed.

The fellow whose duty it was to ring the bell was named Chauth. He was given a Zenith watch. Every day he had to leave at 7 a.m. and go to the railway station or post office to synchronize his watch with theirs. He was also responsible for lighting the lamps. Cities didn't have electricity then. During the day, he cleaned twenty or thirty hurricane lamps and lanterns, filled them with oil, and kept them ready to take to each room in the evening. After the lighting of lamps, incense was burned and taken around for its fragrance.

At the start of the rehearsal Mehtaji called roll, although nobody was ever late. Remember, we were afraid. Sohrabji himself would arrive there five minutes ahead of time, and if anybody showed up even two minutes late it would be very bad for them. Sohrab Ogra was a great actor, the best comedian on the Parsi stage up to now. The photo of him as Sikandar Khan was known even in England.

When a show was going on, this is how the curtain changes worked. A man would be sitting on a chair with a notebook. A thin thread was strung from his position to where the curtain was, and at the end of the thread was a tiny bell which could only be heard by the curtain puller. When that bell was rung, the curtain went up or down. He also had a switch to send a signal to the orchestra. The switch turned on a red light that meant it was time for a once-more.

It wasn't as though we were forced to pay attention during rehearsals. When Sohrabji explained things, the performers wanted to hear what he was saying and learn from him. Well-known artists came to train with him. They had to spend six months just sitting in the audience watching performances, so that they could see for themselves the standard of the company, the method of delivering dialogue, the kind of atmosphere that prevailed. After this training, they would go out and earn a name all over India.

Just imagine how we had to hustle during rehearsals and performances! The truth is, the New Alfred's discipline had no equal. I'll tell you about the management of shows and the regulations on time. If the show was to begin at 9:30 p.m., the first bell rang at 8. It was a huge bell hanging on a chain, like you see in temples. It had to be struck exactly one hundred times. The second bell was rung at 9:15, fifty times. The third bell got only twenty-five strokes, and then everybody got in line for the invocation prayer. Even if your part was only in the last scene of the third act, you still had to be in the theatre at 8:30.

The boys were all handled by the master who taught the dancing class. They had to put on their powder and stand in line for him to check their makeup, see whether they had applied *kajal* correctly to their eyes. Whatever flaws he found had to be corrected. The adult artists put on their make-up and appeared in front of Sohrabji for review. There was no fooling around, no dawdling.

The rule about costumes was that you had to hang them inside out when you took them off. There were long clothes lines, and pegs for the leading actors. That was where the costumes were hung. Down below were boxes to store underwear. You couldn't wear your own clothing, you had to put on those clothes. Everything was kept washed, ready for use. The stage jewelry, necklaces, and earrings had to be carefully stored inside those boxes. The costume manager would hang out everything during the day, but when the artist finished his work he had to leave the costume turned inside out, just so. Those were the kinds of rules we had to follow.

Fida Husain's account of his early life in the New Alfred Company gave insights into the atmosphere, the economic situation, the administration, artistry, and high standards of the professional companies in the early twentieth century. Not all Parsi drama companies were as well-organized and disciplined as the New Alfred, yet this important company provides an indication of the competence and modes of functioning of the Parsi stage at its peak.

Throughout this conversation, Fida Husain's demeanor remained modest and polite. Occasionally he interjected, "That was one of my best roles," or "The audience really appreciated me in that," underscoring the significance of pleasing the public in those days. If a given drama did not prove popular, the company's existence was in jeopardy.

Fida Husain also revealed a character that was generous and supportive. He readily acknowledged virtues in other individuals, be they artists or laymen. About himself he was humble and spoke little, expanding on others at length without reserve. Such grace and cordiality are rare things.

When we met the next day, our talk turned to the Moonlight Theatre. Fida Husain Saheb worked in Calcutta in the Moonlight Theatre for twenty years. When he left in 1968, the owners shut the theatre down. At the time he joined in 1948, the Moonlight had been running several years. It was owned by the four Mehrotra brothers. The youngest of them was the mainstay of the Moonlight, and with him Fida Husain began his account:

Govardhan Babu may have been the youngest, but none of the others could stand up to him. If anybody crossed him, he would threaten to leave for Japan. He was the one who organized the short program format for the Moonlight Theatre: a motion picture together with half an hour's worth of dance, *qavvali*, ghazal, and comedy. This was very popular, and there were four shows every day. Over the course of ten years, the total income after expenses came to Rs 15,000, and with that the Mehrotras bought the Bharat Woolen Mills.

The Mehrotras had heard of my fame and were extremely keen that I join their company. Even though it was a small outfit, they engaged well-known artists like Patience Cooper and Kajjan, offering them a lot of money. Patience Cooper was very beautiful. She was an Anglo-Indian, one of three sisters.

Govardhan came to meet me when I was working for the Shahjahan Company in Karachi. He talked at length about how he wanted to expand the company, but the program was short, just those few small acts plus the film. The tickets cost at most a rupee or twelve annas. The Moonlight Theatre contained a total of 750 seats, and business was booming. It was war time, and Calcutta was full of soldiers.

He invited me to his hotel and offered me Rs 150 a month as salary. The Shahjahan Company was inactive at the time, so I was sitting idle, but Manik Lal didn't approve of my leaving. He thought that if I quit, everybody else would too. I didn't tell him the truth. I kept the matter a secret and went off to Calcutta, saying I had some family business to attend to.

When I got to Calcutta, I saw a long line of customers waiting to buy tickets for the Moonlight Theatre. They were all wearing *lungis* and smoking *bidis*. This was not the audience I was used to. There wasn't a single Marwari gentleman in that line; they were all factory workers. This was a big problem for me. I went inside, and Govardhan greeted me very cordially. I told him the deal was off. At first he was silent, but after a moment he said, "All right, never mind." Although he had advanced me a month's salary, he didn't want any of it back. In fact, I had spent most of it already. Thus ended my first trip to Calcutta to join the Moonlight Theatre.

Seven or eight years later, I went back for good. But in the meanwhile, I did many things. The Marwari theatre was thriving in Calcutta, and Marwari plays were running in the Grace Theatre. Bharat Vyas was doing *Ramucharna*. Some wealthy businessmen based in Kanpur, Padmapat and Kamlapat Singhania, persuaded me through their agent to join the Marwari stage. These Marwaris were devotees of Narsi Mehta. When I performed that role with Ganpat as Lord Krishna, the Singhanias reserved a sofa with their mother for the entire run, paying in advance. The mother used to touch my feet and beseech me to intercede with Lord Krishna on her behalf. In the winter season, they presented Ganpat and me with warm blankets, on the assumption that Narsi and Krishna must feel the cold too.

Calcutta had just been declared an emergency area. One day, I was in the Grace Theatre watching *Kankavatir Ghat.* The play was going magnificently, and I was really enjoying it. When I stepped outside during the intermission, I got word of the emergency from the *Statesman.* The public reaction was to panic. This was in 1942, when Japan was about to strike. Pandemonium ensued, and the actors became very agitated. I had rented a room at No.1 Mandir Street near the Moonlight Theatre. The actors came to my room, crying, "Rescue us, get us out of here. Bombs are going to fall." They were all distraught, even Patience Cooper, who was living on Theatre Road. She sent word to me, "Master, only you can help us, otherwise we will all starve. We must get away from here."

This was the state of things in Calcutta. When I received the proposal from Kanpur, I immediately accepted it. I rounded up a large staff, taking many from the Moonlight. I decided to purchase some stage properties. Manik Lal's company had left a quantity of stage flats, props, costumes and so forth in a Calcutta warehouse. Their agent told me I could have the lot for free if I paid the Rs 300 owing in rent. I paid him Rs 1000, and got Rs 40,000 worth of properties in return.

Thus I formed the Narsi Theatrical Company and set off for Kanpur in a caravan, taking along Nawab Mistri, the scene painter from the Moonlight. Finance was provided by Kailash Babu Singhania. The company was very successful, but three months after we arrived in Kanpur, a commotion broke out there too. Kanpur was a manufacturing center, the munitions industry was based there.[5] The city officials came to our rescue, sponsoring three shows a month for the police. I was often invited to their homes along with the dancer Mauli and Patience Cooper.[6] The company lasted eight months, until Gandhi's Quit India movement began. The unrest that broke out then was so great, it was like the rebellion of 1857. I shut down the company, dismissed the staff, and left for Muradabad.

The day after I reached Muradabad, the manager of the Babu Roshan

[5] Fida Husain implies that there was an exodus from the city due to threats of bombing, causing a drop in ticket sales.

[6] Fida Husain may be suggesting that his role was to chaperone the starlets, who presumably had been invited by the local officials to perform at private parties.

Lal Company from Delhi showed up. Babuji had long been trying to persuade me to sign on with him. His company had been running twenty years, but the Hindu audience took no interest in it. He would put on *Laila Majnun* for two days, get full houses, and that was it. I joined the Babu Roshan Lal Company and produced *Narsi Mehta*. For 300 nights we performed this play in Delhi. D.P. Shrivastav, Sir Jagdish, and Jugal Kishor Birla attended. People saw it twenty times over, and I was awarded 150 medals. The gold ones I turned over to my daughters to wear. The silver ones I melted down; they amounted to Rs 1400. I had no interest in wearing medals, but I kept some as remembrances: the medal from the State of Bikaner, the Maharaja of Patiala's cup, the medal from Tonk, and the Jaipur medal.

I stayed in Delhi for three years. The various newspaper photographs of me date to this period. There were many fine reviews in the papers in Karachi, Lahore, Bombay, Banaras, and Allahabad. However, in those three years of working, I became thin and weak. I also staged *Krishna Sudama*, and we performed two shows every Sunday. I developed chest pain, and when I felt ill I told the company I could no longer do the two Sunday shows. The whole operation was on my head. The managers started gossiping in their tent, saying Fida Husain was putting on airs. Word got back to me, and as soon as I heard what they said I sent in my resignation. They begged and pleaded, sent emissaries to cajole me, but I didn't waver.

After I quit the Babu Roshan Lal Company, I was about to leave for Bombay when the Raja of Indargarh came to Delhi. He formed a company called the Shri Mohan Theatrical Company and hired me. I acquired the stage properties and costumes from the princely state of Charkhari for Rs 7000. Out of passion for theatre—and for Sharifa—the Maharaja of Charkhari had purchased the Corinthian Company, but he was unable to make a go of it. The company owned 110 curtains and 400 wings. The costumes were studded with real gemstones and gold. One of them, the dress of the Turki Hur,[7] could not be worn by a female actress, it was so heavy. Two huge trunks were filled just with shoes, perhaps a thousand pairs. All of these properties were valued at forty lakhs.

Agha Hashr was in Charkhari too. He had been offered Rs 50,000 to write *Sita Banvas*. He took Rs 30,000 in cash and spent the other Rs 20,000 on liquor. The whole world knows that. Are you aware of Agha Saheb's position at the time? His Highness called him *baba*. The most powerful princes respected him. One time, the royal party was driving to the theatre in a motor car with the headlights on. Agha Saheb was in his cups. For three months, *Bharat Milap* ran and earned much money. The raja came from Indargarh to see it, on the company's condition that he not meet

---

[7] The heroine's costume from the play *Turki Hur* by Agha Hashr.

23. Fida Husain in *Krishna Sudama*

personally with any actor. You never know about these rajas and maharajas, what they will get up to. He stayed on the ground floor of the Swiss Hotel, and upstairs stayed Husn Bano, the film actress from Bombay. She was Sharifa's daughter, a pretty girl, and she was playing Sita in *Bharat Milap*. Although it was a small part, I was paying her Rs 3000 a month as salary and Rs 1000 extra to stay in the Swiss Hotel, because the audience was in love with her films. Her name was a big draw. Abdul Rahman Kabuli was playing Dasharath.

Well, the Raja of Indargarh fell for Husn Bano. He called me to his hotel room. He was sitting on the sofa with his minister and behind them stood his secretaries and bodyguards, all wearing turbans and carrying revolvers.

The raja addressed me warmly, "Fine play, first-class. You've really outdone yourself!"

"Thank you."

Pannalal was the raja's private secretary. He was close to the maharani too. Every evening she drank two bottles of liquor—fermented pomegranate juice, ginger beer, everything. Then she listened to performers who sang to the accompaniment of the *daf*. Finally she took a full dose of morphine by injection and went to bed. Royal ways were really something—God forbid!

Pannalal said, "His Highness wishes to meet Husn Bano." When I heard this, the ground lurched under my feet. Masterji avoided such things entirely.

"What can I do for you?" I replied.

His Highness grew impatient. "I want you to arrange for me to meet her," he said.

I was incensed. But what could I do? He was a king. "Look, Your Highness," I replied. "This is against my law. I cannot do it."

"Why not? Here I have invested all this money in the company. Don't I have the right? I'm the king, and you're an impudent good-for-nothing."

"Fine," I replied, "Why don't you call someone who's used to such things?"

"Okay, I'll call Manik Lal. He'll provide me with whatever I want."

"Good," I responded.

"But this is wrong on your part. I've spent so much money, and you dare to deny me? Such conceit!"

I stood up and said, "Listen, Your Highness," in such a firm voice that the minister and the others gesticulated for me to stop. "No one will say a word." The whole of Delhi was on my side, and I feared no one. I was on good terms with all the officials, the court, the magistrate. They were devoted to me because of my role as Narsi Mehta. Kings and princes had no authority over them.

"It's a straightforward matter," I continued. "The respect you command is like a mountain, mine is but a fingernail. You preserve your honor, and I'll preserve mine." Then I left. I wrote a notice, had it typed, and sent it by telegram, saying I was quitting. The management too wanted the matter to be hushed up, otherwise how could the show go on? Thus ended my stay with the Shri Mohan Theatrical Company.

Next I went to Bombay and joined the Ranjit Studios of Chandulal Shah as a permanent employee for Rs 500 per month. They asked me to do a comic role in their next picture, but I refused. Before long, I left and went back home for a month.

The Shri Mohan Company in the meantime had extracted Rs 40,000 from the princely state of Indargarh. Manik Lal and Sultana were clever at that. The raja was in a state of anxiety, with no entertainment in the offing. He sent for me through the lawyer Tavakali, an old friend.

"Masterji, I take back everything I said," the raja apologized. "Brother, please form a new company. The Shri Mohan Company is washed up."

Tavakali Saheb persuaded the raja to give me Rs 8000, saying, "This is for Fida Husain's damages. Consider it a penalty or whatever, but please pay him. Where would you like the company to be formed?"

I wasn't about to start another company, but I said, "Let's try Calcutta." The raja said, "Indore."

I said, "No, sir, it won't be successful there. You'll get your investment back only from Calcutta."

The entourage left for Calcutta, and everyone stayed in the Minerva Hotel. A film crew from Talvar Productions was staying in the same hotel. For seven days I deceived His Highness by pretending to look for land on which to build the new theatre. He believed I was going to start another company, and after seven days he left. I received a check from Lloyd's Bank. I got that money for free.

Plus I got to work in three motion pictures in Calcutta. One of them was *Arabian Nights* with Kanan Bala. My job was to intone the *azan*, the call to prayer in Arabic, during the title sequence when the pigeons fly up into the sky. For that I was paid Rs 500. I'll tell you an amusing story about that film. Madan Studios had built a wall, and on top of the wall they constructed the whole set with the mosque, minarets, and so on. When the shooting was over and they were tearing down the set, a bunch of Muslim villagers showed up and started protesting. "The mosque is being destroyed, the mosque is being destroyed," they shouted. Together with Agha Hashr and a couple of other Muslim colleagues, I pacified them, explaining that this was a movie set, not a real mosque.

I played the chief medical officer in Talvar Productions' film *Tute Sapne*. And one other role, I forget which film. Mr Kapoor of His Master's Voice had urged me to leave the theatre, saying it would ruin my voice. He helped me get work in cinema. But how could Fida Husain find satisfaction in *filim-wilim*? I was too much in love with the theatre. I earned Rs 2000 from those pictures, plus the Rs 8000 I had pocketed, and I was happy.

Fida Husain was very popular among the Marwaris. In the evenings I used to go to music parties at the house of Lala Shri Ram on Harrison Road. That is where I met Sita Devi, sitting modestly in the corner by herself. She was introduced to me as the wife of Gaur Babu, who had come to Calcutta from Dhaka to pursue his MBBS. She had a lovely face and was dressed simply and tastefully. Her ghazal-singing left a lasting impression on my heart. She had a sweet, tuneful voice and a tall figure.

At the urging of my friends, I formed the Hindustan Theatre and hired Sita Devi for Rs 300 per month. On the first day of rehearsal, everybody thought I had lost my mind. The poor girl couldn't speak her lines. I thought it over and hired Muhammad Bhai, a master of seven languages, to coach her in Hindi. She was a quick study, really sharp. In eight days she had her part memorized, and not only that, she was so keen that she wouldn't even let her master get up for meals. The new company opened with *Narsi Mehta* in the Minerva Theatre. It was so popular that the four front rows of Rs 100 tickets were completely sold out. The play ran for three months in 1946, and the money poured in. The rental on the theatre hall was Rs 500 per night, and we performed two nights a week, Tuesdays and Fridays.

The next play, *Hamen Kya Chahiye*, passed muster but was not a money-maker, so we quickly mounted *Krishna Sudama*. Sita Devi played Sharda and I was Sudama. It was a hit. The fourth play was being cast when Mr Jinnah took Calcutta for a wild ride. The murder and mayhem were such that we had to shut the company down.

I still had plenty of money, and it was burning a hole in my pocket. When I got home, I decided to go into business. Enough of the theatre! With my partner, Banvari Lal, I started trading in wood, turning the furniture and properties I had collected from the Raja of Indargarh into beds and cart frames. Gladly I gave Banvari Lal the profit from the first three wagonloads, that's how generous I was. When it came time to deliver my own wagons, they caught fire on the way to Rawalpindi. Thus I lost the Rs 8000 I had acquired for free, along with my own Rs 2000. It was not in my fate to profit from easy money.

Next I lived in Ramnagar. They had a club that performed the Ram Lila, so I figured, why not start doing drama? The plays I directed were so popular that the entire Hindu populace became my followers. Then I was invited to Karachi to direct plays for the Sindhis. For three months, things went swimmingly, until Pakistan was created and riots started. Then I went to Bombay and from there went back to Calcutta. I performed the drama *Durgadas* to help rebuild the temple on Zachariah Street, earning a name for myself among the Hindus. Mangturam Jaipuria called a meeting and announced, "Mahmud Ghaznavi came to India to tear down temples, but Fida Husain came to build them."

Then I produced *Bhagat Singh*, which was very popular. It had a lot of sets, including a scene of the entire State Assembly. Vipin Babu played the role of Saunders. Everything was managed by Gaur Babu, who provided all the properties. The whole thing was sponsored by the Minerva Theatre. My old Hindustan Theatre company was about to be absorbed by Gaur's Bengali company, but I got upset and had a falling out with Sita Devi and Gaur Babu. I was about to accept an offer of Rs 5000 from Delhi, when

Govardhan Babu sent for me. I joined the Moonlight, but then it shut down during the riots. Patching up my quarrel with Sita, she and I left for Kanpur to join the Sarasvati Company. We stayed there for six months. Then I went to Bombay to work in films, but that didn't pan out, so I returned to Calcutta and joined the Moonlight once more. The Moonlight ran for twenty-four years, and for twenty of them I was in charge. It's a long story, the Moonlight, so I will tell you about it tomorrow.

The next day Fida Husain was in an excellent mood. Before I could ask any questions, he explained, "You've really got me hooked. I spend the entire day and night lost in thoughts about the old days. When I try to sleep, I see all these things pass before my eyes like scenes from a film. Let me tell you about another incident, before I get to the Moonlight. It's really interesting."

The company had gone to the North-West Frontier Province, and it was there that I was surrounded by dacoits one day. I had gone to book a ticket in the railway office and was counting my change, when all of a sudden I felt a pistol pressed against my chest. A finger was on the trigger. I was sweating bricks, I was so scared. They took my money and told me to shut up. The truth was that they hadn't been given free passes to our performance, and now they were getting even.

The police got word and captured one of the dacoits, but in the meanwhile I was whisked away to their hideout. It was a huge house surrounded by high walls, with pistols and rifles hanging everywhere. In the corner was a heap of hashish that looked like a pile of cowdung. The chief of the gang told me the police were going to make me identify the criminal in a line-up. If I didn't cooperate, they would be my friends for life. I could call on them at any time. But if I pointed to the right man, they would carry me off along with my wife on her bed. They thought Kajjan was my wife.

I told them I wasn't going to cooperate with the police. They returned all the money in a little purse, and we drank tea together. Then the police dragged me into the station, where I met Wadera, the judicial magistrate, who had just come from his prayers. I saw the dacoit who had captured me in the line-up, but he had shaved off his beard and hair. When they asked me to identify the suspect, I said, "He's not here." Three times they threatened me and asked me again, but I refused to identify him. Finally everybody was released, me included. That was a real fix. When they put that pistol to my chest, I almost soiled my clothes. Really, I'm telling you the truth, why would I try to fool you?

Fida Husain was silent a few minutes, as though he wanted to say something else before starting in on the Moonlight. I didn't wish to disturb him. At last I said, "There's no hurry to get to Calcutta. Wherever you are, let's go there. There's no hurry to reach Calcutta." He laughed, and I did too. The destination was still far in the distance.

You see, I worked in the theatre for fifty years. I started with the New Alfred where I stayed for twelve years. After that, I was in the Alfred Company. Here's how I got involved with the Alfred. When the New Alfred closed down, I went to Lahore to work in a film, but that project failed, and from there I went back home to Muradabad. I'd been there just three days when a telegram arrived from Ajmer, inviting me to join a small company. There was this businessman named Bakhshi Ilahi who had made a lot of money as the India agent for Caesar's cigarettes. He had a concubine in Delhi who used to drive around in a big Chevrolet. Must have been worth twenty lakhs. They say she had these fat gold bricks, and whenever she needed cash, she would produce one of them. Her brother had formed this little company.

So I left for Ajmer and joined the company. We had to leave for Jawara in Madhya Pradesh the next day to perform at the request of the Nawab. After I played the role of Majnun for a couple of days, Nawab Saheb asked me to take up the drama *Khubsurat Bala*. He was so pleased with my performance that he awarded me a medal. Then the Raja of Ratlam invited us to perform there. He was bosom buddies with the Nawab of Jawara—they used to eat their meals together. It wasn't a huge distance between Jawara and Ratlam, so off we went. But I didn't care for the atmosphere that developed in the company at Ratlam. It was so different from the New Alfred—full of Punjabi actors and strange people. I didn't like it.

The Alfred Company owned by the Madans, the one with the actress Munni Bai, was stationed in Indore at the time. I headed straight there and joined my friends Dinshah Irani and Manilal Madhur. We talked things over, and my terms for employment were settled. I took the company straight from Indore to Nauchandi, assuming the risk myself. In those days, the manager and director of a theatrical company had total control. Mehrji Sarves was the director; he was Madan's son and Jahangir's father-in-law.[8] The manager was Dinsha Antiya, a Parsi. The assistant manager was Are Khan Saheb.

---

[8] Possibly a misprint for *sarveyar,* Engl. "surveyor." Mehrji Surveyor is mentioned as a director in other accounts, but not as a member of the Madan family.

I suggested to them, "Let's go to Nauchandi from Delhi."

"To the fair?" they replied, dubiously.

Despite their doubts, when the Alfred Company went to the Nauchandi fair in Meerut, it earned so much money that the management was able to pay all the back salaries owed the performers. You may not know it but the Nauchandi fair is very famous, as a religious festival and an agricultural exhibition. Both communities, Hindus and Muslims, participate in it. The area has a temple dedicated to Chandi Devi as well as a saint's tomb. The saint's death anniversary and the goddess's festival occur at the same time.[9] It's a good example of both communities in India holding a fair together. It used to be a huge event: three or four theatrical companies each year, several circuses, films, traveling cinema. People came from all over UP, and it proved to be very profitable for the Alfred Company.

I suggested that the company travel next to Muradabad. There we performed *Sita, Nagputra, Shalivahan, Dil ki Pyas,* and *Ganesh Janm*. The Muradabad audience was enchanted with such elaborate stagecraft, and for twenty days we raked in the money. Then Muharram started. In both Rampur and Muradabad, Muharram lasts for seven days, and during that time nobody goes to the cinema. In Rampur, the nawab used to enforce this, but the custom was the same in Muradabad and had been so for a long time. The company did not want to shut down the show, however, and this created some trouble. The assistant manager, that Khan Saheb, alleged it was because of Fida Husain that there was agitation in the town. Supposedly there were rumors that the company was going to be set on fire. He and his two sidekicks were jealous of me, envious of my voice. They had convinced the manager and director that I was behind the Collector issuing an order to shut down the company lest there be a riot. But it was not my fault.

The company was about to leave for Bareli when I was called in and given my final salary. I told them that I was blameless and said good-bye. It's a matter of destiny that as soon as that company went to Bareli, they fell on hard times. When they got back to Calcutta, they were on their last legs and soon folded up. By contrast my good times really started when I got to Calcutta, and my career shot way up even though I didn't know anybody when I first arrived. I had never been to Calcutta before. The New Alfred Company traveled to Rangoon and to Sri Lanka, they went to every city in India, but they never came to Calcutta. That was because the Madano

---

[9] The temple is dedicated to Nauchandi, a manifestation of the goddess Chandi, and the shrine is that of the Muslim saint Bala Mian, aka Syed Salar Masood Ghazi.

owned all the cinema halls and wanted a share of the profits, and the New Alfred wasn't about to give them any of their money.

In 1948 I returned to Calcutta once more, and from then until 1967—for twenty years in all—I was in the Moonlight. This was the company which I ran according to my own lights. Up till then, I had mainly worked as an actor in various companies. In some I was the director as well, but to a great extent I had to follow the wishes of the owners. But it was different in the Moonlight. It had its owners too, but they were businessmen who were concerned only with the amount of the monthly profit. Whatever I wanted, however I wished to do things, they never interfered with any of that. They gave me a lot of respect and thought of me as a member of their family, and in return I worked with full dedication and considered the Moonlight my own company.

The first drama we mounted was *Puran Bhagat*. This had been newly composed by B.C. Madhur of Bombay. I took some staff from the Minerva Theatre and called some from Delhi and Bombay, and we had a strong troupe, but the problem was that the gentry class didn't want to come to the Moonlight. The Moonlight Theatre had a reputation from before as being a low-class place with cheap ticket prices. The Marwari audience that frequented the Minerva and Corinthian theatres didn't turn out, despite the drawing power of myself and the other top artists. So the company was running at a loss.

The second production was Randhir's *Nayi Manzil*, a social drama. It was quite popular, but again the gentry did not attend in large numbers. The play ran for one month and one week. Then we put on our third play, *Nal Damayanti*. This made a big splash. The heroine of *Puran Bhagat* was Amina Khatun; she also starred in *Nayi Manzil*. She had a tall figure and a full voice. Kamala Gupta from Orissa was the heroine in *Nal Damayanti*, a beautiful girl, lovely singer. *Nal Damayanti* also played for about a month, but in the middle of it, Hindu-Muslim riots broke out. A curfew was imposed, and it was not possible to hold a four-hour program. As a result the company had to be shut down again; this was in 1948. But the owners told me not to let the staff go. They wanted to adapt the program somehow.

Nonetheless, I went and joined a company in Kanpur, the Sarasvati Theatrical Company. Along with the Moonlight staff, I was offered a big salary, and we all left for Kanpur. I have already told this story. I patched up my quarrel with Sita Devi and she went to Kanpur too. We performed many dramas there. *Krishna Sudama* was a hit, and *Narsi Mehta* was our currency note. Most popular of all was *Rani of Jhansi*. The main role in it was that of Major Ellis. The actor who was cast for that part ran off after two days, so I performed Ellis. People said I was good at imitating the English accent in Hindi and pretending to smoke a pipe.

After six months, that company shut down, and I went to Bombay to join the film industry. I didn't like the factionalism there, and finding housing was a huge problem. I saw a nice flat in a far-off place, very well set up, but they were asking Rs 15,000 as key-money, and I couldn't even afford Rs 5000. Plus the company that I had joined wouldn't use me. There was so much corruption. If your contract was for Rs 15,000, half of that was supposed to go to the director and half went to the artist—that was how you got casted. The director was pretty famous, but still, I couldn't go along with this, so I left.

Here I couldn't help interjecting, "Did that happen on the stage too?" Fida Husain replied:

Not like that exactly, but company directors did receive a lot of hospitality. A certain actress would cook chicken and bring it to the director, another would make a *pulao*. But I never accepted even *pan*, I never got into the habit. Bribery affects the work later on. If you accept somebody's favors, then you have to be partial toward that person. Wherever I've worked, I've maintained discipline. I was in the military for twelve years—in the New Alfred Company. Old habits die hard!

At any rate, I couldn't get used to Bombay. My heart wasn't in films, because I kept thinking about the Moonlight Theatre. People had told me that the Moonlight owners were very angry with me. I heard that they didn't even want to meet with me. But B. C. Madhur convinced me otherwise and took me to their office in the Esplanade. All four brothers were sitting there: Shri Babu the finance man, Vishveshvar Babu the controller, Salig Babu in charge of religious matters, and Govardhan Babu who made things happen. I never could have imagined the welcome. Govardhan said, "Look Masterji, you don't need to go anywhere else now. It's your company, you take over." So I joined the Moonlight once more.

This time, I organized a drama program that lasted two and a half hours. Now the Hindi-speaking audience was mainly Marwari. Marwaris like their *papad,* they like their *amras*, they need dal and everything else: you know their table. They are the same way in the theatre. In two and a half hours, they had to have comedy, songs, and dance, and if the drama didn't feature an exciting plot, no matter how famous the artists involved, the show would be a flop. Instead of taking a risk on new stories, I had some plays from the

Gujarati theatre translated into Urdu and they passed muster, one hundred per cent.

We offered two shows a day with a motion picture thrown in. The picture started at 3:30 or 3:45 p.m. The system was that we had a screen set up on a wagon. In less than three minutes, the stage would be cleared and the screen moved into place. Behind it, the set for the first scene of the next theatre show would be arranged while the film was being screened. The movie ended at 6:00 p.m., and at 6:15 the drama would begin and go on for two and a half hours. There was only one show at night, and no picture after that.

This program ran six days a week. Later we introduced Marwari-language dramas on Tuesdays and Fridays. Marwar has many stories of its own on wonderful subjects. We based our dramas on tales like *Gangaro Teli*, *Jagdev Kangali*, *Dhola Maravan*, *Bin Binari*, and *Ramucharna*. *Bin Binari* was about a 60-year-old bride and her 20-year-old husband. It was very funny, a great play. The money rolled in.

The most popular shows at the Moonlight were *Krishna Lila* which opened in 1955, *Desh ki Laj* at the time of the war with China (1962), and the old *Narsi Mehta* in shortened form. While other companies came and went, the Moonlight kept getting a good audience and making a profit. This was because we satisfied the audience's desires. They got tired of the old plays after a while, so we changed the drama every month. Then there was the heroine. Other companies only found actresses who were temporary, or they tried using courtesans, which didn't work out. The main reason for the Moonlight's success was Sita Devi. She was a good actress who spoke her lines with conviction, and her dramas were always well received.

In 1967 the Moonlight shut down because of me. I began to get some pain in my head due to high blood pressure or who knows what, and I started treatment with several different doctors. Not only that, my family members wanted me to quit and come home. My sons, daughters-in-law, and grandchildren all descended and persuaded me to go back to Muradabad with them. I made an excuse to the company owners and told them I'd be back a month later. I placed the company in the hands of the assistant managers, but I really intended to leave for good. Desperate telegrams arrived from the owners, begging me to return. Sita Devi wrote such a sorrowful letter to my wife that she broke down crying. "Masterji, we can't go on without you. If you don't come back, a hundred people will lose their livelihood," and so forth.

Finally I returned to Calcutta. The Mehrotra brothers invited me home to a big family conference. Vishveshvar Babu asked me what it was I really intended to do. I told him I was ready to retire and leave the Moonlight

Theatre. He said that was fine, but I'd have to bury it with my own hands. The brothers were not interested in running it themselves. It was up to me to finish it off. Reluctantly I said farewell to everyone. The company was wracked with sorrow, everyone felt bereft. Nobody who wanted to work was really left high and dry, however. In Calcutta troupes were always being formed and dissolving. But they felt downcast nonetheless. Notices went out and fifteen days later—that was the rule—the company was dissolved. Everyone got their final pay and departed.

There were several old men I felt responsible for. One of them, Muhammad Bhai, had been Sita's tutor. He was 90 years old. I asked the Mehrotras where he would go, what would become of him. They told me not to worry and set up a trust so that he would receive a regular salary. Then there was Charlie. He was kept on as a gate-keeper. And one other fellow who ages back had taught me the part of Surdas, I kept on as my personal servant, in a manner of speaking. He lived in Howrah, but he died soon after.

I had to pack up all of my effects, thirty-five years worth of gear. I gave the furniture to a friend and left the wooden almirahs behind. Still a lot remained, mostly books, all of the dramas. This had been my profession.

Thus ended the story of the Moonlight. The company folded on my account, let there be no question about that. It's a difficult task to keep a company under control. It's not something everyone can handle. You need to have authority, and you need to have tact. The actresses played all sorts of games and made demands. The owners were not going to put up with that. It was my job to humor them, to somehow soothe their false hurts. People used to misunderstand, think there was some relationship between us. That was far from the reality. There wasn't even scope for a relationship to develop. In twenty years in the Moonlight and before that in the Corinthian, I never got involved in anything like that. And there was no question of drinking or intoxication. I never smoked *bidi*s or cigarettes. In this regard I was different, I set myself apart from others in the theatre line, and in the film line.

Many Marwaris, shopkeepers, and merchants from Bara Bazar used to come to see plays and listen to *lavani*. We provided some songs based on tunes from Rohtak and Haryana. We had trumpet, clarinet, violin, and piano. In the percussion section there was *dholak*, tabla, and *daf*, which was used for Marwari rhythms. The orchestra was located directly below the stage, in front, so that the audience couldn't see the heads of the musicians. On flute we had Chandrakant, the one who now accompanies Lata and has become so famous, and Alok who is with All India Radio. It was a fantastic team—twelve musicians, all permanent employees.

The music in the plays followed the film style. The tunes were selected by Amar Singh Jaisal the clarinet player, Subhan Master the harmonium player, and myself—mostly myself. We took the best musical phrases from film tunes and fit them together so that the audience couldn't tell which film the songs were from. In addition, we had a music director, Hakim Saheb, from His Master's Voice. He was a trumpet player. He composed some of the songs independently. Kamal and Ramsingh wrote the lyrics, using the *sher-o-shairi* style in Hindi. The words were those that the public was fond of. Duets were also sung. Every play had at least ten or twelve songs, and in a two and a half hour program, a good portion of it was music. We had an electric guitar and everything.

You won't believe it, but in the last fifteen years I've seen only three films: *Mughal-e Azam, Pakeezah,* and another one with Dharmendra and Hema Malini.[10] I don't care for the stories nowadays. Where are the stories from before, like those of Shantaram? I loved the direction of Debaki Bose and P.C. Barua—they were my favorites. I saw all of Mehboob's pictures, and I never missed anything of Shantaram's either. I was fond of English films too. When I lived in Calcutta, I always went once a week to see an English movie.

I acted in a number of films. My first role was in the *Ramayan*, in which I played a priest. The director was Prafulla Roy, and that was the only film of his I worked in. I appeared in two scenes with songs in them; that's why I was casted. My next picture was *Mastana*, directed by Charu Roy. I was the hero. With me were Master Gama and a girl named Lila. She was from Lahore and was a Muslim, but they gave her a Hindu name. Later she worked in the Bombay Talkies' film, *Bhabhi*.[11] My third film was *Insaf*, in which I played Banvari, a peasant. This character was very popular with the audience. I had three songs, one of which I learned from a sadhu.

Then came *Daku ka Larka*, another film directed by Charu Roy.[12] I was the secondary hero. And the fifth film I was in was *Dil ki Pyas*. Sohrab Modi directed it, but Charu Roy had his hand in it too.[13] It was very popular and was remade in Bangla as *Jiban Sangini* by Babulal Chokhani. Next, I had a very good role in *Khudai Khidmatgar*. I played the king's commanding officer. The king was a Muslim but the commander was a Hindu. Then came *Matvali Mira* in which I played the role of Raidas. The part was

---

[10] The third film is likely *Sholay* (1975).

[11] Lila may have worked in *Bhabhi* (1957), but the film was made by the director-producer team of R. Krishnan and S. Panju, not by Bombay Talkies, which was not active after the early 1950s.

[12] The chronological sequence is somewhat off. *Daku ka Larka* was released in 1935.

[13] *Dil ki Pyas* was directed by Sohrab Kerawala, whom Fida Husain apparently confuses with Sohrab Modi.

supposed to go to K.C. Dey, but he demanded too much money and so I was given the role. Mukhtar Begam played Mira.

After that came a four-reel film sung to *nagara* beats in Nautanki style. As soon as the *nagara* was struck, the sound equipment blew a fuse. They had no idea of the volume of the *nagara*. Basant Churuvali from Rajasthan was in that film, and she and I sang question and answer passages in *chaubola, lavani*, and other meters. Her voice seemed to come down from the sky, it was so strong. Mine was no less.

All of the plays of that time were musicals. How could the public be entertained without music and dance? Just as we took popular stories and turned them into plays, we took people's favorite tunes and used them. We would fit new words to the film songs that were the most current and successful. Sometimes the audience didn't understand the original song, but they liked these song parodies very much. We had some fine music masters who composed their own songs too, but most of the songs were copies of popular tunes from Hindi films.

These songs were all linked to dramatic situations, and as the drama was unfolding, when an opportunity arose, a song would start up. For example, in *Krishna Sudama* when Sudama's wife says, "When there's no food in the house, what's the need for a platter?" and her neighbor replies, "I'll spread out my sari and pour rice into it for you," the Brahmin lady sings, "This is not my clothing, it's a piece of my heart."

In 1931 when Gandhi launched his campaign against the British, the famous actress Hirabai popularized a song from the drama *Vatan*:

> Dear God, what troubles afflict these residents of Hind!
> At every step for our sake they suffer injustice.
> Those who came as our guests have turned into our oppressors,
> The masters of the house have been thrown out and dispossessed.

Not only was *Vatan* performed during the non-cooperation movement, this song was sung all over India. It fit the times and the situation. The audience supported the Congress Party then, the movement was at its height, and this song became very popular.

In another play, there was a duet between two friends, one of whom is rich and the other poor. One friend says:

> In this blind, selfish world, who can be a friend to another?
> Seeing utter darkness, even one's shadow wants to hide.

The other friend responds:

> The meaning of friendship will I prove through my deeds.
> If you offer the sweat of your brow, I will give my life's blood.

The duet goes on like that, for a long time. I took the tune from a picture of Ramesh Sahgal's called *Station*, the one in which Sunil Dutt first performed.[14] I wrote my lyrics to that melody and mounted the play in 1955 in the Moonlight; it was called *Insan Chahiye*.

One of the songs from *Narsi Mehta* became very popular. It was based on an old folksong: *chhoti bari suiyan re jali ka mora kadhna*. I set these lyrics to that tune: *kahna mere man ki bat mohan se jake*. The play came out in 1939 at the start of World War II in the Corinthian Theatre on Dharmatolla Road. This play was a huge hit and played for one thousand nights in cities throughout India.

Krishna Lila was also a big draw, especially the songs. It has a very famous duet between Yashoda and Krishna. The song was based on an old *bhajan* by Surdas that I adapted. I added the response part to it, wrote my own lyrics. Sita Devi played Yashoda and the actress Kanaklata played the part of Krishna. This particular scene lasted an entire hour, and the whole thing was written in question-answer format. Another popular song of those days was from the film *Nagin*: *tan dole mera man dole*. I took that tune and fit these words to it: *sun rasiya mere tan basiya*. It was a duet between Radha and Krishna and became a big hit.

In the social drama *Parivartan*, which refers to events in 1922, I sang a ghazal on stage. This particular Hindi ghazal was on everyone's tongue all over India: *jane kya kya hai chhupa hua sarkar tumhari ankhon men*.[15] Another song from this play became so well known that women in Hindu households everywhere began singing it—and they still do: *nirbal ke pran pukar rahe jagdish hare jagdish hare*.[16]

Women began performing on stage, I believe, in 1910 or 1911. The first actress was Bijli in the Balivala Theatre in Bombay. After her, there were others in the Alfred, like Putlibai, the mother of Gohar of Ranjit Studios. After that, gradually women began joining other companies. On the Hindi-Parsi stage, Gauhar became the most famous. She was Jewish. There was Miss Mary Fenton, an Anglo-Indian, even before Patience Cooper. Kavasji married her, and Jahangirji was their son. After that the most respected actress was Sharifa. The first *Mother India* that the Madan Theatres produced, Sharifa acted in that. Coming towards the present, Sita Devi was number one in the Parsi theatre. She lasted a long time, longer than other heroines. She maintained both her voice and her character, kept herself strong in every way, and the public consistently favored her. Angurbala was

---

[14] Sunil Dutt's first film was actually titled *Railway Platform*.
[15] "Who knows, oh lord/master, what all is hidden in your eyes?"
[16] "Powerless beings are crying out for you, oh Jagdish, oh Jagdish."

an artist in His Master's Voice, although she also performed on stage. She played Raja Indar in the Parsi theatre long before Sita Devi.

I cut my first record in 1933, with a ghazal by Dagh on one side, and a ghazal of Tabish Lahori on the other. It sold a lot of copies. Singers used to get only Rs 80 for recording two sides, no matter how famous they were. K.C. Dey organized a campaign to increase our recording royalties. He met with Mr. Kapoor, the general manager for His Master's Voice for all of South Asia, including Burma and Sri Lanka. Kapoor agreed that the company was making a huge profit, and he sided with us. After three months of discussion with headquarters in London, they agreed to give the top artists like K.C. Dey 5%, and the rest of us 2.5%. But that wasn't the end of it. K.C. went to bat for the poets, musicians, and music directors too. And he got them royalties of 2.5% also. He made everybody agree to boycott the studio until the royalties were settled. Luckily, the company went along with it, and after that I received a royalty check every six months.

The dramas that I recorded were many. Usually, a single play filled four records, but sometimes three or six. About thirty plays, all directed by me, appeared as records: *Krishna Avatar, Sanyuktaharan, Prithviraj, Subhadraharan*. I used to possess all those records as the artist was given one complimentary record per play. I still have recordings of my songs, but the dramas I've loaned out to people over the years and they haven't returned them. Only one recording is still with me in Muradabad, *Bhagat Singh*.

The session had lasted more than an hour, and Fida Husain had sung each of the songs as he made reference to them. His breath control was a bit weak, but without any instrumental support he sang one song after the other as though it was all in an ordinary day's work. Some of those songs went back twenty-five years and some thirty. One last question remained. "We keep hearing about Nautanki, Svang, and so on. How were these different in terms of the songs?" Instantly, the answer came:

In Nautanki, the main thing is the kettledrum, the *nagara*. It will drive a man wild. When I was very young, the following incident occurred: Nautanki players from Hathras had come to town. Their drumming and singing were out of this world, men lost their hearts to them entirely. It was the hot season, and we were sleeping outside in the courtyard. When the *nagara* started up, I couldn't contain myself. I crept out of my bed and went onto the roof, then jumped down and ran off to the show. I watched the performance and came back before the first *namaz* and went to bed.

The man who delivered water to our house was very fond of me, but he reported to my uncle, "The prince was swaying to the music last night near the stage."

"No, he was sleeping," my uncle retorted.

"Well, not really, sir," the water-carrier answered. "He was actually living it up, listening to the *nagara* right there in front of the stage."

My uncle used to wear *kharaun*—wooden clogs with a peg between the toes. He took off one of those and smacked me about the head, throttled me good. So that was Nautanki.

In Svang, there is no *nagara*. Instead, the *dholak* is used for percussion, and plenty of it too. Svang is also called Desi. Then there's that other style, Kalgi and Turra, sung to the accompaniment of the *chang*, the Indian mouth-harp, and in question–answer form. Each of these kinds of music yields its own pleasure. The words of the songs and the sound of the percussion combine and tug at the heart like a kiss. They still preserve their power, even today.

I felt a unique joy in the recollection of these sounds heard long ago, the twang of the *chang*, the beats of the *dholak* and the *nagara*. This man had immersed himself in music and lived his life in the theatre. How much he had given to it, and how much he had received! Fida Husain Saheb worked in the theatre for fifty years. Theatre was his livelihood, but it was not merely a means of earning a living, it was something much more. The theatre satisfied his inner need to be a singer. It provided the basis for him to express his inner self as an actor. Truth be told, he preserved the theatre, and the theatre preserved him. His cause was not social reform or love of country, nor was he concerned with uplift of the theatre. But whatever he put into practice was good for society, the nation, and the theatre. He placed emphasis on decency of character, and the companies in which he served stressed morality. He maintained the living tradition of the Parsi theatre for a very long time.

The Parsi theatre was attentive to providing entertainment for its audience, and with this in view it included song, dance, and spectacle. Being perhaps a bit overly conscious of its audience, the Parsi theatre became rather lightweight. This cannot be denied. Nor can it be refuted that a large part of the history of the Hindi theatre *is* the Parsi theatre.

If we consider the Hindi theatre to have started in 1850, then until 1950 or so, for a hundred years, this theatre was kept alive through the medium of the Parsi theatrical companies. There was no other commercial stage in this period. Amateur clubs existed which formed and dissolved, according to their convenience and the needs of the hour. Doubtless the Parsi troupes' exaggerated plots and stagecraft were opposed in the twentieth century. The modern theatre developed to a great extent as a reaction against these characteristics. Nevertheless, it was the Parsi theatre that continued the tradition of theatre for almost a century, forging a link. Fida Husain Saheb is in one sense the final link in that chain. His dedication, steadfast character, devotion to communal harmony, and large-hearted nature are exemplary. The central Sangeet Natak Akademi honored Fida Husain with its annual award in 1985. I too wish to congratulate him on this occasion. I salute him and offer my wishes that God may protect him and keep him among us for a long time to come.

Part 3

7

Self and Subjectivity in Autobiographical Criticism

The autobiographical writing of actors and playwrights constitutes a unique resource for the study of theatre and cultural history. As seen in Chapter 2, theatrical memoirs are invaluable historical documents fortuitously preserved in published form. But they are also the life-stories of distinct individuals. Their narrators tell of childhood, of growing up, of entering the wider world and struggling for success. Through these compelling narratives of personhood, the reader glimpses the interplay of memory and experience. The felt quality of the actor's life, his constructions of self and others, his modes of performing his identity are on display. These autobiographies present the reader with a medium through which to explore the subjectivity of the theatrical personality, alternately masked and unmasked in its many guises.

It has often been noted that first-person accounts make strong claims to veracity. The autobiographer's version of the past is valorized as being more authentic, offering a closer vantage point than other kinds of writing.[1] Yet autobiographies like other textual artifacts are fabricated, composed by design. They are crafted under specific conditions for specific audiences, by authors with their own agendas. Like all stories, these narratives involve selection and edition. They are

---

[1] Arnold and Blackburn (2004): 4; Smith and Watson (2001): 27–32, 123–5. On the authority of experience in travel narrative, see Fisher (1998): 897.

situated within particular times, places, and social systems, and can never be free of mediation. Indeed, the process of representing one's own life is highly charged, and the narrator may resort to hyperbole and polemic as much as to balanced remembering and recording. Nor can amnesia and silence be avoided, for memory is only partially under conscious control. Conventional gestures within the text strive to reinforce the autobiographer's authority. The narrator may make forceful declarations of the truthfulness of his act of self-presentation, persuading the reader that his intentions are sincere. But the status of the text as a purposeful project remains, complicating any simple apprehension of the "facts" that it alleges to convey.

The four autobiographies in this book are no different. They require the reader to go beyond simplistically equating first-person narration with impartial reporting or candid self-exposure. In contrast with Chapter 2 and its highlighting of the documentary value of autobiography, the focus in this chapter is upon concepts of the self and the ways in which divergent understandings of the self inform the reading of autobiographical texts. Two well-established constructs of selfhood from the Anglo-European tradition begin the discussion, following which the "problem" of the existence of the self in India is explored. The chapter then proposes the utility of concepts of relationality and performativity for critically engaging with the autobiographical self across diverse cultural, spatial, and temporal planes. It explores the theoretical ground for a more complicated reading of autobiography in general, with the aim of bringing greater rigor to these life stories from the Parsi theatre in particular.

The Sovereign Self and the Fractured Self

Autobiography is concerned, in one of its simplest definitions, with the description (*graphia*) of the individual human life (*bios*) by the self (*autos*).[2] The concept of selfhood thus undergirds the genre in a fundamental way. In the last several decades, the critical study of autobiography has focused attention on the possibility that multiple ideas of the self, the person, or the individual exist, and that these

---

[2] Misch (1950): 5, cited in Smith and Watson (2001): 113.

vary according to the cultural milieu. Arnold and Blackburn characterize the dominant premise of life history research as the notion that "personal lives reflect culture-specific notions of the person or self."[3] The study of autobiography in India offers a case in point. The discussion of the genre has often invoked the assumption that the sense of self in India is at variance with the self in the West. In this way of thinking, the difference that marks the "Indian self" resides outside the text. It inheres in the makeup of the civilization, the culture, and society, and is largely immutable.

The hypothetical contrast that allows for the demarcation of the Indian self, however, is usually with a very specific kind of Western self. This is the "sovereign self," as it is commonly termed, associated with the European Enlightenment. Other models of the self exist in the West, but the concept of the sovereign self enjoys a kind of hegemony and affects the reading of autobiography everywhere. This concept dates to the late-eighteenth and early-nineteenth centuries, when reading and writing autobiography became well established in Western Europe. Notions of the individual in that period were informed by the liberal humanism of the Enlightenment, as well as by Romanticism and, eventually, the self-made man of the industrial revolution and Social Darwinism.[4] The self was equated with the autonomous individual who was capable of self-mastery and self-knowledge. It was assumed to be unitary and universal.

Narratives of this transcendent, unified self became the canonical autobiographies, the master texts of the genre. Autobiographers such as St Augustine, Rousseau, Goethe, and Benjamin Franklin were viewed as enlightened individuals who understood their relationship to others and the world as one of separateness in which they exercised the agency of free will. Their works imparted the idea of the great man of Western humanism, focusing on those whose public deeds and accomplishments shaped their times. It was taken for granted that these autobiographies were to be read for instruction and inspiration. Neither was the self problematized, nor was the writing of the self at issue; the emphasis was rather on the life (*bios*) and its importance

---

[3] Arnold and Blackburn (2004): 4.
[4] Smith and Watson (2001): 112.

as a model. Since the self was taken to be perfectly neutral, it was assumed that the autobiographer took an objective view of his own life. In other words, the narrator was not distinguished from the subject. The narrator was assumed to speak self-evident truths.[5]

The assumptions embedded in this paradigm of selfhood are widely shared as part of a commonsense strategy of reading autobiography. Many readers bring expectations of authorial awareness and agency to their experience of autobiography. They look for a coherent summation of a life's course in the text, from a narrator who is self-reflective and self-determined. Reader reception of autobiographies as reliable, eyewitness documents requires a tacit equation between an omniscient narrator and a sovereign self.

The sovereign self eventually yielded to the fractured self of modernism. Freud's discovery of the unconscious undermined the idea of the person as a rational actor, positing subversive forces within the individual that threatened self-awareness and self-control. The theories of Marx and Althusser regarding economic and ideological determinism challenged the status of the individual as an autonomous agent. Poststructural linguists who questioned the transparency of language also eroded the liberal-humanist notion of selfhood. "What had been assumed by earlier generations . . . to be a universal 'self'—achieving self-discovery, self-creation, and self-knowledge—became, in the wake of multiple theoretical challenges of the first half of the century, a 'subject' riven by self-estrangement and self-fragmentation."[6]

With this radical shift in ideas of the self, the task of autobiography was understood very differently. It now involved imposing order and pattern upon disparate pieces that in themselves did not form a whole. According to Gusdorf, the autobiographer's job was "to reassemble the scattered elements of his individual life and to regroup them in a comprehensive sketch."[7] The interpretation of autobiographical texts no longer focused on representations of the exemplary life but rather emphasized the self in the making. Centerstage was now occupied by the act of writing, insofar as it was through self-narration that both the self and the life assumed a particular shape and image.

[5] Olney (1980): 20–1.
[6] Smith and Watson (2001): 124.
[7] Gusdorf (1980): 35.

In this more complicated concept of the self, the question of the truthfulness of life narrative came to the fore. If autobiographical writing was an artistic process, an attempt to create an identity, the reader could no longer access it directly for the truth of the self. Rather, self-representation had to be approached as encoded truth, which might yield a psychological design through its patterning rather than a factual one. Hart described the reader as "in search of an evolving mixture of pattern and situation—pattern discerned in the life recovered, pattern discovered or articulated in the self or 'versions of self' that emerge in that recovery, pattern in the recovery process."[8] In consequence the reader took on a more active and discerning role. She was obliged to attend to the constructed nature of the self, decoding its elements as it was selectively represented by the narrator.

The reading strategy that devolved from the fractured self thus eschewed the easy assumption of identity between narrator and self. Autobiography appeared not as a site of truth, but as evidence of a creative intervention. Newly foregrounded was the element of artistry, which elevated autobiography to the status of other literary genres. Autobiography was deemed a cultural artifact with its own conventions, themes, and tropes, and the autobiographical text became the subject of literary criticism. The reader approached it, then, more like a novel than like a history. It was interpreted through a battery of critical tools, including new criticism, structuralism, and formalism. Treated in these kinds of ways, autobiography came to resemble the oral histories, tales, and other types of life narrative that anthropologists were analyzing for insight into other cultures.[9]

The Absent Self

Against these two concepts of selfhood from the West, the self in India has been predominantly conceived in terms of lack or absence. The reasons for this lie, in part, with the circumstances under which knowledge of India was acquired by the European powers during the colonial era. In the Orientalist attempt to comprehend Indian civilization, priority was given to the textual traditions of Hinduism,

---

[8] Hart (1970): 492.
[9] Peacock and Holland (1993): 370.

Buddhism, and Indian philosophy. These were understood as stressing the denial of the self in daily life and valorizing the eventual achievement of selflessness. India was a land of spirituality, the opposite of the materialistic West, where the goal of human life was to achieve the absorption of the *atman*, the self, in the *brahman*, the ultimate reality. Concepts such as karma and rebirth allowed for self-knowledge and liberation, but only over the cosmic cycle of ages, not within a lifetime.

When India came under the anthropological gaze, the image of Indian society and self transmuted to form an even starker contrast with the individualism of Western Europe. Indologists had already described the caste consciousness of traditional India. Then with Dumont's exposition of caste and hierarchy in *Homo Hierarchicus*, the idea that collective identities dominated Indian culture and society received further reinforcement. Dumont argued that approaching India through focus on the individual was fundamentally misconceived.[10] Anthropologists Marriott and Daniel also held that the sense of self in India was weaker or less individuated than its Western counterpart. They viewed the boundaries of the ego as porous, characterizing the self as fluid, "reflexively structured through its relations to other 'selves' and not in terms of an autonomous and interiorized individuality."[11] The paradigm for understanding India became that of collectivity. Individual agency and the sense of selfhood were established as marginal to Indian thought and behavior.

This set of ideas, too, had implications for the reading of autobiography. Since the Indian self was posited as weak or deficient, readers tended to highlight assertions in Indian autobiographies that denied the self or disparaged it. Self-deprecation tended to be interpreted ahistorically, as an essential trait of Indian culture, rather than taken as a rhetorical stance or literary convention. The reading method sometimes equated faults in the construction of the narrative with a lack in the self. To a large extent, the sovereign self of the West remained the standard by which the Indian self was judged. Because of this overarching framework, the narrator and subject were generally

---

[10] Mines (1994): 5.
[11] Cohen (1998): 178; see also Marriott (1976) and Daniel (1984).

assumed to be identical, despite the incongruence between the agency of the narrator, the one telling the story, and the subject or self, whom the reader viewed as lacking in agency.

The critical treatment of autobiography in India shows the constraints imposed by the model of the weak self. Indian autobiographies were initially assumed to be absent, and then deemed rudimentary or flawed in significant ways. One deficiency was the sense of reticence or shame in committing to the writing of the self. The "embarrassment over autobiography within India," the discomfort associated with projecting one's ego, was first discussed by Waghorne in her study of Rajagopalachari. She pointed out that Gandhi prefaced his autobiography with a complex denial, claiming he was not writing about himself but narrating his self-experiments with truth. Rajagopalachari himself asserted that autobiography should not be written because it violated Indian traditions; he resisted all those who tried to write his story or get him to do so.[12] In similar fashion, Hatcher noted that Ishwar Chandra Vidyasagar wrote only a single chapter on his childhood. This was because, as his son stated, "By writing of his adult life and later years my father would have been violating the spirit of Manu's great injunction that one should not boast after doing a good deed."[13]

As narrators, Rajagopalachari, Gandhi, and Vidyasagar articulated those strands of philosophy and ethics that conflicted with the impulse to tell the story of the self. Their orientation presumably was shared by their intended high-caste readers. Other scholars have sought to explain authorial silence by reference to the dichotomy between public and private spaces in the colonial period. Kaviraj, following Waghorne, upheld the idea that there was an overwhelming embarrassment in regard to autobiography in the Indian context. In the case of Sibnath Sastri, his chosen autobiographer, Kaviraj connected the narrator's reticence not so much to religious rules as to the lack of invention of private life.[14]

Reticence or embarrassment, however, may be narratorial positions with their own intentionality; they need not be read as truths about the

---

[12] Waghorne (1981): 589–91.
[13] Hatcher (2001): 582.
[14] Kaviraj (2004): 95.

self or its lack. Patterns of disclosure and veiling are part of the structure of expression shared across many cultures. Recent work on autobiography in other non-Western locations has shown that professions of modesty and apologies for writing about the self are frequent. In a study of autobiographies of modern Indonesia, Watson identified "the reluctance to expatiate on one's own merits, common to both Western and Eastern notions of decorum and reticence."[15] Reynolds pointed to "the tension between the portrayal of the self and self-aggrandizement" persisting through centuries of Arabic autobiography, dating to the twelfth century.[16] In regard to premodern Chinese autobiography, Wu took note of "the inhibition, probably universally strong until some four centuries ago, against self-disclosure and self-presentation without a religious context."[17] The impulse to profess the insignificance of the self thus is a common thread, related to widely held cultural norms of deference toward others, especially toward patrons and readers. Sentiments of modesty and humility in the autobiographical text may have more to do with the narrator's good breeding than the limits of selfhood.

The Relational Self

The discussion so far shows the theoretical problems with a reading strategy based on the concept of the Indian self as weak or non-existent. A number of readers approached the Indian autobiography by assuming an essential cultural difference between the West with its liberal humanist concept of the self, and India with its religious tradition of self-abnegation and social hierarchy based on caste. But then, in several striking ways the received idea of the absent Indian self was challenged. The work of Mines on personhood in South India opened up the debate on the historical nature and role of individuality in ordinary life.[18] Inden critiqued the Orientalist construction of caste as a determinant in Indian history and sought to establish Indians as rational subjects and knowing agents. Caste as the core symbol of community in India was additionally challenged by Dirks, who traced its

---

[15] Watson (2000): 45.
[16] Reynolds (2001): 3.
[17] Wu (1990): 3.
[18] Mines (1994); see also Mines (2002).

ideological prevalence to colonial rule.[19] These critiques of the collective self were joined by subaltern studies and women's studies approaches, to yield a more variegated field of subjectivities beyond the high-caste male.

Such developments coincided with an almost opposite movement in Western scholarship. Even as historians and anthropologists of India revised the notion of the collective self constructed by Orientalism in the direction of greater individuality, in the West postcolonial scholars, feminists, and black studies scholars questioned the privileging of the Enlightenment concept of the individual with its masculine, European bias. The autobiographical criticism that had earlier enshrined the sovereign subject came to be viewed as a hegemonic reading practice that left little space for the multiple subjectivities of race, class, and nationality.[20] Instead, postcolonial and feminist scholars invoked a new model, the relational self, as a corrective to the unique and separate bourgeois individual.

This model had a very different trajectory from the paradigm of collectivity developed by anthropologists of India. It began with the analysis of (Western) women's autobiography in the 1980s. According to feminist theorists, the model of selfhood in women's narratives was not the autonomous individual but the self as interdependent and identified with a community. Their writings asserted a sense of shared identity with other women across fluid boundaries between self and an other or others. Subsequent scholarship extended the notion of relationality to life narratives by men as well, after considering the role of intersubjective identification with both genders in the process of psychosocial development.[21] Eakin's project of applying the relational self of feminist theory to male-authored autobiographies served as an effective model for complicating the unified, sovereign subject.[22] In these formulations, the relational self derived its strength through solidarity. Identification with community was empowering, not diminishing. The self was everywhere relational, and every life narrative represented the evolving dynamic between the individual and the community.

[19] Inden (1990), Inden (1986), Dirks (2001).
[20] Loftus (2004): 2.
[21] Smith and Watson (2001), 201, 140–1.
[22] Holden (2005): 95.

The relational self represents a significant advance that may be profitably adopted in the reading of autobiographies from India. Dalit autobiography, an ascendant genre that has attracted wide attention, is a clearcut example. Scholars have examined the construction of self in works like Bama's *Karukku*, the autobiography of a Tamil Dalit woman, and the autobiographies of Omprakash Valmiki and Surajpal Chauhan, two male Dalits writing in Hindi. On the one hand, these narratives are said to represent a collective self, or to express a communal voice rather than an individual one. When their narrators recount the pain and trauma of being treated as untouchable, they speak of common experiences that bind individual Dalits together. Nayar considers *Karukku* less an autobiography than a collective biography in which the individual and the community are often elided.[23] In regard to Hindi Dalit autobiographies, Beth notes the deep connection between the individual and the communal self.[24] The strong presence of the latter links these texts to black autobiography, wherein "the unity of the personal and the mass voice remains a dominant tradition."[25]

Yet both Nayar and Beth also identify persistent assertions of individuality in Dalit autobiographies. In Nayar's reading, the unified subject of *Karukku*—the "I"—is replaced by the communal "we" in some places, but the strong voice of a personal "I" emerges elsewhere. The self is foregrounded whenever personal humiliations, feelings, and physical suffering are described, because "pain is singular to the suffering *individual* body."[26] Beth too argues that Dalit subjectivity is more complex than the contrast between individual and community would imply. For Beth, individuality is important to Dalit self-assertion, since it belies the upper-caste assumption that all Dalits are equally backward, illiterate, and uncultured.[27]

Neither Beth nor Nayar introduce the concept of the relational self in their analysis, yet the model is apt. Dalit selfhood develops by

---

[23] Nayar (2006): 84–5.
[24] Beth (2007): 551.
[25] Butterfield (1974): 3, cited in Beth (2007): 565.
[26] Nayar (2006): 89.
[27] Beth (2007): 554.

means of relationships within the family, school, community, workplace, and other social groups. Relationality is a necessary aspect of social existence, particularly for those on the margins of survival. Rather than diminishing the self, relationality is essential for psychological development; it is also a positive attribute of the mature individual. The relational self allows for the coexistence of distinct individual traits and an orientation toward others. Reading the Dalit self as relational eliminates the split, the "critical narrative tension" between individual and communal voices, that seems to trouble Nayar and Beth.

An additional example should illustrate the importance of avoiding essentialized notions of selfhood. Holden, in his study of the autobiographies of Nehru, Sukarno, and Nkrumah, notes that each narrative personifies national sovereignty. In these autobiographies, the political life of the individual is mapped onto the national narrative, so as to inspire colonial subjects to see themselves as citizens. Holden argues that Nehru wrote against the collective or relational self of traditional India, which he understood as a form of subjugation. Nehru's attempt was to construct an autonomous, individual protagonist who symbolized the new nation-state. However, Holden suggests that his life narrative needs to be rethought with greater emphasis on its relationality. Eakin and others have stressed that the autonomous subject of canonical autobiography was more complex and relationally constituted than usually thought.[28] Nehru's autobiography reveals the gendered relationships that preoccupy the narrator—with his invalid wife Kamala, with the emasculated ascetic Gandhi, and with the unruly masses of the feminized nation, Bharat Mata. Holden concludes, "Read relationally, national autobiographies reveal the contradictory manner in which gender is written into national imaginaries after colonialism."[29]

The Performative Self

Finally, we consider the concept that holds the greatest promise for the autobiographies in this volume: the performative self. In the

---

[28] Holden (2003): 16.
[29] Holden (2005): 98.

performative view, identities are not understood as fixed or essentialized attributes. Central to this position is the idea that the autobiographical subject is produced in performance. In Smith's words: "Every day, in disparate venues, in response to sundry occasions, in front of precise audiences (even if an audience of one), people assemble, if only temporarily, a 'life' to which they assign narrative coherence and meaning and through which they position themselves in historically specific identities. Whatever that occasion or that audience, the autobiographical speaker becomes a performative subject."[30] Thus the "self" or interiority that was earlier thought to direct the narration is considered to be an effect of autobiographical storytelling. Different storytelling occasions and audiences call forth different stories from the performative self, yielding sometimes quite divergent narratives of identity.

Performativity in relation to self-narration has occupied many theorists. Bruss's emphasis on the "autobiographical act" marked an important step toward theorizing autobiographical performativity.[31] Bruss was grounded in the speech act theory of Austin, and for her the self was "an arbitrary cultural fact," not an effect of language as postulated by deconstructionism. Nonetheless, de Man's views to some extent echoed Bruss: "We assume the life produces the autobiography . . . but can we not suggest, with equal justice, that the autobiographical project may itself produce and determine the life . . .?" De Man considered autobiography as an instance of prosopopeia or impersonation, that is, the representation of an imaginary or absent person as speaking and acting.[32]

The performative turn was buttressed by Butler, who argued that gender identity is performatively constituted: "There is no gender identity behind the expressions of gender; that identity is performatively constituted by the very 'expressions' that are said to be its results."[33] Butler deflected attention away from specific "acts" towards the regulatory effects of discourses on gender identity and gendered bodies. Autobiographical occasions revealed the power of discourse

---

[30] Smith (1998): 108.
[31] Bruss (1980): 300.
[32] Smith and Watson (2001): 139.
[33] Smith (1998): 109.

operating through reiteration to construct the "self." In Eakin's formulation, the performative model shifted the emphasis from the textuality of the self to the "ceaseless process of identity formation."[34] He conceived of life narrative as an interactive mode of constituting identity in which self and culture frame each other.

The focus on performativity gains special salience in the interpretation of oral histories and the life-narratives of autodidacts. Lejeune found that the autobiographies of everyday French men from the nineteenth century employed a public discourse structured by class, code, and convention. Popular autobiographical texts did not copy reality; rather, they created verisimilitude by imitating narrative forms that constituted the lingua franca.[35] In "The Autobiography of Those Who Do Not Write," Lejeune recognized the prevalence of collaborative authorship. In ghostwritten autobiographies, the author's signature no longer guaranteed that the featured self and the writer of the story were identical. A person's life could appear through someone else's narrative, or be put together by a third party.[36] Lejeune noted that even when the author and the narrator corresponded, "a *life* (that is, a written and published story of a life) is always the product of a transaction between different postures."[37]

In his critique of ethnological projects in life writing, Lejeune underscored the role of nostalgia and voyeurism, decrying the conversion of the experience of the other into an object of the gaze. He probed the process whereby the reading middle-class public became consumers of the "memories" of forgotten people who had been encouraged to "speak," often to prop up an idealized or exotic picture of the past.[38] He concluded that "by no means [is it] clear that the illiterate individual (peasant, artisan, worker) has in fact been enfranchised through ... ethnographic intervention, achieving 'authority' over his or her own life in the spirit if not the letter of the author's signature."[39]

---

[34] Eakin (1985): 36.
[35] Eakin, Foreword, in Lejeune (1989): xxi.
[36] Lejeune (1989): 190.
[37] Ibid.: 197.
[38] Ibid.: 207–11.
[39] Eakin, Foreword, in Lejeune (1989): xviii.

Against Lejeune's dejected verdict, some critics viewed the "failure" of the performative self to create coherence as a potential source of resistance. The multiple demands placed on the autobiographical subject to reiterate conflicting discourses produced gaps, ruptures, and transgressions, which for Butler signaled the "possibility of a variation on ... the rules that govern intelligible identity." According to de Certeau, the autobiographical subject could tactically adjust, redeploy, and transform discourses of identity. He argued for the capacity of "the weak" to strategically combine heterogeneous elements of discourse and use them to their own ends.[40]

The performative model of self emanates from poststructuralist theory, and theorists like Bruss, Eakin, and Lejeune restricted themselves to analyzing European autobiographies. Nevertheless, their methods acknowledge a large pool of autobiographical subjects, including the illiterate and self-tutored, and their work can constructively engage with life narrative from India. In the collection titled *Telling Lives in India*, the performative self as such is not theorized, although Arnold and Blackburn emphasize the affinities between written and oral histories and speak of subjects "writing or performing a 'life' that they know will please, move or possibly incite their readers or auditors."[41] Several case studies in the book highlight the reticence of the narrators, usually women, relating their strategies of avoidance to codes of modesty and honor. Whereas the volume contributors tend to characterize these silences as deliberate omissions, as self-censorship, an alternative reading is suggested by Butler's premise of performativity, namely that the autobiographical subject is "amnesiac, incoherent, heterogeneous."[42]

As an illustration, Narayan's portrait of Kangra women's life stories emphasizes the performance of suffering. In her study, high-caste women avoided naming living relatives, especially men, as agents of their suffering, but Dalit women's narratives lacked this reticence. Their self-dramatizations showed the influence of the mass media, especially melodramatic Hindi films and television serials, and they invoked a discourse of nationalism and female righteousness, a possible

---

[40] Smith (1998): 110–11.
[41] Arnold and Blackburn (2004): 13.
[42] Smith (1998): 110.

outcome of their contact with an activist organization.[43] Considered within the terms of Lejeune and other theorists of performativity, this case points to the dialogical process of self-narration. Among the upper castes, dominant discourses interact with experience to shape performances of gendered identity. Among lower castes, institutions of popular memory such as the media and the more egalitarian discourses embedded in them increasingly serve as sites from which life stories are interiorized. Through appropriating different forms of life-knowledge and authority, the possibility exists that such groups may transform social relations as well as construct a more dynamic image of selfhood.[44]

Taking the analysis one step further, Parry argues that "memories" are often powerful narratives that have been internalized and stored for use on autobiographical occasions. His case study of a "thumb impression man" probes the consequences of modernization and rapid social and economic change on the telling of personal history. Somvaru, an employee of a large steel plant, saw himself in some ways as a modern man enlightened by progress. As an illiterate untouchable, however, he could not imagine an audience for his life story and was, in Parry's words, silenced by ideology. After eliciting his story over a period of years, Parry came to see Somvaru's performance of self as "a kind of patchwork made up of accounts of incidents which may have been triggered by real experiences but which are now represented in wholly conventionalized and formulaic terms, and which appear to be internalized versions of stories drawn from the larger cultural repertoire; of recollections of previous recollections, and of previously unverbalized memories."[45] This study echoes the ways in which performance creates the self through recitation and repetition, shaping memory itself, which then recirculates and assimilates stories from a wider repository.

If autobiography is a performance that creates the self, if every self is performative, then what of the lives of professional performers, adepts who play roles on stage, and their autobiographies? This chapter concludes with the proposition that a kind of doubled performativity

---

[43] Narayan (2004): 243–4.
[44] Smith and Watson (2001): 144–5.
[45] Parry (2004): 286.

inhabits theatrical memoirs. The actor's self is twice-created, or twice-born, to adopt a Sanskritic usage. The reference to high-caste ritual is not entirely incongruent, insofar as it suggests the elevation that the charismatic actor undergoes. On stage, he becomes the king, the hero, the warrior, even the leading lady, overwriting the abject self of social origins. Performing his role or character, he transforms into a vigorous, impassioned, eloquent actor-self whose look, gestures, and style are consumed by his public. The act of impersonation is his metier, and he is recognized or identified with his most popular character. His performance even continues off-stage, in the interactions with fans and patrons who relate to him through his stage persona. Interiorizing his role, he may alter his presentation of self in everyday life, e.g. Sundari's wearing his hair long, or Fida Husain's yogic bodily regimen. At his most successful he becomes an icon, and his image circulates independently of his body, through advertising, photography, and the media.

Inscribing this subject in autobiographical writing presents a dual challenge. In the theory of performativity, the self does not exist prior to its recitations, and an autobiographical story is already the recitation of a recitation. Here however, the self as an actor has one set of recitations, one performative identity to inhabit, and the self as narrator has another. Congruence is possible, but disjunctures are more likely. Consider the differing narratives of gendered identity as found in Sundari's narrative. While speaking of his career as a stage performer, Sundari recounts with compelling candor his self-transformation from male to female. Yet as a social actor Sundari's story concerns his unrequited love affairs with female fans and his battle with his unenlightened family and caste fellows to contract a companionate marriage. Just as the impoverished Nayak boy seized the opportunity to become a leading female impersonator, the aging narrator capitalized on the chance to promulgate normative discourses of romantic love and conjugality. Both moves arguably expand social boundaries and challenge dominant norms. The complexities of reading theatrical memoirs are thus magnified, and yet the interplay of performative identities with their gaps and instabilities makes them doubly interesting.

8

Voices and Silences: Reading the Texts

This final chapter offers critical readings of each of the four autobiographies. The points of entry chosen here illustrate the value of reading these narratives intertextually. Some of their shared themes have already been discussed. Historical motifs in the autobiographies and their character as ethnographic commentary have been treated in Chapter 2. The introductions preceding each translation summarize issues related to authorial style and translation. They also consider the manner in which each autobiographical text was elicited, assembled, and written.

The readings in this chapter, by contrast, engage directly with the performative self or selves voiced in these life stories. They query such classic autobiographical themes as childhood and destiny. They also explore authorial intentions and probe the topics about which the authors remain silent. The readings respond to each autobiography as a complete and unique whole, yet also survey them comparatively for greater insight. These sketches, it is hoped, will encourage readers to examine their own responses to the narratives and develop additional strategies for unfolding their multilayered meanings.

The Muted and the Voiced

In her study of the Bengali autobiography by Rashsundari, Sarkar outlines the paradoxical position of "muted groups" such as women in nineteenth-century Bengal. She cites the Ardeners to argue that muted groups lacked access to public modes of articulation and could not set cultural standards or norms. Instead, they laid claim to "a sliver of existence," to practices and beliefs outside the prevailing culture. Dominant groups viewed the sphere of the muted as a "wild zone" beyond their knowledge and wished to gaze upon it, to enter it to fill the gaps in their understanding. Thus the writing of women, once it was published, found a ready market among men who desired to see what had previously been hidden from view.[1]

The communities of performers from which the Parsi theatre autobiographers hailed could also be considered muted groups. Just as the upper-caste woman violated nineteenth-century norms of female propriety by writing her autobiography, so too the early-twentieth-century actor in writing his life could be said to have crossed a line. As Seizer convincingly shows, professional actors associated with popular theatre in Tamilnadu are still stigmatized and must counter mainstream perceptions of being disorderly and of bad character.[2] A longstanding prejudice construes actors as lacking a fixed identity and therefore dangerous in their liminality. The actor as autobiographer, however, asserted self-regard, self-mastery, and self-determination. The knowability of the actor through his writing negated the culture's understanding of the performer as a vessel, a mere mask. His writing could engage the voyeurism of the reader, driven by desire to perceive the actor's secret world.

Theorizing the Parsi theatre as a wild zone and the actor as a shadowy subject whose partial visibility exerts a great lure has a certain appeal. It hints at the complex structure of avoidance and attraction that binds the spectator-reader and the actor-author, creating a reading public for theatrical lives. In Sundari's and Fida Husain's stories, the narrators at times play to the voyeurism of their readers by exoticizing the theatre world. Yet these memoirs also advance claims for their subjects' bourgeois sensibilities. They articulate the civilizing virtues of theatrical entertainment and testify to their subjects' public reputations. In their social origins, the four authors came from subordinated groups of lower caste and class. But as artisans they were not among

---

[1] Sarkar (1999): 115.
[2] Seizer (2005).

the most abject, and as *qasba*-dwellers they were not particularly isolated. Assuming the roles of narrators, moreover, while they are silent on certain subjects, in their very forthrightness they create an overall impression of sophisticated audibility not normally associated with subordinated groups.

Indeed, these autobiographies belie to a significant extent the hypothesis that their subjects were made mute through subordination. Although not univocal, these narratives speak in voices that are often bold, daring, and feisty. Their subjects on occasion talk back to those in power, breaking with conventions of deference. They articulate opposition to systems they deem unfair and unjust. To differing degrees, the autobiographies all construct their subjects as righteous individuals, as defenders of a larger moral order. In the next section, I consider the diverse ways in which each narrator constructs the self through choice of voice and tone. The stylized voices in which the narrators speak are various, but each crafts a performative presence that both entertains the reader and affirms the worth of the self.

Performing Humility and Superiority

Betab is not a deep student of human nature. He does not show any unusual insight into the human condition, and it cannot be claimed that his autobiography stands out for its psychological acuity. Nonetheless, his narrator balances the tendency to boast about his good deeds with a self-mocking tone that imbues his narrative with a robust sense of detachment. His ironic perspective on the affairs of the self and the world communicates a stance that modern readers may find very palatable. Betab's self-consciousness, however, stems from a stylized voicing of self that predates modern literary modes. In the opening sections of the narrative, he claims through various turns of phrase that he is worthless, he is nothing. This posture recalls the conventional self-denigrating stance of the Urdu poet, especially the narrator of the lyric ghazal, an abject lover in pursuit of an unforgiving beloved. It further echoes the deprecation of the self found in contemporaneous Urdu autobiographies, such as that of Zakariyya, a religious teacher of the Deoband school, or Zakira Ghouse, a woman from an aristocratic Hyderabad family. The exaggerated humility with which these narrators tell their life stories follows a long tradition in Persian and Urdu prose. The opening of Zakira's autobiography is reminiscent of Betab's foreword, even as it encapsulates the larger heritage. In it, she recites a couplet by Ghalib: "My purpose is simply to relate what actually happened./ I don't consider it a credit to my character to talk about myself."[3]

The preferred voice in Betab's narrative too claims that the self is worthless, even as it recounts his striving and determination. To narrate his adventures and accomplishments, Betab adopts the Sufi vocabulary of mysticism, invoking well-worn rhetorical usages of Indo-Islamic literature. He styles his autobiography after a Sufi journey, labeling its sections or chapters *manzil*, way-stations along the path to God. The metaphor of life as a journey is by no means exclusive to Sufism, and Betab also uses words such as *yatra*, with its connotations of sacred procession or pilgrimage. For the playwright, furthermore, travel was not just figurative, since the career required frequent journeys. Still, Betab's search for the guidance of enlightened men and reference to the stages of life as points along a path toward spiritual progress make evident the Sufistic subtext.

Equally, Betab aligns himself with Indic (i.e. Sanskritic) narrative and didactic traditions. In manzil 3 he compares his exile from home by his stepmother to the departure of Ram for the forest at Kaikeyi's instigation, alluding to the *Ramayan*. He explicitly takes on the instructional mantle of Ved Vyas, the sage who authored the Sanskrit *Mahabharat*, in manzil 10 when he expounds upon the significance of his first step toward honesty. Describing the five coins he received instead of four, he aggregates a raft of Hindu mythological references that play upon the numbers four and five.

Whether adopting Urdu's lofty tone or propounding a Hinducentric worldview, Betab both articulates and undermines the premodern paradigms to which he is heir. His persona as *na-chiz* (unworthy one) continually gives way to earthy descriptions of activity, achievement, and self-esteem. On more than one occasion, his fondness for moralizing is matched by his blatant fascination with money and wealth. As he confesses in manzil 10, he was a disciple of Charvak,

---

[3] Vatuk (2004): 151.

the materialist philosopher of ancient India. Even in this statement, the tone is sardonic. The comment is both self-revealing and an exaggeration, a display of knowledge. Whether feigning abasement or erudition, Betab comes across as cocky and confident. Despite evidence of insouciance and occasional hypocrisy, Betab wins the reader with his solid self-respect.

The singularity of Betab's voice can be judged in comparison with that of Radheshyam Kathavachak. If Betab claims to be worthless, Radheshyam claims just the opposite. The voice of Brahmanical confidence, of god-given superiority, guides his narrative. Unlike Betab, Radheshyam does not speak with irony; he means what he says. His pedantic tone controls the storytelling, which unspools like the endlessly elaborated exegesis of sacred legend. He seems sure of his audience and his power over them. He is self-dramatizing and melodramatic, at times overweening and arrogant.

Behind Radheshyam's authoritative voice, however, lurks a more defensive attitude. His autobiography reveals that the abiding struggle in his life was between his association with the Parsi theatre and his Brahminhood. His attachment to Brahminism emerges gradually in the narrative, gathering force in the later pages, but its seeds are apparent from the start. As a performance of self, Radheshyam's story is very much a performance of Brahmin identity, but not in ideal terms. It shows the strategies of an individual struggling with Brahminhood under the duress of participation in the commercial theatre.

Radheshyam asserts throughout the narrative that theatre was not his primary pursuit. On the one hand, he documents the salaried positions he held in the companies and expresses pride in his earnings. On the other, he repeatedly states that playwriting was only a hobby or passion (*shauq*) for him. His ambivalence toward his profession may have stemmed from the assumption of subordination that went along with "service," work for hire. But it must also have flowed from the fear of pollution. Radheshyam insisted upon his physical purity, sticking to a simple diet and having his own food prepared separately from others in the theatre company. He bathed and performed *puja* regularly, especially before important rehearsals and performances. Following each successful theatrical run, he went on pilgrimage with his wife. He also kept his distance from the taint of the stage by maintaining a scribal and directorial role, rather than acting, except in one instance.

The stylized postures known as *nakhre*, performances of prideful rejection or coy dalliance, inhabit Radheshyam's text. Romantic traditions in South Asia complicate the game of courtship by building in lovers' quarrels, acts of withdrawal and pique, meant to defer and increase the pleasure of love in union. The beloved's attitude of petulance is a coded indicator of interest, a demand to be courted and esteemed. Radheshyam's narrator voices his self-importance using these gestures. More than once he claims unavailability for theatrical work due to reasons of health. He plays rival companies off against one another to increase his desirability. It was common in the competitive theatre business to practice oneupmanship and boast of one's importance. What is different in Radheshyam's case is that he was working out an inner division. Wearing two hats, as *kathavachak* and company *munshi*, Radheshyam maximized his leverage with company bosses who were compelled to kowtow because of their desire to obtain his valuable playscripts.

Although Radheshyam seems at times bombastic about his contribution, the strategy that worked best for him was to bring his Brahminical knowledge base directly into the mainstream of the Parsi theatre. This he did through championing the mythological genre. With predecessors like Talib and Betab, he was certainly not the first to write mythologicals for the Parsi stage. Nonetheless, he put an unprecedented dose of *dharm* of the *sanatan* variety into the *dharmik* play, as the mythological was tellingly called in Hindi. The infusion of Sanskritized language and lore was critical to this process and a logical outcome of his Brahmin upbringing.

The Brahminical heritage could thus serve Radheshyam's career in the theatre, but his ambivalence grew as he aged. Adhering to the four-stage division of life, he began to retire from the world when he turned fifty. He renounced earning money, halted sexual relations with his wife, and devoted himself to social service and prayer, attempting to regain the simplicity and good health that had marked his childhood. But soon he was drawn back into worldly affairs and family tragedies. In the final meditation in his autobiography, he envisioned the force of unbridled lust overwhelming Indian civilization. He exhorted emerging playwrights to avoid obscenity while maintaining amusement. To what extent had he succeeded in living up to his own high ideals? Radheshyam's life-narrative with its divided voice discloses the cracks in the mirror.

Unitary and Decentered Selves

Of all the texts, Sundari's narrative comes the closest to crafting the bourgeois self of colonial modernity. It opens with a plotting of the simultaneous growth of the Gujarati theatre and Sundari's own life course. The autobiography thereby locates its subject explicitly in historical time, an essential element of the master narrative of the Enlightenment self.[4] The narrator assumes an omniscient third-person voice which looks back to before Sundari's birth. Shortly, this voice enters the subject and switches to the first-person. The speaking "I" retains the omniscient vision; it knows the past and the future, the internal and the external. The "I" describes the inner being of the boy-child, reflects upon what nurtured his "inner actor" growing up. Already, the autobiography stands apart for its investment in creating interiority. If Sundari's voice sounds to modern ears the least stylized, the least given to self-deprecation or self-aggrandizement, it is because it is closest to the seemingly reliable, balanced narrator of "realistic" autobiography in the West.

The form of the narrative recapitulates this pattern, insofar as the text is composed along the classic lines of the *bildungsroman*. More precisely, it follows the model of the *künstlerroman*, the story of the development of an artist. Such narratives emplot the subject's education over the course of a period of apprenticeship involving various encounters with mentors. Following these stages of growth, the subject abandons youthful folly and becomes integrated into society. The effectiveness of the *bildungsroman* as a template for the exemplary life hinges on the eventual resolution of conflicts, often between different concepts of education and social value. Narratives of this type culminate in "the acceptance of one's constrained social role in the bourgeois social order, usually requiring the renunciation of some ideal or passion and the embrace of heteronormative social arrangements."[5]

---

[4] Smith (1998): 110.
[5] Smith and Watson (2001): 189; see also 70, 107.

Jayshankar's autobiography chronicles in linear fashion the growth of a sensitive individual through various episodes of training to a pinnacle of professional success. He appears first as a spirited and gullible child, by nature drawn to music and oral performance. Preternaturally suggestible, he is easily reduced to convulsive weeping by the lament of Damayanti in one of his father's recitations. This sensibility presages his uncanny ability to merge with feminine roles later on stage. He is also superstitious and ignorant of common morality, with a tendency to hoard and steal. He proceeds from this childhood phase of immaturity to school, where he becomes overtly rebellious, bunking class and barely passing first grade. His parents, knowing their offspring to be more interested in performing than studying, arrange for him to join a large theatre company.

Jayshankar encounters a more ambiguous terrain when he apprentices himself to Dadabhai Thunthi. Here too his story hones to the pattern of gradual progress by steps. The new regime in the Parsi theatre company is as strict as that of the village schoolmaster, but Thunthi is also a father figure, a pillar of strength and wisdom. Jayshankar becomes the star pupil, masters the Urdu language ahead of the other newly recruited boys, and begins to perform feminine roles, replacing the Bengali actresses in the company. When Thunthi retires, Jayshankar gains his mentor's blessing and moves on.

In Bombay his education enters a new phase. He gains a music guru, studies the methods of experienced actors, and trains intensively, debuting as the heroine Sundari at the age of twelve. At this juncture, he undertakes his program of personal observation of women, supplemented by readings from Gujarati, English, and Sanskrit literature. These methods help him internalize his female characters as well as copy the markers of femininity fashionable among women from well-to-do families. Yet Jayshankar's narrative voice places less emphasis upon an intuitive approach to femininity and instead stresses his studied, rational search for a method of acting. His move beyond the teaching of his gurus to his own system of studied self-absorption in the role foregrounds the artist's personal struggle to define himself, to embrace his inner actor. His triumph as a female impersonator lies in his ability to apprehend the feminine through his own differentiated sense of self, a self which always deeply identified with women.

Effective performance is predicated upon a process of individuation, and the autobiography enacts the emergence of that newly individuated self.

Ultimately, Jayshankar comes to a personal recognition of the rules of family, community, and society. An impassioned voice of protest accompanies his struggles against the repressive pedagogical techniques of the school and the theatre company. The tenor of his outcry is sharp as he confronts archaic marriage practices that deny his romantic ideals. His voice of resistance in the name of individual freedom is firm. But the artist must eventually capitulate and sacrifice his quest for romantic passion in order to be reconciled with the social order. After two earlier failed marriages, he finally finds a compatible partner in Champa. Forsaking his self-centered fantasies and entering the hierarchical order of adulthood, Jayshankar gains wealth and satisfaction after this marriage, which coincides with the close of the most active phase of his career.

Read against the linear progress of Sundari's story, Fida Husain's narrative is fragmented, circular, and digressive. His voice, although co-created in an interview situation through the filtering of his interlocutor, retains a chatty, informal manner. In contrast to Sundari's high artistic seriousness, Husain cracks jokes and makes fun of himself and others. He is alternately garrulous and moralizing. A second voice in the text, that of Dr Pratibha Agraval, frames the narrative and intrudes from time to time. Representing the scholar and patron, this voice is moderate, reasoned, condescending. At times it narrates in the third person; at times it disappears. The two voices intertwine in a sort of dance, with Agraval leading at first, even trying to trip up her partner as she needles him about his way of life. Husain pivots around her, countering her moves spiritedly. Eventually he performs a lengthy solo, looping memories through each other, defying her now weakened attempts to lead.

The voice of the autobiographical subject in this way succeeds in subverting the power imbalance inherent in the ethnographic encounter. Fida resists molding his tale to a prefabricated trajectory such as that of the *bildungsroman*. Nonetheless, his voice is constituted within the terms of the dialogue, and he incorporates his interlocutor, the middle-class other, into his self-representation. Understanding the conditions of the interview and the stakes involved in the oral history, he complies with the request to explain the folkways of his theatrical subculture. He willingly delivers his memories and his repertoire, but hardly ventures into the realm of the personal. It is as though in Agraval's presence he can only call forth laudable acts, praiseworthy habits such as his bodily self-mastery. The self that emerges in the text is thus collaborative, decentered, unstable. Despite the resistance that Husain articulates, the discourses of others exert a persistent pressure upon his presentation of self, pushing and pulling in different directions.

Instruction as Intention

These theatrical memoirs may speak in many distinct voices, but they are agreed on the purpose of writing autobiography: it is to instruct others in the exemplary life. Betab in his foreword asserts, "Beneficial it is when those who have achieved prestige or accomplishment write their life histories." His autobiography was first published in a monthly journal for young men and was obviously intended for their betterment. Later he elaborates, "What is the main purpose of publishing an autobiography? It is so that people may derive educational value from someone else's life story, so they may shape themselves in another's positive image." (manzil 27) When challenged about the truthfulness of his story, he justifies presenting only his blameless side, saying: "Why should I make my *Ram-kahani* a *Kam-kahani*? What benefit would youngsters derive from that? Young boys would not gain any instruction from it. Mothers, sisters, and daughters should not roam in the garden of obscenity, picking fragrant flowers. Propriety is not defended by painting a picture of the naked truth." (manzil 27) The instructional objective and the notion of self-narrative as exemplum fit the pattern of Indo-Islamic religious autobiography. According to Metcalf, the genres of *tazkira* and *apbiti* focus upon "a person whose essential character is a given and whose life story is best told by recounting episodes—anecdotes—which yield lessons for moral understanding."[6] Betab's anecdotal style and his emphasis on the didactic import of his experiences resonate with this pattern. He joins a succession of

---

[6] Metcalf (2004): 120.

Urdu literary forebears who were intent upon the moral improvement of their auditors and readers.

Attached as he is to Sufi metaphors of the spiritual journey as a pilgrim's progress, Betab is also comfortable assuming the posture of a Hindu sage such as Vyas or Shukdev Muni. He moralizes on his departure from home by referring to Ram's exile to the forest. The parable in which he renounces greed by returning the extra coin to his boss is adorned with references to Hindu deities. After his conversion to the Arya Samaj, Betab's text becomes overtly didactic. He dispenses practical advice, such as not to burn coal in a room without ventilation. He expounds on the ten traits of *dharm* that Ram embodied, a kind of Ten Commandments. He defines what it means to tell a lie, providing examples as if to a schoolchild. He even inserts a long poem that he wrote on the occasion of his daughter's marriage, instructing the young wife on her marital duties. The didactic literary sensibility of Betab's time hovers nearby as he pens his text to fulfill the promise of instruction.

Radheshyam and Sundari write under the same warrant, edifying their readers by holding up their own actions for imitation. The effect of their authorial intentionality, while meant to paint themselves in a positive light, also robs their histories of inner conflict and difficult choices. While this tendency is in keeping with Radheshyam's self-serving tone, it often works against Sundari's persona, crafted to create interiority. Even Sundari's obvious acts of mischief, such as slapping the troupe manager Sakharam in the train, are converted into moral victories. His village, his upbringing, his family of origins—all are depicted as idyllic and pure. Expunged of moral failing by definition, Sundari's parents incur no responsibility for the transactions through which his labor is sold and he becomes, in effect, an indentured servant of a theatrical company.

Fida Husain brings a more complex method to the task of teaching through storytelling. He allows himself to be shown in the wrong, but whenever he makes a mistake, he then corrects it. He establishes himself as willing and able to improve, giving proof of the development of his moral character. Consider his dedication to music and theatre, described as an uncontrollable passion that developed in adolescence. This motif is common in theatrical memoirs, but two things stand out in this text. First, Husain narrates a good cop/bad cop scenario, splitting the responsibility for his self-correction between two male authority figures. Neither his father nor his uncle approves of theatre as an appropriate line of work, but Husain's father is depicted as tender and kind-hearted, a man who weeps when his son disobeys, whereas his uncle is the brutal enforcer who repeatedly beats him.

The division between benevolent and punitive parent-figures allows for Husain's eventual reconciliation with his family without loss of face. This occurs after his most flagrant transgression—running away to join a theatre company—when his father comes to Meerut to arrest him. First he persuades his father that the theatre company is a site of surveillance and discipline. Then he promises to follow his father's itemized list of prohibitions and vows to never abandon his familial duties. This narrative module recurs throughout the autobiography: Husain errs and then he learns from his error. His actions deliver a message of accepting one's own fallibility, while at the same time endorsing dominant norms related to masculinity, family, and kinship.

The second lesson that emerges from the conflict between Husain's passion for theatre and social rules is that adversity can be overcome through dedication and self-sacrifice. Like a yogi enduring physical torments to enhance his spiritual power, Husain undergoes round upon round of punishment in order to follow his inborn love of theatre. His body becomes a site of sacrifice, purified for the impure work of song and dance by the physical abuse of his elders. For a while, he follows the daily discipline prescribed by a sadhu to regain the use of his damaged vocal cords. The most graphic description of persecution is reserved for the day he runs away. Here the sado-masochistic details in the text give a melodramatic quality to the narrative, but they also reinforce the lesson that prolonged suffering brings its own reward. The attachment to theatre, rather than making the boy wayward, renders him capable of self-transformation. His primal transgression through determination and sustained suffering is converted into a heroic act.

Husain's ability to learn from his mistakes and endure in the face of adversity follow him through the narrative as he contends with the tough discipline of the theatrical companies and the ups and downs of the acting profession. He describes himself as an actor who was always in demand. As soon as he quit one company, another wanted him. He claims never to have sat idle for even a day in his life. His own virtues and the success flowing from them stand in contrast to the misdemeanors of others around him. Narrating the incident when he was fired from the Alfred Company, he portrays his actions as blameless and asserts that destiny smiled on him afterward, whereas the Alfred Company without him went into rapid decline. Similarly, Kajjan's initial rejection of him is fatefully overturned when he becomes her director and paramour later on. Destiny's hand is visible in his business affairs too. He suffers a loss from his furniture enterprise because the principal amount he invested was acquired without him fulfilling his contractual duties. As he sums it up, "It was not in my fate to profit from easy money." One's moral compass must finally be aligned with fate and destiny. This teaching goes beyond perseverance and proves to be the most subtle to impart.

Childhood and Destiny

Memories of childhood take two forms in these autobiographies: the period is either romanticized, or it is viewed as harsh, a time of endurance. Betab and Fida Husain's narratives follow the latter pattern. Both boys defied parental authority and departed from home on bad terms, although Fida Husain soon was reconciled with his father. Betab's subsequent journey is framed as the quest of a deprived youth for all that was missing at home, especially knowledge and opportunity. Interestingly, Betab does not chronicle his life-story as a smooth movement from rural to urban, running parallel to the transition from youth to adulthood. When he went to Delhi, he stayed with caste fellows from his area, and his supervisor was a relation; his *qasba* connections sustained him. Visiting Bombay for the first time, he registered the rudeness of big city life in the Parsi *seths*' lack of hospitality. Similarly, the city of Calcutta took on a menacing form when he fell ill there. Although he built a house in Muzaffarnagar after his theatre days ended, he never returned to dwell in his hometown. Now a prosperous song-writer, he spent his last years in comfort in Bombay.

Radheshyam and Sundari grew up in families that practised the performing arts and made their living from them. They did not have to struggle against familial expectations when they joined the theatre world, and their accounts are full of nostalgia for the simplicity, harmony, and salubrious environment of their early days. As gifted singers, both boys were recruited by Parsi theatre companies when they were quite young. Sundari left for Calcutta with the full consent of his parents. Radheshyam's entry into the theatre was delayed for some years. He had already found a patron in Rukmini Bibi, who objected to his joining the New Alfred Company, and it may be that the extra income he might have brought to his family was not urgently needed. Radheshyam followed his father's profession of reciting *katha* and maintained this role throughout his life. When he joined the Parsi theatre, it was as a playwright, not a singer-actor. Radheshyam experienced no rupture with his family or dislocation from his childhood home. He maintained his residence in Bareli despite long periods away and established his publishing house on the site of his birth. The outcome might have been very different had he, like Sundari, left home early, become a child star, and played the heroine.

To explain his success, Radheshyam appears caught between taking credit for his own machinations and asserting that everything was divinely destined to occur. He marveled at the reversal of fortune when he purchased the neighboring mansion that had once been the local headquarters of itinerant Parsi theatre companies. Playing the host, he accommodated Sohrabji Ogra and other company elders in the very quarters that they had commanded when he was a boy living in a hut nearby. Radheshyam suggests this was an indication of *karmaphal*, insinuating through Ogra's suggestion that he was rewarded by God for his service to Hindi and the advancement of drama. He also speculates that past *samskaras*, subtle influences that derive from birth, breeding, and deeds, guided his career. Additionally, he credits *ashirvad*, the auspicious words of mentors, as a guiding force in his life, particularly the recognition he received from Madan Mohan Malviya, who bestowed a blessing on him at the start of his career as a playwright.

Silences Maintained and Broken

Silences speak loudly in each of these autobiographies, accompanying the facile, loquacious, and contemplative voices that fill their pages. Betab gives no information about his early education, probably because he felt so strongly that it had been neglected. He does not say how he acquired letters or mention which language he learned first. Why and how he turned to playwriting in Hindi is only cursorily treated. He divulges nothing of his reading habits, nor does he describe how he conceived and composed his most popular plays, particularly his mythologicals. The only book he mentions is Dayanand Sarasvati's magnum opus, *Satyarth Prakash*, which he studied daily when he converted to Arya Samaj beliefs.

The immediate cause for his adopting Hindi was, of course, the insistence of Parsi directors who foresaw a sea change. Betab may have been swayed toward Hindi by Dayanand's express views on the role of the language. However, his move does not seem to have been simply a matter of script or to have been motivated by communal sentiments. Scant antagonism toward Muslims enters his narrative; in fact, he praises an assortment of Muslim teachers and expresses the highest regard for the playwrights Hashr and Ahsan. It appears that the adoption of Hindi as a language of narrative, dramatic dialogue, and abstract thought came bundled with associations to religion and Sanskritic knowledge that were potent adjuncts to the nationalist consciousness in formation. The switch to Hindi also facilitated the re-use of oral traditions that Betab knew well, from erotic Braj lyric songs to the the hymns of *nirgun sants* to the Puranic corpus of tales and legends.

Radheshyam's position on the language question is quite distinct. Coming at the matter as a UP Brahmin raised on Vaishnava *bhakti* poetry, his allegiance to Hindi exists from the start. When he takes to playwriting, he declares his fervent love for the language and his disquiet at Hindu playwrights masquerading under Urdu pseudonyms. The impropriety of cloaking the Hindu epics in Urdu garb profoundly disturbs him. Once or twice he espouses Hindu–Muslim unity, but the sentiment seems hollow. His account of the atmosphere in the New Alfred Company in the mid-1920s is phrased in terms of rivalry between ascendant Hindus such as himself and decadent Muslims such as Agha Hashr, with his penchant for women and wine. It appears that Radheshyam fomented antagonisms by enrolling Hindus in the New Alfred and casting his favorites, usually Gujarati Nayaks and North Indian Brahmins, in preference to Parsis and Muslims.

Radheshyam earned the ire of Muslim viewers on more than one occasion. When his social drama *Parivartan* was performed, he ignored critiques voiced by Muslims, but then with *Masharqi Hur* he sought endorsements from the Urdu luminary Hasrat Mohani to stave off negative reactions. In Chapter 4 he describes himself as "a perpetual victim of the Muslim faction" (*musalman parti ka . . . sada shikar*), referring to negative criticisms of his play *Shakuntala* in the press. Since he includes only favorable reviews of his work among the testimonials in the autobiography, it is difficult to gauge the content and measure of public debate, but even these stray remarks suggest that the instances Radheshyam does mention were likely only part of the story. The disquieting conclusion is that Radheshyam was more than superficially infected by the communal politics of the 1920s. Indeed, through the popularity of his oeuvre he may have contributed directly to the growing anti-Muslim sentiment.

Fida Husain's narrative, while in one sense verbose, contains substantive gaps, especially in regard to his early life and religious identity. The text does not mention his childhood or education, nor is his family's lineage and traditional occupation addressed. The reader does not learn whether he was a Sunni or a Shia. It is as though Fida Husain's identity as a Muslim has been blotted out. Husain was a successful impersonator of Hindu gods and saints, yet he says nothing about the accommodations that were required of a Muslim actor performing these roles. Nor does he mention whether his portrayal of Hindu holy figures ever provoked the audience to react in a communal way, as was the case when Muslim actresses were decried for playing Sita and Draupadi. He mentions the general threat of Hindu–Muslim violence at the time of Partition and recounts that he was once implicated in a dispute about performing plays during Muharram. Aside from these elliptical references, Fida Husain's experiences and self-image as a Muslim remain a mystery. He expresses no hint of sympathy with the political movement for Pakistan, nor does he mention whether he or his family ever considered whether they would remain in India or migrate at Partition.

Husain's silence on religious matters contrasts with Radheshyam, who positions himself explicitly as a Brahmin in his autobiography and describes rifts in the theatrical companies based on religion, region, and caste. Husain's stance is no doubt strategic; he was, after all, in the minority community. Nonetheless, Muslims formed a large part of the personnel in the Parsi theatre in the twentieth century, although probably not as great a percentage as in the late nineteenth. It would be of interest to learn how they adjusted to the surge in Hindi-language productions and devotionally-imbued tales of Hindu gods and saints. Husain's example suggests that they not only embraced these roles on stage but suppressed their Muslimness in non-theatrical, public contexts as well. The textual erasure of Husain's Muslim identity may emanate from the officially secular culture of the post-colonial state and its representatives in the urban theatre world. Throughout his career, Husain was lauded as a performer who convincingly mimed Hindu spirituality through the medium of his Muslim body. In bringing these two strands together, he embodied the hallowed ideal of India's composite culture. It is thus to be expected that his autobiographical self too subsumes his Muslim identity within the nationalist, putatively secular terms of reference that so often deny the separate status of minority communities.

Even more veiled than his religious orientation is the fact that Husain enacted women's roles for at least twelve years. Unlike Sundari, who discusses his experiences as a female impersonator with some candor, Husain barely acknowledges this phase of his career. He gives no hint of the relations between the grown-ups and the boys with whom he was clubbed in the New Alfred, aside from mentioning that the latter were heavily guarded. Nor does he discuss how he graduated to playing men's roles, what transactions were required to reach that position. Sundari played women exclusively until his exit from the commercial stage, whereas Husain's early period when he starred as a heroine was eclipsed by his subsequent career in male roles. Possibly he chose to recall only the latter, especially his performances as Hindu holy men, because he received greater acclaim for them. Certainly the era during which female impersonators reigned on the Parsi, Gujarati, and Marathi theatres was distant from the vantage of the 1980s, the point from which he looks back. Was it a source of embarrassment as well? Husain's narrative provides no answer.

Husain is also cautious in discussing his relations with female artists. Although he teamed up with the actress Sita Devi and credits her with the success of the Moonlight Theatre, he claims that as a director he had no time for dalliance. Only in the case of Kajjan, an actress known for her courtesan background, does he suggest a romantic relationship. The more dominant theme in the autobiography is that he was a good husband and provider. He visited home regularly, in accordance with the vow made to his father, and retired to the bosom of the joint family in old age. His sons are successful, his daughters are happily married, and he adores his grandchildren. He never mentions his wife, keeping her hidden and preserving family honor. His life story thereby reproduces the image of a self in harmony with heteronormativity, sidestepping the ambiguous zones of gender and sexuality that flourished in and around the Parsi theatre.

Radheshyam is more forthcoming about the "wild zone" of gender shifts and sexual opportunity in the proximity of the stage. A believer in the separation of the sexes in the name of morality, he could not remain entirely aloof from actresses and women nor, perhaps, from men who played women's roles. Radheshyam's rapport with Sohrabji Ogra was linked to his support for the policy of barring women from the stage. In contrast with the Parsi Alfred and Madan Theatres, the New Alfred hired female impersonators exclusively to play women's roles. Radheshyam not only approved of the practice, he considered it the "nature" of certain men, especially Nayaks, to enact women. He saw no impropriety in men playing the heroine. Even the great Malviya had played the role of Shakuntala, and this was as it should be in the days when women covered their heads and practised conjugal fidelity.

The advent of actresses for Radheshyam was an evil attributable to foreign influence. When men and women played the hero and heroine they became as if husband and wife, and when they spoke to each other directly on stage, it created an adverse effect, especially on female spectators. Understanding both his own success and that of the New Alfred as dependent upon attracting respectable families to the audience, Radheshyam saw his position as righteous and beyond reproach. The autobiography, however, hints that Radheshyam had his lapses. He expresses acute discomfort in the presence of actresses, likening the licentious atmosphere backstage before an Agha Hashr play to a latrine. At the same time, he was powerfully attracted toward the beautiful young women in the Corinthian Theatre and found it difficult to concentrate while guiding their rehearsals. He was entranced on the set of the film *Shakuntala*, where he encountered a foreign lady (*gori mem*) who handled the scenario book and offered him a cough drop. In the most unusual confession in the autobiography, he describes how he sought the company of a Hindu courtesan, supposedly as a model for the character of Chanda in his play *Parivartan*, since he otherwise could not compete with a playwright like Agha Hashr. Breaking the silence, the text in this way suggests that Radheshyam tasted the forbidden fruit he so staunchly preached against, and probably more than once.

Operating on a very different principle, Sundari's story offers an abundance of heterosexual liaisons and love affairs for the reader to savor, while completely occluding the element of homosexual desire. The modern audience familiar with his reputation as a transgendered performer might seek in his tale evidence of his attraction toward men. And yet one looks in vain for signs of same-sex preference in the narrative. Sundari's dysfunction, according to the autobiography, has nothing to do with an inclination that clashes with heteronormative social rules. Instead, in the chapter entitled "My Married Life," he describes several extramarital relationships with women, painting himself quite the Casanova, while obliquely touching on the circumstances of his three marriages.

The chapter is odd because little is actually said about Sundari's conjugal life, and much of what is relayed seems fanciful and novelistic. He focuses on his romantic attachments, first to a child widow, then to a Parsi girl who is a Theosophist, then to a wealthy married Hindu lady. The latter two are clearly women of superior social status. These romances are depicted as full of pathos, tragedy, and melodrama. The women are said to be of the sort that Jayshankar would have liked to attach himself to permanently. It is probable that they are variations upon the feminine roles he played on stage or was exposed to through his readings in vernacular literature. A close look at such sources might well show that the romantic scenes with women in his autobiography imitate the dramatic scripts and novels of his time.

Through a fragmented narrative, this chapter also recounts the rocky course of Sundari's multiple marriages. He tells of the breakdown of his first marriage only toward the end of the chapter, whereas the wedding itself is described in the first part. The basic dilemma is that Sundari desires an educated wife but is matched with unsophisticated brides from his community according to the dictates of his parents. His first wife was 11 when he was married to her at 14. She developed a crippling disease, and they never lived together. His second wife cohabited with him in Bombay, but he rejected her on account of her backwardness and illiteracy. He tried to educate her in the manner of social reformers of his day, but this effort failed. During the period of their marriage, he avoided going home and became suicidal. Without divorcing either woman, at the age of 30 Jayshankar finally finds a compatible partner in Champa. She agrees to his stipulation to never enter the theatre, preserving his status and her innocence, and he acknowledges her as the goddess Lakshmi for her hospitality and service within the joint family.

Sundari's compliance with heteronormative arrangements is hence troubled, but not, by his own account, due to gender confusion. Yet one wonders at the ease with which he identified with women as a child and youth and was called Plum Girl by his grandfather. For years he worked with Bapulal Nayak in an intense professional relationship that may well have had an intimate aspect. He enjoyed the adoration of male fans who gifted him expensive objects like books and binoculars. Was his silence a defensive tactic to shore up his respectability? Did it hide a traumatic past, a history of exploitation and abuse? Was it occasioned by amnesia? Or were there simply no words for "the love that dare not speak its name"?

Curiously, it is Betab of all the autographs who finds the words to express his passionate feelings for another male. With complete acceptance of his youthful emotions, Betab relates how he fell head over heels in love with a boy actor. "The beauty of the entire world seemed to be contained in his face. A secret pain now settled in my heart. . . . I wanted to buy him items from the bazaar, present him gifts like scarves, silken handkerchiefs, fine stockings, fancy combs." (manzil 11) In naming this desire, Betab resorts to the circumlocutions of the Parsi stage and Urdu ghazal. His beloved is an *apsara*, one of the nymphs who attend upon Indra in his heavenly court (*indar sabha*). He, the lover, is tormented, anxious, restless with yearning (*betab*), but he cannot reveal his desperate love. He is a patient, the beloved his doctor, but he cannot ask him for a prescription or cure.

Then realism intrudes, but not of a psychological sort. The love affair remains idealized, treasured in memory. As he looks back on his infatuation, Betab's narrator is philosophical. The nature of events is transitory, and after the beloved leaves town with the company, the feeling subsides. Betab's practical side also counsels him to keep his adoration unspoken in order to preserve his reputation. There is a touch of didacticism as the wisdom of later years intrudes to contain the burning force of youthful passion. Nevertheless, the episode is fascinating in its frank exposition of the homoerotic energies activated through cross-gender role playing. Betab's lack of inhibition in articulating his desire suggests the positive valence connected to romantic attachment within a homosocial milieu. What is most striking is the effective use of a conventionalized vocabulary of love to suggest the depth of inner experience and at the same time create the distance necessary to its public articulation. By successfully performing the persona of a vulnerable lover, Betab wields the autobiographical medium to speak of what so often remains unspoken. His breakthrough stands as a triumph of the art of self-narration. It encourages readers to find in these stories the audacity of theatrical subjects, who are insistent that they be heard, even as they perform voice and perform silence.

APPENDIX 1

Historical Personages and Institutions

Abdul Rahman Kabuli: Actor of tragic or stately roles, probably a Pathan. Associated with New Albert, then joined New Alfred and performed in Radheshyam's plays.

Ahsan Lakhnavi, Mehdi Hasan: Turn-of-the-century playwright from lineage of Urdu poets. Authored *Khun-e Nahaq* (based on *Hamlet*), *Dilfarosh* (based on *Merchant of Venice*), *Chalta Purza*, *Chandravali*.

Alfred Theatrical Company: Leading nineteenth-century company founded in 1871. Flourished under actor-manager Kavasji Khatau from early 1880s until his death in 1916; then his son Jahangir ran the company.

Apu, Framji: Acted in Gaiety Theatre, became joint proprietor of Victoria Theatrical Company and then joint proprietor of third Parsi Theatrical Company of Bombay.

Arya Samaj: Important Hindu social and religious movement, founded by Dayanand Sarasvati in 1875. Its principles influenced literary and theatrical production, bringing agenda of moralistic nationalism.

Bajan, Dorab: Actor in Victoria Company and Natak Uttejak Company, joint proprietor of third Parsi Theatrical Company with Apu brothers.

Bal Gandharva, aka Narayan Shripad Rajhans (1886–1967): Leading female impersonator and singing actor in the Marathi musical theatre.

Balivala, Khurshedji Mehrbanji (1853–1913): Famous comic actor and one of the Parsi theatre's most successful actor-managers; associated with Victoria Theatrical Company from the early 1870s until his death.

Balsara, Manik Shah (b. 1883): Manager of Alfred Company, joint proprietor of New Alfred beginning in 1918.

Baroda, Maharaja Sayajirao Gaekwad III (1863–1939): Noted patron of visual arts, classical music and dance, founded University of Baroda.

Barua, Pramathesh Chandra (1903–51): Film actor in silent era, then directed melancholy love stories in Bengali and Hindi (*Devdas*).

Betab, Narayan Prasad (1872–1945): Major playwright of the Parsi theatre; composed over thirty dramas. Ushered in Hindi-language plays with his *Mahabharat* and *Ramayan* written for Khatau's Alfred Company.

Bhagat Singh (1907–31): Revolutionary and nationalist martyr, accused of killing J.P. Saunders and hanged by the British.

Bharatendu Harishchandra (1850–85): Considered the father of modern Hindi and the Hindi theatre, synthesized traditions from Sanskrit, English, Bengali, and popular forms in literary dramas.

Bharatpur, Raja Kishan Singh (r. 1918–28): Drama patron and aficionado.

Bhatkhande, Pandit Vishnu Narayan (1860–1936): Major figure in spreading classical Hindustani music to broad middle-class constituency.

Bhavnani, Mohan Dayaram (1903–62): Hindi film director associated with Kohinoor and Imperial Studios in the 1920s; independent producer in 1931–2.

Bhogilal: Actor, female impersonator, dance coach in New Alfred; became director in 1924.

Bhojak, Jayshankar Sundari (1889–1975): Legendary actor, director of the Gujarati theatre, achieved fame in feminine roles in Mumbai Gujarati Natak Mandali at Gaiety Theatre.

Bijli: Actress of Parsi stage; appeared in *Zanjir-e Gauhar* in 1907.

Bose, Debaki Kumar (1898–1971): Bengali and Hindi film director, 1930s–50s.

Charkhari, Maharaja Arimardan Singh Ju Dev (1903–41, r. 1920–): Prince of state in Madhya Pradesh, theatre patron, commissioned Agha Hashr to write *Sita Banvas*.

Charvak: Founder of heterodox philosophical system denying existence of soul and reincarnation; stressed material pleasures of life.

Chaube, Ramkrishna: Actor in New Alfred Company in the 1920s and early 1930s, director of Shahjahan Theatrical Company in the 1940s.

Cooper, Patience (1905–54): Anglo-Indian actress from Calcutta, performed in Bandmann's Musical Comedy, Parsi Elphinstone, Corinthian theatres, became a star of the silent cinema.

Corinthian Theatrical Company: Important twentieth-century company founded in Calcutta by the Madans.

DAV/Dayanand Anglo Vedic schools and colleges: Institutions found across North India, established to implement the educational mission of the Arya Samaj.

Dagh Dihlavi, Nawab Mirza Khan (1831–1905): Classical Urdu poet.

Dangi, Manik Lal (1902–64): Born in Jodhpur, acted in the Alexandria, New Alfred, and Corinthian companies. Ran the Shahjahan Theatrical Company from 1939 on.

Daniel Dada/Daniel David: Jewish director, briefly owned the Parsi Imperial Theatrical Company in 1927.

Dave, Ranchhodbhai Udayram (1837–1923): Early Gujarati playwright, company manager; his *Lalita Dukhdarshak* (1866) was the first play performed by the Gujarati Natak Mandali.

Desi Natak Samaj: Pioneering professional theatre company of Ahmedabad, established in 1889 by Dahyabhai Dholshaji.

Dey, Krishna Chandra (1893–1962): Music director and actor, became blind at 14, specialized in singing saint roles (*Chandidas, Bidyapati, Devdas*).

Dhaulpur, Raja Nihal Singh Lokendra (r. 1873–1901): Patron of playwright Hafiz Abdullah, manager and owner of the Indian Imperial Theatrical Company.

Dholshaji, Dahyabhai (1867–1902): Schoolteacher, dramatist, company owner, wrote over twenty Gujarati plays and constructed several playhouses.

Dil, Munshi: Author of *Laila Majnun* and *Nadir Shah*, plays performed in the Alfred and New Alfred companies. Later wrote dialogues for films (*Tansen*, 1943).

Dinshaw/Dinshah Irani, aka Dinshaw Painter: Parsi scene painter, worked in New Alfred Company and in Madan Theatres, Calcutta; known for his trick scenes and illusions.

Dvivedi, Mahavir Prasad (1864–1938): Early-twentieth-century Hindi editor and publicist whose journal, *Sarasvati*, set the standard for the modern literary idiom.

Elijar/Elizar/Elizer: Jewish actor in New Alfred and films of the 1920s and early 1930s (*Alam Ara*).

Elphinstone Theatrical Company: Old Parsi theatre club, founded in 1863 as an amateur club at Elphinstone College, performed English dramas. Went professional in the early 1870s and switched to Gujarati and then Urdu plays.

Fenton, Mary (1846–96): First celebrated actress of Parsi stage. Daughter of an Irish soldier, born in Landour. Performed as idealized Indian woman in Alfred Theatrical Company (*Gamreni Gori, Bholi Gul, Tara Khurshid, Kalyug*).

Fida Husain Narsi, aka Prem Shankar (1899–2001): Singer, actor, and director in the Parsi theatre tradition. Worked in New Alfred Company as female impersonator, later managed several companies in Calcutta, including Moonlight Theatre (1948–68).

Gaiety Theatre: Built by C.S. Nazir in 1879, still extant as Capitol Cinema, opposite Bombay's Victoria (now Chhatrapati Shivaji) Terminus.

Gauhar, Miss: Leading actress in revival of Hindu mythologicals, played Draupadi in Betab's *Mahabharat* and Sita in his *Ramayan* with Alfred Company. May have been the same as singer Gauhar Jan.

Gauhar Jan (1873–1930): Classically trained singer, early recording star. Sang for princes all over India. Close associate of Amritlal Nayak until his death.

Girnara, Dayashankar Vasanji (d. 1909): Well-known actor, artistic director and partner of Mumbai Gujarati Natak Mandali from 1889 onward.

Gohar, Kayoum Mamajiwala (1910–85): Popular film actress of the 1920s and 1930s, common-law wife of Chandulal Shah. Starred in Ranjit Studio's films scripted by Betab.

Gujarati Natak Mandali: Founded in 1878 by three partners, including Narottam Bhaichand.

Gupt, Maithili Sharan (1886–1964): Pioneer in composing modern poetry in Khari Boli Hindi; after Independence honored with the title "National Poet."

Hashr Kashmiri, Agha (1879–1935): Prolific playwright of Parsi theatre plays in Urdu and Hindi. Attached to numerous companies and briefly ran several companies himself. Best-known for *Yahudi ki Larki, Silver King*, Shakespearean adaptations, and Hindu mythologicals (*Sita Banvas*).

Husain Bakhsh Painter, Ustad (d. 1932): Set designer and painter, active in the twentieth-century Parsi theatre until his death.

Husn Bano: Film actress from the 1930s to 1960s: *Desh Deepak, Hind Kesari, Hurricane Hansa, Bahen, Amar, Ganga Jumna*.

Ibrahim, Muhammad Ali: Joint proprietor who revived Alfred Theatrical Company in the decade following 1881; established New Alfred together with Manikji Master in 1891.

Indargarh, Raja Umrao Singh (1924–98): Ruler of small princely state in Rajasthan.

Indian Imperial Theatrical Company of Agra: Nineteenth-century company owned and managed by Hafiz Abdullah under the patronage of the Raja of Dhaulpur.

Jaipur, Raja Sawai Ramsingh II (1835–80): Patron of the arts, established Ramprakash Theatre in 1878, recruited Dadabhai Thunthi to train actors and put on performances.

Jamadar Theatrical Company: May have originated in what is now Pakistan; toured Rajasthan, Delhi, UP, and the Punjab between 1898 and 1902.

Jauhar, Harikrishna: Hindi dramatist associated with Parsi Alfred and

Corinthian, wrote *Pati Bhakti, Vir Bharat*. Adapted former for a popular silent film.

Jhalawar (Rajasthan), Raja Bhavani Singh (1886–1929): Notable patron of poetry and the theatre.

Kabra, Kaikhushro Navrojji (1842–1904): Social reformer, newspaper editor, theatre pioneer. Established Victoria Theatrical Company, wrote trilogy of *Shahnama*-based plays in the early 1870s. In 1876 founded Natak Uttejak Company, built a playhouse near Crawford Market.

Kabra, Bahmanji Navrojji (1860–1925): Gujarati playwright who wrote popular social dramas for the Parsi theatre (*Gamreni Gori, Bholi Gul*), younger brother of K. N. Kabra.

Kaiser-i Hind Press, Delhi: Established in 1887 and owned by Munshi Babu Ramchandar, managed by Lala Devi Sahay.

Kajjan, Jahanara (1915–45): Popular singing actress, daughter of the courtesan Suggan and the Nawab of Bhagalpur. Often paired with Master Nisar as romantic leads.

Kapariya, Mehrbanji: Joint proprietor of New Alfred with Manik Shah Balsara from 1918 on.

Kapoor, Prithviraj (1906–72): Scion of India's leading film family, actor in over fifty silent and sound films, actor-manager of Prithvi Theatres, the pre-Independence traveling drama company.

Khambata, Jahangir (1856–1916): Actor in Victoria, Alfred, and Hindi theatrical companies. Founded Empress Victoria Theatrical Company in 1876.

Khatau, Jahangir Kavasji: Son of Kavasji Khatau and Mary Fenton. Succeeded father in 1916 as director and owner of Alfred Company, ran it until 1927.

Khatau, Kavasji Palanji (1857–1916): Famous singer and tragedian, tutored by Jahangir Khambata, achieved renown opposite paramour Mary Fenton. Managed Alfred Company for thirty years.

Khori, Edalji Jamshedji (1847–1917): Early Gujarati playwright. Many of his plays were translated into Hindustani and performed by the Victoria Theatrical Company.

Kirloskar Company: Leading Marathi-language dramatic company, founded in 1875, flourished until around 1935. Developed *sangitnatak* form.

Lala, Mohan (1885–1938): Popular Gujarati actor and contemporary of Jayshankar, trained by Nathuram Sundarji Shukla and Mulshankar Mulani.

Madan Company/Madan Theatres: Joint stock company owned by the Madan brothers. Focused on acquiring theatre companies in the 1890s, then expanded into film exhibition and distribution. Produced silent films based on Parsi theatre plays and two blockbuster talkies (*Shirin Farhad, Indrasabha*).

Madan, Jamshedji Framji (1856–1923): Joined Elphinstone Dramatic Club in 1868, popular as female impersonator; bought Corinthian Hall, then Elphinstone and other Parsi theatre companies, developed vast entertainment empire.

Madan, Jeejeebhoy Jamshedji (J.J.): Film director, entrepreneur; third son of J.F. Madan. Directed Patience Cooper in *Nal Damayanti*, *Pati Bhakti*; *Savitri*, first Italian-Indian co-production; and multi-song *Indrasabha*.

Malviya, Madan Mohan (1861–1946): Leader of the Indian National Congress, founder of the Banaras Hindu University and Sanatan Dharm Mahasabha in Allahabad.

Mangeshkar, Lata (b.1929): Top-grossing Bombay playback singer, dominated Indian film music from the 1950s through the 1990s.

Marconi, T.R.: Talented Italian cameraman, joined Madan Theatres film production company in the 1920s; films include *Savitri*, *Indrasabha*, *Zehari Saap*, and the Tamil *Vimochanam*.

Master, Manikji Jivanji: Joint proprietor of Alfred Company (1881–6), started New Alfred with Muhammad Ali Ibrahim in 1891, retained ownership until 1932.

Mauli: Anglo-Indian dancer coached by Master Champalal; worked in Kanpur with Fida Husain and later joined several other companies.

Mehrji Surveyor: Actor in Empress Victoria Company of Jahangir Khambata, later founded the Parsi Ripon Theatrical Company.

Minerva Theatre: Well-known playhouse on Beadon Street in Calcutta, established on the site of Great National Theatre.

Mir, Ezra/Ajra (1903–93): Hindi film director, born Edwin Myers. Started as Parsi theatre actor in Calcutta, worked in Hollywood and several Bombay film studios. Chief producer of Government of India Films Division (1956–61).

Mirabai: Sixteenth-century Rajasthani Vaishnava singer renowned across North India for her *bhajans*.

Mistri, Dadabhai Edalji, aka Edu Kalejar: Actor, dramatist, and partner in the Parsi Theatrical Company with the Apu brothers.

Mohan, Master: Female impersonator, comic actor in Madan Theatres; appeared in silent films (*Nal Damayanti, Pati Bhakti*), early talkies (*Shirin Farhad*).

Mohani, Hasrat, aka Syed Fazl ul-Hasan (1875–1951): Urdu poet, journalist, freedom fighter, led All India Muslim League in 1921, later espoused communism.

Moonlight Playhouse: Established in 1939 on Tarachand Dutta Street, Calcutta. Converted into Moonlight Cinema in 1968.

Moonlight Theatre Company: Last successful Parsi theatre company of Calcutta, which Fida Husain managed from 1948 until 1968.

Mudaliar, Pammal Sambandha (1875–1964): Prolific Tamil playwright, actor, director; founded Suguna Vilasa Sabha in 1891; wrote theatrical memoirs in six volumes.

Mukhtar/Mukhtyar Begam (1911–82): Accomplished singer, actress of Urdu stage and cinema (*Ankh ka Nasha, Dil ki Pyas, Indrasabha, Shravan Kumar*). Wife of Agha Hashr.

Mulani, Mulshankar (1868–1957): Prolific poet and dramatist of Mumbai Gujarati Natak Mandali; wrote eight historicals, eight socials, and nine mythological dramas.

Mumbai Gujarati Natak Mandali: Established in 1889, attained artistic and commercial success under Dayashankar Girnara, Jayshankar Sundari, and Bapulal Nayak.

Munni Bai (1903–66): Twentieth-century Parsi stage actress, child star with Victoria Company, worked for Madan Theatres, Gujarati Natak Samaj, and other companies.

Murad, Murad Ali: Urdu playwright from Bareli, leading dramatist of the Alfred Theatrical Company under Khatau and later the New Alfred of Ogra.

Mysore, Maharaja Krishnarao Wodeyar (1884–1940): Great connoisseur of North and South Indian music and well-known patron of the arts.

Nagari Pracharini Sabha: Society for the propagation of Devanagari, founded in 1893 for the promotion of Hindi language in education and government.

Nanak Chand Khatri (d. 1914): Punjabi owner of the New Albert Company, active around 1910.

Narsi Mehta: Gujarati saint-poet of the fifteenth century, known for extreme generosity and devotion to Krishna as a *gopi* in Ras Lila.

Narsi Theatrical Company: Founded in 1942 by Fida Husain, folded after eight months due to the Quit India movement.

Nat Mandal: Training institute and amateur drama company, founded by Jayshankar Sundari in 1949 under the auspices of Gujarat Vidya Sabha, Ahmedabad.

Natya Shodh Sansthan: Calcutta institute and theatre archive, directed by Dr Pratibha Agraval.

Appendix 1   343

Naval Kishore Press: Foremost publishing house in colonial India, established in Lucknow in 1858.

Navin, Balkrishna Sharma (1897–1960): Hindi poet, nationalist, and editor of *Pratap*.

Nayak, Amritlal Keshavlal (1877–1907): Celebrated female impersonator, actor, and director, joined Alfred Company in 1888, became assistant director in 1892.

Nayak, Bapulal (1879–1947): Famous actor, director, co-owner of Mumbai Gujarati Natak Mandali from 1899. Played romantic hero opposite Sundari.

Nayak, Narmada Shankar Tribhuvan: Female impersonator in New Alfred Company, played female lead in *Turki Hur* (1924) and acted in films through the 1950s.

Nayak, Vadilal Shivram: Influential music director, composed over 500 songs for more than 40 plays. Many of his scores were published in the Gujarati script.

Nazir, Kunvarji, aka Cowasji Sohrabji Nazir (1846–85): Actor, director, founded the amateur Elphinstone Dramatic Society and later turned it into a professional company.

Nazir, Nazir Beg, aka Nazir Akbarabadi: Actor, director, and playwright active between 1888 and 1913; disciple of Hafiz Abdullah.

Nehru, Motilal (1861–1931): Lawyer, legislator, president of the Indian National Congress; father of Jawaharlal Nehru.

New Albert Theatrical Company: Twentieth-century company owned by Nanak Chand Khatri. Toured Bareli in 1910–11 and performed a composite version of *Ramayan*.

New Alfred Theatrical Company: Offshoot of older Alfred Company, formed around 1891 by Muhammad Ali Ibrahim and Manikji Jivanji Master. Became the leading twentieth-century company under Sohrabji Ogra and retained eminent position until the 1930s.

Nisar/Nissar/Master Nisar: Versatile singer/actor, played Parvati, Chintamani, Uttara, Draupadi in Parsi mythologicals; played hero opposite Kajjan on stage and screen.

Novelty Theatre: Constructed by K.M. Balivala and his partner Moghul in 1887, it seated 1400.

Ogra, Sohrabji Framji (1858–1933): Well-known comic actor and director of Alfred and New Alfred theatrical companies. Staunch opponent of actresses appearing on stage.

Parsi Imperial Theatrical Company: Twentieth-century company, home of director Joseph David; its playwright was Nazan.

Parsi Theatrical Company of Bombay: Very early Parsi drama company, founded by citizens of Bombay in 1853. Another company with the same name established in 1876. Third formation arose in 1898 under joint proprietorship of four *seths*; Betab was associated with it.

Patel, Dadabhai Sohrabji, aka Dadi Patel MA (1844–76): Highly educated scion of a mercantile family, became Victoria Company director in 1869.

Patel, Dhanjibhai Navroji (1857–1937): Parsi playwright, actor, poet, and photographer; wrote and illustrated an important Gujarati-language history of the Parsi theatre.

Pathak, Dina (1923–2002): Gujarati actress and director, founding member of IPTA, known for innovative work in the Gujarati theatre.

Phulchand Marwari/Phulchand Dangi (1898–1962): Jodhpur-born female impersonator, worked with many twentieth-century theatrical companies.

Prasad, Jaishankar (1889–1937): Leading modern Hindi poet and dramatist, founding member of Chhayavad group. His closet dramas were mostly historicals (*Skandagupta, Dhruvaswamini*).

Premanand (1636–1734): Foremost composer of *akhyan*; *Nalakhyan* considered his finest.

Premchand, Munshi, aka Dhanpat Rai Shrivastav (1880–1936): Celebrated fiction author in Hindi and Urdu, used fiction as instrument of social and moral reform.

Prithvi Theatres: Traveling Hindi-language theatre company founded by Prithviraj Kapoor in 1944, closed in 1960 after many tours throughout India.

Putli: Actress of Parsi theatre and 1920s silent films (*Sati Sardarba, Cinema ki Rani, Bap Kamai, Bulbul-e Paristan*).

Radheshyam Kathavachak (1890–1963): Influential dramatist, wrote on Hindu mythological themes for Parsi theatre. Worked for the Alfred and New Alfred companies, 1910–30.

Rai, Himanshu (1892–1940): Actor and film producer, founded Bombay Talkies in 1934.

Ranina, Nanabhai Rustamji (1832–1900): Parsi author, journalist, publisher; made early adaptations of Shakespeare into Gujarati and penned several comedies.

Ranjit Film Company/Movietone: Film studio active from 1929 to the late 1960s, started by Chandulal Shah, best known for socials and satires, e.g. *Gunsundari*.

Ratlam, Maharaja Sir Sajjan Singh: Ruled a princely state in central India until 1947.

Ripon/Parsi Ripon Theatrical Company: Founded by Mehrji Surveyor, the company traveled as far as Burma and the Straits Settlements.

Roy, Charu (1890–1971): Formally trained painter, set designer, and director influenced by Franz Osten (*Loves of a Mughal Prince*).

Roy, Prafulla (b.1892): Bengali film director in the 1930s. His *Ramayan*, released in 1934, was made in Hindi.

Sagar Film Company: Extant from 1930 to 1939, produced Ezra Mir's Parsi theatre-derived films. Director Mehboob was schooled here.

Sahukar, Raghubir: Female impersonator from Maharashtra, worked with Bal Gandharva's company and then New Alfred.

Saigal, Kundan Lal (1904–46): Legendary actor and singer in Hindi and Bengali films of the 1930s and 1940s.

Sen, Tapas (1924–2006): Founding member of Indian People's Theatre Association (IPTA), created memorable lighting schemes and special effects for *Angar, Kallol, Setu*.

Shah, Chandulal (1898–1975): Film director and industry mogul, established Ranjit Movietone in 1929 and produced over 150 films by 1950.

Shahjahan Theatrical Company: Prominent twentieth-century company established by Manik Lal Dangi.

Shaida, Pandit Tulsidatt: Playwright of Parsi Alfred and Corinthian of Calcutta, author of *Nal Damayanti, Bhakt Surdas*. Wrote screenplay for the silent film *Dhruva Charitra*.

Shantaram, V., aka Rajaram Vankudre (1901–90): Influential Hindi and Marathi actor, director, and producer (*Admi, Shakuntala, Dr Kotnis ki Amar Kahani*).

Sharifa Bai (d. 1968): Actress in Alfred and Madan Theatres, starred in *Ankh ka Nasha* and *Dil ki Pyas*. In the 1930s, performed in films (*Shirin Farhad, Desh Deepak, Huntervali*).

Singh, Yuddhvir (1897–1983): Gandhian freedom fighter, staunch Arya Samajist, pioneering homeopathic doctor; Betab's family doctor. Received a Padma Bhushan in 1977.

Sita Devi: Actress from East Bengal, long-time associate of Fida Husain; performed with Minerva and Moonlight Theatres in Calcutta in the mid-twentieth century.

Sultana: Heroine of comic plays, one of three sisters (Sultana, Raziya, and Meenu). Stage-name Meena, known in films as *Shakuntala*.

Surdas (late fifteenth–sixteenth century): Saint and poet of Krishnaite devotionalism, known for *Sur Sagar*, compendium of thousands of songs which circulate to this day in oral tradition.

Survijay Natak Samaj: Founded in 1914 in Surat by Lavji Bhai Mayashankar, based in Delhi and Bareli and toured performing plays of Hindi playwrights.

Talib Banarasi, Vinayak Prasad (1855–1922): Urdu/Hindi playwright, born in a Kayasth family. Wrote dramas for the Victoria Theatrical Company.

Thakar, Jasvant (1915–90): Gujarati director, actor, and educator, established the Gujarat branch of IPTA, played a vital role in developing modern Gujarati theatre.

Thunthi, Dadabhai Ratanji: Actor, director, owner associated with Victoria Company around 1870; by 1897, led the Alfred Company.

Tonk, Raja/Nawab Saadat Ali Khan (r. 1930–47): Poet and patron of arts, sponsored touring companies such as Jubilee and Alexandria.

Torney, Ramchandra Gopal (1890–1960): Film director in Hindi and Marathi, headed Sarasvati Cinetone from 1931 until 1942.

Ugra, Pandey Bechan Sharma (1901–67): Hindi author of popular fiction in the 1920s. Story collection *Chaklet* charged with obscenity for tackling homosexual relationships.

Varma, Raja Ravi (1848–1906): Renowned artist from the princely state of Travancore, famous for painting scenes from the *Ramayan* and *Mahabharat*.

Vibhakar, Nrusingh/Nrisimha (1888–1925): Wrote six Gujarati dramas, most dealing with nationalism and social reform (*Sneh Sarita, Sudhachandra, Madhu Bansari*).

Victoria Theatrical Company: Foremost nineteenth-century company, established in 1868 by K. N. Kabra. Pioneered Urdu-language drama, toured South and Southeast Asia, went to England, pioneered employment of actresses. Balivala was its artistic director until his death in 1913.

Vyakul, Vishvambhar Sahay: Director, playwright, founded Vyakul Bharat Theatrical Company in Meerut. Drama *Buddhadev* lauded by Premchand and others.

Zeba, Kishanchand: Popular Urdu playwright in the 1920s; wrote *Kaya Palat, Bivi aur Beva, Padmini, Danvir Karan, Shahid-i Vatan*.

APPENDIX 2

List of Plays and Films

Plays

Achhuta Daman 'The Inviolable Robe'—Hashr 1903.
Amrit 'Ambrosia'—Betab 1908. Opened in the Coronation Theatre, Bombay, April 29, 1908.
Angar 'Coal'—Dutt 1959. Modern Bengali drama about a coal mining disaster.
Ankh ka Nasha 'Eye's Delight'—Hashr 1924.
Asir-e Hirs 'Captive of Desire'—Hashr 1902. Based on Sheridan's *Pizarro*.
Bazm-e Fani 'Fatal Union'—Ahsan 1898, adaptation of *Romeo and Juliet*.
Bharat Milap 'The Reunion [of Lord Ram] with Bharat'—playwright, date unknown.
Bhul Bhulaiyan 'Labyrinth'—Ahsan 1901. Adaptation of Shakespeare's *Comedy of Errors*.
Bilvamangal, aka *Bhakt Surdas* 'Surdas, the Devotee'—Hashr 1915.
Chalta Purza 'Shrewd Operator'—Ahsan.
Chandrabhaga—Nayak 1909; based on earlier drama, *Kala Dev*.
Chatra/Chitra Bakavali—Murad 1887.
Devkanya—Mulani 1908.
Dharmi Balak 'Righteous Child,' aka *Gharib ki Duniya* 'World of the Poor'—Hashr 1930.
Dil Farosh 'Merchant of Hearts'—Ahsan 1900; based on Shakespeare's *The Merchant of Venice*.
Dil ki Pyas 'The Heart's Thirst'—Hashr 1932.
Dorangi Duniya 'Two-Faced World'—B.N. Kabra (Guj).
Draupadi Svayamvar 'Draupadi's Self-Selection of Bridegroom'—Radheshyam 1929.
Ganesh Janm 'The Birth of Lord Ganesh'—Betab 1928. Opened Aug. 16, 1928, Alfred Theatre, Calcutta.

Gorakhdhandha 'Labyrinth'—Betab 1912. Adaptation of Shakespeare's *Comedy of Errors*. Opened July 31, 1912, Quetta.
Gulru Zarina, 'Zarina, the Flower-faced'—Nazir 1897; Abbas Ali Abbas.
Haman, aka *Sitam-e Haman, Khandan-e Haman*—Raunaq 1880; Murad 1885.
Hamari Bhul 'Our Error'—Betab 1937.
Hava'i Majlis 'The Heavenly Assembly'—Ali 1879.
Harishchandra—Dave 1875.
Husn-e Farang 'The Foreign Beauty'—Betab 1904. Opened Royal Coronation Theatre, Karachi, 1902.
Indar Sabha 'The Court of Indra'—Amanat 1853.
Ishvar Bhakti 'Devotion to God'—Radheshyam 1929.
Jugal Jugari—Mulani 1902.
Kamlata—Mulani 1904.
Kasauti 'Touchstone'—Betab 1903. Based on *Dorangi Duniya*. Opened Novelty Theatre, Bombay, July 12, 1903.
Khubsurat Bala 'Beautiful Affliction'—Hashr, 1909.
Khudadad—Murad 1890.
Khun ka Khun, aka *Khun-e Nahaq* 'Blood for Blood'—Ahsan, 1898. Adaptation of Shakespeare's *Hamlet*.
Krishna Charitra—Mulani 1906.
Krishna Janm 'The Birth of Lord Krishna'—Betab, 1902. Opened in Karachi, 1902.
Krishna Sudama 'Krishna and Sudama'—Betab 1920.
Kumari Kinnari, or *Mother India*—Betab 1928. Opened Alfred Theatre, Calcutta, Dec. 1928.
Madhu Bansari—Vibhakar 1917.
Mahabharat—Betab 1913. Opened Delhi, 1913.
Maharshi Valmiki 'The Great Sage Valmiki'—Radheshyam 1932.
Masharqi Hur 'Damsel of the East'—Radheshyam 1926.
Mayur Dhvaj 'Peacock Emblem'—Betab 1902. Opened in Karachi, 1903.
Meghmalini—Vibhakar 1918.
Mitha Zahar 'Sweet Poison'—Betab 1905. Adaptation of Shakespeare's *Cymbeline*. Opened Victoria Theatre, Bombay, 1905.
Murid-e Shak—Hashr 1899. Based on Shakespeare's *The Winter's Tale*.
Nand Battisi—Mulani 1907.
Parambhakt Prahlad 'Prahlad, the Supreme Devotee'—Radheshyam 1921.
Parivartan 'Change'—Radheshyam 1925.
Patni Pratap 'The Splendor of the Wife'—Betab 1919. Opened in Calcutta, 1919.

Pratap Lakshmi—Mulani 1914.
Qatl-e Nazir 'The Murder of Nazir'—Betab 1901. First performed by Jamadar Theatrical Company, Ludhiana, 1900.
Ramayan—Betab 1915. Opened in Bombay, 1915.
Rukmini Mangal—Radheshyam 1927.
Samaj 'Society'—Betab, 1929. Opened Alfred Theatre, Calcutta, Sept. 1929.
Sangat ke Rang—Girnara 1908.
Sangit Lilavati—Adhyapak 1888.
Sati Draupadi—Jhaveri 1914. Said to be basis for Betab's *Mahabharat*.
Sati Parvati 'Parvati the Faithful'—Radheshyam 1939.
Satyavadi Harishchandra 'Harishchandra the Truth-sayer'—Talib 1892.
Saubhagya Sundari—Mulani, 1901. Based on play by Shukla said to be adaptation of Shakespeare's *Othello*.
Shahi Faqir 'The Royal Ascetic'—1917. Fida Husain's first female role.
Shakuntala—Betab 1945. Performed by Prithvi Theatres.
Shirin Farhad, aka *Dagh-e Hasrat*—1901. In Calcutta, Sundari played Shirin.
Shravan Kumar 'The Boy Shravan'—Radheshyam 1916. Performed by Survijay Natak Samaj in 1916; revised and performed by New Alfred, Delhi, 1928.
Shri Krishna Avtar 'The Incarnation of Lord Krishna'—Radheshyam 1926.
Sita Banvas 'Sita's Forest Exile'—Hashr 1927; opened in Charkhari State, 1928.
Sitamgar—Khori 1874.
Sneh Sarita—Vibhakar 1915.
Sone ke Mol ki Khurshed 'Khurshed for the Price of Gold'—orig. Khori, adapted into Hindustani by Marzban (1871).
Sudhachandra—Vibhakar 1916.
Turki Hur 'The Damsel from Turkey'—Hashr 1922.
Vatan 'Homeland'—1931. Playwright unknown; hailed as explicitly nationalist play.
Vikram Charitra 'The History of Vikram'—Mulani 1901.
Vir Abhimanyu 'Abhimanyu, the Warrior'—Radheshyam 1916.
Zahri Sanp 'Poisonous Snake'—Betab 1906. Opened Victoria Theatre, Bombay, June 27, 1906.

Films

Alam Ara (1931)—India's first sound film, dir. Ardeshir Irani, based on a play by Joseph David, starred Master Vithal and Prithviraj Kapoor.
Arabian Nights (1946)—dir. Niren Lahiri, starred Kanan Devi and Robin Majumdar.

Barrister's Wife, aka *Barrister ki Bibi* (1935)—dir. Chandulal Shah, dialogue and lyrics by Betab.

Bhabhi (1957)—dir. R. Krishnan and S. Panju, starred Balraj Sahni.

Daku ka Larka (1935)—dir. Charu Roy, starred Anwari.

Devi Devayani (1931)—dir. Chandulal Shah, inaugurated Ranjit Movietone, screenplay by Betab. Starred Gohar, Miss Kamala, D. Bilimoria.

Dil ki Pyas (1935)—dir. Sohrab Kerawala, starred Mukhtar Begam.

Insaf (1937)—dir. Jagatrai Pesumal Advani, starred Leela Chitnis.

Jhansi ki Rani, aka *The Tiger and the Flame* (1953)—dir. Sohrab Modi, lyrics by Radheshyam Kathavachak.

Jiban Sangini (1942)—dir. Gunamoy Bannerjee, starred Ratin Banerjee and Chhabi Biswas.

Khudai Khidmatgar (1937)—dir. Vithaldas Panchotia, starred Rampyari.

Mastana aka *Diljani* (1935)—dir. Charu Roy, starred Leela and Sheela.

Matvali Mira (1940 or 1947)—dir. Prafulla Roy and K. Sharma, starred Mukhtar Begam.

Mughal-e Azam (1960)—dir. K. Asif, starred Prithviraj Kapoor, Dilip Kumar, Madhubala.

Pakeezah aka *Pure Heart* (1971)—dir. Kamal Amrohi, starred Meena Kumari, Raj Kumar, Ashok Kumar.

Prabhu ka Pyara aka *God's Beloved* (1936)—dir. Chandulal Shah, dialogue and lyrics by Betab. Starred Gohar and Raja Sandow.

Radha Rani aka *Divine Lady* (1932)—dir. Chandulal Shah, screenplay by Betab.

Railway Platform (1955)—dir. Ramesh Saigal, starred Sunil Dutt.

Shakuntala (1931)—dir. J.J. Madan, dialogue and lyrics by Radheshyam Kathavachak.

Shakuntala (1931)—dir. M.D. Bhavnani.

Shirin Farhad (1931)—dir. J.J. Madan, lyrics by Agha Hashr, starred Master Nisar and Jahanara Kajjan.

Sholay (1975)—dir. Ramesh Sippy, starred Dharmendra, Hema Malini, Sanjeev Kumar, Amitabh Bachchan.

Zahri Sanp/Zehari Saap (1933)—dir. J.J. Madan, screenplay and lyrics by Betab.

Glossary of Hindi and Urdu Terms

akhara: guild or club of folk performers, site of public competitions.
akhyan: long narrative poem, recited on religious occasions.
amad: song or dance item introducing a character on stage.
amras: pureed mango pulp, favorite sweet dish in western India.
arti: ceremony performed for worship of a deity, offering of tray with incense, fruits, flowers.
ashtapadi: hymn or composition of eight lines, characteristic verse form of the *Gita Govinda*, lyrical poem praising the love of Radha and Krishna, written by Jayadeva in the twelfth century.
baba: saint or holy man; kinship term meaning father or grandfather; used affectionately to address a young child.
Bahurupiya: solo performer, specialist at changing costumes with amazing speed.
Bapu: "father," "grandfather," affectionate name for Mahatma Gandhi.
bhabhi: sister-in-law, wife of one's brother.
bhai, bhai saheb: brother, elder brother.
bhajan: devotional song, frequently sung by a group.
bhakri: unleavened flatbread made of millet or sorghum.
bhakti: devotional faith, adoration, emotional attachment.
bhang: intoxicating beverage prepared from ground hemp leaves.
Bhavai: Gujarati folk theatre dating to fourteenth century; treats satirical and intercommunal topics.
bidi: inexpensive leaf-wrapped cigarette.
biradari: community based on affiliation by kinship.
Brahmabhatt Brahmin: subcaste of Brahmins whose rank was contested in the early twentieth century; Betab was a Brahmabhatt.
chakravyuh: circular battle formation. In well-known episode of *Mahabharat*, young Abhimanyu, son of Arjun, succeeds in penetrating it but fails to

find his way out; being martyred, he becomes an emblem of youthful heroism.

chaprasi: messenger, peon.

chaubola: poetic stanza of four lines, sung to standard tune in Nautanki folk opera.

chaupai: quatrain which is predominant meter in Tulsidas's *Ramcharitmanas*.

chhand: meter in general, or specific meter of 28 measures.

chhappay: Hindi poetic stanza of six metered lines.

daf: frame drum or tambourine.

dal: cooked dish made of stewed pulses, onions, and spices.

darshan: sight, vision, view; act of viewing a sacred image.

dharm: righteousness, religious observance, duty.

dharmik: religious, righteous; dramatic genre, often translated as "mythological."

dharmshala: resting house or place of retreat.

dholak: small double-headed barrel drum played with folk and devotional singing.

dhoti: single cloth tied around waist in the case of men; simple white sari worn by women.

Dhruv and Prahlad: youthful devotees of lord Vishnu, celebrated in song and popular drama for loyalty in the face of adversity.

divan: minister, secretary.

ghazal: Urdu love lyric, representing pinnacle of Indo-Muslim literary culture in eighteenth and nineteenth centuries.

havan: sacrificial fire into which sacred oblations are offered; *havan* rituals are at the core of Arya Samaj practice.

Hidayak-ul Balaghat: Urdu book on prosody and rhetoric based on original in Persian, used as standard text.

imarti: a deep-fried orange confection, similar to the popular *jalebi*.

islah: traditional pedagogical method in Urdu poetry; teacher corrects student's compositions.

jhulna: to swing, to sway; a poetic meter.

jhumar: rhythmic folk dance and accompanying song, from *jhumna*, to sway, wave.

kajal: lampblack, collyrium; used as cosmetic to enhance eyes.

Kam-kahani: "the story of Kam," refers to mythological Cupid figure who incites love affairs; *kam* also means sensual pleasure, lust.

katha: story, tale; legends of gods, recited in ritual performances.

kathavachak: one who performs *kathavachan*, recitational genre based on deity's story.

Glossary of Hindi and Urdu Terms 353

Kathiawar Brahmins: Gujarat-based caste, includes well-to-do Audichya Brahmins.

kavitt: four-line stanza of 31 or 32 syllables.

khichri: stew of rice and dal; metaphor for mixture, mixed language.

Kurukshetra: "field of the Kurus," region near Karnal, north of Delhi, where war occurs between Pandavas and Kauravas in *Mahabharat*.

lavani: genre of folk poetry in Maharashtra, adopted in Hindi and Urdu in the nineteenth century.

lila: play, sport, pastime; episode in life of deity performed in folk drama.

lungi: men's garment, unstitched rectangle of cloth wrapped around the waist.

manzil: destination, stage, halting place.

maulsari/maulsiri: Spanish cherry tree.

mujra: musical session with erotic dance.

munshi: scribe or clerk; hired playwright.

Nautanki: style of North Indian folk drama, featuring stories of romance and martial prowess.

Padya-Pariksha: Betab's primer on poetic technique.

pakhawaj: double-headed variety of drum.

pan: betel leaf with areca nut, lime, catechu, spices, and occasionally tobacco; considered a digestive.

pauranik: of or from Puranas; mythological genre of plays.

pingal shastra: Hindi system of prosody, based on reckoning of *matras*.

prasad: food offered to deity.

prashasti: poem of praise; eulogy or panegyric.

puja: worship or adoration of image with flowers, incense, sandalwood, and so forth.

qasba: small town or provincial settlement.

qavvali: Sufi devotional song featuring lead singer and chorus.

Ram-kahani: "the story of Ram," expression for one's life story, especially aspects that evoke pity.

Ram Lila: dramatic performance of Ram's story, usually based on Tulsidas's *Ramcharitmanas*.

Ras Lila: devotional drama enacting episodes from life of deity Krishna.

raso: narrative literary genre in Apabhramsha, early Hindi, Gujarati, and Rajasthani.

sakhi: female companion to heroine, minor female role in dramas.

samskaras: inborn faculties and instincts, or cultivated influences and impressions, carrying over from one birth into another.

sanatan dharm: "the eternal faith," i.e. Hinduism. Contrasts with reformist movements such as Arya Samaj or Brahmo Samaj; connotes traditional, conservative form of religious ideology.

Sarasvati: goddess of learning, poetry, and music.

Sarasvatichandra: colossal Gujarati novel by Govardhanram Tripathi, published between 1888 and 1904.

Satyarth Prakash: Dayanand Sarasvati's manifesto (1875), guiding text of Arya Samaj.

seth, sheth: title for merchant, trader, or businessman.

shaikh: Muslim elder or saint.

shervani: long, tight-fitting man's dress coat that buttons down the front.

shloka: Sanskrit stanza of two verses, each of sixteen syllables.

shor: noise or outcry; renown.

shuddh hindi: pure Hindi, i.e. Sanskritized Hindi.

sulfa: small ball of tobacco smoked in a *huqqa*.

Svang: specific genre of versified drama performed to traditional melodies; similar to Nautanki.

taziya: model of shrine of Hasan and Husain, taken into street during Muharram.

tukbandi: versification or composition of rhymes.

Turra-Kalgi: agonistic verbal art originating in Maharashtra in the nineteenth century, used for religious and philosophical disputation.

ustad: teacher or master, of poetic tradition, musical knowledge, or other art.

vaidya: practitioner of indigenous medical system, usually Ayurveda.

yajna: sacrificial act or offering sanctioned in Vedas.

yajnashala: building or site for conducting Vedic sacrifices; temple.

Bibliography

Agraval, Pratibha, ed. 1986. *Mastar Fida Husain: Parsi Thiyetar men Pachas Varsh*. Calcutta: Natya Shodh Sansthan.

Arnold, David and Stuart Blackburn, eds. 2004. *Telling Lives in India: Biography, Autobiography, and Life History*. Delhi: Permanent Black.

Babayan, Kathryn. 2008. " 'In Spirit We Ate Each Other's Sorrow': Female Companionship in Seventeenth-Century Safavi Iran," in *Islamicate Sexualities: Translations across Temporal Geographies of Desire*, Kathryn Babayan and Afsaneh Najmabadi, eds. Harvard Middle Eastern Monographs, 39 (Cambridge: Harvard University Press), 239–74.

Banarasi Das. 1981. *Half a Tale. A Study in the Interrelationship between Autobiography and History; the Ardhakathanaka*, trans., intro., and annotated by Mukund Lath. Jaipur: Rajasthan Prakrit Bharati Sansthan.

Betab, Narayan Prasad. 1937, 2002. *Betabcharit*. 1st ed., Patiala: Ramrakha Ram; 2nd ed., New Delhi: Rashtriya Natya Vidyalaya.

Beth, Sarah. 2007. "Hindi Dalit Autobiography: An Exploration of Identity." *Modern Asian Studies*, 41:3, 545–74.

Bhattacharya, Rimli. 1995. "Actress-Stories and the 'Female' Confessional Voice in Bengali Theatre Magazines (1910–1925)." *Seagull Theatre Quarterly*, 5 (May), 3–25.

———, ed. and trans. 1998. *Binodini Dasi: My Story* and *My Life as an Actress*. Delhi: Kali for Women.

Bowring, Richard. 1987. "The Female Hand in Heian Japan: A First Reading," in *The Female Autograph: Theory and Practice of Autobiography from the Tenth to the Twentieth Century*, Domna C. Stanton, ed. (Chicago: University of Chicago Press), 49–55.

Bruss, Elizabeth W. 1980. "Eye for I: Making and Unmaking Autobiography in Film," in *Autobiography: Essays Theoretical and Critical*, James Olney, ed. (Princeton: Princeton University Press), 296–320.

Butterfield, Stephen. 1974. *Black Autobiography in America*. Amherst: University of Massachusetts Press.
Chatterjee, Sudipto. 2008. *The Colonial Staged: Theatre in Colonial Calcutta*. Calcutta: Seagull Books.
Cohen, Lawrence. 1998. *No Aging in India: Alzheimer's, the Bad Family, and Other Modern Things*. Berkeley: University of California Press.
Daniel, E. Valentine. 1984. *Fluid Signs: Being a Person the Tamil Way*. Berkeley: University of California Press.
Darukhanawala, H.D. 1939, 1963. *Parsi Lustre on Indian Soil*, 2 vols. Bombay: G. Claridge & Company.
Das Gupta, Hemendra Nath. 1934. *The Indian Stage*. Calcutta: Metropolitan Printing & Publishing House.
Datta, Amaresh, ed. 1987. *Encyclopaedia of Indian Literature*, Vol. 1. New Delhi: Sahitya Akademi.
Delta. 1876. *Romyo ane Julyat*. Bombay: Fort Printing Press.
Dirks, Nicholas B. 2001. *Castes of Mind: Colonialism and the Making of Modern India*. Princeton: Princeton University Press.
Eakin, Paul John. 1985. *Fictions in Autobiography: Studies in the Art of Self-Invention*. Princeton: Princeton University Press.
Fisher, Michael H. 1998. "Representations of India, the English East India Company, and Self by an Eighteenth-Century Indian Emigrant to Britain." *Modern Asian Studies*, 32:4 (Oct.), 891–911.
Garga, Bhagwan Das. 1996. *So Many Cinemas: The Motion Picture in India*. Mumbai: Eminence Designs.
Gupt, Somnath. 2005. *The Parsi Theatre: Its Origins and Development*, translated and edited by Kathryn Hansen. Calcutta: Seagull Books.
Gusdorf, Georges. 1980. "Conditions and Limits of Autobiography," in *Autobiography*, James Olney, ed., 28–47.
Hansen, Kathryn. 1998. "*Stri Bhumika*: Female Impersonators and Actresses on the Parsi Stage." *Economic and Political Weekly*, Aug. 29, 2291–2300.
———. 1999. "Making Women Visible: Gender and Race Cross-Dressing in the Parsi Theatre." *Theatre Journal* 51:2, 127–47.
———. 2001. "The *Indar Sabha* Phenomenon: Public Theatre and Consumption in Greater India (1853–1956)," in *Pleasure and the Nation: The History and Politics of Public Culture in India*, Chris Pinney and Rachel Dwyer, eds. (Delhi: Oxford University Press), 76–114.
———. 2002. "Parsi Theatre and the City: Locations, Patrons, Audiences," *Sarai Reader 2002: The Cities of Everyday Life* (New Delhi: Centre for the Study of Developing Societies), 40–9.
———. 2003. "Languages on Stage: Linguistic Pluralism and Community

Formation in the Nineteenth-Century Parsi Theatre." *Modern Asian Studies* 37:2, 381–406.

———. 2006. "Ritual Enactments in a Hindi 'Mythological': Betab's *Mahabharat* in Parsi Theatre." *Economic and Political Weekly*, Dec. 2, 4985–91.

Hart, Francis R. 1970. "Notes for an Anatomy of Modern Autobiography," *New Literary History*, 1:3 (Spring), 485–511.

Hatcher, Brian A. 2001. "Sanskrit Pandits Recall Their Youth: Two Autobiographies from Nineteenth-Century Bengal." *Journal of the American Oriental Society*, 121:4 (Oct.–Dec.), 580–92.

Holden, Philip. 2003. "Imagined Individuals: National Autobiography and Postcolonial Self-Fashioning." Working Paper Series No. 13, Asia Research Institute, National University of Singapore.

———. 2005. "Other Modernities: National Autobiography and Globalization," *Biography* 28:1 (Winter), 89–103.

Inden, Ronald. 1986. "Orientalist Constructions of India." *Modern Asian Studies* 20:3, 401–46.

———. 1990. *Imagining India*. Oxford: Basil Blackwell.

Kabra, Kaikhushro Navrojji. 1869. *Bejan ane Manijeh*. Bombay: Ashkara Press.

Kathavachak, Radheshyam. 1957, 2004. *Mera Natak Kal*. 1st ed., Bareli: Radheyshyam Pustakalay; 2nd ed., New Delhi: Rashtriya Natya Vidyalaya.

Kaviraj, Sudipta. 2004. "The Invention of Private Life," in *Telling Lives in India*, David Arnold and Stuart Blackburn, eds, 83–115.

Khambata, Jahangir Pestanji. 1914. *Mahro Nataki Anubhav*. Bombay: Parsi Ltd. Press.

Khori, Edalji Jamshedji. 1870. *Rustam ane Sohrab*. Bombay: Ashkara Press.

Kosambi, Meera, trans. and ed. 2008. *Feminist Vision or 'Treason Against Men'? Kashibai Kanitkar and the Engendering of Marathi Literature*. Ranikhet: Permanent Black.

Kumar, Udaya. 2008. "Autobiography as a Way of Writing History: Personal Narratives from Kerala and the Inhabitation of Modernity," in *History in the Vernacular*, Raziuddin Aquil and Partha Chatterjee, eds. (Ranikhet: Permanent Black), 418–48.

Lal, Ananda. 2004. *The Oxford Companion to Indian Theatre*. Delhi: Oxford University Press.

Lejeune, Philippe. 1989. *On Autobiography*, edited and with a foreword by Paul John Eakin, translated by Katherine Leary. Minneapolis: University of Minnesota Press.

Loftus, Ronald P. 2004. *Telling Lives: Women's Self-Writing in Modern Japan.* Honolulu: University of Hawaii Press.

Lokuge, Chandani. 2001. *India Calling: The Memories of Cornelia Sorabji, India's First Woman Barrister.* New Delhi: Oxford University Press.

Malhotra, Anshu. 2009. "Telling Her Tale? Unravelling a Life in Conflict in Peero's *Ik Sau Sath Kafian.*" *Indian Economic and Social History Review,* 42:4, 541–78.

Marriott, McKim. 1976. "Hindu Transactions: Diversity without Dualism," in *Transaction and Meaning: Directions in the Anthropology of Exchange and Symbolic Behavior,* Bruce Kapferer, ed. (Philadelphia: Institute for the Study of Human Issues), 109–42.

Mehta, Kumudini A. 1960. "English Drama on the Bombay Stage in the Late Eighteenth Century and in the Nineteenth Century," unpublished PhD thesis, University of Bombay.

Metcalf, Barbara D. 2004. "The Past in the Present: Instruction, Pleasure, and Blessing in Maulana Muhammad Zakariyya's *Aap Biitii,*" in *Telling Lives in India,* Arnold and Blackburn, eds, 116–43.

Mines, Mattison. 1994. *Public Faces, Private Voices: Community and Individuality in South Asia.* Berkeley: University of California Press.

———. 2002. "Memorializing the Self: The Autobiographical Will and Testament of Narayana Guruviah Chetty, Madras City, 1915," in *Everyday Life in South Asia,* Diane P. Mines and Sarah Lamb, eds (Bloomington: Indiana University Press), 69–80.

Misch, Georg. 1950. *A History of Autobiography in Antiquity,* trans. E.W. Dickes. London: Routledge & Paul.

Mishrabandhu (Ganesh Bihari, Shyam Bihari, and Shukdev Bihari Mishra). 1975. *Hindi Navratna,* 6th ed. Hyderabad: Ganga Granthagar.

Mudaliar, Pammal Sambanda. 1998. *Nataka Metai Ninaivukal* (Chennai: Ulakat Tamilaraycci Niruvanam), trans. by Venkat Swaminathan in "Over Forty Years Before the Footlights," *Sangeet Natak,* Nos. 121–2 (July–Dec. 1996), 25–39, and No. 123 (Jan.–Mar. 1997), 25–44.

Namra, Vidyavati Lakshmanrao. 1972. *Hindi Rangmanch aur Pandit Narayanprasad Betab.* Varanasi: Vishvavidyalay Prakashan.

Narayan, Kirin. 2004. "Honor is Honor, After All: Silence and Speech in the Life Stories of Women in Kangra, North-West India," in *Telling Lives in India,* Arnold and Blackburn, eds, 227–51.

Nayak, Amrit Keshav. 1908. *M.A. Banake Kyon Meri Mitti Kharab Ki?* Bombay.

Nayar, Pramod K. 2006. "Bama's *Karukku:* Dalit Autobiography as Testimonio." *Journal of Commonwealth Literature,* 41:2, 83–100.

Nijhawan, Shobna, ed. 2010. *Nationalism in the Vernacular: Hindi, Urdu, and the Literature of Indian Freedom—An Anthology.* Ranikhet: Permanent Black.
Olney, James, ed. 1980. *Autobiography: Essays Theoretical and Critical.* Princeton: Princeton University Press.
Orsini, Francesca. 2009. *Print and Pleasure: Popular Literature and Entertaining Fictions in Colonial North India.* Ranikhet: Permanent Black.
Panchotia, Bhailal Bulakhidas. 1987. *Jayashankar Sundari and Abhinayakala.* Bombay: Bharatiya Vidya Bhavan.
Parry, Jonathan P. 2004. "The Marital History of 'A Thumb-Impression Man'," in *Telling Lives in India,* Arnold and Blackburn, eds, 281–318.
Patel, Dhanjibhai Nasarvanji. 1931. *Parsi Natak Takhtani Tavarikh.* Bombay: Kaiser-i Hind Press.
Peacock, James L. and Dorothy C. Holland. 1993. "The Narrated Self: Life Stories in Process," *Ethos,* 21:4 (Dec.), 367–83.
Rajadhyaksha, Ashish and Paul Willemen. 1999. *Encyclopaedia of Indian Cinema,* rev. ed. New Delhi: Oxford University Press.
Ranina, Nanabhai Rustamji. 1865. *Shakespeare Natak.* Bombay: Ashkara Press.
Reynolds, Dwight, ed. 2001. *Interpreting the Self: Autobiography in the Arabic Literary Tradition.* Berkeley: University of California.
Rudolph, Susanne H. and Lloyd Rudolph. 2002. *Reversing the Gaze: Amar Singh's Diary.* Boulder: Westview Press.
Sarkar, Tanika. 1999. *Words to Win: The Making of* Amar Jiban: *A Modern Autobiography.* Delhi: Kali for Women.
Seizer, Susan. 2005. *Stigmas of the Tamil Stage.* Durham: Duke University Press.
Shodhan, Amrita. 1999. "Review: *Sundari: An Actor Prepares.*" *Seagull Theatre Quarterly,* No. 22 (June), 90–1.
Sisson, Charles Jasper. 1926. *Shakespeare in India: Popular Adaptations on the Bombay Stage.* London: Oxford University Press.
Smith, Sidonie. 1998. "Performativity, Autobiographical Practice, Resistance," in *Women, Autobiography, Theory: A Reader,* Sidonie Smith and Julia Watson, eds. (Madison: University of Wisconsin Press), 108–15.
Smith, Sidonie and Julia Watson. 2001. *Reading Autobiography: A Guide for Interpreting Life Narratives.* Minneapolis: University of Minnesota Press.
Sundari, Jayshankar. 1976, 1989. *Thodan Ansu: Thodan Phul: Jayshankar "Sundari" ni Atmakatha.* 1st ed., compiled by Dinkar Bhojak and Somabhai Patel, Ahmedabad: Gandhi Sombarsa; 2nd ed., compiled by Somabhai Patel and Dinkar Bhojak, Unjha: Asait Sahitya Sabha.

Tharu, Susie and K. Lalita, eds. 1991. *Women Writing in India: 600 B.C. to the Present*. 2 vols. New York: The Feminist Press.

Vatuk, Sylvia. 2004. "*Hamara Daur-i Hayat:* An Indian Muslim Woman Writes Her Life," in *Telling Lives in India,* Arnold and Blackburn, eds, 144–74.

Waghorne, Joanna Punzo. 1981. "The Case of the Missing Autobiography," *Journal of the American Academy of Religion*, 49:4 (Dec.), 589–603.

Watson, C. W. 2000. *Of Self and Nation: Autobiography and the Representation of Modern Indonesia*. Honolulu: University of Hawaii Press.

Weintraub, Karl J. 1975. "Autobiography and Historical Consciousness," *Critical Inquiry*, 1:4 (June), 821–48.

Willmer, David. 1999. "Theatricality, Mediation and Public Space: The Legacy of Parsi Theatre in South Asian Cultural History," unpublished PhD thesis, University of Melbourne.

Wu, Pei-Yi. 1990. *The Confucian's Progress: Autobiographical Writings in Traditional China*. Princeton: Princeton University Press.

Index

Abhinetrir Atmakatha (Binodini Dasi) 26
Achhuta Daman (Agha Hashr) 121
actors, as autobiographers 316, 317
Adhyapak, Keshavlal Shivram 199, 203
Agraval, Lala Devi Sahay Vaishya 67, 68
Agraval, Pratibha 246, 248, 249–51, 252–4, 255–6, 323
Ahsan Lakhnavi, Mehdi Hasan 21, 82, 113, 114, 123, 150
Alam Ara 157, 270
Alauddin 111
Alfred Theatrical Company 10, 21, 92
   Betab and 52, 53–4, 85, 91–2, 95–6
   and female actresses 19, 168
   Fida Husain and 284–5
   and Madan Theatres, merger with 23, 139
   split in 16, 116
   See also Parsi Alfred; New Alfred Theatrical Company
Ali Baba 111, 112
Amar Abhinetri Jiban (Binodini Dasi) 35
Amar Jiban (Rashsundari Debi) 27
Ammulal 126, 134, 135
Amrit (Betab) 83
Anandlahari (Bapulal) 241, 242
Angar 268–9

Angurbala 292–3
Ankh ka Nasha (Agha Hashr) 137
apbiti, genre of 27, 324
Ardhakathanaka (Banarasi Das) 27, 28
Arnold, David 28, 29, 301, 312
Arya-Kumar 35–6, 57, 60
Arya Samaj 38
   Betab and 51, 53–4, 57, 58, 86, 88–9
Atharva Brahmin Sabha 55, 96
autobiography
   and concept of selfhood 28, 300, 302
   Dalit 308–9, 312–13
   definition 30, 300
   and fractured self 302–3
   genre of 26, 27
   ghostwritten 311
   and identity making 302–3
   instructional objective of 324
   vs. life narrative 29–30
   and memories 313
   of muted groups 315–16
   non-western 306
   and performative self 309–14
   and relational self 306–9
   selection and edition in 299–300
   and sovereign self 29, 301–2, 304
   See also Indian autobiography

Babu Roshan Lal Company 277–8
Baburnama 27

362　　　　　　　　　　Index

Bakhsh, Husain 272
Bakhsh, Rahim 72, 117, 124
Bal Gandharva 43, 171, 237
Balivala, Khurshedji Mehrbanji 10, 11, 12, 15, 91, 182, 214, 265
Balivala Victoria Theatrical Company 11, 115–16, 121, 266
　and Vinayak Prasad Talib 91, 116, 143
Balkrishna (Radheshyam) 132
Balram 108, 109, 128, 162
Balsara, Manikshah 136, 138, 140
Banarsi Krishna Theatre (Delhi) 41
Bareli 110–11, 113–14
Bekas, Babu Dhanpat Ray 71
Bengali theatre 3, 35
Betab, Narayan Prasad 17, 21, 37, 38, 45, 51–9, 60–108, 139, 140, 144, 160
　Agha Hashr Kashmiri, opinion of 82
　and Alfred Theatrical Company 52, 53–4, 85, 91–2, 95–6
　and Arya Samaj 38, 51, 53–4, 57, 58, 86, 88–9
　Atharva Brahmin Sabha, establishment of 55, 96
　autobiography, analysis of 35, 37, 317–19
　　childhood memories in 327
　　commissioning of 57
　　denial of self in 60, 61
　　Hindi as language of narrative 329
　　Hindu-centric worldview in 318
　　instructional objective of 324–5
　　language of 55–6
　　Pandit Durgaprasad's role in writing of 57, 60
　　serialization in *Arya-Kumar* 35, 57
　　structure of 58
　　Sufi subtext in 318
　　translation of 55–6
　autobiography, comments on 90
　birth and early childhood 61–2
　Bombay, arrival in 78–9
　and Brahmabhatts 55, 96
　Chaudhri Shibbaray's ashram, account of 67, 68–9
　and cinema 25, 52
　departure from home 64
　early poetic skills and training 52–3, 62–4
　education 41, 45–6
　and Hindi language 39, 51, 54, 94–5, 329
　and Jamadar Drama Company 53, 75–9
　Kaiser-i Hind Press, employment at 53, 67–8, 69–70, 73, 76
　and Madan Theatres 52, 54, 95, 96, 97
　and *Mahabharat* 39, 43, 51, 58, 91, 93–4, 120, 143
　marriage of daughter 97–8
　Murad Ali Murad, meeting with 53, 74
　and mythological genre 19, 51, 52
　and Parsi Theatrical Company 53, 79–83, 84
　personal reform program, account of 87–8
　as a publisher 41
　Ranjit Film Company, employment with 98–9, 101
　as screen writer for films 55
　sexuality and 72–3, 334–5
　Shor Saheb, meeting with 65–6
　and Urdu language 45–6, 51, 63–4

Index

Vidyavati Namra's biography
of 56–7
vow of truthfulness 87–90
widow remarriage, views on 84
and *Zahri Sanp* 53, 82, 119
Betab Printing Works 60
Beth, Sara 308
Bhagat Singh 282, 293
Bharat Milap 248, 278, 279
Bhavai 7, 39, 45, 47, 171, 186
Bhave, Vishnudas/Vishnu Amrit 5, 35
Bhogilal 42, 119, 121, 122, 129, 135
and New Alfred 133, 136
and *Vir Abhimanyu* 124, 125–6
Bhojak, Dinkar 176, 177–8, 179
Bhojak, Jayshankar Sundari 18, 20, 21, 39, 42, 43, 170–4, 181–245, 198, 244
abduction, rumor of 173, 231–2
acting skills, development of 192–3
autobiography
analysis of 36–7, 175–80, 314, 321–3, 326–8
Dinkar Bhojak's role in 176, 177–8, 179
Hindi translation of 178–9
instructional element in 325
publication history of 176–8
sexuality in 333, 334
Somabhai Patel's role in 176, 177
awards and recognition 174–5
B.B. Panchotia's biography of 179–80
Bal Gandharva, meeting with 237
Bapulal Nayak, association
with 172, 173, 174, 200, 203, 208–9, 211–13, 214, 229, 244, 334

Calcutta, stay in 189–91, 193–5
childhood 182, 183–5
Dadabhai Thunthi, association
with 170, 171, 191, 197, 203, 204, 322
Dayashankar Girnara, assessment
of 235–6
in *Devkanya* 173, 238
as director 239–40
early influences on 182–3, 186–7, 188–9
education of 41, 45, 186
family 182–3, 185–6
as female impersonator 20, 171, 172, 173, 192, 209–11, 322, 331
and Gaiety Theatre, association
with 200–1
as Gandhian 239
in *Haman* 171, 193
and Lakshmikant Natak Samaj
173, 242, 243
as Lalita in *Jugal Jugari* 172, 213–15
married life 40, 172, 217–29, 334
and Mumbai Gujarati Natak
Mandali 18, 172–3, 198, 199, 203–4, 205–6, 243–4
music, training in 208
and Nat Mandal 173
as Rambha in *Vikram Charitra* 172, 211–12
Sarasvatichandra, influence of 209
as Sarita in *Sneh Sarita* 173, 174, 239
as Shirin in *Dagh-e Hasrat* 172, 173, 212–13
as Sundari in *Saubhagya Sundari* 172, 198, 207, 208, 209–11
Thanthaniya Theatre, account
of 196–7
theatre makeup, account of 195–6

traditional folklore, revival of 173–4
and Urdu 46, 191–2
Bhojaks 19–20, 39, 47, 182
Bhul Bhulaiyan (Ahsan) 114
Bijli 42, 292
bildungsroman 321
Bilvamangal or *Bhakt Surdas* 120, 130, 143
Blackburn, Stuart 28, 29, 301, 312
Bombay Amateur Theatre 4
Bradlaugh Hall (Lahore) 41
Brahmabhatts 38, 55, 58, 96, 97
Bruss, Elizabeth W. 310, 312
Buddhadev (Vyakul) 129, 130, 144
Butler, Judith 310, 312

caste 39, 306
and collective identity 304
censorship 38, 44
Chalta Purza (Ahsan) 21, 131
Chandrabhaga (Bapulal) 173, 235
Chandravali 111, 112
Charkhari, Maharaja of 25n.36, 144, 160, 278
Cheta Chamar 39, 54, 94, 139
child labor 45
cinema 21, 23, 157
Betab's move to 52, 55
and decline of Parsi Theatre 25
Radheshyam and 103, 105, 167
collective self, notion of 306–7
and Dalit autobiography 308
Cooper, Patience 19, 42, 292, 276, 277
Corinthian Theatre 22, 155, 286, 292
and female performers 168

Coronation Theatrical Company 21, 25n.36, 115, 160, 278
Hindi drama and 144

Dagh-e Hasrat 212–13
performance in Karachi 231, 232
Dalit autobiography 308
and relational self 308–9
women's 312–13
Dangi, Manik Lal 164
Daniel Dada 136, 137
Daniel, E. Valentine 304
Das, Babu Shyam Sundar 93
Das, Banarasi 27, 28
Das, Tribhuvan 182, 183
Dasi, Binodini 26, 32, 35, 36
De Certeau, Michel 312
De Man, Paul 310
Debi, Rashsundari 27
Desh ki Laj 248, 288
Devi Devayani (Betab) 55
Devi Devayani (film) 98–100
Devkanya (Mulani) 237–8
Dhanji Garak 7
Dholshaji, Dahyabhai 198, 199, 203, 238
Dil ki Pyas (Hashr) 159
Dirks, Nicholas B. 306
Draupadi Svayamvar (Radheshyam) 105, 150
Dumont, Louis 304
Durgaprasad, Pandit 57, 60
Durlabh, Ramji Raval 130, 190

Eakin, Paul John 307, 309, 311, 312
education, advent of 40–1
Elijar 270
Elphinstone Dramatic Society 6
Elphinstone Theatrical Company 10, 11, 13, 22
Empress Victoria Theatrical Company 11, 34

Index

English theatre 265

farcical plays 7, 9
female autobiographies 31–2, 315–16
female impersonator(s) 8, 14–15, 18, 40, 42, 168, 170
   Bal Gandharva 43, 171, 237
   Fida Husain 247, 331
   Jayshankar Sundari. *See* Bhojak, Jayshankar Sundari
   Madan Mohan Malviya 121
   Nayaks as 20, 105, 119, 332
   New Alfred and 19–20, 332
female performers 15–16, 155
   Fida Husain's account 292–3
   New Alfred's rule against 40, 119, 155, 247, 261
   and Parsi Alfred Company 134
   Radheshyam's views on 168
   See also individual female actresses
Fenton, Mary 10, 16, 19, 20, 42, 182, 292
Fida Husain Narsi 40, 45, 47, 105, 151, 165, 170, 246–9, 250, 253, 255–9, 287, 294–5
   Agha Hashr, account of 278
   and Alfred Theatrical Company 284–5
   autobiography
      analysis of 36, 37, 246, 316–17, 323–4
      compositional history 249–51
      erasure of Muslim identity 330–1
      as ethnographic encounter 252
      instructional element in 325–7
      memories of childhood 327
      structure 251
      style 249, 251
   and Babu Roshan Lal Company 277–8
   capture 261–2
   dietary habits and routine 253, 255, 256
   family 256–7
   as female impersonator 139, 247, 331
   female performers, account of 292–3
   film performances 281, 290–1
   and Hindustan Theatre Company 282
   influence of Marathi theatre on 43
   interest in music 247, 258, 259, 260
   in *Krishna Sudama* 279, 282
   loss of voice 259–60
   and Moonlight Theatre Company 246, 248, 263–4, 275–6, 283, 286, 287, 288–9
   music in drama, views on 266, 289–90, 291–2
   as *Narsi Mehta* 44, 137, 246, 248, 278
   and Narsi Theatrical Company 248, 277
   and New Alfred Company 17, 247, 260–1, 275
   New Alfred's rules and regulations 269–71, 272–5
   North-West Frontier Province experience 283
   Pratibha Agraval, meeting with 248, 255–6
   and Ranjit Studios 280
   relationship with father 263
   relationship with female actresses 331–2
   and Sarasvati Theatrical Company 286–7
   and Shri Mohan Theatrical Company 278–80, 281
   and Sita Devi 248, 281–2, 286

Firdausi 6
Fisher, Michael H. 28–9
Folly of Indian Princes, The 7
Freedom to Native Females 7

Gaekwad, Sayajirao, Maharaja of Baroda 216–17
Gaiety Theatre 12, 41, 172, 173, 200–1, 230, 233
Gandhi, M.K. 239, 261, 305, 309
Ganesh Janm (Betab) 55, 97, 140, 267
Gangavataran 132, 155
Gauhar Jan 42, 43, 82, 83, 139, 182, 292
gender, representation of 19–20, 39–40
Ghanshyam 106, 108, 150–1, 154, 165–6
Girnara, Dayashankar Vasanji 181, 201, 202, 203, 235–6
Gorakhdhandha (Betab) 21, 54, 91
Grace Theatre 276
Grant Road Theatre 4–5, 6, 8, 11, 16
Gujarati, as language of Parsi theatre 6, 8, 10
Gujarati Natak Mandali 181, 198
Gujarati theatre 3, 18
  ethnicity of 39
  and mythological dramas 119–20, 237–8
  and Parsi theatre 42, 170
Gulru Zarina 113
Gusdorf, Georges 302

Haman 171, 193, 203
Hamen Kya Chahiye 282
Harishchandra 143, 187, 189
Harishchandra, Bharatendu Babu 143
Hart, Francis 37, 303

Hashr Kashmiri, Agha 22, 25n.36, 40, 41–2, 74, 82, 93, 116–17, 121, 137, 144, 214, 255, 278, 329
  and cinema 21, 157
  and New Alfred 123
  Radheshyam, meeting with 123–4
  and Shakespeare Theatrical Company 21, 156
  Surdas 120, 143
Hatcher, Brian A. 305
Helen Theatrical Company 22, 23
Hindi 46
  Betab's shift to 39, 51, 54, 94–5, 329
  as language of Parsi theatre 18, 19, 54, 294–5
  New Alfred and 145
  Premchand's views on 143–4
  Radheshyam and 102, 117, 154, 329
  and Survijay Natak Samaj 144
  as symbol of nationalism 39, 51
  Vyakul Bharat Company and 144
Hindu Vidhva (Vishvambharnath Kaushik) 154
Hindustan Theatre Company 282
Holden, Philip 309
Husn Bano 42, 279, 280
Husn-e Farang (Betab) 74, 78

identity, performativity and 310–11
Ilachi Kumar, story of 188
Indar Sabha 13, 15, 71, 93, 143, 160, 181, 266–7, 268
Inden, Ronald 306
Indian autobiography 26–9
  colonial modernity and 28
  deliberate omissions in 305–6, 312
  indigenous genres of 28
  print culture and 30–1

public figures and 31
self-deprecation in 304
theatre memoirs and 32–5
weak self and 304, 305, 306
women and 31–2
See also Dalit autobiography
Irani, Dinshah 134, 207, 267
Ishvar Bhakti (Radheshyam) 105, 149

Jamadar Theatrical Company 53, 70, 71–3, 75–9
Jauhar, Harikrishna 144, 155, 160, 266
Jessawalla, Dosebhai 32
Joshi, Framji 8, 10
Jugal Jugari (Mulani) 172, 213–15

Kabra, B.N. 20
Kabra, K.N. 9, 10
Kabuli, Abdul Rahman 117, 124, 126, 160, 269–70, 279
Kaiser-i Hind Press 46, 53
  Betab's employment in 67–8, 69–70, 73, 76
Kajjan, Jahanara 2, 21, 157, 247, 276, 332
Kamlata (Mulani) 229–30
Kanak Tara (Talib) 115, 143
Kanan Bala 281
Kanitkar, Kashibai 32
Kapadia, Jamshed 197, 198
Kapariya, Mehrbanji 136, 137, 138
Kapoor, Prithviraj 266
Kapur, Anuradha 178
Karanjiya, Framroz 136, 152
Karukku, construction of self in 308
Kasauti (Betab) 80–1
Kathiawari Natak Mandali 230, 237
Kaviraj, Sudipta 28, 305
Khambata, Jahangir 11, 33–4, 36, 54, 143, 265

Khanna, Dinesh 175, 179
Khatau, Jahangir Kavasji 16, 95, 134, 158
Khatau, Kavasji Palanji 10–11, 16, 19, 53, 54, 91, 95, 131, 214
  See also Alfred Theatrical Company; Parsi Alfred Theatrical Company
Khatri, Nanak Chand 117, 118, 122, 123
Khori, Edalji Jamshedji 6
Khubsurat Bala (Agha Hashr) 104, 116–17, 143, 284
Khurshid-e Zarnigar (Murad Ali Murad) 74
Kirloskar Company of Maharashtra 132
Kolhatkar, Sripad Krishna 35
Krishna Charitra (Mulani) 173, 238
Krishna Janm (Betab) 78
Krishna Lila 248, 288, 292
Krishna Sudama (Betab) 278, 279, 282, 286, 291

Lakshmikant Natak Samaj 173, 242, 243
lavani 44, 46, 53, 64, 110, 121, 289
Lavji Bhai 147
Lejeune, Philippe 311–12, 313
life narrative 29, 30, 303

M.A. Banake Kyon Meri Mitti Kharab Ki? (Amrit Keshav Nayak) 34
Madan Theatres/Madan Company 22–3, 150, 155, 163
  Betab and 52, 54, 95, 96, 97
  female actresses in 168
  Radheshyam and 105, 157–8, 159
Madan, J.F. 15, 22–3, 24, 25
Madhu Bansari (Vibhakar) 240

Index

Mahabharat (Betab) 19, 39, 42, 43, 51, 54, 58, 120, 143
   Cheta Chamar 54, 94, 139
   performance in Delhi 91–3
Maharshi Valmiki (Radheshyam) 105, 160
Mahlarees, The 7
Mahro Nataki Anubhav (Khambata) 33–4
Malviya, Madan Mohan 18, 121, 133, 153, 168, 260
Mamajiwala, Gohar Kayoum 55, 99–100, 292
Mamajiwala, Seth Qayyum 84
Marathi theatre 3, 12, 35, 38, 43, 104, 119, 132, 143
Marriott, McKim 304
Marwari, Phulchand 42
Marwari theatre 276–7
Marwaris 281, 286, 287–8, 289
Masharqi Hur (Radheshyam) 105, 145, 146
   Hasrat Mohani's comments on 139–40
Master, Manikji Jivanji 18, 116, 126, 136
Mayur Dhvaj (Betab) 78
Meghmalini (Vibhakar) 173, 241
memoir, genre of 29, 37, 178. *See also* autobiography, genre of
Metcalf, Barbara D. 324
Minerva Theatre (Calcutta) 41
Mines, Mattison 307
Mitha Zahar (Betab) 81
Modi, Sohrab 21
Mohan Lala 205, 233–4
Mohan, Master 42, 150, 160
Mohani, Hasrat 139–40, 330
Moonlight Theatre Company 41, 248, 255, 288–90
   and Fida Husain 246, 248, 263–4, 275–6, 283, 286, 287, 288–9
Mudaliar, Pammal Sambanda 35
Mukhtyar, Miss 42, 160
Mulani, Mulshankar 20, 173, 180, 204, 213, 214, 230, 233, 238–9, 242
   and Kathiawari Natak Mandali 230, 237, 238
Mumbai Gujarati Natak Mandali 18, 172, 173, 182, 199, 203–4
   collapse of 242–3, 244–5
   and Dayashankar Girnara 181, 201, 202, 203, 235–6
   and Jayshankar Sundari 18, 172–3, 198, 199, 203–4, 205–6, 243–4
   and national movement 239, 240
Munni Bai 42, 284
Murad, Murad Ali 20, 53, 74, 113
music 14
   in drama, Fida Husain's account 266, 289–90, 291–2
Muslims 113, 193
   and Parsi theatre 18–19, 331
Myers, Ruby 19
mythological drama 130, 237–8
   Betab and 51, 52
   comic subplots in 43
   nationalism and 43, 51
   Parsi theatre and 19, 43
   popularity of 38
   Radheshyam and 46, 102, 104–5, 320

Nagari Pracharini Sabha 93
Nal Damayanti 144, 286
Namra, Vidyavati L. 56–7
Nand Battisi (Mulani) 173, 233
Narayan, Kirin 312

Index

Narsi Mehta 120, 278, 282, 286, 292
   Fida Husain as 44, 138, 248, 280
Narsi Theatrical Company 248, 277
nationalism
   cultural changes and 38–9
   Hindi as language of 51
   Hindu, Radheshyam and 104
   and mythological genre 43, 51
Natya Shodh Sansthan 258
Nautanki 293–4
Nayak, Amritlal Keshavlal 20, 21, 34, 42, 53, 80, 81, 82–3, 119, 181, 234–5
Nayak, Bapulal 174, 207, 233, 235, 239–40, 241, 242
   meeting with Maharaja of Mysore 215–16
   meeting with Maharaja of Baroda 216–17
   and Mumbai Gujarati Natak Mandali, ownership of 173, 243
   as playwright 235, 241, 242
   and Sundari, association with 172, 173, 174, 200, 203, 208–9, 211–13, 214, 229, 244, 334
Nayak, Narmada Shankar Tribhuvan 20, 21, 42, 119, 136, 137, 138, 148, 149, 155
Nayak, Pandit Vadilal Shivram 204, 208
Nayaks 19–20, 119, 171
   as female impersonators 105, 119, 332
Nayar, Pramod K. 308
Nazir, C.S./Kunvarji 6, 10, 11, 12, 74–5, 113
Nehru, Jawaharlal, autobiography of 309
Nehru, Motilal 18, 105, 114–15, 149, 153

New Albert Company 117, 122
   Radheshyam and 104, 117–18, 121–2
New Alfred Theatrical Company 17–18, 23, 116, 131, 151, 153–5, 123, 261, 275
   Bareli, tour of 111, 114, 116, 121
   closure of 155
   discipline in 18
   female actresses, employment of 155
   female impersonators in 19–20, 332
   female performers, rule against 18, 40, 119, 168, 247, 261
   Fida Husain and 247, 260–1
   gender segregation policy of 18
   Hindu actors in 138–9
   and Madan Company 150
   Master Nisar and 270
   Muslim actors in 155
   new ownership of 136
   Parivartan, staging of 136–7
   Prahlad, staging of 135
   Premchand's discussion of 144–5
   Radheshyam and 102, 103, 104, 105, 108, 112, 113, 122, 123, 136, 142, 148
   rules and regulations, Fida Husain's account 269–71, 272–5
   Sati Parvati, staging of 140
   sets and costumes 125
   Shravan Kumar, staging of 147, 148, 149
   Shri Krishna Avatar, staging of 140–2
   Sohrabji Ogra and 144, 247. *See also* Ogra, Sohrabji Framji
   Vir Abhimanyu, staging of 104, 122, 123
Nisar, Master 21, 42, 118, 124, 157, 270

Non-Cooperation Movement 161, 241, 291
Novelty Theatre 12

Ogra, Sohrabji Framji 18, 42, 43, 104, 112, 116–17, 121–4, 125, 129, 131–2, 133, 135–6, 144, 153, 181, 247, 269, 271, 272, 274, 332
oral performance, theatre biographies as archive of 26, 30, 37, 44–5

Panchotia, B.B. 179–80
Pandit, Vijayalakshmi 115
Parambhakt Prahlad (Radheshyam) 105, 129, 130, 132–3, 135, 145, 153
  comedy in 43
  Gopivallabh Upadhyay's review 161
  police surveillance of 38, 44
Parekh, D.N. 8
Parivartan (Radheshyam) 105, 131, 134, 135, 136–7, 138, 145, 247, 292
Parsi Alfred Theatrical Company 116, 134, 139
  female performers in 134, 168
  and Madan Company 144, 150
Parsi Dramatic Corps 5, 7
Parsi theatre 3–5, 17, 21, 25, 45, 160, 170–1, 294–5
  amateur 8–9
  in Calcutta 22, 25
  cross casting in 43–4
  decline of 23–5
  expansion and consolidation 9–17
  and female performers 15–16
  gender representation in 19–20
  and Gujarati language 6, 8, 10
  and Gujarati theatre, connection between 42, 170
  Hindi, shift to 19, 54, 160

  Indo-Muslim culture and 18–19
  music in 14
  Muslims and 331
  mythological genre and 18, 19, 38, 43
  Parsi influence on 9, 10
  rural dramatic forms, influence on 44–5
  and *Shahnama* genre 6, 10
  Shakespearean productions and 6
  sources of 6
  spectacle in 267–8
  Urdu as language of 10, 14, 18
  visual realism in 14
Parsi Theatrical Company 116
  Betab's employment in 79–83, 84
Parsi Victoria Company 11
Parsis 3, 4, 6, 9
Patel, Dadi 11, 12
Patel, Dhanjibhai N. 33, 36
Patel, Somabhai 176, 177
Pathak, Dina 174
Pati Bhakti (Harikrishna Jauhar) 144, 160
Patni Pratap (Betab) 95
performative self 309–14
playhouses. *See* theatre houses
Prasad, Jaishankar 142
Pratap (journal) 134, 142
Premchand, Munshi 46, 102, 105
  essay on Parsi theatre 143–7
print culture, and Indian autobiographies 30–1
printing press
  Kaiser-i Hind 46, 53
  Radheshyam's 128–9
  theatrical memoirs and 41
Prithvi Theatres 266
professional actresses. *See* female performers
Puran Bhagat 286

Index

Putlibai 84, 292

Qatl-e Nazir (Betab) 44, 53, 75, 77–8

Radheshyam Kathavachak 21, 45, 47, 102–6, 110–69
  Agha Hashr, meeting with 123–4
  autobiography, analysis of 36–7, 106–9
    anti-Muslim sentiments in 329–30
    Brahminical heritage, influence on 319–21, 330–1
    childhood memories in 327–8
    composition history of 108–9
    gender and sexuality in 332–3
    instructional element in 325
    and modern Indian history 37, 38
    style of 106
    translation 106–7
  Bareli, account of 113–14
  Brahminical influence on 38, 43
  childhood 110–14
  and Congress Party 105, 133
  early training in music 114
  education 41, 45
  female actresses, views on 168
  and film industry 25, 105
  and Gujarati theatre 43
  Hindi language and 39, 102, 117, 154, 329
  Hindu-Muslim relations, views on 113–14
  Hindu mythology, influence of 46
  and Hindu nationalism 104
  and *Ishvar Bhakti* 105, 149
  as *katha* performer 104, 105, 106, 114, 115, 117, 119, 120, 121, 130, 131, 136, 146, 148, 150–2, 157, 163
  and Madan Theatres 105, 157–8, 159
  and *Maharshi Valmiki* 160
  married life 40
  and *Masharqi Hur* 105, 139–40, 145, 146
  and mythological genre 19, 102, 104–5, 320
  Nehru family, account of 115
  and New Albert Company 104, 117–18
  and New Alfred Company 17, 102, 103, 104, 105, 108, 112, 113, 122, 123, 136, 142, 148, 153–5
  and *Parivartan* 105, 131, 134, 135, 136–7, 138, 145, 247, 292
  Premchand, interaction with 149–50
  publishing business of 41, 102, 103, 120, 128–9
  and *Rukmini Mangal* 105, 142, 146
  and *Sati Parvati* 106, 140, 147, 164
  screen play of *Shri Satyanarayan* 161, 162
  and sexuality 137, 167, 168
  and *Shakuntala* (film) 157–8
  and *Shakuntala* (play) 159–60
  and *Shri Krishna Avatar* 105, 140–2, 145–6
  and Sohrabji Ogra, relationship with 121–2, 332
  and Survijay Natak Samaj 130, 131, 132

Radheshyam Ramayan 103, 113, 117, 121, 150

Radheshyam Vilas 120

Rai, Himanshu 162

Raja Chitrakut Mahal 110, 112, 128–9

Rajagopalachari, autobiography of 305
Ram Janm (film) 165, 166
Ram Lila 45, 113, 138
　Betab and 65
　Radheshyam and 103, 104, 110
　Sundari and 171, 187
Rama Theatre (Delhi) 41, 70
Ramayan
　New Albert Company's production of 91, 104, 117–18, 121–2
　Parsi Alfred Company's production of 139
　Radheshyam's version of. See *Radheshyam Ramayan*
Ramkrishna, Chaube 42, 149, 155, 164
Ranade, Ramabai 32
Ranchhodbhai 182
Rani of Jhansi 268, 287
Ranjit Studios 280, 292
　Betab and 98–9, 101
relational self 306–9
relationality 307, 309
　and performativity 300
religious plays 121
　Gujarati theatre and 119–20
Ripon Theatrical Company 115, 116
Rudolph, Lloyd 28
Rudolph, Susanne H. 28
Rukmini Bibi 112, 120
Rukmini Mangal (Radheshyam) 105, 142, 146
Rup Sundari 75, 76–7
Rustam and Sohrab 6

sabhas, formation of 39
Sahitya Kala Mandal 185
Sahukar, Raghubir 270
Sangam Theatre 41, 91, 124, 132
Sangat ke Rang (Girnara) 173, 235
Sangit Lilavati (Adhyapak) 189, 199
Sarasvati Theatrical Company 286–7
Sarasvati, Swami Dayanand 31
Sarasvatichandra 46, 172, 209, 217, 225
Sarkar, Tanika 32, 315
Sarkari, Naslu 15
Sati Draupadi 120, 143
Sati Parvati (Radheshyam) 106, 140, 147, 164
Satyavadi Harishchandra 115
Saubhagya Sundari (Mulani) 172, 204, 205–6, 207, 211–12, 238
　Jayshankar's portrayal of Sundari 172, 208, 209–11
　performance in Karachi 21, 173, 230–1
　performance for royalty 215–16
　success of 210–11
Savai Madhosingh, Maharaja of Jaipur 117
Seizer, Susan 316
self 300–1
　absent 303–6
　collective 306–7, 308
　concept of, and autobiographical genre 300, 302
　culture-specific notions of 301
　denial of 303–4
　deprecation of 304, 317–18
　fractured 302–3
　Indian vs. western concept 301, 303–4, 306
　narration, performativity and 310
　performative 309–14
　relational 306–9
　sovereign 301–2, 304
Setu, illusion in 268
Shah, Chandulal 52, 55, 98, 280
Shah, Wajid Ali, and *Indar Sabha* 181
Shahjahan Theatrical Company 106, 164
Shahnama, and early Parsi theatre 6, 10

Shakespeare Theatrical Company 21, 156
Shakuntala (Betab) 55
Shakuntala (film; Radheshyam) 105, 157–8
Shakuntala (play; Radheshyam) 159–60, 330
Shantaram, V. 162, 270, 290
Sharifa Bai 25, 42, 132, 134, 135, 137, 160, 278, 292
shetias 5
Shibbaray, Chaudhri 67, 68
Shirin Farhad 21, 157, 172, 212
Shor Saheb 65–6
Shravan Kumar (Radheshyam) 105, 130–1, 144, 156
  version for New Alfred 147, 148, 149
Shri Desi Natak Samaj 198, 199, 203
Shri Krishna Avatar (Radheshyam) 105, 140–2
  Premchand's review of 145–6
Shri Mohan Theatrical Company 248, 278–80, 281
Shri Radheshyam Pustakalay 103, 108, 153
Shri Satyanarayan (Radheshyam) 161, 162
Shriradheshyam Kirtan 113
Shriradheshyam Vilas 113
Shukla, Nathuram Sundar 120, 204
Singh, Dr Yuddhvir 58, 60
Sita Banvas (Agha Hashr) 248, 255, 278
Sita Devi 42, 248, 258, 281–2, 286, 288, 292, 331–2
Sita Vanvas 132
Smith, Sidonie 28, 310
Sneh Sarita (Vibhakar) 239–40
social drama, genre of 20
Sone ke Mol ki Khurshed 10, 181

Sorabji, Cornelia 32
Sudhachandra (Vibhakar) 173, 240
Sultana 42, 280
Surdas (Agha Hashr) 120, 123–4, 143
Surdas, of Survijay Natak Samaj 130
Surveyor, Mehrji 115, 116
Survijay Natak Samaj 105, 130, 131, 132, 168
  closure of 147
  and Hindi theatre 144
Svang 45, 113, 294

Tagore, Rabindranath 31
Talib Banarasi, Vinayak Prasad 21, 91, 116, 143
talkies. *See* cinema
Tamil theatre 35
tazkira, genre 28, 324
Thakur, Debendranath 31
Thanthaniya Natak Mandali 191
Thanthaniya Theatre (Calcutta) 41, 196–7
theatre biographies/memoirs 32–5
  and cultural formation 37, 38–41
  and doubled performativity 313–14
  evolution of 26
  and history 36, 37–8
  in Marathi 35
  as narratives of personhood 299
  and oral performance 26, 30, 37, 44–5
  and theatrical history 41–4
  See also autobiography
theatre houses
  Bombay Amateur Theatre 4
  establishment of 12
  European style 7–8
  Gaiety Theatre 12, 41, 172, 173, 200–1, 230, 233
  Grace Theatre 276

Grant Road Theatre 4–5, 6, 8, 11, 16
Novelty Theatre 12
Rama Theatre 41, 70
sacralization of 43, 127
Sangam Theatre 41, 91, 124, 132
Thanthaniya Theatre 41, 196–7
Victoria Theatre 12
theatre journals 34–5
theatrical companies 11–12, 42
artistic growth of 17–18
establishment of 10
expansion of 116
gender representation in 19–20
Indian royalty and 24–5
litigation and 44
rivalry between 11, 81
Thunthi, Ardeshar 205
Thunthi, Dadabhai Ratanji 10, 12, 46, 191–2, 193n.11, 197
and Jayshankar Sundari 170, 171, 203, 204, 322
Trivedi, Lavji 130

Umrao Singh, Raja of Indargarh 278, 279–80, 281
Urdu 10, 13–14, 39, 18, 91, 181
autobiographies, self-deprecation in 317–18
Betab and 45–6, 51, 63–4
Jayshankar Sundari and 46, 191–2
as language of Parsi theatre 18, 20–1, 113
Usha Aniruddh (Durgadatt Pant) 132, 161
Utthan (magazine) 97, 98

Vatan 291
Veersalingam, Kandukuri 31
Vibhakar, Nrusingh 239–41
Victoria Theatre 12

Victoria Theatrical Company 10, 11, 12, 13, 21, 23, 266
female performers in 15
and New Alfred Company, rivalry between 54
Vidyarthi, Ganesh Shankar 133–4, 142
Vidyasagar, Ishwar Chandra 31, 305
Vikram Charitra (Mulani) 172, 205, 211–12
Vir Abhimanyu (Radheshyam) 42, 104, 118, 119, 120–1, 124, 129, 130, 153, 260
casting in 125–6
comedy in 43
Gopivallabh Upadhyay's review 161
New Alfred Company and 122, 123–4
performance in Delhi 124–7
Premchand's review of 144
publication of 128
Vir Bharat 144
Vyakul Bharat Company Limited 129–30, 144, 168
Vyakul, Vishvambhar Sahay 129–30, 132

Waghorne, Joanna Punzo 29, 305
Watson, Julia 28
Weintraub, Karl J. 28
widow remarriage, Betab's views on 84
Wodeyar, Krishnarao, Maharaja of Mysore 215
women's autobiographies, selfhood in 307

Yahudi ki Larki (Agha Hashr) 21

Zahri Sanp (Betab) 53, 54, 82, 119, 143

www.ingramcontent.com/pod-product-compliance
Lightning Source LLC
Chambersburg PA
CBHW021815300426
44114CB00009BA/188